C000297381

The Shell Guide ⸺⸺⸺⸺

to Germany ⸺⸺⸺⸺⸺

The Shell Guide to Germany

John Ardagh

Consultant and Research Assistant

KATHARINA ARDAGH

SIMON & SCHUSTER

LONDON · SYDNEY · NEW YORK ·
TOKYO · TORONTO

First published in Great Britain by
Simon & Schuster Ltd in 1991

Simon & Schuster Ltd
West Garden Place
Kendal Street
London W2 2AQ

Simon & Schuster of Australia Pty Ltd
Sydney

British Library Cataloguing-in-Publication Data available

ISBN 0-671-71021-4

Design and layout: Susie Home
Maps: Graham Douglas

The author and Publisher would like to thank all the
organizations who loaned transparencies for use in this book.

Front cover picture: Brandenburg Gate, Berlin
The Telegraph Colour Library

Typesetting: Ace Filmsetting Ltd, Frome, Somerset
Printed and bound by: Butler & Tanner Ltd, Frome, Somerset

Contents

CHAPTER ONE

Introduction

Germany Today

THE NEW UNITED Germany has been much in the news recently. With their changing emotional moods, their high serious culture, their brilliant economic efficiency, the Germans are a people who evoke fascination and admiration, sometimes envy and fear. But how well do we know them or their country today? For many people, it is not the most obvious of holiday destinations. It lacks the exotic, sunsoaked appeal of Mediterranean lands; it is thought to be mostly flattish, urbanized and over-organized; and for some people the very idea of it still evokes the ugly wartime past.

These clichés can give a false picture. Maybe I'm biased, for my wife is German and we have countless friends there: but I have always found Germany a delightful and stimulating country for holiday tourism. Not only is it full of diversity – from the hilly folksy south to the breezy maritime north – but many of its smaller towns are quaintly picturesque, and its old inns invitingly cosy. What's more, despite the strength of the Deutschmark, this is not an expensive country (hotels and restaurants tend to offer better value than in Britain). And it's a country that makes things very easy for the visitor, for German orderly efficiency is a reality – and so is German warmth of hospitality. It is rare to find the two so well combined. If you leave an item of clothing in a hotel bedroom, it will usually be rapidly forwarded; if you break down on an *Autobahn*, a patrol car will quickly come with free help. The countless excellent museums are duly open at the times stated, and their contents are explained in meticulous detail – often in English as well as German. Most educated people speak English, especially in tourism; or they'll gladly let you try out a few phrases of poor German, without being intolerant about it like the French. All the above applies to former West Germany: the East, though full of historic interest, still has much catching up to do, both in tourist infrastructure and in standards of service.

The Federal Republic, as we know, has been a great success story ever since the war. Many foreigners today fear that the new larger Germany will be too successful, and too dominant, with a return to nationalist arrogance. Time will tell. For the moment, I do not see much sign of a new assertive nationalism, except within the kind of small extreme-Right fringe that exists in any country. For many years now, West Germans have looked towards the European Community as a substitute for their old destructive nationalism that led to world wars; and today most Germans still see a tightly integrated Europe as the best way forward. In this context, after monetary union, it may become as meaningless to talk about 'German dominance' as, say, 'Californian dominance'.

It is true that Germany is not a country with a long democratic tradition. In the 18th century it was still a patchwork of some 300 separate 'free cities', kingdoms and principalities, many of them feudally run. In the Bismarck era, after unification, parliament still had little real power. And the Weimar Republic of 1919–33 had such a weak Constitution, and so little experience of stable democracy, that it was not able to withstand the rise of Nazism. However, the Nazi nightmare and then the 1945 defeat were so total and traumatic that, after the division of the country into two, the West Germans were shocked into making a completely new start, and into learning true democracy. They were given enlightened help by the Western victors, and they devized a model Constitution that has since been liberally applied. Power has alternated between two moderate centre-focused parties,

the Christian Democrats and Social Democrats, under a succession of mostly excellent Chancellors. So wary are the Germans of any return to bad old ways that any scandals or abuses of power tend to be vigilantly rooted out, alike in federal and local affairs, where adminstration is highly efficient, German-style. And a system of proportional representation ensures that a fair balance of opinion is achieved without thereby encouraging extremist parties. Other countries, including Britain, could learn a lot about democracy from the Germans.

The spirit of partnership is notably evident in labour relations, where a strong legal framework helps employers and unions to work together for the good of the firm. Strikes have thus been extremely few. In larger companies, workers have seats on management boards; even in smaller ones they tend to share in the goal of profitability. They are encouraged by the open-minded, benevolent attitude of most employers – and by welfare services that are among the best and most generous in Europe. The health service works superbly, with hospitals well staffed and equipped.

The Catholic and Protestant Churches play a big role here, owning and running many public hospitals. The Churches in West Germany are very rich, for they derive over ten billion DM a year from a special income tax levied voluntarily on some 90 per cent of the population, and they use much of this to fund welfare projects. About half of West Germans are Catholic (mainly in Bavaria and the Rhineland) and about half Protestant (in East

Cologne's joyous carnival: costumed clowns dance in the street.

Germany, the vast majority are Protestant). The old pre-war antagonism between these two confessions has largely died away and ecumenicism is now *à la mode*. Instead, conflicts have developed within each Church – among Catholics, on moral and sexual matters (as in other countries), and among Protestants between conservative 'pietists' and Left-inclined radical 'peaceniks'.

If I have painted a fairly rosy picture of Germany today, does this mean that all past demons have been exorcized? Yes and no. Certainly the terrible legacy of Nazism seems to have been more-or-less digested, finally. Until the early 1970s the subject was largely taboo: its history was poorly taught in schools, and people would shy away from discussing it. But now, with a change of generation and the growth of outspokenness in society, the taboo is lifted. Many civic councils have staged exhibitions of their town under Nazism; the Press and media have been full of debates, articles and programmes on the subject; and many Germans you meet will now talk about it frankly. This does mean that some elderly ones will launch into prickly self-justification ('I never knew about the death camps', 'I was just doing my duty as a soldier', or even 'Hitler had some good ideas at first, but then went too far'), while many young ones vocally resent being held guilty for the sins of their grandparents. So it is wise to tread tactfully, when starting a conversation on the subject. But neo-Nazism, that often exaggerated scare, is of very limited influence, confined to sentimental SS veterans who are now dying out, and to a few young hothead thugs. The new far-Right Republikaner party is unpleasantly racist and xenophobic, but not Nazi – and it too has a strictly limited appeal.

However, there are some general traits in the German social character, still widely persisting, of which I am not a great admirer. The Germans are a very legalistic people, and they devize rules and laws for all kinds of little things that might better be left to common decency. Faced with any decision, they tend to apply the rules unthinkingly rather than use common sense. They hate to break the law, or see someone else breaking it, in however minor a way, for it offends against their profound need for *Ordnung*. Hence they wait sheepishly for a pedestrian traffic-light to turn green, even when there is no car in sight. And they like to mind your own business for you: if you walk down the street with your shoe-laces undone, in France or Britain no one will notice, but in Germany you'll soon be told, and not just for your safety's sake. If anything is out of place, it makes a German feel uneasy. *Ordnung muss sein*, in all ways. Even small children in public places are disliked because they tend to behave restlessly and messily, as children do: while Latins drool over neighbours' children, Germans continually lodge complaints about them, or are reluctant to rent flats to a young family.

It follows that the Germans are very litigious – and this has increased with modern affluence, for they have more money to spend on lawyers' fees. One Berliner sued a next-door tennis club of which he was himself a member, because the ping of ball on racquet disturbed his siesta: you would have thought he could have sorted it out more amicably. And if a man offends his neighbour, by making a noise or a mess, or even by having a tree that sheds leaves into his garden, the recourse is often to solicitors' letters. The Germans tend to be suspicious of neighbours, or of any stranger until proved a friend.

In fact, I have often noted the contrast between the warmth of German private life and the stiffness and coolness of public life, and the curious hiatus between public and private morality. A person will feel loyalty, affection and moral obligation to his family, close friends and others whom he knows and trusts; towards other citizens he feels little concern, even if they are in trouble, and to the authorities his sense of duty tends to be cool and rational, a matter of wanting to preserve efficient order. The Germans take great trouble with their little circle of true friends: but the Anglo-Saxon concept of a wide ever-shifting circle of loose acquaintances, of casual friendships quickly struck up and as quickly forgotten, does not mean much to them.

Alike to strangers and friends, they tend to be scrupulously polite, but in a rather formal way. They make much play with titles, and anyone who is a director or professor will expect to be thus addressed – 'Ja, Herr Oberregierungspräsident', 'Nein, Frau Justizrat'. If someone has not just an ordinary degree but a prized doctorate, in whatever subject, you must make sure not to leave out the 'Doktor', in a letter or in conversation, or you may cause offence. And, except among family and real friends, the use of Christian names is still quite rare, notably in an office context: girl typists sharing a room, of the same age and background and on cordial terms, will remain on Fräulein terms. The Germans draw a sharp distinction between work and private life,

and will seldom make social friends with office colleagues, except at the higher professional level. And, as with French and other Continental languages, the dual form of 'you' (intimate du and formal Sie) adds to this gulf between friendship and other social contacts, and heightens the social reserve.

These formalities are the outward signs of a society that in many ways is still conformist, highly competitive, intolerant of weakness and failure. Or rather, the weak (elderly widows, the handicapped, etc) are excellently looked after by public institutions, but the ordinary citizen does not want to know. And to fail in your career is a great stigma. The success ethic and the work ethic have made West Germany prosperous, but they do not make it a gentler and more caring society in which to live.

It is true that all the above social traits are being modified and contested by a younger generation, more informal and tolerant, more open to outside influences. Younger people are less respectful of titles than their elders, more ready to use Christian names and du (this is widespread among students, but still not so common inside offices). They are also less legalistic, readier to obey the spirit rather than the letter of the law, less subservient to authority, less impelled by the hard work and success ethics, less suspicious of neighbours, less hostile to other people's children. And they are readier to form informal groups to help handicapped or lonely people, or the despised Turkish immigrant workers.

All this is especially true of the Greens, who have made such an impact on Germany since the early 1980s. Many Greens have excellent ideas and are gentle, humane and sensible people. But some are fanatics, obsessed by their anti-bourgeois, anti-industrial ideology, ultra-intolerant of all that they dislike. In reaction against bourgeois materialist conformism, they and the other so-called *Alternative* have developed their own anti-materialist conformism, where messy hair and clothing, chaotically untidy flats, organic foodstuffs, use of bicycles instead of motor-cars, are all part of the creed. And so the contrast in Germany between two rival sets of values and lifestyles, each hating the other, is much sharper than in most Western countries. It is hard to be somewhere in the middle, an easy-going, messy liberal but certainly no *Alternative*. You have to choose: for example, it would be hard in Germany to be a vegetarian spiritualist *and* to love computers and other high-tech wizardry (as my own son does). If you try to hold the balance, each side will denounce you as belonging to the other.

However, the Greens' concern for the environment has certainly made an important contribution to this tight-packed industrialized country that was over-using its resources. The Greens spotlighted some of the dangers, they rallied a large part of German opinion, and so they obliged the larger parties, in power in Bonn and the *Länder*, to adopt many of their ideas and to apply them. As a result, West Germany today has the strictest anti-pollution rules in Europe; it took the lead in introducing catalytic convertors and lead-free petrol; and refuse bins are carefully colour-coded to ensure recycling of paper, glass, etc.

But the Germans are always prone to excess, and to anxiety, and it could be argued that their new obsession with environmental problems has been carried to absurd limits. Health hazards, soil erosion, noise, tree sickness, damage to the landscape – all such ills are endlessly discussed at dinners or political meetings. Once, my hostess at a dinner in Munich, herself no Green, said without a trace of irony, 'Don't eat the skins on those potatoes: they might have been grown near a motorway.' The Greens, of course, are the keenest crusaders. I know of a case where 20 of them kept vigil beside an old oak tree for a fortnight, day and night, to prevent it being cut down to make way for a supermarket. And they won. But some critics of the Greens feel that they are more concerned about trees than people.

Many of them have at least been concerned about such people as the Turks and other southern immigrant workers, often regarded as little more than semi-people by Rightist elements and the gutter Press. The Germans before the war had more than a hint of xenophobia: today they are extremely well disposed towards West Europeans, and they treat perfectly well their tiny Jewish community, which now numbers only 28,000, compared with 550,000 before 1933. Anyone who dares to make anti-semitic remarks is pounced on, for this is still a sensitive issue, and rightly so. But the Germans are not too keen on Poles, or Sicilians or other swarthy South Europeans if they behave too noisily. And they have not welcomed joyfully the 1.4 million Turks now in Germany, much the largest single component of the *Gastarbeiter* population ('guest workers' – a somewhat ironic term) that began to flood into Germany in the 1950s and '60s, to help with the 'economic miracle'.

At worst, the Turks are cruelly exploited by unscrupulous employers of casual labour, as Günter Wallraff recounted in his terrifying book *Ganz Unten ('Lowest of the Low')*. Or else they are treated with cool indifference by ordinary Germans who fear and dislike their funny Muslim habits. The Turks, it must be said, do not always make it easy to be liked, for they are under pressure from their own Islamic fundamentalists *not* to try to integrate; a Turkish girl with a German boyfriend will not find things easy. However, the situation is not as bad as it has been painted, and it is improving; actual violence is very rare, and racist feeling of this kind is probably worse in France today than in Germany. Turks and other *Gastarbeiter* are legally covered by the German welfare services and wage agreements, and most employers treat them well; and many Church associations, as well as Green groups and others, go out of their way to befriend them and try to make them feel at home. In 1990, the major danger was that the rise of mass unemployment in the former GDR would foster ill feeling against foreign workers all over Germany.

These immigrants were a major asset to German industry during its heady years of rapid expansion. But if the post-war German economy has been such a success-story, it must be put down mainly to other human factors: to the Germans' capacity for thorough organization and disciplined hard work, at all levels from shop-floor to top management. Their main weakness is an inability to improvize, to adapt quickly and imaginatively when something unforeseen occurs; their strength is to work out a technique, then follow it with meticulous precision and efficiency. They do not have great engineering colleges or business schools, in the French or American manner. But they are excellent at in-service training, and they have a highly effective system of apprenticeship, which trains some 700,000 school leavers a year in a wide variety of skills. Experts believe that this is the main reason why productivity levels are so much higher than, for instance, in Britain.

In schools, too, education is generally of a high level academically; pupils are disciplined and well motivated, especially for such subjects as learning English. The weakness of German education is that it hardly extends outside the classroom: the school day generally ends at 1 pm, and there is very little of the extra-curricular activity that is such an important part of the whole school experience in some other countries. More serious is the malaise that for many years has affected German universities, due sustantially to over-crowding and under-funding. Anyone with the *Abitur*, the higher school leaving certificate, has a right to a university place, more-or-less wherever he or she chooses, and can then prolong his or her studies indefinitely. The result is a swollen student population, inadequately catered for on amorphous campuses, taught by professors who have little personal contact with their pupils, and weighed down by an over-heavy official bureaucracy: the universities are run by the *Länder*, and have hardly any autonomy.

In this rich and normally efficient country, higher education is badly organized and poorly funded. Yet German cultural life benefits from lavish official subsidies: some 50 opera houses, 70 orchestras, over 100 theatres and nearly 1,300 museums all receive this largesse, and attract big audiences. The sheer range of cultural activity is amazing, and standards of performance are generally high. The weakness – but Germany is not alone in this, in the West today – is that individual creativity, that of the writer, artist or composer alone in his workroom, is at a low ebb. Since the heyday of Günter Grass and the late Heinrich Böll, the German novel is in the doldrums; few modern artists of note have appeared; film-making, after a fertile flush in the 1970s, has relapsed into mediocrity, and so has play-writing. On the margin of the arts, German television too is remarkably dull, though often worthy and serious. One main reason for this is that the TV stations are controlled by the various federal *Länder*, in a manner that is intended to ensure a fair political balance but, in practice, stifles creative boldness.

In most other ways, however, West Germany's post-war federal system has been a success. It brings decision-making closer to the people, it creates a fertile spirit of competition between the *Länder*, it has provided (like Europe) an alternative focus to outmoded nationalism, and it reflects a genuine historical diversity, in a country where local patriotism has always been strong. 'I feel Bavarian first, European second, and German third', one Münchner told me. Bavarians, extrovert, jovial and sentimental, especially feel this kind of loyalty (their *Land* was a separate kingdom until 1918): but so do cosy, ponderous Swabians and jolly Rhinelanders, and the people of those two proudly independent Hanseatic ports, Hamburg and Bremen. Since the war, West Germany has been divided into eleven *Länder* including Berlin, varying in size from North-Rhine Westphalia with 16.7 million people to Saarland (1,050,000) and Bremen (660,000), and they have now beeen joined by the five reconstituted East German *Länder*. The federal system leaves each *Land* government in charge of education, culture, welfare, justice, and some aspects of economic policy.

German diversity is such that many regions have their own dialect, still in wide daily use; and even educated people speaking standard *Hochdeutsch* will have a regional accent. Your voice tends to mark your regional origin; as in Britain it also marks your class. Some cities, too, notably Berlin and Cologne, retain their own dialect which a villager from only 20 miles away might find hard to follow. Small wonder that some Germans still think of distant parts of their country as alien: but this mutual ignorance has much diminished since the war, under the impact of television, tourism, and big shifts of population. In particular, the arrival in West Germany of some 13 million German refugees from the East – from Silesia, East Prussia, etc, as well as the GDR – caused a tremendous shake-up in the old population patterns, as Silesians for example poured into Swabia.

Cities and medium-sized towns play a crucial role in Germany. Many have a long tradition of autonomy, dating from the days when they were 'free imperial cities' under the Holy Roman Empire or members of the powerful Hanseatic trading league. There has never been one super-dominant city in the manner of London or Paris: even Berlin never played quite that role. And after the war, with Berlin isolated, West Germany was led by a number of dynamic cities of roughly equal importance, all in intense competition – Hamburg, Munich, Frankfurt and others, with Bonn as the smaller, somewhat dull and artificial, federal capital. With no one city to set the pace and provide a national focus, this situation has encouraged a certain self-regarding provincialism (even Munich is provincial in a way), though the other side of this coin is that a *Land* capital like Stuttgart or Hanover has far more importance and self-confidence, and a far higher cultural and business profile, than such foreign equivalents as, say, Lille or Manchester. As Berlin becomes the capital again, it will provide the focus that Germany probably needs. But it will still not dominate as Paris does. Germany is too decentralized for that.

Most of the cities were badly bombed, and have been rebuilt in a style that is often too metallic and concrete-laden. Some of their former beauty has gone for ever: yet redeeming features survive, enhanced by new traffic-free piazzas and walkways, with gardens, fountains, and the folksy comic sculptures that are much in vogue. Munich is still impressively baroque; Hamburg has a serene patrician dignity. And some cities belie their poor reputation. Frankfurt-am-Main is not just a 'Mainhattan' (its nickname) of brash banks in glass-and-steel skyscrapers: Goethe's home town is also a vibrantly cultured place, with a charming rebuilt *Altstadt* and some of the best museums in a country full of superbly laid-out museums. Even the vast Ruhr conurbation, around Essen and Dortmund, has a delightful rural fringe of lakes and wooded hills, along the valley of the river Ruhr which today is idyllically pastoral – believe it

or not. And mighty industrial Stuttgart, the city of Mercedes, Bosch and Porsche, nestles in a leafy vale where terraced vineyards slope almost to the main station.

Many smaller and medium-sized towns, too, have a great individuality and sense of history, as well as handsome old half-timbered buildings, well restored. Among my favourites are Bamberg, Goslar, Lemgo, and little Bad Wimpfen above the river Neckar. By contrast, very few of the villages in Germany are really picturesque or interesting, far fewer than in Britain or France. One main reason is that in the 1950s and '60s many German farmers and villagers, in their eagerness to modernize and brush away the past, tended to tear down their old homes and replace them with modern villas, more comfortable but less graceful.

However, after a period of obsession with modernism, the Germans have now been returning to their traditions – it is one aspect of the 'Green' movement. An old half-timbered house, that in the 1960s might have been removed to make way for a supermarket, is now carefully preserved. There's a vogue, too, for *Freilichtmuseen*, outdoor heritage museums where old farmhouses and other rural buildings are collected from all over a region and reassembled in a park, together with old farm implements and furniture – an artificial solution, maybe, but better than letting rural tradition vanish unseen.

The Germans also sedulously keep up their folklore pageants and festivals, above all the pre-Lenten jollity known as *Fasching* in Bavaria, *Fastnacht* in Baden-Württemberg, and *Karneval* in the Rhineland where it is especially vigorous. At Elzach in the Black Forest, masked fools dressed in red with large

Some Historical Dates

BC

800–100 Germanic tribes invading from the north and east push into lands long settled by Celtic tribes.

60–20 The Romans invade, build forts at Trier, Cologne, Mainz, etc, then advance towards the Elbe.

AD

9 Roman Army defeated by Germanic leader Arminius on Teutoburg hill (nr Bielefeld). Romans withdraw to fortified line linking Rhine to Danube.

314 Roman Emperor Constantine, after introducing Christianity, sets up bishopric at Trier, builds palace there.

4th–5th C Vandals, Goths, Huns and others break through Roman defences, pour westward; Roman Empire collapses.

481 King Clovis, Frankish leader, sets up Merovingian dynasty, embracing Germany and most of France.

768–814 Frankish leader Charlemagne forges an empire covering most of western Europe, sets up his court at Aachen.

800 Charlemagne crowned Emperor by the Pope. He is the first to weld the Germanic tribes into one unit. But his empire is split up after his death.

936–973 Reign of Otto the Great.

1152–1190 Reign of Frederick Barbarossa, of the Hohenstaufen dynasty. The term 'Holy Roman Empire' is first used to denote the Germanic realms.

13th C Under leadership of Lübeck, foundation of the Hanseatic League, a powerful trading association of some 200 towns and ports, mostly in north Germany.

1356 The Holy Roman Emperor is henceforth elected by a 'college' of princes and bishops. In practice he tends to be a Habsburg, ruling in Vienna, and Germany is still parcelled into some 200 independent units.

1386 First German university is founded at Heidelberg.

1440 Johannes Gutenberg in Mainz develops modern printing.

late 15th C Golden age of Augsburg, thanks to Fugger the Rich and other merchants.

early 16th C Flowering of culture and science in Nuremberg, during the Renaissance, with Albrecht Dürer.

1517 Martin Luther's revolt sparks off the Reformation.

1521 Luther arraigned before Diet of Worms.

1524–5 Peasants' Revolt, brutally suppressed.

1555 Peace of Augsburg officially sanctions Protestantism in some areas; partial victory for Reformation.

1618–48 Thirty Years' War devastates Germany, reducing its population from c. 21 to 13.5 million.

1648 Peace of Westphalia ends war, guarantees equality of rights to both faiths, but endorses parcellization of Germany into c. 300 separate sovereign units.

1701 Prussia becomes a kingdom, under Friedrich I.

1714 Elector (prince) Georg of Hanover becomes George I of England; union of England and Hanover lasts till 1837.

1740–86 Brilliant reign of Frederick the Great, who defeats Austria, makes Prussia into a major European power, and Berlin into a major European capital.

1803–15 Napoleonic Wars. Napoleon occupies much of Germany, defeats Prussia, abolishes Holy Roman Empire.

1815 After Napoleon's defeat, Congress of Vienna sets up a new German Confederation with only 39 sovereign states. Prussia is enlarged to include Westphalia and Rhineland.

1848 Popular uprising leads to creation of German National Parliament in Frankfurt, but with poor results.

1862 Bismarck comes to power as Prime Minister of Prussia.

1866 Prussia defeats Austria, annexes Hanover and Hesse, forms new unified North Germany.

1867 Karl Marx publishes *Das Kapital* in Hamburg.

1870–71 Franco-Prussian War. Prussia defeats France at Sedan, annexes Alsace-Lorraine. Proclamation at Versailles of the German Empire, under Wilhelm I of Prussia. Germany now fully unified.

1830–90 Period of rapid industrialization, especially in Ruhr. Population grows from 41 to 65 million in 1871–1911.

1882–86 Carl Benz and Gottlieb Daimler invent the motor car, in Karlsruhe and Stuttgart respectively.

1875 Social Democratic Party founded.

1888 Wilhelm II comes to throne, dismisses Bismarck (1890).

1914–18 First World War: Germany allies with Austro-Hungary against Russia, France and Britain, invades neutral Belgium and reaches river Marne, but then bogged down in four years of trench warfare in France.

1916-17 Battle of Verdun: c. 800,000 die.

1918 Kaiser Wilhelm abdicates, Germany becomes a republic, surrenders to Allies.

1918–19 Communist revolts in Berlin and Munich are put down. Weimar Republic is proclaimed. Treaty of Versailles exacts huge reparations on Germany, restores Alsace-Lorraine to France.

1923 Hitler's Munich *Putsch* fails.

mid-1920s Terrible galloping inflation erodes German economy.

1929–33 Great Depression; unemployment reaches six million.

1933 National Socialists (Nazis) emerge as largest single party in Parliament, Hindenburg appoints Hitler as Chancellor. After Reichstag fire, Hitler suspends civil rights, starts to rule as dictator.

1935 Nuremberg 'race laws' against Jewish citizens.

1936 German troops re-occupy demilitarized Rhineland.

1938 Hitler annexes Austria, then the German-speaking Sudeten areas of Czechoslovakia.

1939 Hitler invades Poland, precipitating world war.

1940 Germans overrun France and Low Countries.

1941 Hitler invades Russia, but fails to take Moscow. United States enters the war against Germany.

1945 Defeated Germany is divided into four zones, Berlin likewise; Russians begin to communize their zone.

1948–49 Russians blockade West Berlin, but Allied airlift (plus Berliners' spirit) foils their bid to subdue it.

1949 Federal Republic of Germany and German Democratic Republic are created; division of Germany is complete. Konrad Adenauer becomes first West German Chancellor.

1953 East Germans revolt against Communist regime, without success.

1955 West Germany joins NATO, then becomes founder member of European Community (1957).

1961 East Germany builds the Berlin Wall.

1969–70 Willy Brandt becomes first Social Democrat Chancellor, launches Ostpolitik, begins to ease tensions with East Germany and Soviet Union, wins guarantees for Berlin.

1971 Erich Honecker succeeds Walter Ulbricht as ruler of East Germany.

1972 Munich hosts Olympic Games.

1974 Helmut Schmidt succeeds Brandt as Chancellor.

1977 Wave of Leftist terrorism by 'Baader-Meinhof gang'.

1983 Helmut Kohl, Christian Democrat, confirmed as Chancellor; the Greens emerge as a political force.

1987 First visit to West Germany by Erich Honecker.

1989 Honecker resigns under pressure, then on 9 November the Berlin Wall and all the East–West frontier are thrown open, as Communist regime disintegrates.

1990 March: general election in East Germany brings Christian Democrats to power. July: monetary union between the two Germanies. October: Germany reunifies. December: first pan-German elections, Kohl re-elected Chancellor.

11

decorated hats run through the town beating people with blown-up hogs' bladders; at nearby Rottweil, rival groups of fools jump through the Black Gate. The whole Carnival razzamatazz, however mindless and silly, has been a means for an anxious nation to seek out its identity and restore broken links with past tradition untainted by politics, nationalism or ideology (the Nazis never tried to appropriate Carnival, as they took over and thus tainted so many of the lovely old German folksongs and drinking-songs).

The Germans remain lovers of sport and keep-fit activities. They are the world's leading spa-cure addicts, and some 6 million of them a year go to take a cure (often reimbursed by social security) in one of the 200 or so designated health spas, most of them in the hilly areas of the south and south-west that are rich in mineral waters. These range from elitist Baden-Baden to simple down-market places. One medical rule of a cure is that you must not bring your spouse with you, for a complete break with home is part of the treatment (a *Kurgast's* ailment is often diagnosed as psychosomatic, due to family tensions). So here are all these mostly middle-aged people, separated from their beloveds maybe for the first time in decades. The *Kurschatten* (spa romance) is as common in Germany as the shipboard romance once was on Cunard liners. And the divorce lawyers are familiar with it.

The Germans also remain lovers of hiking, in their forests and upland pastures where the well-kept paths are clearly signposted. Some woodlands are today affected by 'acid rain' sickness, as you can see if you look at the dying tops of trees. But this is not as widely noticeable as I had expected.

It is a truism to say that North and South Germany are very different. The south and south-west parts tend to have the prettiest scenery, hilly and wooded, and to be strongest on cosy, quaint *Gemütlichkeit*. These are gentle regions of vineyards and half-timbered houses, old hilltop castles and baroque churches, whereas the north is flatter and windier, turned towards Scandinavia, Britain and the sea. The people of the south and west, notably Bavarians and Rhinelanders, like to drink and sing with gusto in their taverns, swaying together arms linked; in the north, people are more stolid and reserved, but also maybe more reliable, and in the big cities such as Hamburg they are more liberal and serious. This, at least, is the classic generalization, though in reality the pattern is more complex. And the north in its own way has much to offer the visitor. The scenery may be flattish: but areas such as the Weser valley and Lüneberg Heath have their own quiet pastoral beauty, and some of the old towns are just as lovely as in the south. Here the older buildings tend to be of red brick, whereas towards the Black Forest and Alps the rural housing is more often of wood with low thatched roofs. But nearly everywhere, north and south, there is half-timbering.

The West German part of this book is divided in 34 itineraries, grouped by *Land*, some dealing with just one city, some with a string of towns or a mainly rural area. Only in one or two small cases does an itinerary stray across a *Land* border. I start in Aachen, because in a sense that is where Germany's history as a nation began, in Charlemagne's town; also because it is the first city you will come to, if you drive from the French or Belgian ports.

I then work south, then up to the far north, then over to Berlin. The last section of the book deals, in rather less detail, with the former territory of the GDR. I should explain that all that I have written above, in this introductory survey of German society, applies to West Germany. The people of the GDR are equally German and they share many of the same characteristics: but more than 40 years of Socialism have left them with very different problems and mentalities.

Getting There

For travel from Britain to south or central Germany, there are various ferry services to the Dutch and Belgian ports, Hook of Holland, Zeebrugge and Ostend: these crossings take four hours or more. But, seeing that a car travels far quicker than a boat, much the fastest journey is to take the short 75 to 90 minutes' crossing (Sealink or P&O) from Dover to Calais, or the even quicker hovercraft to Calais (daylight hours only), then pick up the *autoroute* just west of Dunkerque that will bring you via southern Belgium to Aachen and then Cologne, or via Luxembourg to the Moselle or Strasbourg. It is motorway almost all the way. These are the routes I take myself, when going to south Germany, and from the London area they are one or two hours quicker than going via the Dutch or Belgian ports (Calais to Cologne takes about four hours). If you live in East Anglia or the Midlands and want to get to north Germany, it might be quickest to go from Harwich or Felixstowe to Hook of Holland or Zeebrugge.

One pleasant means of travel from Britain to north Germany is to take a Scandinavian Seaways ferry from Harwich to Hamburg. This overnight crossing takes 21 hours, and the ferries go on alternate days: they are large, smooth and comfortable, with good cabins, pleasant food and plenty of amusements. This sealine also offers inclusive holidays at small rural hotels in north Germany.

Incidentally, between France, Germany and the Benelux countries, the frontiers are now control-free, with no passport or customs checks, and you seldom need to stop the car. If you do not want to take your own car to Germany, various airlines offer fly-drive schemes that enable you to fly to an airport and hire a car there.

Documents Needed

Passports are required, but not visas for EC citizens. You must have a current national (or international) driving permit, and proof of third party insurance; a Green Card is not essential, but advisable. As for free medical care, if before you leave you ask your local DHSS for form E111, you will be entitled to use the German health service on the same conditions as the Germans, if you are an EC citizen (others must pay full medical costs, and would be well advised to take out insurance).

Motoring in Germany

The West German road network is as excellent as you might expect, with some 8,200km of motorway, Europe's highest figure. Some of these *Autobahnen* date from Hitler's time and have since been rebuilt: they are constantly being repaired, so that you have to slow down and drive along narrower 'lanes' divided by yellow studs, in face of oncoming traffic – not advisable after dark if you are not yet used to driving in Germany. The *Autobahnen* have the usual blue signs and 'A' numbers. Other main roads have 'B' numbers; minor roads are not numbered, but the signposting is clear. Roads are well surfaced; even in rural areas they mostly have paved edges and white lines down the middle. This German neatness does tend to make country driving a somewhat urban experience, and you may start longing at times for a real rustic road with unmade edges and the occasional bump.

There are no tolls on West German roads. The speed limit is 50kph in built-up areas, 100kph on other roads – except for the *Autobahnen* where along most sections there is *no* speed limit, despite Germany's high level of fatal car accidents. The 'recommmended' limit of 130kph is seldom observed by the many Germans who have power-ful cars – and the macho executive type tends to be an aggressive driver. So, unless you have a fast car too and relish speed, you might be advised to keep off the fast lane of an *Autobahn* where the Audi 200s, BMW 700s and big Mercedes go throbbing by at speeds of up to 250kph, angrily flashing their lights behind you if you dare to dawdle at a mere 150kph or so. For me, this is the single most unpleasant aspect of touring in Germany. Today, a contrast-ing hazard comes from the masses of east German 'Trabis' still unused to West German speed: beware of them too, should one of them swing out from the slow lane.

However, on lesser roads the Ger-mans are well disciplined drivers, even pedantically so. In or out of a car, they rather like to mind your business for you, so that if you park where you

shouldn't, or have your lights on wrongly, or turn when you shouldn't, they will seize the chance to tell you so. In towns, keep carefully to your lane. All this may sound tedious. However, let me add that parking tends to be easier than in most European countries, and city traffic jams less heavy. In towns there are lots of meters or public car parks; in rural areas you can park anywhere. Vandalism is less of a problem than in many countries; even so, it is unwise to leave luggage visible in the car.

Accidents and Breakdowns

Seat belts are compulsory, for front and rear passengers. Rules against driver-drinking are severe, and the Germans take this seriously: the legal limit is about equal to half a litre of beer. The police can impose spot fines for speeding and other offences, rang-ing from roughly 20DM to 70DM: if you are doing more than 25kph above the limit, you could be taken to court. If you are involved in an accident, you must expect the police to make a detailed report, which takes time. If you break down on a road, you must place a warning triangle behind the car. The emergency phone number in towns is 110, in the country 19211; along the *Autobahnen* there are free emergency phones about every km. The main German automobile club, ADAC, operates frequent patrols, and will often fix your car free if the prob-lem is a minor one. They are usually very helpful and efficient: but you will get best service from them if you can produce the card of an affiliated club, such as the AA or RAC.

Maps

There are several useful series. One,

Neuschwanstein, most flamboyant of Bavaria's 'royal castles'. Fotobank

published by ADAC in a 1:200,000 scale, marks the minor roads and viewpoints very clearly but gives no relief contours. Kümmerly und Frey has the whole of Germany in one clear 1:500,000 map, while the *Grosse V.A.G. Atlas* (1:300,000) has many city centre plans too. But for town plans the red and green *Michelin* guides remain unsurpassed. For the larger German towns, *Falk* publish a very useful series of blue-and-yellow detailed fold-out street plans.

Petrol

This costs very slightly less than in Britain, and can be bought by credit card at many service stations. The West Germans have moved over to lead-free petrol ahead of the rest of Europe, and it is easily obtainable everywhere.

Hotels and Other Accommodation

Nearly all hotels in Germany are individually owned and family-run. There are few chain hotels and motels in the cheaper ranges, though you will find some more expensive ones. The leading German chains are Steigenberger and Maritim; some foreign chains are also represented, such as Crest, Holiday Inn and Mercure. But many smaller privately-owned hotels do group together for joint publicity and marketing. Perhaps the best is the Romantik Hotels association whose 60 hotels, generally upper-medium price, are mostly in old buildings of character. Gast im Schloss, also good, is an assocation of nicely converted castles, not all of them expensive, and some still run by their old family owners. The Silencehotels, linked to France's Relais du Silence, tend to be in quiet secluded settings. The Ring Hotels are a large and diverse group, some of them dullish city hotels for businessmen, others with more character.

Room prices are about average for the Continent, i.e. cheaper than in Britain. It pays to share a room if you can, for a double one is usually only about 50 per cent dearer than a single one. German hotels are not officially graded, but the gables in the red *Michelin* guide will give some idea of standards. This lists a fuller selection than I have room for in this book, where at the end of each sub-chapter I have recommended about one in five of the good hotels in the area: the local tourist office will supply a fuller list. At 1991 prices, these are the price-brackets I use in my lists, for a double room with buffet breakfast:

CATEGORY A: over 250 DM

CATEGORY B: 180 – 250 DM

CATEGORY C: 120 – 180 DM

CATEGORY D: 80 – 120 DM

CATEGORY E: under 80 DM.

Standards of service, comfort and cleanliness tend to be high in Germany, even in cheaper hotels and guesthouses. So you can safely go down market without finding broken fittings or bugs in the bed. Most German hotels are run very professionally, but not too impersonally. Many old rural and small-town inns date back centuries, and were not bombed in the war; modern ones, too, are frequently built in local traditional style, which may mean gabled roofs and flowery balconies. Modern-style buildings are less common. Inside, especially in south Germany, you can expect to find cosy traditional decor, maybe with panelled walls, discreet alcoves, even four-poster beds in some places. It is all very *gemütlich*, though in Bavaria it can verge on kitsch.

There are some peculiarities that might puzzle a first-time visitor to Germany. As in most of Central Europe, duvets are the norm rather than sheets and blankets; twin beds put together are much commoner than a double one; and the Germans like their beds rather hard, with small, thin pillows, for this is considered healthy. You can get extra pillows if you ask. Many hotels pursue the tradition of leaving a chocolate or sweet on the pillow as a goodnight gift. And one great asset of German hotels is that nearly all provide a help-yourself buffet breakfast, included in the room price. This will usually offer juices, some fresh fruit, cereals (maybe including muesli), sliced meats and cheeses, various rolls and breads, boiled eggs, tea and the always excellent coffee, and in smarter hotels cooked dishes such as bacon and scrambled eggs. After this feast, you may hardly need more than a light snack at lunch. Service is always included in the hotel bill, and there is no need to leave a tip, except for a full meal (see p. 17).

A small hotel is often called *Gasthof* or *Gasthaus*; a pension or guesthouse is *Fremdenheim*, while bed-and-breakfast in a private home is usually announced by the sign *Zimmer frei* (if all the rooms are taken, the sign *besetzt* goes up). In some rural areas you can even stay on a farm, maybe one that has been turned into a guesthouse by its owners, or in a converted farm building rented on a self-catering basis (*gîte* in French). Local tourist offices will provide lists of such places.

Camping

There are some 2,000 registered sites, graded officially, and standards tend to be high. Even the simpler grades offer a shop, toilets and washhouses; in the top grades you may find supermarkets, discos and swimming-pools. A full list of sites, with all details, is provided by the German camping club, DCC, Mandlstr. 28, Munich 40, tel. 33 40 21.

Restaurants, Food and Drink

All in all, this is a most civilized and agreeable country for eating and drinking. The food, much more varied and interesting than is often supposed, is generally good value. Really expensive restaurants exist of course, but they are fewer than in Britain or France: most are of average cost, serving dishes over a wide price range. Thus, even in a place that looks quite smart, if you take a simple dish with a soup or salad, you need not spend much; and even if you order just a snack and a beer, no one will mind. It is all very flexible. In this book, a short selection of restaurants is given at the end of each itinerary; for reasons of space, we have left out many other good ones, but a tourist office will supply a full list. At 1991 prices, these are the brackets we use for a full meal for one, drinks included:

CATEGORY A:	over 70 DM
CATEGORY B:	50–70 DM
CATEGORY C:	30–50 DM
CATEGORY D:	20–30 DM
CATEGORY E:	under 20 DM.

Another asset of the West German scene is that many simpler traditional places (the *Gaststätte*, *Gasthaus* or *Kneipe*) fill the triple role of eating-place, pub and café: at the same table they will be ready to serve one person a glass of beer or wine, another a coffee, a third a snack, a fourth a full meal. Helpings are usually large. Many of these places will be serving some hot dishes all day, not just at normal meal-times; and cold snacks will still be available after the kitchen has closed at night. In such places, it is usual to share a table with strangers, and you should wish them '*Guten Appetit*' and then '*Auf Wiedersehen*' in the courteous German manner. A big central table, the *Stammtisch*, may be reserved for habitués, usually older men who drop in for a gossip. The bill includes service, but the waiter or waitress should get a tip of two or three per cent: do not leave this under the plate, but give it direct when you pay.

Many Germans today have become diet-conscious, and the younger ones are noticeably slimmer than their elders. Even so, Germans traditionally still have hearty appetites. After their sizeable breakfast, many still take a mid-morning snack known as *Brotzeit* (bread-time), consisting maybe of cheese or cold meat with bread, on offer in many restaurants. Again in mid-afternoon, the equivalent of the English tea and sandwiches is *Kaffee und Kuchen* – coffee with large creamy cakes, taken in a café. This tradition is kept up by older middle-class people, past caring about their waistlines; the young have less time for it. Lunch, with a hot main dish, is still the principal meal of the day; in the evening, most families at home are content with a cold supper of meats, cheese, maybe salad and fruit, etc, known as *Abendbrot* (evening bread). However, when they go out to dinner in a restaurant, they are likely to have a hot meal. And even humble bread itself is deliciously appetizing, in a country with over 200 varieties, such as the rich black *Pumpernickel* rye-bread.

Most Germans' preference is for *gutbürgerlich* cooking – wholesome, fairly simple, generously portioned. It may not be nearly as subtle as French or Italian cuisine, but it is tasty, and nearly always well served and presented. On the other hand, fancy modern *nouvelle cuisine*, with smaller portions and invented dishes, has now become fashionable in many smarter restaurants: in Germany the results are very often pretentious and inept, as well as pricey. Nor are these the places where you can come for a simple dish while others are knocking back the caviar.

My own advice would be to stick to classic German food in traditional restaurants. As well as the many regional specialities (see below), there are basic dishes that you find in most places. Soups are seldom remarkable, the commonest being foreign derivations – *Gulaschsuppe*, vaguely from Hungary, *Zwiebelsuppe*, a version of French onion soup, and spicy Serbian-inspired *Bohnensuppe* (bean soup). While lamb is a rarity, the Germans eagerly devour pork, which is usually of high quality: it comes in a range of dishes, maybe with a sauce, or as a schnitzel or an *Eisbein* (knuckle). Or it makes its way into the endless variety of *Würste* (sausages), which can be spicy or bland, grilled or boiled, or served cold. Beef braised in sauces, or veal schnitzels, or game such as venison in season (more expensive) are also common, while lakes and rivers provide trout, perch and carp, cooked in interesting ways. Vegetables are better in north Germany than in the south, where dumplings often replace potatoes and pork is frequently served with *Sauerkraut* (but this is not as ubiquitous in Germany as you might think). Desserts in restaurants are disappointing: the best cakes and strudels are served in cafés.

Should you tire of German food, you can turn to the hordes of foreign restaurants, run mostly by the nationalities that account for Germany's large 'guest worker' minorities – Turkish, Greek, Yugoslav, Spanish and Italian (plus the inevitable Chinese). These places are quite cheap, and mostly they have the standards of service and tidiness that their German clients expect. There are plenty even in smaller towns, where some old half-timbered building, looking very German, may bear the sign 'Trattoria Siciliana' or 'Balkan Grill'.

Generally speaking, the cuisine of the south is more subtle and interesting than in the north: but the latter too has its specialities. This round-up follows the order of the chapters in this book.

North-Rhine Westphalia

Westphalia is noted for its smoked meats, especially ham: this is made from boneless pork, smoked over juniper berries and resin-free wood. It is served with rye bread such as *Pumpernickel*, another local speciality. You will also find sausages braised in beer and *Pfefferpothast*, a peppery goulash. In the Bergische Land east of Cologne, a traditional afternoon meal is the Kaffeetafel – coffee with fresh waffles, breads, fruit, apple syrup and much else. The Rhineland, oddly, has little gastronomic tradition and its local dishes are quite basic: *Himmel und Erde* (heaven and earth), an old paupers' dish, is apple mousse and potatoes with blood sausage. In Cologne, *Halve Hahn* sounds like a half-chicken but in fact is cheese with a rye roll; *Kölsche Kaviar* is in fact no pricey delicacy but just black pudding with rye bread. There are no wines north of Bonn, but the beers are good: the clear, highly-fermented *Kölsch* of Cologne, the dark, sweetish *Altbeir* of Dusseldorf, and the many beers of Dortmund, Europe's leading brewery town.

Rhineland-Palatinate

Despite all the vineyards, wine is little used in local cooking, which has few specialities. In the pubs of Mainz, also around Frankfurt, you'll find a curious snack called *Handkäs mit Musik* – a soft, ripe and odorous local cheese, doused in white wine and smothered in chopped onions (these produce the *Musik*, i.e. tummy-rumblings, later). In the Hunsrück they eat *Festessen* (sauerkraut and pease-pudding with ham).

Baden-Württemberg

The cuisine of Baden, French-influenced, is Germany's most sophisticated, and includes wine-based sauces, delicious smoked hams, quenelles, subtle ways with snails and trout, and the famous *Schwarzwalderkirschtorte* (Black Forest cherry gâteau). Cherries and other fruit go to make the excellent local fruit brandies, such as *Kirschwasser* (cherry brandy). The cuisine of Swabia is less refined, but very tasty. Dishes include *Maultaschen* (mouth pockets), a kind of spinach-filled ravioli eaten usually in soup; and *Zwiebelbraten*, beef in onion sauce. Many meat dishes are accompanied by the renowned Swabian *Spätzle*, crinkly flour noodles, delicious when properly *handgemacht*. *Pfannkuchen*, pancakes also made of flour-and-egg, are sometimes cut up and put in *Flädlesuppe*.

Bavaria

This at heart is a heavy peasant cuisine, but well-flavoured and quite varied. Sausages of all kinds are popular, notably the boiled white skinless sausages (*Weisswürste*) of Munich, and the grilled spicy *Bratwürste* of Nuremberg and Regensburg. Try also *Schweinshaxen* (huge knuckles of pork) and *Leberkäse*, which despite its name contains no cheese and little liver, but is a baked dough made of minced meat and smoked bacon. *Semmelknödel* (dumplings made from stale bread) are often served with meat dishes, while *Leberknödel* (liver dumplings) find their way into soups. The Gruyère-like cheeses from the Allgäu are among Germany's best; and pretzels and white radishes are often nibbled with a glass of beer. Some corners of Bavaria have their own specialities, for example Nuremberg's *Lebkuchen* (spicy gingerbread) and Bamberg's carp cooked in beer. Franconia, being a wine region, tends to have more refined cooking than beery southern Bavaria. But Franconia has its notable beers, too, i.e. the curious smoked beer of Bamberg and the strong Kulmbach ale.

Hesse
True local dishes are very few. But Frankfurter sausages originate from the region, and a green herb sauce accompanies some dishes. Frankfurt has a special dry white apple wine, *Äppelwoi*.

Lower Saxony
The fish dishes, notably eel, are much the same as in Schleswig and Hamburg (see below). *Grünkohl mit Pinkel*, cabbage with black pudding sausage, is one common dish. In the Lüneburg Heath area, the sheep which browse on the juniper and heather produce a delicious fragrant mutton, *Heidschnucken*: on local menus you'll find it cooked in various ways, mostly with mushrooms and cranberries. It is expensive. Strong tea is drunk in coastal areas. The favoured alcoholic drink is *Korn* (Schnaps): in some parts of Friesland, *Korn* by tradition is drunk from a long tin spoon, together with smoked eel, eaten with the fingers.

Hamburg and Bremen
In both these cities, and all over Schleswig and Friesland, the smoked or grilled eel is excellent, as well as the local herring done in a variety of ways. *Labskaus*, originally a sailors' dish eaten at sea, is a humble mix of pickled corned beef, herring, potato, beetroot and fried egg – rather an acquired taste. You might do better with Hamburg's remarkable eel-plum-and-vegetable soup (*Aalsuppe*), or a Bremen dish such as *Kükenragout*, a delicious stew of chicken, veal, sweetbreads and clams, cooked in white wine.

Schleswig-Holstein
The Bremen and Hamburg dishes are found here too, also such curiosities as *Grosse Hans* (dumpling with bacon and cherry sauce) or a mixed platter of beans, pears and bacon. The Holstein dish best known abroad, *Holsteinerschnitzel*, is seldom seen on local menus. But Busum has an excellent shrimp soup; Sylt is noted for its *Friesentorte* (plum clafoutis with cream); Lübeck does varied things with marzipan. *Rote Grütze*, red fruits with custard and wine, is a delightful Schleswig-Holstein dessert now found all over Germany.

Berlin
Some common and basic German dishes originate from Berlin, such as *Eisbein*, knuckle of pork served with sauerkraut and pease-pudding or mashed potatoes, and *Kasseler Rippenspeer*, a smoked and fried pork rib that comes not from Kassel but from Berlin where a butcher called Cassel invented it. *Bulette*, a spicy meat-ball, is popular. As for drinks, the very popular *Berliner Weisse mit Schluss* is pale wheaten beer with a dash of raspberry or woodruff syrup which turns it red or green.

Glossary of Some Common Terms Found on Menus
(not already mentioned above)

Abendessen	supper, dinner
Braten	roast
Eier	eggs
Forelle	trout
Frühstück	breakfast
Gans	goose
Geräuchert	smoked
Gemüse	vegetables

Hirsch, Reh	venison
Huhn, Hähnchen	chicken
Kartoffeln	potatoes
Knoblauch	garlic
Lachs	salmon
Lamm	lamb
Mittagessen	lunch
Nieren	kidneys
Obst	fruit
Rindfleisch	beef
Schinken	ham
Schnecke	snail
Schwein(efleisch)	pork
Spargel	asparagus
Speck	bacon
Topf, Eintopf	stew, casserole

Beer, Wine and Other Drinks

Almost all restaurants are licensed for serving alcohol, while pubs (*Kneipen*) and taverns (*Weinstuben, Bierstuben*) are extremely numerous. Many of these serve some food, too.

Beer is the commonest of drinks, and quite cheap. There are some dark beers and other varieties, but mostly Germans drink the kind of light beer known as 'lager' in Britain. *Pils* is one general term for it, no longer directly related to its origin in the Czech town of Pilsen.

Germany produces much wine, about four-fifths of it being white. Very little of it, at least in restaurants, is the kind of cheap table wine that you find in Mediterranean countries; so it is relatively pricey and is normally drunk in smallish quantities. You can always order it by the large glass (*Viertel*) or smaller glass (*Achtel*, i.e. one-eighth of a litre) if you do not want a full bottle. Germans do not drink wine heavily during a meal, but they like to go on sipping it afterwards; their style of wine, mostly light and fruity, lends itself to this. Wines are officially graded

into *Tafelwein* (blended table wine), *Qualitätswein* and, at the top level, *Qualitätswein mit Prädikat*, which is subdivided according to the timing and manner of the grape-picking: for example, *Spätlese* wines are from late-picked grapes, giving full flavours, while for *Auslese* wines the grapes have been picked separately, to produce an elegant bouquet. The best species of grape include Riesling, Müller-Thurgau, Sylvaner, Spätburgunder and Trollinger.

The main wine-producing regions are in the Moselle valley, the middle Rhine, the Pfalz, Baden, the Heilbronn/Stuttgart area, and Franconia. The wines of the Moselle, mostly from Riesling grapes, are mainly white and fairly dry but fruity; the harvesting is done late. A distinctive full-bodied red wine comes from the Ahr valley, south-west of Bonn. The Rheinpfalz wines are fruity and high in alcoholic content; some of the output is *Liebfraumilch*, far superior to the sugary stuff sold under that name in Britain. The Rheingau, on the north bank of the Rhine around Rüdesheim, produces full, dry white wines that are among the finest in Germany. In southerly Baden, French grape varieties are used, to produce subtle white wines, mostly dry, some sweeter; the few reds are excellent, too. In the Stuttgart and Heilbronn areas, you find light, very fruity wines both white and red, many from sweet Trollinger grapes; the reds are a pale luminous colour, delicious to drink on their own, but seldom robust enough to accompany meat. Franconian wines, grown mostly in the Main valley near Würzburg, tend to be dry and strong; they are marketed in green circular flagons known as *Bocksbeutel*.

In St Mary's church in Lübeck, an altarpiece of the Virgin Mary (1518).

Museums, Shops, Banks:

Opening Hours and Closing Days

NB: museums in Germany are generally closed on Mondays but open all other days; In the text of this book, under each museum, we give closing days only when there is an exception to this rule. Only a few private museums, and those of wide public interest such as open-air theme parks and zoos, are open daily.

As for shopping, an irritating law dating from the 1950s makes it illegal for shops to remain open after 6.30pm on weekdays, or 2pm on Saturdays (5pm on the first Saturday in the month), or to open at all on Sundays (save for bakers from 11am to 3pm). Exceptions are allowed to a few food shops near main stations, for the benefit of 'travellers'. This absurd law, much contested, has recently been modified slightly, to allow late closure on Thursdays, up to 9pm. Apart from this, German hours are normal. Shops mostly open at 9am. Banks tend to be open 8.30am–1pm, 2.30pm–4pm (some remain open over lunch in city centres); all close at weekends, save for exchange bureaux at airports and big railway stations. In villages and small towns, most shops, post offices and other offices close for lunch.

Public Holidays

The main national public holidays are: 1 Jan; Good Friday and Easter Monday; 1 May; Ascension Day; Whit Monday; third Wed in Nov (Day of Prayer and Repentance); 25/26 Dec. As from 1991, the German National Day, and the most important public holiday, will be 3 October, the date of unification in 1990. There are also some special religious holidays in mainly Catholic areas: 6 Jan, 15 Aug, 1 Nov. Corpus Christi day, in May or June, varying with the date of Easter, is a holiday in most regions, too.

Architecture and Art

The principal surviving Roman monuments in Germany are at Trier; other fragments can be found at Cologne and Regensburg. Later, Carolingian architecture (8th–9th century) found expression in the palace chapel at Aachen, also in St Georg on Reichenau island and other churches. The Romanesque style began to develop in the 10th–11th century, with St Pantaleon church in Cologne and St Michael in Hildesheim; then Rhineland Romanesque reached its apogee with the mighty cathedrals of Mainz, Speyer and Worms, all with double chancels. The 12th century was a great period of monastic building, for example the Romanesque abbey of Maria Laach, the Cistercian abbey of Eberbach. The 13th century marked the transition from Romanesque to Gothic, with the arrival of the pointed arch and ribbed vaulting, as witness Bamberg and Limburg cathedrals, and Maulbronn abbey.

The greatest Gothic cathedrals (13th–14th century) are at Cologne, Freiburg and Regensburg, all French-influenced. In north Germany, Gothic churches were built of brick, e.g. St Mary's, Lübeck. The Late Gothic period was marked by lofty hall-

Temperature and Rainfall Chart

Average temperatures in centigrade (to convert to Fahrenheit, multiply by 9, divide by 5, add 32):

		BERLIN	HAMBURG	MUNICH
January	max	9	2	2
	min	−12	−2	−5
April	max	22	13	13
	min	−2	3	3
July	max	32	22	23
	min	9	13	2
October	max	21	13	17
	min	−1	6	9

Rainfall in most cities is around 2–3 inches a month, but a little more in the south. In the Black Forest it reaches around 6 inches a month.

churches, notably the Frauenkirche in Munich. This was also a period of important secular building, when burghers created handsome town halls and patrician mansions, some in brick, some half-timbered: there are good examples in Bamberg, Brunswick, Frankfurt, Goslar, Lübeck, Regensburg and many other towns.

The influence of the Italian Renaissance can be seen in south Germany, for example in the town hall and the Fugger funeral chapel at Augsburg (early 16th century), and at Rothenburg. Further north, the Renaissance has left fewer traces, though the Weser Renaissance buildings of the Hameln area are distinctive. Baroque architecture began to emerge in Bavaria in the later 17th century, under the impetus of the Vorarlberg school: it has left a fine legacy in Munich, also in Würzburg and other parts of Franconia where Balthazar Neumann and the Dientzenhofer brothers were its greatest exponents: witness the Residenz at Würzburg and the Vierzehnheiligen chapel near Bamberg. Many Gothic and other earlier churches had their interiors refurbished in ornate baroque style, or in the light and exuberant rococo that followed it. In Bavaria, Ottobeuren abbey designed by Fischer is a marvellous example of baroque, while Zimmermmann (Wies church) and Cuvillies (the Residenztheater in Munich) were masters of the rococo. In the early 18th century, baroque spread to Berlin, with the work of Andreas Schlüter.

The late 18th century saw the arrival of the neo-classical movement (Schloss Solitude at Stuttgart, Walhalla near Regensburg and the illustrious Brandenburg Gate in Berlin). This in turn gave place to mid-19th-century neo-Gothic, much promoted by the Romantics, which produced some extravagant hilltop castles such as Neuschwanstein and Hohenzollern. Around 1900 *Jugendstil* (Art Nouveau) made its impact, with Darmstadt as its creative centre. Then in 1919 Walter Gropius founded the Bauhaus, and his ideas and those of Mies van der Rohe had worldwide influence. Since the war, German architecture has been noted for its striking modern churches with beautiful stained glass, and for some superb museums – designed, for example, by Mies van der Rohe in Berlin, James Stirling in Stuttgart, Hans Hollein in Mönchengladbach.

Painting and Sculpture

The first truly great German painters emerged in the 15th century, with the Cologne school, led by Stephen Lochner and some anonymous artists such as the Master of St Veronica. At the same period, in Nuremberg and other parts of Franconia, religious wood sculpture flowered wonderfully, with the work of Tilman Riemenschneider and Veit Stoss. In the Renaissance period of the 16th century, south Germany was again the main focus: Albrecht Dürer worked in Nuremberg, and Albrecht Altdorfer in Regensburg, while the two Hans Holbeins came from Augsburg. Lucas Cranach and Matthias Grünewald were other great artists of this period. The 17th and 18th centuries produced few painters of note, but brilliant architects.

The landscape painter Caspar David Friedrich was the most gifted member of the Romantic movement of the early 19th century. There were few notable German Impressionists, apart maybe from Max Liebermann and Lovis Corinth: but Expressionism had great influence in Germany, where it centred around the Brücke group (Kirchner, Schmidt-Rotluff, and for a while Emil Nolde). The Blauer Reiter group of Munich included Franz Marc, August Macke, the Russian-born Wassily Kandinsky and Paul Klee, the Swiss. In the earlier half of the 20th century, Otto Dix, George Grosz and Max Beckmann were powerful satiric realists who protrayed the misery of Germany between the wars, while Ernst Barlach was a gifted sculptor and Max Ernst a leading Surrealist. Best known of post-war artists are the 'action sculptor' Joseph Beuys and the painter Georg Baselitz.

Glossary of German Words (Other than Food Terms) Used in the Text

Allerheiligen	All Saints
Alt	old
Altstadt	old part of a town
Badisch	from, or of, Baden
Bahnhof	railway station
Bau	building
Bayerisch	from, or of, Bavaria
Berg	hill, mountain
Brücke	bridge
Brunnen	fountain
Burg	fortress, castle
Bürgermeister	mayor
Denkmal	memorial
Dom	cathedral
Dorf	village
Fachwerk	half-timbering
Fasching	carnival in S. Germany
Fest	festival
Festsaal	banqueting hall
Festung	fortress
Frauenkirche	Church of Our Lady
Freiherr	minor member of the nobility
Freilichtmuseum	open-air museum of rural life
Fürst	prince
Gasse	alley
Gasthaus, Gasthof	simple hotel, inn
Gaststätte	simple restaurant
Graf	count (title)
Hafen	port, harbour
Hauptbahnhof	main station

Hauptstrasse	main street
Heimat	home, homeland
Herzog	duke
Hexe	witch
Höhle	cave
Hof	courtyard, mansion
Insel	island
Jagdschloss	hunting lodge
Jugendstil	*Art Nouveau*
Junker	former Prussian landowner
Kaiser	emperor
Kammer	chamber, room
Kapelle	chapel
Kloster	monastery, convent
Kneipe	pub
Kunst	art
Kur	spa cure
Kurgast	spa visitor taking a cure
Kurhaus	assembly rooms at a spa
Kurpark	park in a spa
Land	State of the Federal Republic
Landesmuseum	regional museum
Landgrave	Count in charge of a sizeable region
Landtag	*Land* parliament building
Margrave	Count of a *Mark*, former frontier district
Marienkirche	St Mary's Church
Markt	market, market square
Messegelände	trade exhibition grounds
Münster	large church with cathedral status
Palast	residential palace or castle
Pfarrkirche	parish church
Rathaus	town hall
Ratskeller	Rathaus cellars, used as restaurant
Residenz	palace
Rittersaal	knights' hall
Sammlung	collection
Schloss	castle, château
Spielbank	casino
Stadt	town, city
Stiftskirche	collegiate church
Stiftung	foundation
Strand	beach
Stube	room used for drinking, pub
Tor	gate, gateway
Tracht	local traditional costume

Turm	tower
Verkehrsamt, Verkehrsverein	tourist office
Wald	forest
Weingut	wine-growing estate
Weinlehrpfad	explanatory footpath in vineyards
Weinstube	wine-tavern

Symbols Used in Accommodation, Food and Drink Recommendations

H = Hotel
R = Restaurant
B = Beer Garden, Beer Cellar
P = Pub (*Kneipe*)
W = Wine Tavern
C = Café
D = Disco, Dance Hall

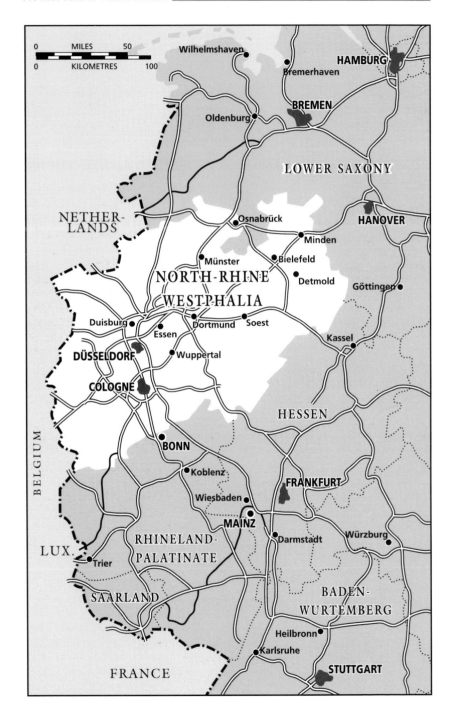

CHAPTER TWO

North-Rhine Westphalia

(Nordrhein-Westfalen)

THIS IS THE most populous of the *Länder*, by far, with some 17 million people. It embraces the great Ruhr industrial conurbation, the Rhineland cities of Bonn, Cologne and Düsseldorf (its own political capital), and such other important towns as Aachen and Münster. It is currently ruled by the SPD. It was formed in 1946 from the territories of north Rhineland and Westphalia which had belonged to Prussia since the early 19th century; the Rhineland had previously been annexed by France in 1801–14. After 1919 the left bank of the Rhine was demilitarized, and when Hitler illegally reoccupied it in 1936, the Anglo-French acquiescence paved the way for World War Two. As for Westphalia, Napoleon briefly made it a kingdom in 1807–13, with his brother Jerome as its monarch; then the Prussians made it a province, with Münster as its capital.

The *Land* is above all industrial, but there is much large-scale farming too, on the Westphalian plain and by the middle Rhine, where towards the Dutch border the houses have a distinctly Dutch look. The forested hills of the Sauerland and Bergishes Land to the east, and of the northern Eifel to the south-west, are popular holiday and leisure areas. In the Rhineland, the people are mainly Catholic; they are easy-going, gregarious, given to jokery and jollity – as you can see especially at carnival-time. The Westphalians are mostly Protestant and have the more reserved temperament of north Germans.

Aachen and Düsseldorf

AACHEN (pop. 245,000), Germany's most westerly city, could well be the first that you visit if you drive from Britain. This is apt: for though it is not Germany's oldest city, it played a leading role in early German history – in the time of Charlemagne (Karl der Grosse) who made it his capital, in his bid to unite Franks, Saxons Bavarians and others into a single empire. The amazing cathedral that he founded in c. AD 800 survives today as one of the finest Christian treasure-houses of Germany; and around it is a small but very picturesque Altstadt, well restored after the bombing that flattened much of Aachen. In fact, there's much of interest in this town that also contains one of Germany's leading science and engineering colleges, and whose diverse industrial output ranges from needles and umbrellas to machinery and rolling-stock. The huge open-cast lignite mines in the region are an important source of energy for industry.

Aachen is also a well-known spa town, with the hottest springs (brine and sulphur) in north-west Europe: they are used for treating rheumatism, gout and sciatica. They attracted the Romans, who built thermal baths, and also Charlemagne: after years of restless campaigning, constantly moving his court, he finally settled in Aachen in 794 – partly for strategic reasons, partly because he loved swimming in these waters. He built a palace here from which he ruled his great empire, which stretched from Spain to the Baltic and down to Austria, and he died at Aachen in 814. Soon after this, the empire broke up: but from 936 to 1531, Aachen was Germany's coronation city, and 32 kings were crowned in its cathedral. After this its influence declined.

Of Charlemagne's palace few traces survive today, save for its chapel, which has given the town its French name, Aix-la-Chapelle ('the spa with a chapel'). This octagonal basilica, with its two-storey arcaded gallery, forms the heart of the present-day **cathedral**, whose Gothic chancel was added in 1355–1414. It is a weird building, quite small, rather dark, but full of wonders. Suspended under the dome of the octagon is a huge brass candelabrum, the gift of Frederick Barbarossa; on the high altar is the Pala d'Oro, a sumptuous 11th-century altar frontal decorated with scenes of the Passion; and close by is the ambo, an amazing small pulpit of gilded copper adorned with precious stones. As if this were not enough, in the chancel you will find the Shrine of Charlemagne, a wonderful ark-like golden reliquary, while up in the gallery is the marble imperial throne (probably not Carolingian but made about 100 years later). The cathedral's Treasury (*Domschatzkammer*, open daily) contains many dazzling objects – notably the golden jewel-studded Cross of Lothair (990), and the 13th-century gold-and-silver Shrine of the Virgin.

Just north of the cathedral, in the heart of the old town, is the 14th-century **Rathaus**, one of the finest in Germany, looking more like a feudal castle than a town hall. It was built on the site of Charlemagne's palace (of which two towers, the Granusturm and Marktturm, still survive). Inside, you can see the chamber where the treaty marking the end of the Austrian War of Succession was signed in 1748, and the much-restored but still splendid Kaisersaal where the kings were crowned: it holds the crown jewels, and is lined with lively 19th-century murals of the life of Charlemagne. Here each year the Charlemagne Prize is awarded to someone judged to have done the most for European unity.

Near the Rathaus, in Krämerstrasse, is the very picturesque old Postwagen inn (1657), still open as a restaurant. This old heart of the town is full of curiosities – old city gates, half-timbered houses and statue fountains, such as the dolls' fountain (*Puppenbrunnen*), made of bronze dolls whose arms can be twisted. Best of the town's museums are the nearby Couven Museum, in Hühner Markt (period furnishings, and a reconstructed 18th-century pharmacy, in an elegant bourgeois home); the Suermondt-Ludwig Museum, Wilhelmstr. 18 (mediaeval sculpture and carvings, 15th–17th century Flemish, Dutch and German paintings); and, most interesting, the **International Newspaper Museum**, Pontstr. 13 (cl. Sun). This is in an old house almost next to the one where in 1850 Paul Julius von Reuter founded his famous news agency, using carrier pigeons. It contains some 120,000 world newspapers, and has fascinating exhibits showing how the Press reacted to major events of the day, from 1848 to the present time.

MÖNCHENGLADBACH (pop. 260,000), north-east of Aachen, is an old textiles and machinery producing centre that has recently acquired other distinctions. First, its ambitious new Abteiberg Museum of modern art, in the heart of the old town, is a striking modernistic building by the Viennese architect Hans Hollein: it is devoted to avant-garde works by Beuys and others. Secondly, the western suburb of Rheindahlen contains NATO's operational HQ for north and central Europe, also the HQ of the British Army of the Rhine: here you'll find cricket pitches, an Anglican church, and other manifestations of the British way of life.

Plutocratic **DÜSSELDORF** (pop. 570,000), on the Rhine, is a town of little charm but considerable interest. It is the *Land* political capital, also *de facto* the economic and commercial capital of the nearby Ruhr: suitably, its skyline is dominated by the skyscraper office headquarters of Thyssen and Mannesmann, two of the Ruhr's multinational corporate giants. Everything

in Düsseldorf breathes money. After Frankfurt, it is Germany's leading centre of international banking and finance, with over 2,000 foreign firms including some 400 from Japan: the Japanese have made this their foremost trading centre in Europe, and the resident colony of Japanese citizens, 6,000, is the largest outside Japan. It's a wealthy city, with a *per capita* income 25 per cent above the federal average, and is said to contain more millionaires and big jewellers than any other. More than elsewhere in Germany, here in smart society you are judged by your money and how well you display it.

Yet this is also a lively city of the arts (it can afford it), with a true cultural heritage. It was just a Rhine fishing-village until the 14th century, when it became the residence of the Dukes of Berg. In the 17th century the Electors of Neuburg-Palatinate settled there; and it was one of them, the splendour-loving Johann Wilhelm (1679–1716), known as Jan Wellem, who laid the basis of a cultural tradition. He drew musicians and artists to his court, commissioned baroque buildings and founded the picture gallery (his bronze equestrian statue stands outside the Rathaus). Today the city may have little notable architecture (it was badly bombed), but there are several fine museums; and it's remarkable how many great writers, musicians and artists have been associated with a town best known for trade and money. Heinrich Heine was born and spent his youth here, son of a local merchant. Brahms, Mendelssohn and Schumann all lived a worked here for a time, as did Goethe and the painter Peter Cornelius, while it is thanks largely to the conceptual artist Joseph Beuys (see feature) that Düsseldorf has become

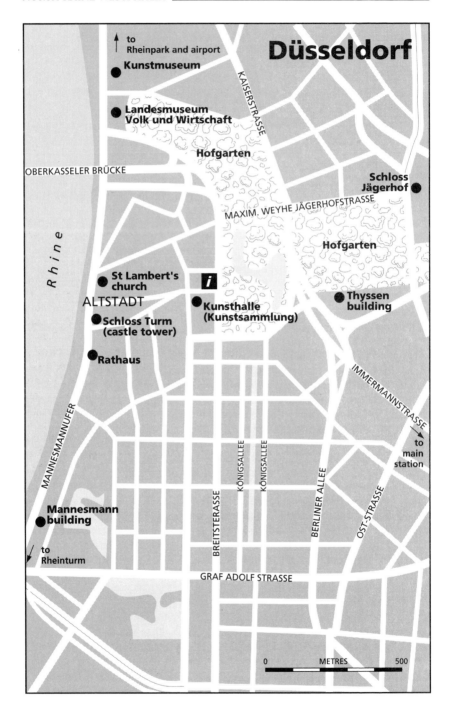

to
Rheinpark and airport

Kunstmuseum

Düsseldorf

KAISERSTRASSE

**Landesmuseum
Volk und Wirtschaft**

Hofgarten

OBERKASSELER BRÜCKE

**Schloss
Jägerhof**

MAXIM. WEYHE JÄGERHOFSTRASSE

Rhine

Hofgarten

**St Lambert's
church**

ℹ️

ALTSTADT

**Kunsthalle
(Kunstsammlung)**

**Thyssen
building**

**Schloss Turm
(castle tower)**

Rathaus

MANNESMANNUFER

IMMERMANNSTRASSE

to
main
station

KÖNIGSALLEE

KÖNIGSALLEE

BERLINER ALLEE

OST-STRASSE

**Mannesmann
building**

to
Rheinturm

BREITSTERASSE

GRAF ADOLF STRASSE

0   METRES   500

Germany's foremost centre for avantgarde art, after Berlin. Theatre and opera are amongst the best in Germany. And Düsseldorf has also become one of the nation's leading centres for graphic design, advertising and fashion. After Munich, this is Germany's smartest town. But it lacks the gentler grace of Munich: its style of high chic tends to be more cool, brittle and arrogant – as you can tell if you watch the hard-faced glamorous ladies in the Königsallee, the city's most fashionable boulevard (see p. 34).

Düsseldorf is notable for its traditional **festivals**. The Carnival in February is the best and biggest in Germany after those of Cologne and Mainz. In July, the Grosses Schützenfest is a riflemen's meeting and a hugely popular festival, along the Rhine banks. On 10 November, St Martin's Eve is marked by a big procession of children bearing lanterns.

Düsseldorf's nightlife is lively all year. Theatre booms, too: the Komödchen, Grabbeplatz (tel 32 54 28), is one of Germany's leading satiric cabarets. The adjacent Altstadt is notable less for picturesque charm than for being the focus of a Soho-like, tourist-geared entertainment industry.

Düsseldorf's main points of interest are spread out fairly close to the Rhine, on its east bank. Starting at the north end, the excellent **Kunstmuseum** is one of the city's two great museums of modern art. The German Impressionists and Expressionists with their bright, rough colours (Kandinsky, Kirchner, Nolde, Macke, etc) are much in evidence. So is Beuys, while one room is devoted to 22 works by the 'Zero' artists of the 1960s and '70s, including Vasarely. Older periods are best represented by two remarkable

Rubens, his *Assumption* and *Venus and Adonis*. Above all I was struck by Otto Pankok's haunting, fiercely emotional series of 60 lithographs that relate the life and Passion of Christ to the sufferings of the Jews under Hitler. Pankok, then a professor of art in Düsseldorf, created this work here in 1933–36 and was attacked by the Nazis for 'blasphemy'. His model for Mary was a gipsy girl who later died in a concentration camp.

The next-door Landesmuseum Volk und Wirtschaft (open daily except Sat) displays a vast amount of world economic and social data by means of graphs, charts and working models: too didactic to be as interesting as it could have been. Further south, a spacious modern building houses the city's other major art collection, the **Kunstsammlung Nordrhein-Westfalen**, with notable works by Chagall, Kandinsky, Léger and Picasso, and some 90 Klees (he taught at the Düsseldorf Academy until sacked by the Nazis in 1933, and by way of atonement this big collection was bought from America after the war). East of this museum stretches the pleasant Hofgarten park, with two lakes and several fountains. On its south side are the two adjacent thin slabs of the 26-floor Thyssen building; and in the far corner is the baroque 18th-century Schloss Jägerhof, housing a small museum of Goethe souvenirs. To the west of the Kunstsammlung, by the river, is one of the city's few interesting churches, St Lambertus, a 14th-century brick hall-church with a 15th-century *Pietà* and some nice modern stained glass. It is best known for its curious twisted spire. Huge Düsseldorf, incidentally, has no cathedral: cynics suggest that the Thyssen skyscraper fulfils this role.

Close to St Lambertus, the sturdy round white Castle Tower (Schloss Turm), surviving relic of the 13th-century city castle, stands at the entrance to the **Altstadt**, a network of narrow traffic-free streets. Here Heine was born in 1797, at Bolkerstr. 53, in a house now destroyed. The Altstadt today, always thronged with visitors, is a heady mix of the smart and tawdry, with kitschy shops next to elegant boutiques, fast-food eateries and jazz clubs beside quaint old pubs in *Fachwerk* houses. At any of these pubs, as elsewhere in the city, you can drink the dark *Altbier* for which Düsseldorf is famous; and in many of them you'll be served by the same species of jolly blue-aproned waiter as in Cologne (see p. 58), known here as 'Zappes'. In the Altstadt, too, in the tourist season, you may see the cartwheel-performing urchins (*Radschläger*) for which the town is also known. It is said that at Jan Wellem's wedding a wheel of his coach grew loose and a boy of ten saved the day by clinging to it and 'cartwheeling' to the end of the parade. Today some small kids eagerly do cartwheels for tourists – and expect a tip.

To the east is the **Königsallee** (known locally as 'die Kö'), a broad boulevard laid out in 1802: it is now the city's assertive focus of would-be glamour, and one of Germany's most famous streets. Swans and ducks glide in the many-bridged canal down its centre, under the plane and chestnut streets. One side is lined with banks, the other with some of Europe's most exclusive shops and cafés. Here the social scene is amazing. Very dandified men and haughtily rich-looking ladies, coldly stylish, some leading poodles as neatly groomed as they, jostle on the pavement with ordinary scruffy folk and beggars, too. But only the former enter the smart shops. The new high-glass-domed Kö-Galerie at no. 60 is a notably trendy arcade. The 'Kö' is at the heart of the city's financial district, and to the west by the river is the 24-floor Mannesmann building, close to the Rheinturm, a TV tower that offers a broad Rhine view from its observation platform (234m). Across the river, Oberkassel is a residential district of tall *Jugendstil* houses: it has plenty of interesting pubs and bistros, patronized more by locals than by tourists. Düsseldorf's actual setting, astride the broad Rhine, is attractive; and there are pleasant river walks, notably by the Rheinpark, a wide stretch of green between the museum district and the huge trade fair grounds to the north.

The striking silhouette of the Thyssen headquarters' skyscraper, in Düsseldorf.

TOURIST OFFICES

AACHEN: Bahnhofsplatz 4, tel (0241) 180 29 65, Markt 39, tel 180 29 60.

DÜSSELDORF: Heinrich-Heine-Allee 24 and Hauptbahnhof, tel (0211) 35 05 05.

Accommodation, Eating and Drinking

AACHEN 5100 (tel. code 0241):

(H)**Aquis-Grana-City**, Büchel 32, tel 44 30. Modern, near cathedral, central but quiet. Thermal baths, indoor pool. Rooms (90) B. Meals (cl lunch, Sat, Sun) B–C.
(H)**Ibis**, Friedlandstr. 8, tel 4 78 80. Modern, well-run, near main station. Rooms (104) C. Meals D.
(H)**Frankfurter Hof**, Bahnhofstr. 30, tel 3 71 44. Near main station. Clean, friendly. No restaurant. Rooms (22) D.
(R)**Gala**, Monheimsallee 44, in Casino, tel 15 30 13. Elegant and fashionable; superb cooking. Cl lunch and Mon. Meals A.
(R)**Ratskeller**, Markt, tel 3 50 01. Picturesque historic tavern in old Rathaus. Meals C.
(R)**Elisenbrunnen**, Friedrich-Wilhelm-Platz 13, tel 2 97 72. Modern, facing the spa gardens and fountain; well-reputed cooking. Meals B–C.
(R)**Zum Schiffgen**, Hühnermarkt 23, tel 3 35 29. In Altstadt, cosy and intimate; good German dishes. Meals C–D.
Attractive, modest restaurants near the cathedral include the **Goldene Rose, Haus am Dom** and **Friesenstube**.

MÖNCHENGLADBACH 4050 (tel code 02166):

(H)**Besch-Parkhotel-Rheydt**, Hugo-Junkersstr. 2, tel 4 40 11. Pleasant old patrician residence in Rheydt district, quiet and cheerful. Rooms (33) C. Meals (cl Sat dinner, Sun) B–C.
(R)**tho Penningshof**, Eickenerstr. 163, tel (02161) 18 10 00. Charming old 16th-century timbered house; excellent Rhenish specialities. Meals (cheaper at lunch) B–D.

DÜSSELDORF 4000 (tel code 0211) An expensive city:

(H)**Majestic**, Cantadorstr. 4, tel 36 70 30. Fairly central; good Italian restaurant. Cl Christmas. Rooms (52) A. Meals B.
(H)**Graf Adolf**, Stresemannplatz 1, tel 36 05 91. Near main station. No restaurant. Rooms (100) A.
(H)**Schnellenburg**, Rotterdamerstr. 120, tel 43 41 33. Pleasantly set by the Rhine near exhibition grounds; attractive and individual. Rooms (50) A–B. Meals B.
(H)**Astor**, Kurfürstenstr. 23, tel 36 06 61. Fairly central; nice welcome. No restaurant. Rooms (16) C.
(H)**Intercity-Hotel Ibis**, Konrad-Adenauer-Platz 14, tel 1 67 20. In station; plain but well run. No restaurant. Rooms (166) C.
(H)**Domo**, Scheurenstr. 4, tel 37 40 01. Near station; cheap but pleasant. No restaurant. Rooms (15) C–D.

Joseph Beuys and the Düsseldorf Art Scene

Commercial Düsseldorf might seem an odd place to be the leading centre of the German avant-garde art scene (along with Berlin). The explanation lies with the late Joseph Beuys, hyper-controversial artist, who lived and worked here – and with history. In the 19th century, under its Prussian rulers, Düsseldorf's Academy of Art became the foremost in Germany. Then after 1945 it developed as a major art school, attracting many avant-garde artists: the abstract 'Zero group', perhaps Germany's most influential post-war art movement, began here in 1957. The young Beuys arrived from his home near the Dutch border, became a teacher at the school, held exhibitions, shocked and thrilled the art world, led leftist and Green protests, quarreled with the stuffy *Land* authorities, was sacked, then reinstated, and died in 1986.

High prices are paid for Beuys' provocative 'action sculptures', which you will find in many German museums. He loved to make sculptures out of rough material – bits of wood and steel, discarded refuse, and especially felt and fat, his private symbols of rebirth. He was a generous idealist with a poetic extremism and a craving for absolutes, essentially Germanic. Whether he was also a great artist, time will tell.

Since his death, Düsseldorf has been losing ground to its rival, Cologne, and many artists have been moving there. In the post-war era, Cologne has also been the foremost art-dealing city of Germany, with some 150 galleries: its Art Fair every November is Europe's most important after that of Basel.

(R)**Im Schiffchen**, Kaiserwerther Markt 9, tel 40 10 50. North-west of the town, one of Germany's top restaurants, with brilliant French cooking and prices to match. Dinner only; cl Sun. Meals A.

(R)**Weinhaus Tante Anna**, Andreasstr. 2, tel 13 11 63. Historic 17th-century wine-tavern in Altstadt. Cl lunch. Meals B.

(R)**Heinrich-Heine-Stuben**, Bolkerstr. 50, tel 13 23 14. Characterful Altstadt tavern, near poet's birthplace. Meals B–C.

(R)**Meuser**, Alt Niederkassel 75, tel 5 12 72. Very personal and family-run, in a private house; local specialities such as bacon pancakes. Need to book. Meals B–C.

(R)**Amadeus**, Belsenplatz 1, tel 58 87 53. Popular local venue in Oberkassel. Very authentic. Meals C–D.

(R)**Zum Schiffchen**, Hafenstr. 5, tel 13 24 21. Large, traditional very sympathetic tavern in Altstadt; friendly service and good local dishes. Meals C–D.

(R)**Confetti's Trattoria**, Düsseldorferstr. 2, tel 57 26 66. Trendy Italian place in Oberkassel, popular with artists, etc. Meals C.

(R)**Koller's Kahn**, Rheinpark. On a boat by the river near Theodor-Heuss bridge. Good for outdoor lunch in summer. Meals D.

Among the many pubs, bars and cafés, especially interesting are:

Königsallee: (C)**Casserole**, no. 92, smart modern pavement café, rich clientele; (D)**Sam's West**, no. 27, leading night-club and bar.

Altstadt: (P)**Zum Uerige**, Bergerstr. 1, famous old brewery pub, rough and simple, good for beer and snacks; (P)**The Irish Pub**, Hunsrückenstr. 13, quite authentic. *Oberkassel:* (P)**Muggel**, Dominikanerstr, youthful bohemian pub, very lively; (P)**Sassafras**, Düsseldorferstr. 90, lively local venue, notably at Carnival time.

The Ruhr – Rural, Cultural, even Industrial

The Ruhr district (*Ruhrgebiet*), named after a river that flows into the Rhine near Duisburg, is far from being merely a tedious industrial eyesore. It has some fine museums and other culture, and can teach a lot about modern Germany history; it is also much less grimy and polluted than it used to be, and is surprisingly rural in places, even quite idyllic. But it does remain the leading industrial area of Europe, producing some 60 per cent of the EC's bituminous coal and 20 per cent of its crude steel. Within a built-up zone measuring some 60 km by 20 km, about 5.5 million people live in a dozen or so industrial towns, Duisburg, Essen, Bochum and Dortmund being the biggest.

Until about 1850 this was rural farmland. Then the fortunate presence of coal and iron-ore in this one area, near the Rhine, led to rapid industrial growth. Family firms such as Krupp and Thyssen built steel mills and engineering works, and later the Ruhr became the powerhouse of the German armaments industry in two world wars: Hitler gained much crucial support from its rich magnates. Despite heavy Allied bombing, its industrial capacity was still 80 per cent intact in 1945, and in the 1950s it played a central role in the 'economic miracle'. But then around 1960 the best mines began to wear thin. The pit closures were carefully programmed over the next years, with generously-funded retraining and early retirement schemes, and the unions co-operated. So, although some 250,000 jobs were lost, there was *not one single strike* – an object lesson for British industry. Output is still at some 60 million tons a year. But the mines near the surface, in the Ruhr valley to the south, are now virtually used up, and it has become necessary to dig further north in the Emscher valley, where the seams are deeper and thus costlier to exploit. So Ruhr coal, once so cheap, is today undercut by imported coal. Since the mid-1970s the steelworks too have faced recession, and their workforce has been cut by over half – but again without strikes. Many workers have left for other areas. The Ruhr has been trying hard to diversify into other sectors: but it is not easy, for new industry prefers to settle in south Germany.

Despite these difficulties, the big Ruhr towns are remarkably spruce and civilized places. In their wealthy heyday they built fine public parks and opera houses, and this heritage survives: Bochum today has one of Germany's best theatres, Essen and Bochum boast superb museums, and you will even find such surprises as Europe's finest museum of icons in dour Recklinghausen. Housing too is impressive: the homes that Krupp and others built for their workers, in the last century, were far superior to the squalid back-to-back dwellings of early industrial England. These estates were models of intelligent paternalism, little cottages with gardens, and many still exist, notably in the western parts of Essen; nicely modernized, they are cosily lived in by today's well-paid workers. Often you will see a Mercedes parked outside old miners' cottages. But, though lifestyles have changed, the Ruhr retains the familiar miners' tradition of being a warm neighbourly community with strong local loyalties.

In response to Willy Brandt's famous appeal in 1965, 'Let us have blue skies over the Ruhr', firms and town councils have spent huge sums on anti-pollution measures – to some effect. Some chemical factories of course are still smelly: but soot and smog no longer cast much pall. The main heavy-industry activity is now on the northern side of the conurbation, roughly between Duisburg and Recklinghausen, where the river Emscher still swirls thick and black. Here and there, between the pits, a few mansions of rural landlords survive incongruously from an earlier era. And the giant satanic mills loom up. I find a certain awesome poetic beauty in these desolate industrial scenes.

On the south side of the conurbation, nature's recent reconquest of the winding river Ruhr valley has been an amazing ecological saga. There was coal-mining here since the 18th century, and this was the first part to be industrialized: hence the Ruhr gave its name to the whole region. Then the mines and factories spread north, around and beyond Essen and other cities; and then the Ruhr valley coal

mines wore thin and were closed. So now, with true Germanic thoroughness and neatness, the coalpits and railtracks have been mostly grassed over, the pitheads removed and the slagheaps planted with trees. The valley has been restored to its pre-industrial state, save for a few tidy suburbs or the dinosaur-like rusting skeleton of some disused ironworks. Today, from the southern suburbs of Essen as far east as Dortmund, you can walk along the wooded heights above views of the changing landscape: here cows graze in water-meadows beside romantic old castles and half-timbered pubs, and colourful sailboats dot the pleasure-lakes where the river widens, as sunbathers lounge on its shore. Not one's usual image of the Ruhr.

Starting from Cologne, this itinerary works north towards the Ruhr. First, in the hilly, attractive Bergisches Land you'll find the 'cathedral' of **Altenberg**, lying amid fields and woods. It's a 14th-century Cistercian abbey, Gothic in style, with some fine stained glass; its services today are alternately Protestant and Catholic. Further north, at **Burg an der Wupper**, a mighty feudal fortress looms high on a hill above the river Wupper, winding in its narrow valley sheer below – a dramatic location. This former home of the Dukes of Berg (sic) has an impressive courtyard: but the interiors were over-restored in the last century, and the lively murals in its old banqueting hall are hardly mediaeval. Concerts are held here; there's also a local history museum.

The industrial town of **Solingen** (pop. 161,000) is Germany's Sheffield, long famous for its knives, scissors and other blades – notably swords in olden days. Its Klingenmuseum (blade museum) has an array of these items, including old surgical instruments and splendid dress swords. To the north-east is **Wuppertal** (pop. 380,000), a big textile-producing centre that straggles for miles along the Wupper valley: it is made up of several separate towns that were not merged until 1929. Wuppertal, a city of culture as well as industry, has diverse claims to fame. First, it was the birthplace in 1820 of Friedrich **Engels**, whose family were local textile magnates (their house still stands, in Engelstrasse): they sent him to work in their sister factory in Manchester, where he collaborated closely with his friend Karl Marx, in London (do you remember Marxism?). Secondly, the **Von der Heydt Museum** has works by many famous French artists (Delacroix, Manet, etc) and a notable collection by a local painter, Hans von Marees (1837–87), who deserves to be better known. Thirdly, the opera house is the home of Germany's foremost modern dance company, created and run by the great **Pina Bausch**: she was born in 1940 in Solingen, trained in New York, then returned to her roots to form her own company, which is funded by the city and *Land*. If she is not touring abroad, it's worth trying to catch a performance of the supercharged Bausch mix of mime and circus, frenzy and incantation, described by one critic as 'a collective therapy session'. Fourthly, Wuppertal is known for its overhead suspended railway, built in 1900, that curves through the town for 13km: invented by a local engineer, this wheelless pioneering precursor of the modern monorail is striking to look at, useful, fast and safe (it has never had an accident). Quite a place, Wuppertal.

To its north you will reach the Ruhr valley at **Hattingen** (pop. 60,000),

mostly modern and industrial but with a charming Altstadt of half-timbered houses and old alleys; it has a church of c. 1200 and a 1576 Rathaus. A lively costumed festival is held here each summer. At **Blankenstein**, just upstream, a semi-derelict fortress stands on a hill above the river (good view from its tower). Here we begin our tour of the rural part of the Ruhr. Cross the river at Hattingen, drive east along the north bank, and you will see remarkable contrasts. There are villas amid meadows, and quiet river vistas: yet you are within the borders of industrial Bochum, fourth largest Ruhr city. You drive through thick woods down steep winding country lanes, to a glen where deer graze; in the nearby coomb, some early mineworks dating from 1700 have been preserved as an outdoor museum.

Cross back south of the river, and you'll come to another of the old castles along the Ruhr valley – the moated **Haus Kemnade**, with a small music museum and a pleasant courtyard restaurant: a *Gastarbeiter* festival (folk groups from Bosnia, Turkey, etc) takes place here every other summer. The castle stands by the pretty **Kemnadesee**, one of the four points between Essen and Dortmund where the river has now been widened into lakes with dams – partly to prevent flooding, and partly for recreation. There are new marinas, where you can take boat-trips or go surfing, sailing or canoeing (but not bathing: the water is still too polluted).

Many of the industrial memorials in the Ruhr valley are concerned with coal-mining. East of the Kemnadesee, at Bommern, you will find the **Muttental** coomb, seemingly deep in the country. But its black earth is crumbly and coaly. Here some early mines have been conserved as an outdoor museum, all clearly explained with signboards. Old coal-wagons stand on a restored railtrack (1829), said to be the oldest of its kind outside Britain; a gate marks the entrance to an old mine-tunnel in the cliff; and the miners' chapel (1820) is now a small museum of mining history. All along the valley is the German miners' emblem of crossed pick and hammer, with their slogan *Glückauf* ('good luck that you come back again', the cry given to miners going down into the pits).

East again, beyond Wetter, is another Ruhr lake, the **Harkortsee**, and beside it stands another industrial memorial – a huge flywheel made by a local firm during the war and then seized by the British Army. In 1986 REME nobly donated it to the town, and now it's a kind of outdoor modern sculpture. **Herdecke** (pop. 25,000), at the lake's far end, is one of several small Ruhr towns whose old pre-industrial core has been lovingly restored: its quaint little Altstadt is now a pedestrian area with cobbled paths, a stream, a church with green onion-dome, and the feel of a village. Its 'Mini-Hotel' has just one room to let.

Back across the river, at Eilpe in the south-west suburbs of industrial **Hagen** (pop. 209,000), is one of the most unusual and interesting of German open-air museums: the **Westfälisches Freilichtmuseum** (Apr–Oct), set in a secluded valley. Here the theme is not rural life but the area's early industrial technology: genuine working exhibits of old-style printing, papermaking, tannery, dyeing and so on are displayed in some 50 old

Fachwerk buildings that have been regrouped here. The machines and instruments, some pre-19th-century, are operated by the museum staff who will also sell you paper, nails, rope, shoes, etc, all made in the old way. The 'village' grocery and pub are in 1900 style, and their wares too – *Schnaps* as grandpa distilled it. The city of Hagen, itself today a dull place, was a centre of the *Jugendstil* (Art Nouveau) movement in the 1900 era: the Karl-Ernst Osthaus Museum, named after its leading local pioneer, is in a *Jugendstil* house that was the studio of the Expressionist painter Christian Rohlfs. It has works by him, Dix, Macke and others.

Leaving the rural Ruhr, we now tour the main industrial cities. **DORTMUND** (pop. 570,000), at the eastern end of the conurbation, is the largest town in Westphalia. From the mid-19th century it developed fast as a centre of heavy industry; and today, despite the inevitable decline of its steel-works, it is still important for engineering, electronics and machine tools. It is also the foremost brewery town in Germany – indeed in the world, after Milwaukee. Six huge breweries turn out six million hectolitres of beer a year: but the inhabitants drink less of the stuff than, say, in Munich.

Dortmund never had much of an Altstadt (its population in 1815 was only 4,000), and what there was the bombs flattened in the war. But a few old churches have been well restored, notably the Gothic Reinoldikirche, with 14th-century statues of Charlemagne and St Reinhold, and the Romanesque/Gothic Marienkirche, with a glorious altarpiece (1420) by Konrad von Soest. The **Museum am Ostwall** has works by such painters as

Beckmann, Macke and Modersohn-Becker, plus action sculptures by Beuys and others – notably Wolf Vostell's pile of 13,000 forks and spoons behind barbed wire. The **Museum of Art and Cultural History** includes a hoard of Roman gold coins and Germanic bracelets of c. 500 BC, found locally. Dortmund has some fine parks: the 170-acre Westphalia Park has children's playgrounds and a miniature railway. Nearby, the modern glass-walled Westfalenhalle, seating 23,000, is one of Europe's largest sports and congress halls. There's a new university in the suburbs. But in student circles Dortmund is best known as the site of the giant central computer, much dreaded and detested, that sifts and allots the candidates to all German universities – with capricious impersonality.

In the western outskirts of Dortmund, at Grubenweg 5, Bövinghausen, is one of the most ambitious of the new Ruhr industrial museums that are being created by restoring old plant *in situ*. It is **Zollern II/IV**, a handsome old minehead that was built in *Jugendstil* in 1898 as a showpiece, Europe's first electrically-operated mine: but it remained in production only till 1954. It is due to re-open in 1992 as a museum of mining and its social history. To the north, on the busy Dortmund-Ems canal at **Waltrop**, is another of these 'museums' – a lock with a huge twin-towered iron shiplift, built in 1899, able to hoist ships of up to 600 tons. It remained in service until 1962. A new lock and lift (for ships up to 1,000 tons) have since been built, on this vital waterway between Ruhr and North Sea. Just to the west – a typical Ruhr contrast – the picturesque old half-timbered village of **Horneburg** is a

centre of strawberry-growing. West again, in industrial **Recklinghausen** (pop. 119,000), you'll find a further surprise – Western Europe's leading collection of icons. This **Icon Museum** has over 600 of these beautiful paintings from the Orthodox Churches, mostly from Greece and Russia, many dating from the 16th century. The showpiece is a huge 16th-century calendar icon from Russia, featuring 600 saints and their feast days. The 16th-century Cretan icons are also striking. The town's large annual Ruhr Festival in May/June features drama, music and ballet from all over Germany.

BOCHUM (pop. 403,000) has plenty of culture as well as heavy industry. Its university is the Ruhr's most important, while its Schauspielhaus has been built up into one of the half-dozen leading repertory theatres in Germany, by two great directors, Peter Zadek and Claus Peymann. In a lighter vein, the new Starlight-Express-Halle is a grandiose venue for musical shows (starting in 1988 with Lloyd Webber). And the Romanesque Marienkirche in the suburb of Stiepel has fine frescoes (c. 1200). But Bochum's main point of interest is its **Bergbaumuseum** (museum of mining), the biggest of its kind in the world. Visitors are taken along 3km of tunnels in a disused mine and are shown mining equipment of all kinds, including special cabins used to rescue trapped miners. Tracing the history of mining in great detail, the museum contains a Roman frieze of mining in Spain c. 2,000 years ago, and stark photos of women mineworkers – in Lancashire in the 1890s, and in Japan where girls worked naked in the mines until the 1960s. From the top of the museum's 60m winding-tower

At Hagen, in the industrial Ruhr: picturesque rural housing in the Westphalian open air museum.

there's a fine view of the region – far more greenery than industry, and the slagheaps neatly landscaped into wooded hillocks.

At **ESSEN** (pop. 620,000), we are no longer in Westphalia but back in the Rhineland. This is is the fifth largest West German city, bigger than Frankfurt or Stuttgart. Though its main growth was in the 19th century, as the heartland of Krupp's industrial empire, it is also a very old town – as you can tell from its churches. Its cathedral (**Münster**), founded in 852, has a 10th-century west chancel based on that at Aachen, and inside are some remarkable treasures. In the church itself is a Gold Madonna (c. 980), said

to be the oldest in existence, and a big seven-branch candelabrum (c. 1000) with geometric patterns; the adjacent treasury (*Schatzkammer*) contains four resplendent 10th/11th-century processional crosses of abbesses and other precious items. The little Gothic Johanniskirche, nearby, has an unusual double-sided altarpiece, while the abbey church in the suburb of Werden is a superb example of Romanesque, with a baroque interior.

The **Folkwang Museum**, quite central, has one of the best 19th- and 20th-century art collections in Germany – German Romantics such as Thoma, French Impressionists (Monet, Manet, etc), some fine Gauguins and Van

Goghs, also Cubists (Leger, etc), German Expressionists (Nolde, Kirchner, etc), not forgetting Ernst and Chagall. The **Ruhrland Museum** in the same building, also not to be missed, deals with local customs and history, and has graphic photos and souvenirs of the dour life of 19th-century miners and steelworkers. Although its last coalmine closed in 1986, Essen today remains a major industrial and commercial centre, headquarters of some of the biggest German firms; its elegant shops bear witness to its vitality. It boasts Germany's tallest Rathaus (106m), built in the 1970s; and Germany's biggest synagogue, which survived the Holocaust and now houses a memorial to victims of Nazism. The huge Grugapark contains a botanical garden, aquarium and sports facilities. In the western suburbs are the Krupp factories and housing estates and to the south the Krupps' Villa Hügel: the villa overlooks the Baldeneysee, another of the Ruhr's pleasure-lakes, and the rural scenery all around is quite idyllic. Essen's main annual festival is the *Lichtwochen* (weeks of light), Oct to Dec, when the huge central shopping centre is brilliantly lit up.

Industrial **Oberhausen** (pop. 224,000), just west of Essen, was the site of the first Ruhr ironworks, in the late 18th century. The modern art gallery in the Schloss has a notable glass collection. And the town's annual festival of short films is famous in cinema history: here, in 1962, 26 radical directors drew up the 'Oberhausen Manifesto' for creative freedom that paved the way for the German 'new wave' of Fassbinder, Herzog, etc. **Mülheim**

(pop. 170,000), astride the river Ruhr, is another Ruhr city that combines heavy industry with a picturesque Altstadt of Fachwerk houses and some fine buildings – the 13th-century Petrikirche, well restored, and the fortress of Broich (open daily), Carolingian with Romanesque, Gothic and Renaissance additions. August Thyssen's steel empire was initially based on Mülheim.

DUISBURG (pop. 518,000), set at the point where the Ruhr flows into the Rhine, claims to be the world's biggest inland port, with 43km of quays and an annual traffic of over 20 million tons: via the Rhine it links the Ruhr industries with the North Sea. It is also the leading German steel town, producing a third of the country's output: but today, with Europe's steel industry in crisis, some of the giant mills have closed or contracted, and they stand looking gaunt and majestically hideous. The few belching chimneys, however unlovely, are at least a healthy sign of activity. You can take a guided motorboat trip of the port (Apr–Oct) past the miles of cranes, barges, warehouses and slagheaps (almost all the mines have closed too). On the cultural side, the **Lehmbruck Museum** of modern sculpture contains a splendid array, from Rodin via Moore and Arp to the inevitable Beuys, with the accent on the *oeuvre* of the local sculptor Wilhelm Lehmbruck (1881–1919). The great geographer and mapmaker Gerhard Mercator lived and worked in Duisburg from 1552 to 1594: the Niederrhein Museum contains a fascinating display of his work.

The Krupp Dynasty and their Villa Hügel

Alfred Krupp (1812–87), founder of the Krupp empire, did more than anyone else to create the industrial Ruhr. He was the kind of paternalist patriarch who combined real benevolence with cunning self-interest. Scared of the rising trade unions, he saw that his employees would be less likely to revolt if he treated them well. So he provided crèches, old people's homes, and better housing and welfare services than were usual in those days (witness the handsome garden-suburb estates near the old main factory in Essen). But he was also tough with workers wanting more pay: the grim strike rallies of that time, and the dour life of mine and mill, are vividly evoked in Essen's Folkwang Museum. Krupp the ironworks magnate moved into heavy armaments, and the firm provided Germany with the weapons for three major wars. Krupp's successors as heads of the dynasty, Gustav and Alfred Krupp von Bohlen, were sentenced at Nuremberg as war criminals, for their part in helping Hitler: but the Americans soon let them regain control of the firm. However, under bad management it then went into decline, and became a public company in 1968. The Krupp family today own very few shares.

For himself and his large family, Alfred Krupp built the amazing **Villa Hügel**, a pompous neo-Renaissance hulk on a hill above the Ruhr valley in the south Essen suburbs. It is now a museum, full of revealing portraits of the Krupps and their powerful friends. Its detailed account of Krupp history glosses over the nastier aspects. A big biennial art exhibition is held in the villa on even years.

TOURIST OFFICES

WUPPERTAL: Pavillon Döppelsberg, Elberfeld, tel (0202) 563 21 80.

DORTMUND: main station, tel (0231) 14 03 21; Südwall 6, tel 54 22 56 66.

BOCHUM: main station, tel (0234) 1 30 31; Rathaus, tel 621 39 75.

ESSEN: main station, tel (0201) 23 54 27 and 810 60 82.

DUISBURG: Königstr. 53, tel (0203) 283 21 89.

Accommodation, Eating and Drinking

BERGISCH GLADBACH 5060:

(H)**Waldhotel Mangold**, Am Milchbornsberg 32, tel (02204) 540 11. In a wooded rural setting just east of Cologne: family-run, attractive; good food. Cl 3 weeks Jun/Jul. Rooms (20) C. Meals (cl Sun, Mon; dinner only) B–C.

BURG AN DER WUPPER 5650 Solingen:

(H)**Haus in der Strassen**, Wermelskirchenerstr. 12, tel (0212) 4 40 11. Old house (1673) near castle; lots of atmosphere. Rooms (25) C. Meals B–C.

SPROCKHÖVEL 4322:

(H)**Rotisserie Landhaus Leick**, Bochumerstr. 67, tel (02324) 76 15. Country house in big garden; comfortable but rather impersonal and formal; 2 restaurants, stylish modern cooking. Cl Mon, 3 weeks Jan. Rooms (12) B. Meals A–C.

DORTMUND 4600:

(H)**Romantik-Hotel Lennhof**, in Barop suburb, Menglinghauserstr. 20, tel (0231) 7 57 26. Charming old half-timbered house in rural setting; pool, tennis; excellent food. Rooms (37) B. Meals B.
(H)**Drees**, Hohestr. 107, tel (0231) 10 38 21. Near Westfalenhalle and park. Modern, well run. Rooms (114) C. Meals C.
(H)**Esplanade**, Bornstr. 4, tel (0231) 52 89 31. Central. No restaurant. Cl Christmas period. Rooms (48) D.
(R)**La Table**, Hohensyburgstr. 200, tel (0231) 77 44 44. Excellent, stylish French restaurant in the casino at Syburg, S of city. Meals A, dinners only. **Neue Ruhrterrasse**, lunch too, B–C.
(R)**Zum Treppchen**, in Hörde suburb, Fassstr. 21, tel (0231) 43 14 42. Attractive old house with rustic décor and beer-garden; very popular. Cl Sun. Meals C.
(R)**Hövels Hausbrauerei**, Hoher Wall 5, tel (0231) 14 10 44. Cosy old pub, rustic-style but central; beer-garden. Meals C.

RECKLINGHAUSEN 4350:

(H)**Die Engelsburg**, Augustinessenstr. 10, tel (02361) 2 50 66. Central (in Altstadt) but quiet. Delightful tavern with good food. Rooms (30) C. Meals A–B.

BOCHUM 4630:

(H)**Arcade**, Universitätstr. 3, tel (0234) 3 33 11. Near station, large and convenient. Rooms (168) C. Meals (cl Sat Sun, 3 weeks Christmas, 7 weeks summer) C–D.
(H)**Schmidt**, Drusenbergstr. 164, tel (0234) 3 70 77. In S suburbs, quiet, modest and welcoming; kitschy décor. Rooms (33) D–E. Separate Vitrine restaurant (tel 31 24 69) is good, B–C.
(R)**Stammhaus Fiege**, Bongardstr. 23, tel (0234) 1 26 43. Old brewery with excellent varied cooking. Cl Thur, July. Meals C.

ESSEN 4300:

(H)**Schloss Hugenpoet**, in Kettwig suburb, August-Thyssen-Str. 51, tel (02054) 1 20 40. Moated 16th-century castle on the Ruhr banks, now a luxury hotel with classy cuisine and a warm welcome. Rooms (19) A–B. Meals A–B.
(H)**Parkhaus Hügel**, Freiherr-vom-Stein-Str. 209, tel (0201) 47 10 91. In Bredeney suburb, beside Baldeney lake. Friendly and personal; serious restaurant. Rooms (13) C. Meals B–C.
(H)**Luise**, Dreilindenstr. 96, tel (0201) 23 92 53. Central. No restaurant. Rooms (29) C–D.

(R)**Ange d'Or**, in Kettwig suburb, Ruhrtalstr. 326, tel (02054) 23 07. Used by top Ruhr tycoons: superlative cooking and setting. Dinner only; cl Sun Mon, June, Christmas period. Meals A.

(R)**Die Schwarze Lene**, in Bredeney suburb, Baldeney 38, tel (0201) 44 23 51. Old house overlooking Baldeney lake; fine food. Cl Thur Jan. Meals B–C.

DUISBURG 4100:

(H)**Haus Reinhard**, Fuldastr. 31, tel (0203) 33 13 16. Central, no restaurant. Cl Christmas period. Rooms (15) B–C.

(H)**Mühlenberger Hof**, in Rheinhausen suburb, tel (02135) 45 65. Charming rustic place with beer-garden. Cl 2 weeks carnival-time, 2 weeks Sep–Oct. Rooms (10) D. Meals (cl Mon) C.

Northern Westphalia and Lippe: Münster to Minden

This itinerary is really in two parts. It begins in northern Westphalia, at the renowned old city of Münster and the moated castles in its area. Then, via the big towns of Osnabrück and Bielefeld, it goes to the former principality of Lippe – to the long hill of the Teutoburger Wald and the old towns of Detmold and Lemgo. The latter is one of North Germany's loveliest.

MÜNSTER (pop. 272,000), Westphalia's historic capital, is one of the most distinguished episcopal and university cities in north Germany. It forms a kind of island of staunch Catholicism in the middle of mainly Protestant Westphalia: in today's ecumenical age, this situation no longer causes tensions, but the city remains devoted to its Catholic traditions. Its lordly past has left it with a wealth of fine architecture, from Romanesque to baroque. But it was terribly destroyed in the war, and despite careful restoration, some of its old character has been lost. Some baroque palaces have never been rebuilt.

Münster was made a bishopric by Charlemagne in 805. In the 13th century it also became a Hanseatic city. Its main claim to fame in history is that the Peace of Westphalia, which ended the Thirty Years' War, was negotiated and signed here (and in Osnabrück) in 1643–8. Until 1803 the city was the seat of prince-bishops, who endowed it with many of its fine baroque buildings. Then in 1806 it was made the capital of the Prussian province of Westphalia. In World War Two it was a bombing target, for the Allies believed that the Nazis were using the university to train their elite; over 90% of the central area was laid flat. But the old circular lay-out of the city is still discernible, with the cathedral at its heart, and a ring-avenue of lime-trees on the line of the old ramparts. The town has little industry, but is a major agricultural market for the rich Westphalian plain. Its university, founded in 1780, whose main campus lies right downtown, is Germany's third largest (after Berlin and Munich), with some 45,000 students. It is no surprise that Münster has almost as many bicycles (260,000) as people. The city has two notable **festivals**: the big Münster-Festival is in early June, while a five-day popular fair called 'Send' is held three times a year, in March, June and October.

The city's focus is the twin-towered Romanesque **cathedral** (1225–65), light and spacious inside. Photos in the porch show the fearful extent of its damage by 1945, but it has since been well rebuilt: the altar, organ and stained-glass are modern, but some 13th-century statues of saints escaped destruction. One curiosity is the elaborate astronomical clock (1540) whose mechanical figures perform at noon. Next to it is the tomb of the brave Cardinal Clemens August von Galen (1878–1946), the local bishop who dared to speak out against euthanasia and other Nazi crimes: he is due to be canonized. In the modern Domkammer (treasury) are various religious art works from the cathedral, notably an 11th-century gold reliquary of St Paul and a 13th-century processional cross. And in the cloister you can see the foundations of the original 8th-century church, where excavations have revealed the skeletons of 343 Carolingian canons! A market is held in the Domplatz every Wednesday and Saturday.

Another remarkable church is **St Lamberti**, built in 1375–1450 as a Gothic hall-church; its high lacework spire is a 19th-century addition. Up in its old tower you'll see three metal cages, where the bodies of three Anabaptist leaders were displayed in 1535: the Anabaptists, a fanatically radical sect preaching polygamy, adult baptism and jointly-held property, briefly seized Münster during the Reformation, but were driven out by an army raised by the prince-bishops, and their leaders were executed. The three bodies were left to rot, *pour encourager les autres*, and the cages were not cleaned out till 1887. The Anabaptist excesses produced a Catholic backlash and for centuries Protestants were not allowed in the town. But today there are lots of them. A town watchman still blows a trumpet from the church tower at noon and at 9pm each day – largely to impress tourists.

The main street of the Altstadt, leading from St Lamberti to the Rathaus, is the austerely graceful **Prinzipalmarkt**, lined with arcaded Renaissance houses, once the homes of merchants. All save a few at the north end have been rebuilt since the war. The 14th-century Gothic **Rathaus** has a superb stepped-gable façade, well restored; its former council chamber (open daily except Sun pm), finely panelled, is where the 1648 Treaty was signed and is now called the Hall of Peace. On its walls are portraits of the sovereigns who signed the treaty. The foyer of the new Rathaus contains interesting scale-models of the city in past times.

To the east is the **Erbdrostenhof**, a stately patrician palace (1757) with a lovely forecourt: its interior, open only to guided tours, is worth seeing for its rococo décor and frescoes, all newly restored. Goebbels in 1942 had detailed photos taken of these, for he feared that the building might be bombed and need to be rebuilt – as indeed happened. Restorers in the 1970s found the photos, and were thus able to copy the interiors exactly. The same occurred with the small round St Clement's church, close by: its lovely rococo décor has been accurately replaced thanks to these.

The **Landesmuseum**, opposite the cathedral, has a notable collection of mediaeval sculpture, altarpieces and stained glass, and exhibits of local history and folk art: but its post-17th-century paintings are unremarkable. West of the cathedral is the university quarter, and beyond it in a green park is the huge and elegant palace of the prince-bishops (1767), now part of the university: the architect, as with many of the town's other baroque buildings, was Johann-Conrad Schlaun. There are pleasant leafy walks along the banks of the little river Aa (the word comes from *aqua*), which winds from the cathedral to the Aa lake, used for boating and other leisure activities. Here there's a well-planned modern zoo with dolphinarium; and the **Mühlenhof**, an open-air museum of local rural life, with some 20 old farm buildings.

On the fertile plain all around Münster, and notably to its south-west, is the distinctive region of the **Wasserburgen** – châteaux surrounded by water. There are dozens of them, some still owned and lived in by the landed families that built them. In feudal days they were given wide moats for defence against attack: then in more peaceful times the moats were kept full because it looked nice. A number of these castles have been gracefully restored, and are worth a visit. Many of them still bear the old family colours, in the form of diamond-shaped motifs on the shutters – yellow-and-black, white-and-red, or black-and-white. Their owners may have lost their political power, but their estates are still large and prosperous: this is a wealthy region of live-stock-breeding and cereals. As well as the water-castles, there are many mellow old redbrick farmhouses.

Just west of Münster is the moated **Haus Rüschhaus**, not so much a castle as a neat little redbrick manor (1745–48); the poetess **Annette von Droste-Hülshoff** (see below) lived here in 1826–46, and there are mementoes of her inside (Apr to mid-Dec). Not far away is **Wasserschloss Hülshoff**, to my mind the loveliest of the water-castles, set in a trim and idyllic deer-park. Its buildings are on two tiny islands, within a moat where swans and carp glide. One holds the outbuildings, the other the redbrick Renaissance castle (1545); its neo-Gothic chapel was added in 1870. The Droste-Hülshoff family had owned the place since 1417, and the poetess was born here in 1797. Some rooms can be visited (daily Mar–Oct), and are kept authentically furnished in the style of her day – very gracious but a bit lifeless. I preferred the memorial to her at Meersburg where she died (see p. 140).

To the south-west, outside Lüdinghausen, is **Vischering**, another striking Wasserburg but different in style, far more feudal and severe. It was built of stone in 1271, as a defensive bastion, and its moat is as wide as a lake. Its interiors contain mediaeval furniture. Concerts are held here in summer, and the park is a nature reserve. **Nordkirchen**, to the south-east, is in another style again. This spacious baroque palace, Westphalia's largest, stands beside a formal lake in a huge park: it was built in 1703–33 for the Prince-Bishop of Münster, and looks almost like Versailles. Now used as a civil-service training school, its rooms can be visited only on Sunday. The park is always open.

Strike north-east across-country, leaving Münster to your west, and you will come to **Freckenhorst**, whose

Stiftkirche is pre-Romanesque: its remarkable baptismal font is inscribed with its date, 1129. Warendorf, to the north, is an old horse-breeding town – and this is horsey country, like many an English shire. At **Osnabrück** (pop. 150,000), just inside Lower Saxony, we are back with modern industry (metalwork, paper, textiles) and also with 17th-century history: just as in Münster, the 1648 Peace of Westphalia was negotiated here, in a room in the (much rebuilt) Rathaus now called the Peace Hall (Friedenssaal, open daily). As in Münster, this room bears portraits of the signatories. Osnabrück, a bishopric since 785, was badly bombed and today is mostly modern and graceless: but a few old streets survive, and there are three interesting churches. This very provincial town surprisingly has a brilliant daily paper, the *Osnabrücker Nachrichten*, famous for its political scoops and interviews in Bonn.

Bielefeld (pop. 312,000) is a big industrial town (engineering, electronics, linen, clothes, food-processing, etc) with little else of great interest. The Kunsthalle museum has some German Expressionist paintings (Beckmann, etc) and even Rodin and Moore amongst its sculptures. There's a farm museum just outside town. Since the 1950s the Bielefeld area has been a major centre of the British Army of the Rhine. **Gütersloh** (pop. 82,000), to the south-west, is a 'company town' choc-a-block with printers and editors – it's the unlikely headquarters of the world's largest publishing empire, Bertelsmann.

From Osnabrück east to Detmold, the Westphalian plain is cut by a long, thin range of wooded hills, the **Teutoburger Wald**. On its crest near Detmold are two famous curiosities, the Arminius monument and the **Externsteine**. The latter is a natural group of tall rocks in odd craggy shapes. They were used as a place of worship first by pagan tribes, then by Christians: carved on one rock is a fascinating 12th-century Romanesque low-relief of the Descent from the Cross. Also visible are a tomb, a pulpit and two chapels, all hewn from the rock. They can be seen clearly from the meadow: but (Apr–Oct) you can climb up new stairways in the rocks for a closer view. The summer solstice, with the sun rising up between the rocks, has long been celebrated here, as at Stonehenge. The Nazis then endowed this rite with some mystic national meaning, and took it over. So it's no longer so popular today.

The giant Arminius statue (**Hermanns Denkmal**) has been a focus of German nationalism for much longer. In c. AD 9 a local chieftain called Arminius (Hermann in German) roused the Germanic tribes to oppose Roman rule, and on this hill he defeated Rome's legions. Soon before German unification in the 19th century, he was made into a national hero, and this hilltop monument to him, on a high pedestal, was erected under Bismarck: it's a 26m greenish-copper statue of a helmeted Arminius raising a sword aloft. The Nazis held rallies here, too. But today it still draws hordes of trippers – less for nationalist reasons than for the wide view from the pedestal's upper gallery.

Below the memorial, at Berlebeck, is a big ornithological park where eagles and other birds live in freedom or in cages. It is near to the **Wesfälisches Freilichtmuseum**, whose open-air display of local rural tradition groups 65 old buildings, 15th to 19th century.

Here you are in the suburbs of **Detmold** (pop. 68,000), which until 1918 was the capital of the principality of Lippe. Though now absorbed into the *Land* of Nordrhein-Westfalen, Lippe is not part of Westphalia and it retains a vivid sense of its own identity. Detmold's handsome 16th-century castle has some Brussels tapestries and princely souvenirs (Bernhardt of the Netherlands' family came from Lippe). The town has large British Army barracks, known locally as 'Little London'.

To the north, also in Lippe, is **LEMGO** (pop.39,000), one of my favourite small German towns, bustling, friendly and intimate. It was a thriving Hanseatic trade centre in the 15th and 16th centuries, hence its legacy of gabled mansions in the delightful Altstadt. Here the unusual old Rathaus consists of eight adjacent buildings – 'It just grew, as the town did', I was told. Behind it is the Nicolaikirche, part 13th-century, with two dissimilar towers: its quiet little square, with lawns and linden trees, has all the tidy cosiness of an English cathedral close. Along the main street, Mittelstrasse, note the carved painted façade of no. 17 (1587), and the modern bronze fountain/sculpture of people and a goat drinking from a

beer-barrel. New and old here go well together: some modern houses in the Altstadt have been built in the same gabled shape as the old ones, and they seem to harmonize. Down Breitestrasse is the **Hexenbürgermeisterhaus** (1568), the beautiful house of the mayor who in the 1670s led an *un*-beautiful witchhunt: alleged witches were tortured so as to extract confessions that they had dealt with the Devil. Some were drowned. The house has a small museum, with details of all this and some torture instruments: but my kindly hosts were not keen for me to visit it. Lemgo is not proud of this episode in its past.

Further north is a beauty-spot known as the **Porta Westfalica**, where the river Weser has driven its way between two wooded hills: each of them is topped by a graceless monument from the Wilhelmine period, one a statue of Bismarck, the other a tower in honour of Wilhelm I. And so you will come to **Minden** (pop. 78,000), a well-preserved city whose cathedral has a superb Romanesque façade; inside is a remarkable 11th-century crucifix. The town's giant lock (*Schachtschleuse*), 85m long, links the Weser to the Mittelland canal: a small museum explains how it works.

TOURIST OFFICES

MÜNSTER: Berliner Platz 22, tel (0251) 51 01 80.

DETMOLD: Rathaus, Langestrasse, tel (05231) 76 73 28.

LEMGO: Haus Wippermann, Kramerstrasse, tel (05261) 21 33 47.

MINDEN: Grosser Domhof, tel (0571) 8 93 85.

Accommodation, Eating and Drinking

MÜNSTER 4400 (tel code 0251):

(H)**Waldhotel Krautkrämer**, Am Hiltruper 173, tel (02501) 80 50. One of several sophisticated rural hotels on city's outskirts. By a small lake to the south: rather smart, but family-owned and friendly, with stylish traditional furnishings. Excellent superior cooking. Indoor pool. Rooms (76) A. Meals A–B.

(H)**Schloss Wilkinghege**, Steinfurter Str. 374, tel 21 30 45. 16th-century water-castle amid parkland on NW outskirts, next to golf-course. Quiet and rural; lovely décor; good food, served on terrace or in atmospheric Schlosskeller. Rooms (38) C. Meals B.

(H)**Romantik-Hotel Hof zur Linde**, Handorfer Werseufer 1, tel 32 50 02. Charming old rural building (1661) in NE outskirts – beams, antiques, log-fire, four-posters and other cosiness. Good food, too, notably game. Rooms (30) C. Meals B.

(H)**Conti**, Berliner Platz 2a, tel 4 04 44. Opposite main station. No restaurant. Rooms (60) C–D.

(H)**Horstmann**, Windthorststr. 12, tel 4 70 77. Also near station, no restaurant. Rooms (24) C–D.

(R)**Altes Brauhaus Kiepenkerl**, Spiekerhof 45, tel 4 03 35. Attractive old brewery-pub; good local dishes. Cl Tue. Meals C.

(R)**Pinkus Müller**, Kreuzstr. 4, tel 4 51 51. Charming old student tavern in old town; brews the city's strong 'Altbier'. Excellent Westphalian cooking, too. Cl Sun. Meals C.

(B)**Kruse Baimken**, Am Staatgraben. Large, very popular beer-garden by north bank of Aasee.

HÖRSTEL-RIESENBECK 4446:

(H)**Schlosshotel Surenberg**, Surenberg, tel (05454) 70 92. Next to a water-castle, a breezy modern ranch-like hotel, friendly and spacious, with good food and the accent on riding and other sports. Own stables. The restaurant's wide windows give on to the riding-hall, so you can watch the horses while you eat. Cl 2 weeks Jan. Rooms (23) C. Meals B–C.

WARENDORF 4410:

(H)**Im Engel**, Brünebrede 37, tel (02581) 70 64. Ancient traditional inn, well modernized, family-run. First-rate food, with accent on lamb and duck. Sauna, solarium. Cl 2 weeks Aug. Rooms (23) C. Meals (cl Fri dinner, Sat lunch) C.

OSNABRÜCK 4500:

(H)**Park-Hotel**, Edinghausen 1, tel (0541) 4 60 83. By a quiet park in W suburbs; indoor pool, minigolf, bowling, etc; cosy Bierstube. Rooms (90) C. Meals B–C.

(H)**Klute**, Lotter Str. 30, tel (0541) 4 50 01. Fairly central. Rooms (20) C–D. Meals (cl 2 weeks July) C.

BIELEFELD 4800:

(H)**Hoberger Landhaus,** Schäferdreesch 18, Uerentrup, tel (0521) 10 10 31. Country house in W outskirts, on edge of wooded hills. Rooms (30) C. Meals C.
(R)**Ente,** Niedernstr. 18, tel (0521) 55 54 55. Downtown and smart, with reputed cooking, especially duck. Cl Sun Mon, 2 weeks July/Aug. Meals A–B. Its **Bistro Tele-Treff** is cheaper (C–D).

DETMOLD 4930:

(H)**Lippischer Hof,** Allee 2, tel (05231) 3 10 41. 18th-century cavaliers' house, well modernized, central; food the best in town. Rooms (24) C. Meals B–C.
(H)**Hirschsprung,** Paderborner Str. 212, Berlebeck, tel (05231) 49 11. Attractive old hunting-lodge, up in the Teutoburg woods. Rooms (10) C–D. Meals B–C.

LEMGO 4920:

(H)**Auf dem Brokhof,** Zur Behrensburg 19, Lüdissen, tel (05261) 4482. A real find! In rolling country N of town, a nicely converted farmhouse, run by charming people. Spacious rooms, hearty rural cooking. Rooms (9) E. Meals (E) for residents only.

VLOTHO AN DER WESER 4973:

(H)**Lütke,** Weserstr. 29, tel (05733) 50 75. Near river, run by Lütke family; unassuming and sympathetic; good German cooking. Rooms (20) D. Meals C–D.

MINDEN 4950:

(H)**Bad Minden,** Portastr. 36, tel (0571) 4 30 55. Well-run modern hotel in S outskirts. Rooms (33) B–C. Meals C.

The Sauerland

The Sauerland, just east of the Ruhr conurbation, is a wild schistous massif rising to 841m, cut by deep valleys and partly covered with forest. Its name means literally 'bitter land', a reference maybe to the rough terrain and poor soil. In the 19th century, the water-power in the valleys encouraged industry: many little factories are still at work today, but most are old-fashioned and they do not look pretty.

Nowadays the Sauerland is above all a vacation area, popular with trippers from the teeming Ruhr. The rivers are good for fishing, and at some points have been widened into lakes now used for water-sports. The highlands to the east offer hiking in summer and skiing in winter, around the big resorts of Schmallenberg and Winterberg.

This route begins just north of the massif, at the market-town of **Soest** (pop. 43,000) on the Westphalian plain. This former Hanseatic city has a pleasant Altstadt full of quaint old houses. Beside the pink Rathaus are two distinctive pale-green Romanesque churches: one, the 12th-century St Patroclus, has a splendid west front and handsome square tower, while the nearby chapel of St Nicholas contains a notable altarpiece (c.1400). In the 14th-century Gothic Wiesenkirche, to the north, is a strange stained-glass window (1520) of the Last Supper: Christ and the apostles are shown eating Westphalian food – boar's head, ham and rye loaves, with jugs of beer.

To the south the river Möhne, a tributary of the Ruhr, has been broadened to form the lengthy **Möhnesee**, whose dam is very famous: in May 1943, a squadron of RAF Lancasters – the 'Dambusters' – bombed it successfully in a bid to disrupt the water supply of the Ruhr industry downstream, and 125 factories were claimed to have been wrecked by the flooding. In today's happier times, the dam is rebuilt and the lake is bright with windsurfers and sailboats. The road leads on southwards through a forest, to reach the Sauerland proper at **Arnsberg** (pop. 78,000), a graceless industrial town that does contain a few fine old buildings, notably the rococo Hirschberger Tor. To the south-west is the Sorpe lake and dam, another of the many big Sauerland dams that have created recreational lakes. And at nearby **Luisenhütte** is Germany's oldest blast furnace (1732), well preserved and open to visits. **Hagen**, south

of the Sorpe, is a charming show-village of black-and-white houses. Around here the scenery is gorgeous, first with broad pastoral landscapes near Allendorf, then with majestic views of dark forests: but at Rönkhausen ugly industry rears its head. At Finnentrop, a detour would lead you to the impressive **Atta** caves and their stalactites (open daily) and to the well-named Bigge lake – none other in Westphalia is bigger.

Grevenbrück and Lennestadt in the Lenne valley are hideous little industrial towns with archaic-looking factories and tall smoking chimneys – far removed from the usual German image of clean modernity. But turn east up this valley, along B236, and you'll soon enter a pleasant tourist area, with riverside inns amid woods, and will come to the big summer and skiing resort of **Schmallenberg**. The original town was burned down in 1822, then neatly rebuilt in a uniform style, with façades all of local slate. From here a scenic road winds onto the heights, past a quarry that explains the local prevalence of the grey slate roofs and slate-tiled upper floors – rather sombre. You can walk to the summit of the **Kahler Asten** (841m), the Sauerland's highest point, for a splendid view of the rolling forests. Nearby **Winterberg**, another big resort, is especially popular with Dutch tourists. From here it's an easy drive south to Marburg (see p. 219).

TOURIST OFFICES

SOEST: Am Seel 5, tel (02921) 10 33 23.

SCHMALLENBERG: Weststr. 32, tel (02972) 77 55.

WINTERBERG: Haupstr. 1, tel (02981) 70 71.

Accommodation, Eating and Drinking

SOEST 4770:

(H)**Im Wilden Mann**, Am Markt ll, tel (02921) 1 50 71. Attractive old *Fachwerk* house in town centre; good Westphalian dishes in its stylish restaurant. Rooms (14) D. Meals B–C.

(H)**Andernach zur Börse**, Thomästr. 31, tel (02921) 40 19. Central; excellent value, good food. Rooms (16) D. Meals (cl Mon) B–D.

ARNSBERG 5760:

(H)**Menge**, Ruhrstr. 60, tel (02931) 40 44. The best in town: pleasant garden, excellent food. Rooms (20) D. Meals (dinner only; cl Sun, 3 weeks July) C.

ATTENDORN 5952:

(H)**Burghotel Schnellenberg**, on Helden road, tel (02722) 69 40. Stylishly converted 13th-century castle amid woods, by Biggesee; lots of sports; baronial restaurant. Cl Christmas, 2 weeks Jan. Rooms (42) B–C. Meals B–C.

There are scores of holiday hotels in or near both Schmallenberg and Winterberg, many of them small and inexpensive. Among them:

SCHMALLENBERG 5948:

(H)**Waldhaus Ohlenbach**, Ohlenbach 10, tel (02975) 462. Mountain views, quiet seclusion, and fine ambitious cooking. Cl mid-Nov to mid-Dec. Rooms (50) B–C. Meals B–C.

(H)**Störmann**, Weststr. 58, tel (02972) 40 55. Classic family-run hotel inside town; garden, notable restaurant. Cl Christmas, 2 weeks Mar. Rooms (39) C–D. Meals B–C.

(H)**Gasthof Alfons Hanses**, in hamlet of Schanze, tel (02975) 473. Simple, friendly, quiet. Cl Nov. Rooms (14) D. Meals (cl Tue) D.

WINTERBERG 5788:

(H)**Waldhaus**, Kiefernweg 12, tel (02981) 20 42. Quiet setting, lovely views, friendly service, superb cooking. Cl mid-Nov to mid-Dec. Rooms (28) C–D. Meals (cl Mon) B–C.

(H)**Berghotel Nordhang**, In der Renau 5, tel (02981) 22 09. Near ski-lifts, newly renovated; small and modest but with remarkable varied cooking. Rooms (11) D. Meals B–C.

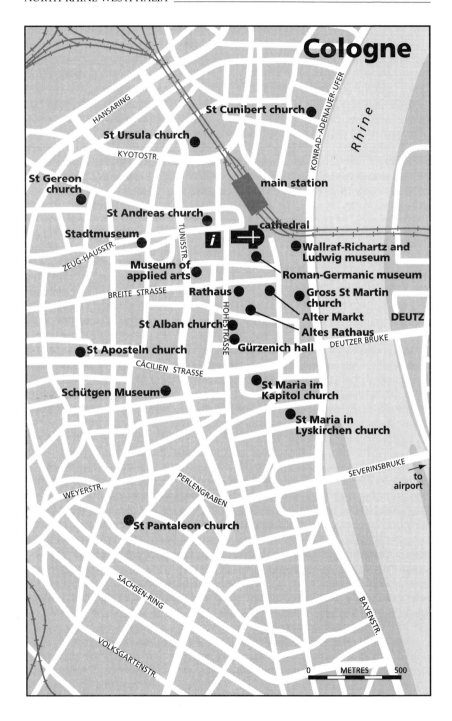

Cologne

HANSARING

St Cunibert church

St Ursula church

KYOTOSTR.

KONRAD-ADENAUER-UFER

Rhine

St Gereon church

main station

St Andreas church

Stadtmuseum

TUNISSTR.

i

cathedral

Wallraf-Richartz and Ludwig museum

ZEUG-HAUSSTR.

Museum of applied arts

TUNISSTR.

Roman-Germanic museum

BREITE STRASSE

Rathaus

Gross St Martin church

HOHESTRASSE

Alter Markt

DEUTZ

St Alban church

Altes Rathaus

St Aposteln church

Gürzenich hall

DEUTZER BRUKE

CÄCILIEN STRASSE

Schütgen Museum

St Maria im Kapitol church

St Maria in Lyskirchen church

SEVERINSBRUKE

to airport

WEYERSTR.

PERLENGRABEN

St Pantaleon church

SACHSEN-RING

VOLKSGARTENSTR.

BAYENSTR.

0   METRES   500

Cologne (Köln)

Sprawling along both banks of the broad Rhine, Germany's fourth largest city (pop. 965,000) is known above all for its soaring cathedral, its mammoth Lenten carnival, and its perfumed toilet water, eau de Cologne. It is the Rhineland's cultural capital, just as Düsseldorf is the political and commercial capital; and the two cities are in fierce rivalry, part in earnest, part in jest. They are also socially very different: Düsseldorf is more snobbish and uptight, Cologne more open, jolly and democratic. With their dark, lithe looks and fun-loving temperament, the Kölner might seem the least 'Germanic' and most Latin-like of Germans – maybe a legacy of old French and Roman influences.

First founded by the Romans in 33 BC, Cologne was elevated to the rank of 'colony' (hence its name) in AD 50, by the Emperor Claudius, whose wife Agrippina was born there. And until the rise of Trier it was the major Roman outpost in what is now Germany. The Romans built walls, parts of which still stand. The city became a bishopric in the 4th century, and had its share of early martyrs. Then Charlemagne raised it to an archbishopric; and by the 13th century it was the largest German city, with 40,000 people. It became a leading member of the Hanse, and a major commercial, cultural and religious centre, with some 150 churches (many of its lovely Romanesque ones are still there). Decline set in later: but Cologne's fame revived in the 18th century when a local Italian chemist distilled flower-blossom into alcohol, to produce what was originally meant as an aphrodisiac but later was marketed worldwide as toilet water, *eau de Cologne*. Under Napoleon the French occupied the city and wrecked 50 of its churches, but they also left a Gallic cultural imprint that survives today.

Badly bombed in the war, then rebuilt, modern Cologne has a variety of industry (cars, petrochemicals, etc), some major trade fairs, and a large university (first founded in 1388). It remains a lively focus for culture, being the main German centre for art dealers (there is a notable art fair each March) and home of Westdeutsche Rundfunk (WDR), the best German TV and radio station for plays and films. Germany's greatest post-war novelist, Heinrich Böll (1917–85), came from Cologne, and many of his books are set in or around the city where he spent much of his life.

The Kölner have a vibrant city patriotism, as strong as any in Germany, and they celebrate this with endless songfulness and whimsical joking: theirs is a city-state mentality, much as in Italy. A Münchner may be proud of his city, but he is foremost a Bavarian; a Kölner's loyalty is to Cologne, not the Rhineland. More than most Rhinelanders, the Kölner are chatty, gregarious, high-spirited, often a bit vulgar, fond of their beer and wine. Like Italians, they love show and spectacle, as witness the boisterous pre-Lenten carnival, and the Corpus Christi procession on the Rhine in May or June. All this, you could say, is one aspect of their Catholicism, whose other side is seen in the serious, deeply moral reflectiveness of a writer such as Böll. It's a cliquey society, given to in-jokes told in the curious *Kölsch* dialect that outsiders cannot easily follow: many of the stock jokes focus on Cologne's two mythical comic characters, short round

Tünnes and tall bowler-hatted Schäl, sometimes seen in effigy. The city's good-natured bohemian informality can be savoured especially in its numerous big pubs (*Kneipen*), among Germany's liveliest. Here the locals drink their clear *Kölsch* beer in slim glasses, and are served by the city's famous beer-waiters, the blue-aproned *Köbes*, whose matey, jokey tradition it is to provoke and insult their customers – a carnival tradition that goes on all year round. Be warned.

Many of the city's main sights, including its two great museums, cluster close to the cathedral and are easy to tour on foot. Others are more scattered; and as traffic is heavy and parking hard, you must be prepared to walk a lot, or take taxis. The **Altstadt**, Germany's largest, two by three km, lies between the Rhine and a broad semi-circular ring-road on the line of the old ramparts. This 'old town' has been rebuilt in a jumble of styles, and a few ugly high-rise blocks have been allowed to mar the view of the cathedral from some angles. The city's overall appearance is not beautiful. But it secretes some fine individual buildings, notably Cologne's 12 remarkable Romanesque churches, most of them now well restored. And in the heart of the Altstadt, in the rebuilt ancient quarter by the Rathaus, you'll find pleasant surprises and contrasts – Roman remains cheek-by-jowl with handsome new glass-and-steel structures or gabled *Jugendstil* houses, and modern sculptures or gargoyles in cobbled alleys or tiny squares, where people sit drinking *Kölsch*. Here are many of the best *Kneipen*. Above this pot-pourri soars the cathedral, dwarfing the rest of the city, and visible for miles across the Rhine plain. Its twin black spires look magical at night, bathed in a silvery floodlighting.

This **cathedral** (*Dom*), one of the greatest of all Gothic buildings, has a curious history. Work on it began in 1248, but was broken off in the 16th century with the façade still unfinished. And so it stayed until the 1840s, when the rise of the neo-Gothic movement brought demands for its completion; the original designs were found, and used, so that the newer parts of the building were able to merge seamlessly with the old, when the job finally was ended in 1880. The cathedral was not too badly damaged in World War Two. Its two great lacework spires rise to 157 metres: you can climb up to the base of one of them (open daily) for a wide Rhineland view. On the outside, the building is aswarm with pinnacles and flying buttresses; inside, the dominant impression is of its sheer size. It has some lovely stained glass, notably in the north aisle. Among its major art works are: the 12th-century golden jewelled shrine of the Magi, in a glass case behind the high altar; the 9th-century Gero crucifix, a poignant sculpture, in a north chapel off the ambulatory; and, in a south chapel, the *Adoration of the Magi* altarpiece by Stefan Lochner, a 15th-century Cologne artist. The tombs of arch-

The towers of Cologne cathedral rise above the Rhine.

bishops and the richly carved choir-stalls are also worth inspecting.

On the cathedral's south side is the marvellous **Roman-Germanic Museum**, housing Germany's finest archaeological collection after that of the Pergamon in Berlin. It was built around its star exhibit, the *Dionysos Mosaic*, which was excavated on this spot in 1941, the adornment of a patrician villa of c. AD 200: this vivid work, with its satyrs, dancers and drunken Bacchus, is made of over a million pieces of glass and ceramic. Above it stands the tomb of Lucius Publicius, a veteran of the Fifth Legion: it was found south of Cologne and moved here. Next to these two showpieces are rooms full of authentic items that illustrate the daily life of the Romans – everything from clothes and shoes to toys, keys and thimbles. There are also superb displays of glass, jewllery and ornaments: much is Roman, but many of the loveliest of these pieces come from the Dark Ages and are Frankish or the work of migrants from Eastern Europe. The huge *Philosophers' Mosaic* (AD 260) is dedicated to seven Greek sages.

A handsome modern building next door, newly opened, houses one of Germany's largest and finest art collections: the **Wallraf-Richartz and Ludwig Museum**, named after its collectors and donors. As in the Roman-German Museum, all is superbly laid out. The main interest centres on paintings of masters of the 15th–16th-century Cologne school, notably the Master of St Veronica and Stefan Lochner (his *Last Judgement* and *Virgin and the Rose Bush* are especially fine). But I liked equally the Dutch and Flemish works of the same period, by the Master of Delft, Rubens, Jan de Beer of Antwerp,

and others. The 17th to mid-19th centuries are less well represented, but upstairs the Ludwig section offers a varied display of 20th-century art: German artists such as Beckmann, Dix and Ernst, some splendid Picassos (e.g. *Harlequin with Folded Hands*), and on to Chagall, Leger, Bacon and others. The modern pop-art movement is represented by Warhol and Rauschenberg, while Niki de Saint-Phalle contributes a curious sculpture, *The Black Nana*. One room contains large canvases by such contemporary German artists as Georg Baselitz.

Just to the west, in An der Rechtschule, is the newly-opened **Museum of Applied Arts** (*Angewandte Kunst*), housed in the building just vacated by Wallraf-Richartz. Its remarkable collection includes Biedermeier furniture, Dutch faïence, Viennese glasswork, *Jugendstil* porcelain, silver and glass, modern Danish and Japanese furniture, and much else.

The **Hohestrasse**, the city's main traffic-free shopping street, modern and ugly but lively, leads south from the Dom. Between here and the Rhine, around the Rathaus and the Alter Markt, is the delightful core of the Altstadt, a network of narrow streets. The imposing **Altes Rathaus**, 14th-century Gothic, is fronted by a lovely Renaissance loggia. Its old tower once bore 124 statues, which the French destroyed in Napoleon's time: now the city council, SPD-controlled, is seeking sponsors for 124 new ones and itself is paying for Karl Marx, while a local feminist politician has sponsored one of a famous mediaeval witch. Typical Cologne jokey liberalism! In the broad **Alter Markt**, where a market is held on Fridays, just two of the old 16th-century houses have survived the war, at nos. 20 and 22. Here you'll find more jokey whimsy, for high up outside one top floor is a modern sculpture of a man crapping, while in the tiny square behind are statues of Tünnes and Schäl with the plaque, 'Here they lived'.

A short step from the absurd to the sublime will then bring you, on the east side of this square, to the **Gross St Martin**, one of the grandest of Cologne's Romanesque churches, noted for its sturdy five-pinnacled tower: nicely restored, it is now used by the local Hispanic community, which explains the white madonna in the nave, distinctly South European. Right next to the Rathaus, and below ground, you can visit three curiosities: the **Mikwe**, a 12th-century Jewish ritual bath, relic of the former ghetto; and the vaulted Roman sewer, below the Praetorium, remains of the Roman governor's palace. The huge **Gürzenich** hall, built for festive banquets in the 15th century and still so used at Carnival time, stands next to the bombed 10th-century **St Alban** church, whose ruins are now kept as a war memorial.

To the south is another important Romanesque church, **St Maria im Kapitol**, sombre outside, glorious within: it has remarkable 11th-century carved wooden doors, a typical Rhenish clover-leaf chancel, and a fine crypt. The Renaissance rood-screen somewhat divides the church in two. Nearby, the little **St Maria in Lyskirchen**, a sailors' church, has 13th-century ceiling frescoes; the sermons here are sometimes delivered in *Kölsch* dialect. Go on south and you'll come to the pleasant St-Severinus district, with another attractive old church. Here you are by the old ramparts and modern ring-road. Along to the west is the

city's oldest surviving church, **St Pantaleon**, an example of 10th-century Ottonian architecture. Back towards the city centre, the former church of St Cecilia now houses the **Schütgen Museum**, devoted to religious art, notably ivory carvings and sculptures of Madonnas. At the western end of the busy Neumarkt is **St Aposteln**, 11th-century Romanesque, with a handsome 13th-century apse; and west again is the battlemented Hahnentor, one of the old city gates.

West of the Dom, the former arsenal (*Zeughaus*) now houses the **Stadtmuseum** which expounds the city's history, from battles and bishops to carnival and toilet water. Finally, an Altstadt tour could end with four notable Romanesque churches to the cathedral's west and north. **St Andreas**, with its high octagonal tower, contains in its crypt the remains of Albertus Magnus, a 13th-century Cologne scholar whose pupils included Thomas Aquinas. **St Gereon**, perhaps the most striking and unusual of all these churches, was built around a 4th-century chapel; its pride is a 13th-century decagon (ten-sided tower) whose ribbed vaulting is most graceful. A crypt with mosaic flooring, early frescoes, and a 17th-century Aubusson tapestry, add to its interest. **St Ursula** has a curious baroque treasure-chamber (*Goldene Kammer*) filled with bones and other relics. St Ursula herself, whose grave is in the church, is the subject of a famous local legend: she, daughter of a fourth-century English king, was murdered here by the Huns along with her virgin companions, who numbered either 11 or 11,000, depending on how you interpret the Latin inscription 'XIMV'. 11 sounds more plausible. **St Cunibert**, last in

The 'Crazy Days' of Carnival

Of all German pre-Lenten carnivals, the biggest and most boisterous is Cologne's: it fits in well with the city's spirit of fun-loving whimsy. Carnivals began as pagan fertility-rites, heralding spring. Later the Church sanctioned them as safety-valves of naughtiness before the solemn duties of Lent. Now they are pagan again, that is, rather commercial – but the fun is also very real. In Cologne, it begins in October with the election of a Carnival Prince and his two henchmen, the Peasant and the Virgin (the Virgin has always been a man, save under the Nazis who hated transvestism). These 'Three Stars', who 'rule' the city during *Karnevel*, are usually small businessmen – and competition is intense, for the honour and publicity are good for trade, even though a Star must pay out heavily, for example for the tons of toffees that he hurls at the crowd in the big parades.

The fun reaches its climax in the *Tolle Tage* (Crazy Days) before Lent. Thursday is *Weiberfastnacht* (Women's Day), when women exact revenge for their long 19th-century exclusion from carnival by cutting off the tie of any male (very Freudian?). On Sunday, school and local groups stage a huge informal procession, with lots of topical satiric floats. Then on *Rosenmontag* (Rose Monday) comes the main parade, with a million lining the route. The acrobatic *Mariechen* (sort-of majorettes) do their pirouettes. And the Prince's bodyguard, in 1820s uniforms stick flowers in their rifle-barrels and studiously disobey orders: they symbolize Cologne's anti-militarist, anti-Prussian tradition.

Alongside the official organized *Karneval* is the big popular booze-up-and-laugh-in, an explosion of local pub-parties and street-parties, of merry crowds with painted clown-faces and zany costumes. Even the dogs wear carnival hats and cloaks. Kölner still adore their carnival, and treat its mad jollity with Germanic thoroughness: 'Anyone not foolish at *Karneval* is foolish the rest of the year', is a saying. The local radio blares out non-stop the dotty carnival songs in Cologne dialect: '*Love me for Three Crazy Days*' is one of them. Is it not true that adultery during carnival has never been grounds for divorce?

date of the city's Romanesque churches, has some fine stained-glass windows and lively Gothic carvings of the Annunciation.

Across the Rhine is the suburb of Deutz, where the Rheinpark offers pleasant riverside walks and vistas. At Brühl, 15 km south of the city, the ornately furnished **Schloss Augustusburg**, former home of the archbishops, is a fine example of the rococo, with a ceremonial staircase by Balthasar Neumann and formal French-style gardens. The nearby **Phantasialand** (open daily), Germany's largest amusement and theme park, was modelled on Disneyland: dolphin displays, rides on a Viking ship, a Wild West town, and an evocation of pre-war Berlin are amongst its attractions.

Germany is the world's third largest producer of lignite (brown coal), and the main deposits are around Kerpen, just west of Cologne, and towards Aachen. It is worth taking a look at this huge-scale open-cast mining, for it is managed with a true German respect for the environment. First, whole areas must be cleared, before the giant craters can be dug, kilometres long and up to 370 metres deep: the farmers and villagers are handsomely compensated, so they do not object too much. The hills of loose earth dug out from each hole are neatly planted with trees; and when a mine is exhausted, it is given back to nature and to human pleasure. One string of old mines has been turned into a huge recreation zone, with 40 new lakes amid woods, where the Kölner now have better scope for swimming, sailing, surfing and fishing than the city's neighbourhood ever offered them before.

TOURIST OFFICE

Am Dom (facing cathedral), tel. 221 33 40.

Accommodation, Eating and Drinking
(Postal code 5000, tel code 0221)

There are numerous quality restaurants mostly serving French cuisine. Local cooking at modest prices can be found at the many lively *Kneipen* (beer and wine pubs) in the Altstadt, notably between the cathedral and the Heumarkt. There are lots of discos, cabarets and late-night bars in this area, too.

(H)**Excelsior Hotel Ernst**, Domplatz, Trankgasse 1, tel 27 01. Elegant, classic and distinguished. Very good food in the **Hanse Stube**. Rooms (160) A. Meals A–B.

(H)**Dom-Hotel**, Domkloster 2a, tel 202 40. Traditional, with marble and tapestries, but well renovated. Restaurant facing cathedral. Rooms (126) A. Meals A–B (Atelier B–C).

(H)**Bristol**, Kaiser-Wilhelm-Ring 48, tel 12 01 95. On ring-road 1 km W of cathedral. Some rooms with carved furniture and four-posters. No restaurant. Rooms (44) A–B.

(H)**Haus Lyskirchen**, Filzengraben 28, tel 209 70. Modern hotel near Rhine, in Altstadt, but quiet. Swimming-pool. Cl Christmas, New Year. Rooms (95) B. Meals (cl Sun) B–C.

(H)**Am Augustinerplatz**, Hohestr. 30, tel 23 67 17. In Altstadt. No restaurant. Rooms (56) B.

(H)**Ludwig**, Brandenburgerstr. 24, tel 12 30 31. Near Rhine and main station. No restaurant. Closed Christmas. Rooms (61) B–C.

(H)**Altstadt**, Salzgasse 7, tel 23 41 87. In Altstadt, near Rhine. Sauna; no restaurant. Cl Christmas, New Year. Rooms (28) C.

(H)**Landhaus Gut Keuchhof**, Braugasse 14, in Lövenich suburb, tel (02234) 760 33. Good restaurant. Cl 2 weeks Dec–Jan. Rooms (43) C. Meals (cl Mon) B–C.

(H)**Spiegel**, Hermann-Löns-Str. 122, in Porz-Grengel suburb, tel (02203) 610 46. Family-run *Gasthof* beside a forest; convenient for airport. Good food. Cl 3 weeks July–Aug. Rooms (19) C. Meals (cl Fri) B–C.

(R)**Goldener Pflug**, Olpener Str. 421, tel 89 55 09. Eight km E of city, in Merheim suburb. Formally elegant but family-run; outstanding Franco-German cuisine. Cl Sun, 3 weeks June/July. Meals A (lunch B).

(R)**Die Bastei**, Konrad-Adenauer-Ufer 80, tel 12 28 25. In a former fortress by Rhine; river views and fine food. Meals A–B.

(R)**Weinhaus im Waldfisch**, Salzgasse 13, tel 21 97 75. Cosy old half-timbered tavern near river, in Altstadt. German cooking. Cl Sun. Meals B.

(R)**Em Krützche**, Am Frankenturm 1, tel 21 14 32. In Altstadt, facing river, with tables outside; elegant. Cl Mon. Meals B.

(R)**Gaffel**, Alter Markt 20, tel 21 46 68. Cologne cooking and ambience, but not *too* pub-like. Meals C–D.

(R)**Alt Köln**, Trankgasse 7–9, tel 13 46 78. Romantic old tavern with local ambience and dishes; garden. Cl Christmas. Meals C–D.

(R)**Alter Wartesaal**, Hauptbahnhof, tel 13 30 61. Former station waiting-room, now a trendy social centre. Meals C–D. Also disco.

(R)**Früh am Dom**, Am Hof 12–14, tel 23 66 18. Facing cathedral: big lively pub with usual jokey waiters. Local dishes. Meals C–D.

(R)**Brauhaus Sion**, Unter Taschenmacher 5–7, tel 21 42 03. Large, typical *Kneipe*, oozing ambience. Food so-so. Meals D–E.

(R)**Päffgen**, Heumarkt 62, tel 21 97 20. Typical Altstadt *Kneipe*, crowded, great fun. Local cooking. Meals D–E.

(P)**Papa Joe's Klimperkasten**, Alter Markt 50, tel 21 67 59. Delightful cosy Altstadt pub with folksy décor, lively ambience; live music in evening. Some snacks.

(P)**Lommerzheim**, Siegesstr. 18, rel 81 43 92. Across the river in Deutz. Packed with bohemians and media trendies.

Bonn and its Neighbourhood

This old university city (pop. 296,000), the birthplace of Beethoven, is gracefully situated where the broad Rhine leaves the hills and enters the Cologne plain. Its older and residential districts still retain some of the charm of any friendly, wine-drinking Rhineland town. But since the war it has become submerged by its role as Federal capital, as big new ministries and embassies have sprawled across the meadows and foothills, and its population has doubled. Yet it is still only the 19th largest West German town ('the Federal village', it is nicknamed), and its myriad civil servants, politicians and diplomats form a somewhat artificial, charmless society, where government is a mono-industry. And today, if reunification means the return of the German capital to Berlin, what will Bonn's future be?

It has existed for 2,000 years, since the time when the Romans built a fort by the Rhine. From 1238 Bonn was the residence of the Archbishop Electors of Cologne, who in the 18th century built two palaces. The university was founded in 1818. So why, in 1949, was Bonn chosen as the Federal capital? Most politicians then believed – or

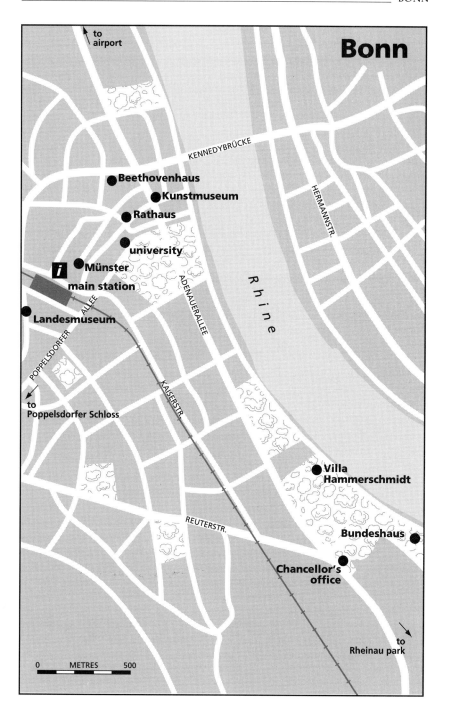

to
airport

Bonn

KENNEDYBRÜCKE

● Beethovenhaus

● Kunstmuseum

● Rathaus

● university

HERMANNSTR.

i ● Münster

main station

ADENAUERALLEE

R h i n e

● Landesmuseum

POPPELSDORFER
ALLEE

to
Poppelsdorfer Schloss

KAISERSTR.

● Villa
Hammerschmidt

REUTERSTR.

Bundeshaus ●

Chancellor's
office ●

to
Rheinau park

0   METRES   500

paid lip-service to the belief – that Germany would soon be reunited, so that a purely provisional site was needed. Frankfurt, Hamburg and Munich were all judged too large and powerful – and would the rest of Germany have ever accepted to be ruled from Bavaria, or south Germany from the far north? Bonn had the advantages of being (a) geographically central; and (b) obscure, without ambitions to a permanent role. What's more, Chancellor Adenauer had a home close to Bonn and was a native of Cologne, and this elderly leader wanted to stay near his *Heimat*. His voice proved decisive. Later, as the division of Europe persisted, and the dream of a united Germany faded, the new government buildings erected so expensively began to appear more permanent. And yet, Bonn as a capital still kept a vaguely makeshift and unreal air, maybe because neither politicians nor public ever fully accepted it as the nation's *Hauptstadt*.

Bonn has retained its earlier roles too, that of residential centre for retired people from Cologne and the Ruhr, and of lively university town with an old campus next to the Altstadt. Just to the south, on what used to be open meadowland by the Rhine, the government quarter has been tacked on. And south again is Bad Godesberg, once a fashionable spa town, now annexed by Bonn and the home of many embassies and senior diplomats' abodes. It is a pretty setting, with pleasant river walks. But the climate, humid and enervating, causes liverishness and lethargy – not the best recipe for effective government. Bonn's cosmopolitan yet oddly provincial ambiance is still much as described in *A Small Town in Germany*, by John Le Carré, who served as a diplomat here. Its bureaucrats, politicians and diplomats have little contact with the rest of local society, but exist in their own milieux, hectic but boring. The senior civil servants have mostly been seconded for a few years from their *Land*, so they do not put down roots, but go back home at the weekends. The authorities, aware of these problems, have tried to make Bonn more cheerful and homelike by lavishing money on opera, theatre and other culture. Despite these efforts, it remains cut off from the authentic life of the country: foreign journalists posted there often complain how hard they find it to make close contact with the 'real' Germany. But the picture may change, if government begins to transfer to Berlin. Early in 1990, work stopped abruptly on several big building projects.

Festivals and events in Bonn include the February Carnival, with Rose Monday parade; 'Rhine in Flames' (illuminations and fireworks along the river, at Bonn and nearby) on the first Saturday in May; 'Bonn Summer' (outdoor music, dancing and theatre, notably in the Markt at weekends) from May to September; *Pützchens Markt*, big popular funfair, in Beuel, early September; and every 3 years in April, September (1992, 1995, etc) the renowned international Beethoven festival.

The **Altstadt**, though rather too commercial and congested, has pleasant pedestrian streets (e.g. Sternstrasse) lined with 17th- and 18th-century gabled houses unscathed by the bombing. Here in Bonngasse is the Beethovenhaus, also the lovely baroque Jesuitskirche, alas normally closed to the public. The Kunstmuseum has a good range of works by

Rhineland expressionist artists, notably August Macke who lived for a while in Bonn. Next to it, on the market square, is the rococo pink-façaded **Rathaus**, built by the Archbishop-Electors in 1737 and now used for State receptions: Kennedy, de Gaulle, Reagan, Gorbachev and Queen Elizabeth are among those to have addressed the crowd from its balcony.

The long orange-and-grey baroque building close by was also built by 18th-century Electors, and is now the hub of the large university: students by the hundred sprawl on the grass of its adjoining Hofgarten, a charming scene in fine weather. But here again Bonn's national political scene has spilled over into the old town, for in the early 1980s this park was the venue for huge anti-Government demos, often staged by the peace movement; they made such a mess that rallies here are now forbidden. **Beethoven's** birthplace, the small, attractive house where he lived until he left for Vienna aged 22, is now a museum; it has various souvenirs, including his viola and the ear-trumpets he used when going deaf.

To the west of the Rathaus is Bonn's finest church, the **Münster**, an elegant piece of 12th-century Rhenish Romanesque, restored since the war. It has a lofty interior with some baroque furnishings, also an 11th-century crypt and a stately arcaded cloister. Across the square, if you enter the Leffus supermarket and go upstairs, you will see most incongruously a tiny 12th-century chapel inside a newer building – an odd illustration of Bonn's layers of history. And Bonn's museums wil take you far back into pre-history: the **Rheinisches Landesmuseum**, just west of the station, displays the skull of Neanderthal Man, found in 1856 in a valley near Düsseldorf. This museum also has an array of Roman and Frankish antiquities, and delightful works by 15th-century Rhenish painters. There's more history in the nearby **Poppelsdorfer Allee**, a broad impressive avenue of chestnut trees that the Electors laid out to link their two palaces, the one by the Altstadt and the handsome Poppelsdorfer Schloss (1715) to the south-west: this too now belongs to the university, and is closed to the public, but its botanical gardens are open on weekdays. The quiet residential streets near here, such as Argelanderstrasse, are lined with ornately elegant turn-of-the century houses and remain a haunt of the Bonn upper bourgeoisie. The Robert Schumannhaus at Sebastianstr. 182 (closed Tue, Sat) has mementoes of the life of the composer, who spent his last two unhappy years in an adjacent asylum, after his attempted suicide by jumping in the Rhine.

To the southeast by the river is the **Government district**, an unremarkable assembly of older and modern buildings. Best of them is the Federal President's residence, the elegant white Villa Hammerschmidt, built in 1860 as a rich man's home. The adjacent residence/office of the Chancellor is ultramodern. The parliament buildings (*Bundeshaus*), converted from a college put up in 1930, are not at all grand, in fact quite suburban, and could well pass for an insurance company office in Wimbledon (guided tours weekdays, by prior appointment, when neither House is sitting). The deputies' office block is a dull skyscraper. To its south by the river is the pleasant Rheinau park, newly laid out, with little lakes. The various ministries are scattered all over town.

Bad Godesberg, officially part of Bonn since 1969, is no longer much used as a spa but with its shaded avenues remains a discreetly graceful place; it is the site of most embassies and diplomats' homes, and the venue for endless cocktail parties. The British Ambassador has a splendid old mansion by the river; the Chinese Embassy looks like a pagoda; and the Americans and Russians have both built themselves gigantic ghetto-like embassy complexes, the one by the river upstream, the other on a hill. Above the spa stands the lofty **Godesberg** tower, all that remains of a hilltop castle built by the Cologne Electors in the 13th century, then blown up by a Bavarian army in 1583 because the Elector of the day had turned Protestant. From its terrace you get a good view of Bonn and the Rhine, with the Drachenfels (see below) almost opposite. In the south-west corner of Bad Godesberg is **Muffendorf**, an unexpected and picturesque 17th-century village, its old timbered houses now in vogue as homes for well-to-do yuppies. It has a pretty church and an old monastery. And the river promenade at Bad Godesberg is delightful for a stroll.

The main road south along the west bank passes below **Rolandsbogen**, a creeper-covered stone arch alone on a hilltop, relic of an 11th-century stone castle. You can walk up to it by a steep path from the road, or drive up by winding back lanes from Mehlem – and be rewarded by a lovely view, or by a meal or drink at the Rolandsbogen restaurant where Adenauer held his engagement party in 1902. Further south along B9 is Rolandseck, where a former main-line station with *Jugendstil* décor has been cleverly converted into an unusual cultural centre and modern art gallery.

On the right bank of the Rhine, east and south-east of Bonn, are a number of interesting places. The village of **Schwarzrheindorf** has a very curious 11th-century church, built on two levels: the upper part was for the archbishop and his court, the ground floor for the lower orders. Vivid Romanesque frescoes decorate the lower church. Further up the river is the pleasant tourist and wine-growing centre of **Königswinter** (pop. 37,000), initial venue of the annual Anglo-German Königswinter conferences that have done so much since the war to restore good relations between the two countries. Behind the town rise the **Siebengebirge** 'seven mountains', wooded hills no higher than 400m but visible from far across the Rhine plain. They have long been central to Rhenish romantic folklore, above all the rocky **Drachenfels** peak, which you can reach from Königswinter on foot or by Germany's oldest rack-railway (1883). The slopes of these hills contain Germany's most northerly vineyards, whose best-known product is *Drachenblut* (dragon's blood): Nibelung legend relates that Siegfried killed the dragon which haunted the Drachenfels, then bathed in its blood. A road east from Königswinter leads up into the Siebengebirge at the Grosse Olberg, which offers fine views over the Rhine. Just off this road is **Petersberg**, a huge hillside hotel that was built c. 1900 as a posh health resort. After 1945 it became an Allied headquarters, was then given to the Federal Government which has since used it for entertaining top guests (Queen Elizabeth, the last Shah of Iran and Brezhnev have all stayed there). It has just been totally rebuilt in a more attractive and modern style.

Inevitably, many of the places of interest near Bonn are connected with recent political history. On a hillside at Rhöndorf, south of Königswinter, is the quiet country villa that was **Adenauer's home** from 1936 until his death here in 1967: you can visit the house with his furniture and books, and the rose-garden that he adored. The adjacent institute has a small museum of his life and times. A path through the nearby woods leads to the secluded rural cemetery where he lies with his family in a modest grave: it is all very discreet and low-key, as with de Gaulle's tomb at Colombey or Churchill's at Bladon. Continue south via Badon Honnef, and past the blackened pillars of Remagen Bridge (see p. 83), and you'll come to the picturesque old town of **Linz am Rhein**, known for its folklore activities, summer festival and carnival. Its newly restored Schloss holds two unusual museums. One has a collection of old electrical organs, pianolas and other mechanical musical instruments, some very quaint; the other is a mediaeval torture chamber, whose attractions include a clamp that squeezed the victim's head until his skull broke. Across the neat cobbled courtyard is a folksy restaurant, the Ritterschänke, where waiters in *Tracht* serve quite good 'mediaeval' dishes.

TOURIST OFFICE

BONN:
Münsterstrasse 20, tel (0228) 77 34 66.

Accommodation, Eating and Drinking
(Bonn postcode 5300, tel code 0228)

(H)**Bristol**, Prinz-Albert-Str. 2, tel 2 69 80. Near station; formal, luxurious, used by top government visitors. Pool, sauna. Smart restaurant, also useful cheaper coffee-shop. Rooms (120) A. Meals A (C–D in coffee shop).

(H)**Steigenberger Hotel Venusberg**, An der Casselruhe 1, tel 28 80. New luxury hotel on Venusberg hill, just W of town, very peaceful. Two restaurants. Rooms (86) A. Meals A–C.

(H)**Rheinhotel Dreesen**, Rheinstrasse 45, Bonn 2 – Bad Godesberg, tel 8 20 20. Classic hotel on Rhine, full of tradition (Hitler and Chamberlain met here). Food so-so. Rooms (68) B. Meals B.

(H)**Schaumburger Hof**, Am Schaumburger Hof 10, Bonn 2 – Bad Godesberg, tel 36 40 95. Spacious, pleasantly old-fashioned hotel by the Rhine. Cl mid-Dec to mid-Jan. Rooms (34) C–D. Meals C–D.

(H)**Haus Hofgarten**, Fritz-Tillmann-Str. 7, tel 22 34 82. Near university; quiet and friendly. Rooms (15) C–D. No restaurant.

(H)**Mertens**, Rheindorferstr. 134, Bonn 3 – Beuel. Across the Rhine; modest and cheerful. Rooms (14) D. Meals D.

(R)**Cäcilienhöhe**, Goldbergweg 17, tel 32 10 01. Above Bad Godesberg, with good views; Italian cooking; popular with politicians. Cl Sun. Meals B. 10 rooms too, C.

(R)**Le Marron**, Provinzialstr. 35, tel 25 32 61. Good French *nouvelle cuisine*. Cl Sat, Sun lunch. Meals A–B.

(R)**Maternus**, Löbestrs. 3, tel 36 28 51. Classic haunt of top politicians, diplomats; food average. Cl Sun. Meals B.

(R)**Bayerische Botschaft**, Brüdergasse 15, tel 65 88 00. Not the 'embassy': but food and service are assertively Bavarian, and good. Put on your *Lederhosen*. Meals C.

(R)**Em Höttche**, Markt 4, tel 65 85 96. Atmospheric old tavern; sound Rhenish and French cooking. Meals B–C.

(R)**Im Bären**, Acherstr. 1, tel 63 32 00. Authentic and stylish old tavern; many Rhenish dishes. Meals C-D, so cheap, but good.

(R)**Bei Wassili**, Hochkreuzallee, Bad Godesberg, tel 31 50 36. Small, friendly, very Greek and nationalist: refuses to serve all Turk-influenced Greek dishes, such as souvlakia. That eliminates most of them. Cl lunch weekdays. Meals D.

(R)**Ermis**, Klufterstr. 40, tel 31 06 91. More relaxedly Greek; ouzo, jovial ambience and retsina. Meals D–E.

(R)**Bahnhöfchen**, Rheinaustr. 116, Beuel, tel 46 34 36. A nice terrace on the Rhine's east bank. Station-turned-pub. Meals D.

(R)**Im Stiefel**, Bonngasse 30, tel 63 48 06. Lively pub in old town; simple local dishes. Cl Sun. Meals D–E.

BORNHEIM 5303:

(H)**Heimatblick**, Brombeerweg 1, tel (02222) 600 37. NW of Bonn, simple and peaceful, with views over the Rhine from its restaurant terrace. Rooms (18) D. Meals C.

KÖNIGSWINTER 5330:

(R)**Bauernschenke**, Heisterbacherstr. 123, tel (02223) 212 82. Old building with rustic décor, cosy ambience, good local wines and food. Meals C–D.

In Bonn, the elegant Poppelsdorfer Avenue leads towards the Rhine.

CHAPTER THREE

Rhineland-Palatinate

(Rheinland-Pfalz)

THE PFALZ (PALATINATE in English) is a former county that for centuries belonged to the rulers of Bavaria; it covers a smallish area west of the Rhine, around Worms and Kaiserslautern. In 1947 it was amalgamated with some former Prussian and Hessian lands, stretching north almost as far as Bonn, to form somewhat artificially the *Land* of Rheinland-Pfalz (pop. 3.6 million). This is a strongly Catholic *Land*, a heartland of the CDU, and its best-known citizen today is Helmut Kohl: born near Ludwigshafen, he was the *Land* Prime Minister in 1969-73, before moving on to higher things in Bonn.

The focus of the *Land* is the mighty river Rhine that flows through it or along its eastern border; its three biggest towns, Mainz, the capital, Koblenz and Ludwigshafen, all lie on its banks. Here is the most scenic stretch of the middle Rhine, curving between wooded hills, lined by ancient castles. It is also the stretch most cloaked in ancient legend, notably those of the Nibelungen that inspired Wagner. Three major tributaries flow into the Rhine in this region: the Main and Neckar from the east, and the lovely Moselle, flowing down from Trier, once the Romans' chief city in Germany. North of the Moselle are the lovely wooded uplands of the Eifel, a popular holiday country. In fact, nearly the whole *Land* is attractively hilly and wooded. Major industry is confined to the Rhine valley around Mainz and Ludwigshafen.

With two-thirds of all German vineyards, this is the major wine-producing *Land*. Well-known vineyards line the Moselle and parts of the Rhine; and a 'wine-road' runs along the edge of the Pfalz hills. The region's wines are mostly white and quite dry but fruity. Harvesting is done late, usually early October: this is the season of boisterous festivals in the wine-towns and villages. The local people, as in so many wine areas, tend to be outgoing, jovial, fond of jokes and fun – as is noticeable at wine-harvest time and during the pre-Lenten carnivals. Everywhere there are pleasant old wine-pubs, or places where you can take part in wine-tastings. And in some vineyards you can walk down *Weinlehrpfade*

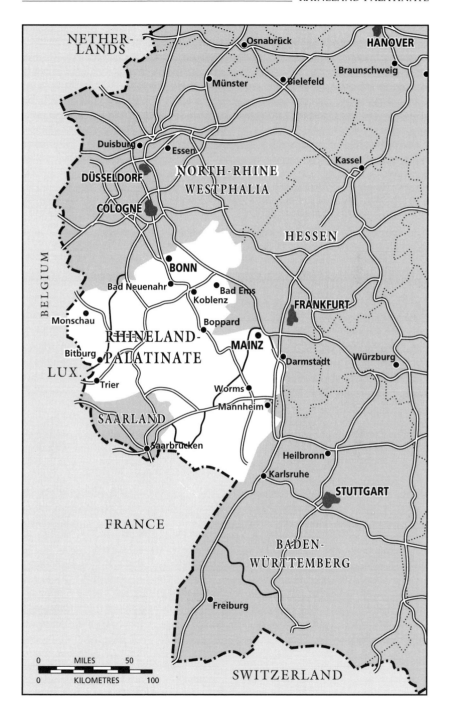

(wine-teaching paths) where placards explain the wines, their produce and other details, all in the best German didactic and methodical manner.

Trier and the Moselle Valley

From the Luxembourg border, the lower Moselle flows past the fascinating city of Trier to the much duller one of Koblenz, where it joins the Rhine. The lovely curving Moselle valley is in many ways more attractive than the Rhine. It is more intimate and less grandiose, as the gleaming river glides quietly between meadows or rocky cliffs; in places the vineyards slope so close to the banks that, from a boat, you could almost pluck the grapes (mostly these are riesling grapes, producing dry white wines). Old white sundials stand amid the vines at some points. The small towns and villages, too, notably Bernkastel, Beilstein and Cochem, tend to be prettier than those on the Rhine. And there's much less heavy industrial traffic. The hilltop castles above the valley, it's true, may be fewer and on the whole less striking: Burg Eltz, however, a few miles away from the river, is one of Germany's most splendid mediaeval fortresses.

TRIER on the Moselle (pop. 95,000), which calls itself 'Germany's oldest city', has more and better preserved Roman remains than any other town in northern Europe – notably the Porta Nigra, the great black gateway that towers up in its middle. Trier for a while was the Roman Empire's capital of the north, and it has marvellous memorials of that period and of early Christian times. It would not be fair to

call it 'just a museum town': but certainly it is a place where the distant past looms mightily. Recent centuries are relatively little represented – save that Trier was the birthplace of Karl Marx.

Around 400 BC a Celtic tribe, the Treveri, formed a settlement here, which was conquered by Julius Caesar in 58 BC. Then in 16 BC the Emperor Augustus officially founded Trier (Augusta Treverorum), as a civil rather than a military town (its 2,000th anniversary was celebrated in 1984). It became a flourishing centre of trade and culture, as can be seen today from the objects in the Rhineland Museum. When the Emperor Diocletian reorganised the Empire in the late 3rd century, he made Trier into the capital of Gaul and an imperial residence. Then under Constantine's rule (306–37) the town had its golden age: when this emperor embraced Christianity, he built up Trier as a religious capital on an equal footing with Rome itself, and in 314 it became the seat of the first bishopric north of the Alps. Constantine created some great civil and religious buildings, and he built ramparts of which the Porta Nigra is part. Trier's population of 80,000, was almost as large as it is today. But later its leading role was taken over by Arles and Byzantium, and in the 5th century it fell to Frankish invaders. However, Charlemagne made it into an archbishopric, and in this role it kept much influence: until 1794 its archbishop was one of the three ecclesiastical Electors of the Holy Roman Empire.

Today Trier's prosperity depends on tourism and the Moselle wine trade, of which it is the leading centre: it has huge underground wine cellars, which can be visited. But despite this vinous tradition, it is not nearly as jolly and fun-loving a place as the Rhine wine towns: its people, somewhat heavy and solemn, are closer in temperament to their Luxembourg neighbours than to Rhinelanders. It is a garrison town of the French forces in Germany, who here number 10,000 with their families. For the best view of town, river and vineyards, drive up to the Petrisberg hill in the eastern suburbs.

The **Porta Nigra** (cl Dec) is the largest and best-preserved gateway of the ancient world. Its dark colour comes from the patina that has formed on its limestone blocks, which weigh up to a ton each and are held together with iron rods. The building is an impressive example of Roman skills in fortification: attackers could be trapped within its outer and inner gates. In the 11th century it was adapted for use as a church, a function that it kept until Napoleon arrived in 1804: if you climb up inside (there's a good view from the tower gallery), you can see traces of the Romanesque apse and later rococo decoration, contrasting oddly with the monolithic military structure. Just below the gate is an 11th-century monastery, now housing a museum of local history; and to the north-east is one of Trier's finest churches, St Paulinus (1754), designed by the great Balthazar Neumann in exuberant rococo style, with complicated ceiling frescoes.

Nearly all Trier's main sights, notably the Roman ones, are quite close together in the heart of town, strung out in a line from the Porta Nigra down to the Imperial Baths. First the wide Simeonstrasse leads to the **Hauptmarkt**, lined with old gabled houses, half-timbered or baroque: this is the kernel of the pedestrian zone of the old part of town, and a popular meeting-place for students, buskers and others. There are varied curiosities here. In the centre of the square is a Celtic cross erected in 958, next to a fountain with ornate Renaissance sculptures. At Simeonstrasse 8 is the house, now an optician's, where Karl Marx spent his childhood; no. 19, the *Dreikönigshaus* (house of the Magi), a finely restored 13th-century Romanesque mansion with coloured arches, was the home of a wealthy merchant. The alley almost opposite, the Judengasse, was a mediaeval Jewish ghetto. The Steipe, on the Hauptmarkt, is a fine 15th-century Gothic mansion now used as a festival hall; round the corner in Dietrichstrasse is the Frankenturm, a rough turreted tower used as a nobleman's dwelling from the 11th century. And most curious of all, at Hauptmarkt 5, is the restaurant recently opened in the old Roman cellars of the cathedral; it is decorated with Roman pottery found *in situ*, and serves Roman recipes (see p. 80).

The vast **Cathedral**, the oldest Christian church north of the Alps, is a fascinating hotch-potch, built and rebuilt over many centuries. It was destroyed in the 5th century, then rebuilt after the 6th; but much of it including the façade is 11th–12th-century Romanesque. Parts of Constantine's original 4th-century outer walls, the granite core of the structure, still survive. The interior is mainly baroque, including the high altar, but there's a fine Romanesque tympanum in the south aisle. The Treasury contains a tenth-century portable altar of St Andrew; locked away in the sacristy is a very precious relic, the so-called 'Holy Robe' of Christ, which Constantine's mother is said to have brought from Palestine. Next to the cathedral is the **Liebfrauenkirche** (1235), one of the earliest Gothic churches in Germany: circular in shape, it was built on an unusual geometric pattern in the form of a Greek cross, and it has a certain austere elegance. Note the 17th-century statue on the black marble tomb of Canon Karl von Metternich.

Beyond the cathedral's Gothic cloister is the superb **Bischöfliches Museum** (episcopal museum), opened in 1988, wonderfully bright and inviting in the best manner of modern German museums. As well as mediaeval statuary and sacred art, it has interesting models of the cathedral as it was in Roman times, and of the recent excavations. Its most amazing exhibit, by far, is the 15 panels of Roman frescoes, dated to AD 326, that were discovered in 1946 in Constantine's palace below the cathedral: they are partly obliterated, but the segments that survive have remarkably fresh colours, and they have been cleverly pieced together. The panels depict the emperor's mother, St Helen, his eldest son Crispus and his wife by a second marriage, Fausta: but this cosy family album had a tragic sequel, for Constantine later had Crispus and Fausta put to death – because they were having an adulterous affair, or so it is believed.

Further south is the huge brick **Basilika** which Constantine built as part of his palace and called Aula Palatina; 30m high and 75m long, it has no pillars or buttresses and is the largest surviving single-hall structure of the ancient world. In Roman times it had a marble floor and statues and was used as a throne room: but it was burned out in World War Two and has since been restored very plainly, with bare walls, for it would cost too much

to bring it back to its former glory. Since the mid-19th century it has been used as a Protestant church. South again, beside a pleasant formal garden, you'll come to the enormous **Rheinisches Landesmuseum** (open daily). This contains some modern art, and local relics from the Paleaolithic, Bronze and Iron Ages (jewellery, pottery, etc): but its main glory is the huge collection of local Roman finds (mosaics, friezes, statues, ceramics, glass, etc), many of them from the settlement at Neumagen, lower down the Moselle. The star Neumagen exhibit is a charming sculpture of a wine-ship with six oarsmen, one grinning broadly. There are also scale models of local Roman fortified encampments.

Close by are the **Kaiserthermen** (imperial baths), among the largest in the Empire after those in Rome itself, and fairly well preserved. You can see the vestiges of the cold and warm water bathrooms, the saunas and toilets, the underfloor heating system, and you can walk through the network of tunnels used for servicing and draining. The baths must have looked splendid, with their marble and statuary: but it seems that they were never actually used, for no sooner were they finished than Constantine moved to Byzantium – rather a waste. Local lords in the Middle Ages used them as a castle and made them part of the city walls. On a hillside to the east, and rather the worse for wear, is the old Roman amphitheatre which could seat 20,000; and to the west, also in poor condition, are Trier's other Roman baths, the second-century Barbarathermen. These were used, over several centuries. Nearby is a Roman bridge over the Moselle.

Returning from here towards the

centre, along **Karl-Marx**-Strasse (yes!), you come to the sturdy bourgeois house where the Prophet of the Left was born and spent his babyhood, before his lawyer father moved the family to the Simeonstrasse. The house belongs to the German Socialist Party (SPD) which acquired it as a memorial in 1931; it was then taken over by the Nazis as a propaganda office. It is now a very well-set-out **museum**, full of documents and photos about Marx's life, the workers' struggle, and the development and philosophy of Marxism. There are first editions of *Das Kapital* and the 1848 *Manifesto of the Communist Party*, and photos of visits by such men of stalwart honour as Erich Honecker. To some visitors, the museum may seem nauseously didactic and committed, but I – certainly no Marxist – found it historically fascinating. Trier seems to be a graveyard of crumbled empires – first Rome's, now the one that Marx's ideas created. This episcopal city, with its long conservative tradition, has never been exactly keen on its most famous son, and has erected no public statue to him. I found it a pleasing irony that his house is now in the heart of Trier's red-light district.

Leaving Trier, the Moselle flows down past Neumagen, site of the Roman finds that are now in Trier's Rhine museum. It comes to **Bernkastel-Kues** (pop. 7,500), a characterful old wine-town known for its excellent Rieslings. In its tiny Markt square, charming Renaissance coloured houses surround a 17th-century fountain-statue of an angel with a sword; down an alley by the Rathaus, the Spitzgiebelhaus (1583) is a very quaint half-timbered gabled building, narrow and oddly-shaped. The suburb of Kues across the

river was the birthplace of Nicolas Cusanus (1401–64), a great scientist, artist and humanist, who founded the Cusanusstift, a hospital for the poor that today is still in use and is open to visits: its chapel is 15th-century, as are the frescoes and altarpiece inside. The ruined Burg Landshut, a former fortress of the bishops of Trier, stands theatrically on a cliff above the town; it is worth driving up, for a superb view of the valley.

Further downstream, the Moselle curves and loops gracefully between vineyards sloping right to its banks – a lovely scene. The smaller road along its right bank leads to the pretty wine-village of **Zeltingen-Rachtig** which has an interesting *Weinlehrpfad* (see p. 72): you can drive between the vines, whose types, produce, etc are clearly explained. On the other bank, the main B53 goes through the attractive wine-villages of Urzig and Kröv, then the duller town of Traben-Trarbach, to reach **Zell**, a charming little wine-producing town in whose square is a curious statue of a black grimacing cat, subject of a local legend (*Schwarz Katz* is one local wine). Next the main road passes below Marienburg convent, towering above a great loop in the river (its terrace offers a fine view of this). At Bremm, where the Moselle makes another sharp bend, the south bank is flattish but the north bank is steep, and its vines cling vertiginously. **Beilstein**, two loops further down, is a delightful little fortified village of old houses and alleys, surmounted by the gaunt ruins of a castle that was owned by Chancellor Metternich: there's a good view from its terrace, but the interior is dull.

The picturesque old town of **Cochem** (pop. 8,000) has neat gardens along the river, beside houses with painted fronts. Its setting is as striking as any on the Moselle. Here, too, a massive fortress (the *Burg*) stands high on the hill above. But its 'fairy-tale' turrets and pinnacles are 19th-century; of the 11th-century original, wrecked in the Palatinate War of 1688–97, only the keep and foundations remain. The chair-lift up to the nearby Pinnerkreuz will reward you with a fine view of castle, town and valley. Below Cochem, the hills become lower and the Moselle more-or-less straightens out. It passes **Treis-Karden**, whose Romanesque/Gothic church of St Castor has a fine carved altarpiece (1420). Above the town are two more ruined castles. At Moselkern a turning left will bring you up to **Eltz** (open Apr–Oct), one of the most magnificent mediaeval castles in Germany. It stands some distance from the river, isolated in a narrow wooded valley – a defensive site chosen by the lords of Eltz, who built it in the 12th to 17th centuries. Its vast high-towered outer walls are an awesome sight; by contrast, the interior (open Apr–Oct) seems almost intimate – a succession of small courtyards with half-timbered façades, pinnacles, and a jumble of irregular gables. The rooms have been intelligently restored, in their original style as far as possible: a tour takes in the hall of banners with its vaulted ceiling, the old kitchen, the ornately decorated bedchamber, the 'treasure chamber' with its jewelled ornaments, and the collection of old weapons and armour.

The Moselle passes below twin-towered Thurant castle, and the handsome ruins of two castles at Kobern-Gondorf, before it reaches the Rhine at

---

The Hunsrück: Where Reitz Filmed Heimat

East of the Moselle valley there stretches the broad rolling plateau of the Hunsrück. This used to be a poor and isolated region, well off the tourist map: yet today it is familiar to millions around the world who have seen Edgar Reitz' masterly 15-hour film *Heimat*, made for WDR TV in Cologne. Reitz was born in 1932 in the little Hunsrück town of Morbach; and his saga of the Simon family from 1919 to 1982, rising from peasant poverty to modern affluence, was based on his own memories. What's more, he made it on location in the area, in several villages that he fused to create his 'Schabbach' – and the precise settings can be visited.

Most of *Heimat* was shot in Woppenroth. At nearby Gehweiler is the cottage used for the exteriors of the Simon house; and at Griebelschied, near the Nahe valley, is the little cemetery where Maria Simon's funeral was filmed, with Anton's optics factory across the road. Fiction becomes more potent than reality!

The valley upstream was once rich in semi-precious mineral deposits; and the double town of **Idar Oberstein** is still a major centre for cutting and polishing such stones and for making costume jewellery. Two museums, open daily, have dazzling displays of agate, amethyst, opal, quartz, etc, drawn from the world over and fashioned locally, as well as precious antiques such as lapis-lazuli frescoes found at Ur in Assyria. At the Weiherschleife gem-cutting mill (open daily), you can see how the rough stones are ground by giant wheels. Built into the cliff-face above the town is a remarkable 15th-century church, reachable by a stiff climb.

The Porta Nigra, Trier, grandest of surviving Roman monuments in Germany.

KOBLENZ (pop. 110,000). This historic town, founded by the Romans, remains today an important wine-trade and traffic centre, at the confluence of two great rivers: yet it lacks much real charm or interest, partly because it was 80 per cent destroyed in the war. Such of the old quarter as survives is between the Moselle and the multi-style Liebfrauenkirche, 13th to 17th centuries. The Romanesque church of St Castor stands on the site where the Treaty of Verdun, dividing Charlemagne's empire, was drawn up in 843. Along the Rhine, where a festival is held in summer, a pleasant promenade leads to the Deutches Eck (German corner), the tongue of land where the rivers meet – so called because the German Order of Knights here set up

its first post on German soil, in 1216. A huge equestrian statue of Wilhelm I stood here, but only its base now survives. On a low hill above the Rhine, just opposite, is the vast fortress of **Ehrenbreitstein**, which you can reach by car or chair-lift. Dating from the 10th century, it was a residence of the archibshops of Trier until sacked by the French in 1799; then in 1816 the Prussians built its existing fortified network of battlements, gateways and long tunnels. It houses a small museum of industrial design, and its terraces offer good views down over the city and rivers. On the second Sunday in August a lavish firework display, 'The Rhine in Flames', is given from the battlements.

TOURIST OFFICES

TRIER: Porta Nigra, tel (0651) 4 80 71.

BERNKASTEL-KUES: Gestade 5, tel (06531) 40 23.

KOBLENZ: Hauptbanhof, tel (0261) 3 13 04.

Accommodation, Eating and Drinking

TRIER 5500 (tel. code 0651):

(H)**Dorint Porta Nigra**, Porta Nigra-Platz 1, tel 2 70 10. Central, well run; lavish breakfast buffet. Rooms (106) B. Meals B–C.

(H)**Petrisberg**, Sickingenstr. 11, tel 4 11 81. Excellent modern hotel, friendly and family-run, on a hill amid vineyards in the suburbs, with a fine view. No restaurant. Rooms (33) C–D.

(H)**Villa Hügel**, Bernhardtstr. 14, tel 3 30 66. Also on a hill in the outskirts, a white *Jugendstil* villa; helpful owners, good food. Rooms (26) C–D. Meals (residents only) C–D.

(R)**Palais Kesselstatt**, Liebfraenstr. 10, tel 4 02 04. 18th-century wine-cellar, elegantly converted, rather formal; good modern cooking. Cl Jan, Sun dinner, Mon. Meals B–C.

(R)**Zum Domstein**, Hauptmarkt 5, tel 7 44 90. Popular wine-tavern with charming courtyard. **Römische Weinkeller** in a basement, part of Constantine's cathedral (see above), has authentic Roman décor and serves recipes from the famous Roman cookbook of Apicius, a gourmet of the 1st century AD. An experience. Meals C.

(R)**Lenz**, Viehmarkt 4, tel 4 53 10. Pleasant wine-tavern, large and sedate rather than jolly. Dinner only; cl Mon. Meals C–D.

LONGUICH 5559:

(R)**Auf der Festung**, Maximinstr. 30, tel (06502) 49 20. Notable wine-list and many special dishes; good value. Cl 3 weeks July, Sun dinner, Mon. Meals B–C.

LIESER 5550:

(H)**Mehn**, Moselstr. 2, tel (06531) 60 19. Unpretentious inn amid vineyards; good food, served outdoors when fine. Cl mid-Dec to mid-Jan. Rooms (25) D. Meals B–C.

BERNKASTEL 5550:

(H)**Moselblümchen**, Schwanenstr. 10, tel (06531) 23 35. Simple, friendly Gasthaus near the river; good food. Cl Feb to mid-Mar, Sun or Mon. Rooms (22) E. Meals D.

(R)**Rotisserie Royale**, Burgstr. 19, tel (06531) 65 72. Old half-timbered house, elegantly decorated; solid fare. Cl lunch, last 2 weeks Dec. Meals B–C.

TRABEN-TRARBACH 5580:

(H)**Krone**, An der Mosel 93, tel (06541) 63 63. Friendly, cheerful; nice river views. Rooms (22) D. Meals (cl Mon) C–D.

BEILSTEIN 5591:

(H)**Haus Lipmann**, Marktplatz 3, tel (02673) 15 73. Enchanting old inn, cosy and picturesque, good food; own wine-cellar just opposite. Mid-Mar to mid-Nov. Rooms (22) E. Meals C–D.

COCHEM 5590:

(H)**Alte Thorschenke**, Brückenstr. 3, tel (02671) 70 59. Old house dating from 1132; baronial décor and furnishings; good cooking. Cl Jan to Mar 15. Rooms (45) C. Meals B–C.

TREIS-KARDEN 5402:

(H)**Brauer**, Moselstr. 26, tel (02672). By the river, family ambience, food very good value. Cl Jan to Feb 15. Rooms (35) D–E. Meals (cl Wed winter) C–D.

KOBLENZ 5400:

(H)**Kleiner Reisen**, Kaiserin-Augusta-Anlagen 18, tel (0261) 3 20 77. Facing river, good service. No restaurant. Rooms (27) C.

(H)**Zum Schwarzen Bären**, Koblenzer Str. 35, tel (0261) 4 40 74. Friendly, warm and first-rate cooking at this wine-house in the suburb of Moselweiss. Cl 2 weeks F, 2 weeks Jul to Aug. Rooms (13) D. Meals (cl Sun dinner, Mon) C.

Eifel Heights and the Ahr Valley

The Eifel is a rolling schistous plateau, thinly populated, between the Moselle, Belgium and Luxembourg; in the border areas, the people, their housing and cuisine have a distinctly Belgian or Luxembourg character. Though little known abroad, the Eifel is a delightful, unspoilt region, with wide vistas and a marvellous sense of space; it's good for hiking or fishing, even skiing in some places. The central part was once volcanic, and some of the old craters are now lovely small lakes. To the north, this route goes through the beautiful Ahr valley, known for its robust red wines, then enters North-Rhine Westphalia on its way to the very picturesque old town of Monschau.

From Tier, the road goes north to the major brewery town of **Bitburg** (pop. 11,700) whose beers you see advertised everywhere under the slogan 'Bitte ein Bit'. The town also has a big US air base nearby, and a cemetery with the graves of SS officers. This led to an international row in May 1985: Chancellor Kohl ill-advisedly selected Bitburg for a ceremony with President Reagan at which both men laid wreathes in the cemetery, to mark the 40th anniversary of the war's end. American Jews protested loudly – but in vain – that the choice of Bitburg was supremely tactless.

A scenic route runs across-country to **Manderscheid**, a small resort amid wild scenery in the heart of the southern Eifel. Nearby is ruined Niederburg castle, and an extinct volcano with four craters, one of them now a tiny lake. The Manderscheid/Daun area is full of these small round volcanic lakes (*Maare*) with clear blue water: among the prettiest are Holz Maar and Pulver Maar, near Gillenfeld, and Schalkenmehrener and Weinfelder Maare, set either side of a road south-east of **Daun**. Gemündener Maar, isolated amid woods just south of Daun, is an attractive spot for boating or bathing. Daun itself (pop. 8,000), a climatic resort set on high ground with wide views over the Eifel hills, is known for its bracing air. A scenic road leads north through these hills to the **Nürburgring**, Germany's principal motor-racing and motorcycle-racing track: you can drive your own car along its 27km circuit (except on race-days), for a modest fee. At its northern end the track loops round the hilltop ruins of Nürburg castle, which makes an odd contrast to the large modern grandstands. Further on, to the left, is **Hohe Acht** (747m), the Eifel's highest point but more hill than mountain: it's a easy walk to the top, where the views are sweepingly impressive.

The road eastwards descends to a valley at **Schloss Bürresheim** (closed Dec), a graceful 14th–17th century building with baroque gables and a formal garden; its interiors are lavishly furnished. The old town of **Mayen** (pop. 19,000), dark-hued from the local basalt, has a 13th-century castle now housing the Eifel folklore museum. Turn north and you'll come to the remarkable Benedictine monastery of **Maria Laach**, in a fine secluded lakeside setting on the edge of the hills. Its 12th-century Romanesque church, powerfully sombre, has modern stained glass and a curious 13th-century canopy above the altar; the monks' Gregorian chant, sung daily at mass (9am) and vespers (5.30pm), is well worth hearing. The monks also run some excellent craft shops for visitors.

After this, it's an anti-climax to reach industrial Brohl on an ugly built-up stretch of the middle Rhine. Our route follows this busy river for a few miles, past ruined Rheineck castle to **Sinzig** (pop. 15,000) whose big 13th-century Romanesque church has an octagonal tower and yellow-and-white façade. A glass case inside holds an oddity – the preserved corpse of the Vogt von Sinzig, an ancient skeleton of uncertain date that was found in the fields. The nearby *Zehnthof* (tithe house) has a pretty courtyard. North along the river, at **Remagen**, you will notice two mysterious blackened towers: they belong to the famous bridge that the American Army captured intact on 7 March 1945, but three days later it collapsed through over-use, killing 18 US soldiers. These events, and their impact on the final weeks of the war, are detailed in a small museum in one tower.

At Sinzig, turn west up the Ahr valley to **Bad Neuenahr** (pop. 28,000). This large spa resort has one of Germany's busiest casinos, much frequented by diplomats from nearby Bonn. The spa treats diabetes and has a graceful Kurpark. Just west is the pleasant old town of **Ahrweiler**, where picturesque houses line the pedestrian zone round the Marktplatz. The road then follows the beautiful winding valley of the Ahr, past attractive wine-villages with outdoor taverns: the Ahr region produces some of the best German red wines. In the little town of Altenahr, with its ruined 12th-century castle, the Ahrgau museum is strong on local history and St Laurentius church (1248) has fine stained glass.

Here you should leave the Ahr and go due west along a minor road, into the gently pastoral little valley of the Sahrbach, quite off the tourist track. It leads to **Kirchsahr**, a remote village whose tiny church secretes an unexpected treasure – a lovely ornate altar triptych whose colours are still bright though painted in c. 1408. To visit, enquire at the redbrick house just below (the church is kept locked for fear of theft).

Beyond Kirchsahr you leave Hesse to enter North-Rhine Westphalia. Back on the undulating Eifel plateau, you will pass the huge white saucer of one of the world's biggest radio-telescopes, before arriving at **Bad Münstereifel** (pop. 17,000). This modern spa centre is also an attractive ancient town with mediaeval ramparts, gates and towers, an 11th-century Romanesque church, and plenty of fine *Fachwerk* houses such as the Windeckehaus in Orchheimerstrasse. At Mechernich, a detour north-east would lead to the impressive old pinnacled fortress of Satzvey, set by a river. But above all in this area you should visit the Rheinisches Freilichtmuseum at **Kommern** (open daily), best of Germany's many open-air museums of rural tradition. In this big, pleasant park, some 50 old farmhouses, cottages and other buildings from the region, 15th to 18th century, have been cleverly reassembled. Two windmills are set to work when the wind allows. And sometimes trained artisans hold displays of old crafts such as basketwork, forging and weaving; or farmers work with old tools, thresh with flails or harvest with scythes.

At Gemünd, you can drive direct to Monschau via Schleiden, or else first go north-west to the big artificial lake created by the Rurdam. Beyond is **Nideggen** whose pink 12th-century Schloss, in ruins since the 16th century, affords a good view from its keep of the hills and the Rur (*not* Ruhr) valley. In the chancel of the 12th-century church are attractive frescoes and statues. A road south-west via Simmerath will then take you to **Monschau** (pop. 12,000), near the Belgian border. This fascinating old town has a dramatic setting, deep in a narrow winding gorge of the river Rur, and by car it can be reached only from the north (B258). It has little bridges over the swirling river; and the Laufenstrasse, Kirchstrasse and other streets are lined with quaint old steep-roofed half-timbered houses. The *Rotes Haus* (red house), built as the home of a prosperous cloth merchant, is now the local museum and has kept its 18th-century furnishings. The best view of the town is from the cemetery on the cliff above.

TOURIST OFFICES

DAUN: Kurverwaltung, Leopoldstr. 14, tel. (06592) 7 14 77.

MAYEN: Alten Rathaus, Markt, tel. (02651) 8 82 60.

BAD NEUENAHR: Bahnhof and Marktplatz, tel. (02641) 22 78.

MONSCHAU: Stadtstr. 1, tel. (02472) 33 00.

Accommodation, Eating and Drinking

DUDELDORF 5521:

(H)**Romantik-Hotel Zum Alten Brauhaus**, Herrengasse 2, tel (06565) 20 57. Former brewery, as its name reveals; furnishings a bit severe, but ambience homely and local cooking sound. Cl Jan. Rooms (15) C. Meals (cl Wed) C.

EISENSCHMITT-EICHELHÜTTE 5561:

(H)**Molitors Mühle**, tel (06567) 581. Converted millhouse run by a friendly family, in an idyllic lakeside woodland setting. Cl Jan. Rooms (30) C–D. Meals C.

MANDERSCHEID 5562:

(H)**Zens**, Kurfürstenstr. 35, tel (06572) 769. Friendly old coaching-inn, with heated pool and big garden. Cl Jan, early Nov to mid-Dec. Rooms (46) C–D. Meals C–D.

DAUN 5568:

(H)**Schloss-Hotel Kurfürstliches Amtshaus**, Burgberg, tel (06592) 30 31. An 18th-century château with fine views, now an excellent stylish hotel with baronial furnishings, sleek bedrooms (one suite's huge bed was bought from the Petersberg near Bonn, see p. 68, where it was slept in by the Shah of Iran, Brezhnev, etc). Superb sophisticated cuisine. Rooms (42) B–C. Meals B.

MAYEN 5440:

(H)**Zum Alten Fritz**, Koblenzerstr. 56, tel (02651). Excellent cooking at this friendly, simple hostelry. Rooms (19) E. Meals (cl Tue, 3 weeks July) C–D.
(R)**Gourmet Wagner**, Markt 10, tel (02651) 28 61. An old building, but ambitious *nouvelle cuisine* in a trendy Art-Deco setting. Meals (Cl Mon, Tue lunch, 2 weeks Feb and July) A–B.

BAD NEUENAHR 5483:

(H)**Giffels Goldener Anker**, Mittelstr. 14, tel (02641) 23 25. Sedate, well-run establishment near the Kurhaus; good food; many cure guests. Rooms (85) C. Meals C.
(R)**Altes Zunfthaus**, Oberhutstr. 34, Ahrweiler, tel (02641) 47 51. Charming old house; very good value. Meals (cl Thur) C–D.

SCHLEIDEN 5372:

(R)**Alte Rentei**, Am Markt, tel (02445) 699. Fine cooking, e.g. saddle of lamb, in a lovely old building. Meals (cl Thur) B; C in the cheaper rustic-style Rentei-Keller, fine value. Six attractive bedrooms, D.

HELLENTHAL 5374:

(H)**Haus Lichtenhardt**, tel (02482) 614. In a rural setting; modern, friendly and unpretentious; indoor pool. Rooms (19) D–E. Meals D–E.

The Rhine from Koblenz to Bingen

This is the most famous and 'heroic' stretch of the entire Rhine, as it forms the 'Rhine gorge' by forging its way through a schist massif. The river turns and twists as it curves, causing sudden swift currents that can be risky even for modern shipping: hence the legend of the siren on the Loreley rock whose songs lured sailors to their doom. The Rhine curves majestically below sloping vineyards, past dozens of old castles on the hilltops and hillsides: nearly all were built in mediaeval times and some are now in ruins, but others have been restored – either in mock-feudal manner in the 19th century, or more discreetly in modern times. Many now contain museums, or even hotels. The villages and small towns in the wine-producing stretches of the river tend to have picturesque houses and lively wine-harvest festivals: but where the river banks are too steep for vines, the villages noticeably have less charm and character.

This is not a quiet river. All year it is busy with big barges, excursion boats and other shipping. Railways and main roads, also heavy with traffic, follow both banks; and this can reduce the pleasure of motoring, for the roads are not wide. One way of seeing the river is by regular boat excursion, starting from Bingen, Koblenz or other points. But without a car you cannot easily visit the castles, villages and vineyards.

Driving south from Koblenz past a huge modern brewery in its outskirts, you will come to a footpath right up to **Stolzenfels**, a vast ochre castle on the hillside: it was rebuilt in neo-Gothic style in 1836 by Friedrich-Wilhelm IV who added the battlements. Its lavish interior is now a museum (closed Dec); the keep offers a good view down over the river. **Rhens**, looking across the Rhine to the high-towered profile of Marksburg castle (see p. 88), is a quaint old town whose half-timbered Rathaus juts out into the main street. Beyond here the river makes an imposing double bend between the vineyards sloping to its banks, just north of **BOPPARD** (pop. 17,000), largest of all Rhineside resorts and maybe the jolliest – at least at wine-festival time. Rows of hotels and *Weinstuben*, nearly all of them advertising *Tanz* and *Stimmung*, line its elegant promenade. The river valley then narrows to a defile, and reaches **Rheinfels** (open Apr–Oct), biggest of all the Rhine castles between Koblenz and Mainz. Built in the 13th century and re-fashioned in the 16th, it was wrecked by the French in 1794, then partially pulled down. But the towering frame of its great vaulted hall survives, and the castle museum has a model of how it looked in 1607, a cross between Carcassonne and Neuschwanstein. You can stroll through its maze of ruins, to inspect the clock tower, pharmacy, brewery, even the gallows. The town just below, **St Goar**, is tediously

trippery: but its old Gothic church has charming 15th-century frescoes.

The curving river passes the Loreley rock on the far bank (see below). Just beyond is **Oberwesel**, a pleasant old wine-town with towers and half-timbered houses: the Gothic Liebfrauen-kirche has remarkable altarpieces, and a triptych showing the 15 cataclysms ending the world. Towering on the hill above is the romantic mediaeval hulk of **Burg Schönburg**, former triple fortress of the Dukes of Schönburg; part is now a Catholic holiday centre and part a delightful hotel (see p. 89). Its owners have painted one of the outer walls bright red – back to what it was in the 16th century when painted walls were a symbol of wealth. The main road then passes opposite the neat and toy-like little white castle of Pfalz, secluded on an islet; it was a toll-house in medi-aeval times. **Bacharach**, shielded from the river, road and railway by a line of ramparts with gateways and tall towers, is a charmingly quaint but thereby trippery old wine-town: its narrow streets are lined with ancient *Fachwerk* houses, many now in use as hotels, wine-pubs or craft shops where arti-sans can be seen at work. The folksy Weinhaus Altes Haus in the Ober-strasse dates from 1368. The Peters-kirche has a Romanesque four-tiered nave. Above the town is another much-restored yet imposing old for-tress: **Burg Stahleck**, now housing a youth hostel. You can drive up for a fine view of the river from the terrace behind it.

Steep terraced vineyards line both banks of the Rhine, on the way to two more high-perched old castles, both much restored: Sooneck, with garden terraces and a tall tower, and Reichen-stein (open Mar–Oct) which has hunt-

Katz Castle, above St Goarshausen on the middle Rhine.   Fotobank

ing trophies and old armour. More interesting is **Rheinstein** (open Mar–Nov), a small castle also set on a high hill, almost sheer above the river, and alluringly floodlit at night. In 1975 it was bought by Hermann Hecker, an Austrian opera singer, who has restored it gracefully (tapestries, suits of armour, new stained glass, and arrays of tin soldiers). Sometimes he organizes opera seminars or stages knightly plays. The climb up the outside stairway is vertiginous, but the view of the river is rewarding. Finally the route comes to **Bingen** (pop. 24,000), not itself a resort but a workaday railway town, overlooked by the grey turreted tower of Burg Klopp.

This former stronghold of the bishops of Mainz now contains the Rathaus: its terrace affords a sweeping view of the Taunus and Hunsrück hills, and of the Ehrenfels ruin and Niederwalk monument across the river (see p. 214). Down to the left, on a little island, you'll see the mediaeval *Maüseturm* (mouse tower), tall and yellowish: its name comes from an old legend about a fiendish archbishop of Mainz who was eaten by mice in divine retribution for burning to death some starving beggars. A less apocryphal event – the saving of Bingen from the Black Death – is commemorated each August by an ancient festival at the hilltop chapel of St Rochus, outside the town.

From Bingen you could make a detour south to **Bad Kreuznach** (pop. 40,000), a sizeable spa town with 15th-century houses on a bridge over the river Nahe. The Karl Geib museum has floor mosaics and other local Roman relics. To the south, a smaller spa with a longer name, **Bad Münster am Stein Ebernburg**, lies close to the Rheingrafenstein rock that towers above the cliff-lined Nahe valley: you can climb the rock, for an impressive view.

Back in Bingen, you should cross the Rhine by ferry to Rüdesheim, which is in Hesse (see p. 214). Driving north up the east bank you will re-enter Rheinland-Pfalz at the pleasant village of Kaub, where the much-restored Schloss Gutenfels towers high on its hill. At a bend in the river further north is the notorious **Loreley**, a high wooded bluff that holds a notable place in German legend. One myth relates that it held the treasure of the Nibelungen; in another, subject of poems by Heine and others, a lovely siren sat on the cliff, singing songs that lured boatmen to their death. Yet the Loreley is hardly worth visiting, for unlike the siren it is *not* beautiful: drive up to its top by the back road, and you'll find merely a mediocre view of the river, and a tatty restaurant overcrowded with tourists.

On the hill above St Goarshausen is **Burg Katz** (Cat Castle), so named by its owners, the Counts of Katzenehlbogen, who built it in riposte to the castle of their rivals to the north, which they dubbed 'Burg Maus': Cat Castle has now been bought by a rich Japanese who has plans to convert it into a hotel. The grey hulk of Burg Maus (not open to visitors) looms above **Wellmich** whose 14th-century church has restored 15th-century frescoes. To the

north you will pass below another pair of warring fortresses, white Sterrenburg and grey Liebenstein: they are known as the 'Hostile Brothers' because of the long 13th–14th-century feud between their owners, rival branches of the same family. North of Kamp-Bornhofen, where the road winds round the Boppard curve, the rugged slopes are too steep for vineyards.

The attractive old village of **Braunach** has a lively wine-festival in early October. From here it's a 20-minute walk or short drive up to **Marksburg** (open daily), whose high-towered silhouette dominates this part of the river. I like it best of all Rhine castles. It is the only one never to have been captured or even partly pulled down, so it survives in its original form: the Landgraves of Hessen owned it till 1803, and today it belongs to a society for the upkeep of old castles, which has tastefully restored without adding false 'feudal' touches. Some parts are 12th-century, the main building is 14th, and the battlements were rebuilt in 1479. The guides, unusually helpful and erudite, show you first the two picturesque half-timbered gun-batteries whose 16th-century cannons face the river. The interior has been kept as authentically mediaeval as possible, and is almost a museum of the life and customs of the times; its 14th-century kitchen can be hired for mediaeval banquets, at which small oxen are roasted whole. There's a torture chamber and, in the little Rittersaal, a mediaeval lavatory that casts its excreta onto the terrace below. In the bedrooms are cradles and looms; the lovely chapel has 13th-century frescoes. The display of armour, from Greek to Renaissance times, has genuine mediaeval pieces and imitations of what Greek hoplites and Roman legionaries wore. As for modern times, on the hill behind the castle are three tall black chimneys belonging to Braubach's silver-mining works, down below.

At Lahnstein, a road leads up to Lahneck (open Apr–Oct), a feudal fortress much restored in the 19th century; from its terrace there's a good view. A detour east up the wooded Lahn valley will bring you to the classic spa resort of **Bad Ems** (pop. 10,000), which has a stately new casino. King Wilhelm I came here for a cure, each year for 20 years: outside the Kurhaus, a flagstone recalls the insult that he gave here in 1870 to the French ambassador, thus precipitating the Franco-Prussian war. From Bad Ems, it's a short drive back to Koblenz.

TOURIST OFFICES

BOPPARD: Theodor-Hoffmann Platz, tel (06742) 62 97.

BINGEN: Rheinkai 21, tel (06721) 18 42 05.

BAD EMS: Lahnstr. 90, tel (02603) 6541.

Accommodation, Eating and Drinking

BOPPARD 5407:

(H)**Klostergut Jakobsberg,** 12km to north, near Spay, tel (06742) 3062. High above the river, an old monastery stylishly converted into a smart hotel; sports centre, indoor pool, interesting cooking. Rooms (110) B. Meals B.

(HW)**Am Ebertor**, Heerstr., tel (06742) 20 81. On the main promenade, pleasant and unassuming; lively wine-garden, where you can dance to music under the trees. Apr–Oct. Rooms (60) D. Meals C–D.

OBERWESEL 6532:

(H)**Burg Schönburg**, tel (06744) 70 27. In an ancient hilltop fortress, a delightful and very romantic hotel, intimate and cosy: beamed courtyards, four-poster beds, friendly owners. Mar–Nov. Rooms (21) B–C. Meals (cl Mon) B.

BACHARACH 6533:

(H)**Gelber Hof**, Blücherstr. 26, tel (06743) 10 17. Very modest, but quiet and welcoming; good food. Cl Jan, mid-Dec. Rooms (32) E. Meals (cl Mon) C.

BINGEN 6530:

(H)**Starkenburger Hof**, Rheinkai 1, tel (06721) 1 43 41. Classic hotel by the railway, facing the river. No restaurant. Cl Jan. Rooms (30) D.

LAHNSTEIN 5420:

(R)**Historisches Wirtshaus an der Lahn**, Lahnstr. 8, tel (02621) 72 70. Historic half-timbered riverside pub once visited by Goethe, now a smart place with first-rate *nouvelle cuisine*. Cl lunch, Thur, 2 weeks Aug. Meals B.

Mainz and the German Wine Road

MAINZ (pop. 190,000), the *Land* capital, stands beside the Rhine on a broad plain; home town of Gutenberg, the pioneer of modern printing, it's a place of much character with an attractive well-restored Altstadt, full of jolly wine-taverns. As befits a city that is Germany's leading wine market, the ambience is relaxed and friendly – almost *too* exuberantly friendly during the famous pre-Lenten carnival. But Mainz has a serious side too: its cathedral is one of Germany's grandest, and the city has played an influential part in German history.

In Roman times it was a major military headquarters. Then in 742 St Boniface, from England, created its archbishopric and made it the main centre of the Church in Germany. Work on the cathedral began in 975. Under the Holy Roman Empire the archbishop held the high rank of Prince-Elector; and when in the 1450s Gutenberg began to print his Bibles in Mainz, this revolution in technology helped to spread the city's influence across Europe. Its university, one of Germany's oldest, was founded in 1476. The Prince-Electors remained powerful during the 17th and 18th centuries; but in Napoleon's day Mainz was for a while annexed to France, and after this it never quite recovered its impor-

tance. In World War II its centre was 80 per cent destroyed by bombing, but has since been well rebuilt: many old buildings have pleasing red-and-white façades. Today Mainz has some flourishing modern industries, including IBM, and it is a major centre of the media: the second German television network, ZDF, has its headquarters here, employing a staff of 3,000.

Mainz is often regarded as the most 'French' of German towns, still marked by the French annexation of Napoleonic times. Many French families have settled here, and French cultural influence is strong, as witnesses the flourishing Institut Français. Maybe, too, the wine tradition gives Mainz much in common with the wine-growing areas of France; the local temperament, relaxed and jovial, given to intrigue and wheeler-dealing, seems in many ways more Latin than Germanic. This is exemplified by Mainz's famous Carnival, where politics and crazy buffoonery go hand-in-hand. After Cologne's, this is the leading carnival in Germany, and it has always been somewhat political, whereas Cologne's is more commercial. It began in the 1830s as an expression of radical student revolt against the harsh conservative rule of the time: in the 19th century, carnival organizers often risked arrest. But after 1918 the carnival was appropriated by the bourgeoisie and its focus shifted from Left to

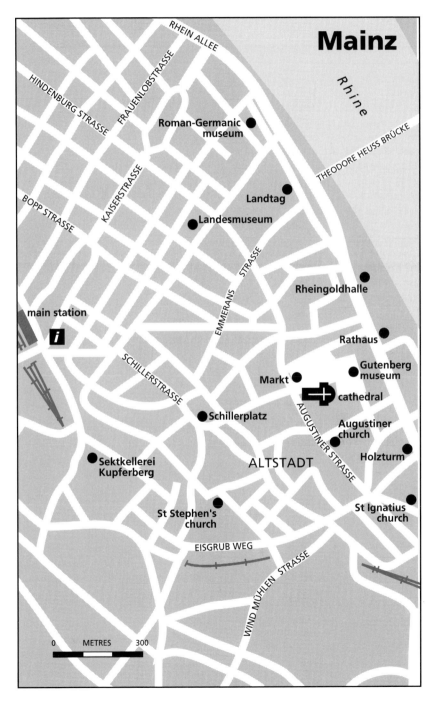

Mainz

RHEIN ALLEE

Rhine

HINDENBURG STRASSE

FRAUENLOBSTRASSE

THEODORE HEUSS BRÜCKE

Roman-Germanic museum

KAISERSTRASSE

BOPP STRASSE

Landtag

Landesmuseum

EMMERANS STRASSE

Rheingoldhalle

main station

i

Rathaus

SCHILLERSTRASSE

Gutenberg museum

Markt

cathedral

Schillerplatz

AUGUSTINER STRASSE

Augustiner church

Holzturm

Sektkellerei Kupferberg

ALTSTADT

St Ignatius church

St Stephen's church

EISGRUB WEG

WIND MÜHLEN STRASSE

0   METRES   300

Right. And so it remains today: the carnival is run not by the city council but by local clubs mostly Rightish in character, and the Socialist mayor has to go along with them. The pre-carnival period is marked by a series of festivities where speakers stand on beer-barrels to make satiric speeches, generally criticizing Greens, students and other radicals: these are widely televised, and they have given Mainz a somewhat reactionary image in the rest of Germany.

Besides the pre-lenten Carnival, Mainz's main annual **festivals** are the Johannisnacht on the third weekend in June (fair on the Rhine banks, much jolly drinking) and a wine festival on the last weekend in August and the first in September.

A tour of the old town on foot could start at the **Cathedral**, which happily was damaged little in the war. This massive reddish sandstone structure, with high pinnacled towers rather than spires, is essentially Romanesque, though with Gothic and baroque additions. Its lofty nave contains the imposing tombs and memorials of a number of its archbishops. Many of the cathedral's side-altars and paintings were sold off by the French under Napoleon, and the murals that you now see high up in the nave are mid-19th-century replacements, but sensitively done. The beautiful late-Gothic cloister leads to the Diocesan Museum which contains some impressive early sculptures: the finest (a man with a headband, a group of 'the damned', and others) are by the 13th-century anonymous 'Master of Naumburg'.

The cathedral gives onto the broad Markt square, whose painted houses are post-war copies of old ones: the square contains an exuberant Renaissance fountain and a curious allegorical modern one, featuring the Romans, Christalnacht, the Greens and other bits of local history. Unusual lanterns prettily light the little square on the east side, leading to the marvellous museum devoted to **Gutenberg** and the history of printing (see box feature). There's a statue of the great man in the nearby Gutenbergplatz. And to the south the **Altstadt** begins, much of it now a pedestrian zone and ideal for a stroll: from the Leichhof square you get a fine view of the soaring cathedral, while the little Kirschgarten is a lovely old cobbled street lined with restored half-timbered houses, some of them 15th-century. The Altstadt's main street, the Augustinerstrasse, is today rather touristy, with cheap Italian and Turkish restaurants, even an Afghan bazaar: but take a look at the Gothic Augustiner church and the Frankfurter Hof, a cradle of Europe's 1848 uprising.

Further on, down a quiet side-alley, is Mainz's oldest surviving house, the 12th-century Wohnturm, built by a Jewish family and still lived in by Jews. Nearby stands the lofty mediaeval Holzturm, part of the old city walls. In this pleasant quarter of 16th-century houses you'll come next to the red sandstone church of St Ignatius, with its painted cupolas and sumptuous rococo interior; outside is a notable 16th-century sculpture of the Crucifixion by Hans Backoffen. The adjacent Kapuzinerstrasse has some nice old houses, some of them wine-pubs: but it is on the edge of the city's red-light district.

Going west from the Altstadt, you will come to the old church of **St Stephan** which contains a wonderful surprise: nine blue stained-glass windows by Marc Chagall, his only work in Germany. When the great Russian-Jewish artist was persuaded by the parish priest to take on the job, he chose the theme of reconciliation – between Christian and Jew, between Germany and his adopted France. The work was carried out in 1976–81, when he was already in his nineties: but the vivid fantasy and the luminous dark-blue hues are typical of Chagall at his best. In the nearby Schillerplatz is another modern work, of a very different kind – one more example of those quirky fountain-sculptures in bronze that the Germans love, this one an allegory of the Mainz carnival. The square and the Schillerstrasse beyond it are lined with fine baroque mansions (one houses the Institut Français). Like many other old buildings in the city, their walls have been smartly restored in white with red borders, and this pattern helps to give Mainz its distinctive look.

Beside the river north-east of the cathedral is the smart new black-and-white Rathaus, next to a modern concert hall, the Rheingoldhalle. In 1982, work on an extension to the nearby Hilton Hotel revealed nine Roman boats dating from the 4th century. From here a promenade along the Rhine leads to a district of big public buildings – the Landtag, the law courts, and two museums. Of these, the Roman-Germanic Museum in the 17th-century Electors' Palace has various antique objects, of no special interest: but the Landesmuseum, modestly housed in the former imperial stables, is more worthwhile. Among its Roman sculptures is the famous Jupitersäule, a triumphal column; and its mediaeval paintings include a copy of Dürer's *Adam and Eve*. Also worth a visit is the

Sektkellerei Kupferberg, near the main station, claimed to be the world's largest cellars of sparkling wine.

WORMS (pop. 73,500), beside the Rhine, is a distinguished historic city. It is closely connected with the legend of the Nibelungen, for here the young prince Siegfried came to the Burgundian court and Hagen threw the Nibelungen treasure into the river. In mediaeval times, Worms was a royal residence and seat of the Imperial Diet: in 1521 Martin Luther was summoned before this Diet and condemned, under the notorious Edict of Worms. But the city ever since has backed Luther; today it is two-thirds Protestant, and in 1868 it erected a sturdy Luther Monument, whose bronze figures depict the Reformation's protagonists. However, the magnificent 12th-century cathedral is Roman Catholic: its exterior is one of Germany's finest examples of the Romanesque, while in the north aisle are five beautiful Gothic reliefs. Among other notable churches, the Gothic Liebfrauenkirche has given its name to the wine produced in its surrounding vineyards – Liebfraumilch, the 'milk of Our Lady' (the dryish version of this wine sold in Germany is much superior to the sweetish liquid exported to Britain). Worms was an important Jewish as well as Protestant centre: its 11th-century synagogue, rebuilt in 1961, is Germany's oldest; the Jewish cemetery, too, is 11th-century and contains over 1,000 ancient steles engraved in Hebrew. The Heylshof Museum (cl Jan) has superb stained glass and porcelain of the 15th–19th centuries; the Städtisches Museum displays Roman and prehistoric remains.

To the south-west of Worms the

Mainz cathedral, in the heart of the city.

Pfalz vineyards begin. The wooded hills of the Pfalz are a prolongation of the Vosges; and as in Alsace the vineyards stretch along the eastern slopes, from Bockenheim south of Worms to the French border. The zig-zag road linking the many wine-villages is clearly marked 'Deutsche Weinstrasse'. A visit at harvest-time is best of all: but nearly all year the growers keep open house in their attractive *Weingüter* (wine stores) in the villages, where at give-away prices you can drink the new, still barely fermented wine.

From Worms a road leads across the plain to reach **Bad Dürkheim** (pop. 18,000), a resort with a pleasant park: in September it holds a well-known sausage-fair-cum-wine-festival. Here wooded hills rise up to the west, and the Wine Road follows their vineclad slopes. First stop is **Deidesheim**, whose venerable balustraded Rathaus has a small wine museum. At the local Romantik-Hotel (see p. 98), Helmut Kohl met Margaret Thatcher on 30 April 1989 and tussled with her about nuclear missiles; after drinking the local wine she confided to the TV cameras, 'It's *very* dry with just a *touch* of sweetness, like me' (giggles all round). A detour to the south-east will lead to **Hassloch**, for a visit to the 'Holiday

Park', said to be Germany's largest: children especially will enjoy the vast model railway and the Frankenstein monster. Continue the detour further and you'll come to **Speyer** (pop. 44,000), an interesting town on the Rhine, whose massive four-towered Romanesque cathedral dates from 1030: its superb crypt holds the tombs of eight Holy Roman Emperors. A Neo-Gothic Protestant memorial church commemorates the Lutherans' protest in 1529 against the Diet of Worms – the name 'Protestant' comes from this. The Historisches Museum der Pfalz (open daily) has prehistoric and Roman exhibits. And the town's wine museum contains the world's oldest surviving bottle of wine still in a liquid state – it dates from c. AD 300!

Back on the Wine Road, **Neustadt** (pop. 54,000) is the region's commercial wine capital; it boasts a 16th-century Rathaus and an amusing modern fountain of spurting pedestals. At Hambach, a road west up the hillside leads to **Hambach Castle** (open daily Mar–Nov) whose history is curious. First built in c. AD 1000, it was wrecked in 1688 during the Palatinate wars; then in 1832 some patriotic radicals demonstrated here, and were the first to raise the black, red and yellow banner much later chosen as the German flag. So Hambach has been dubbed 'the cradle of German democracy'. Now restored in mock-feudal style, it is sometimes used by the Federal Government for state ceremonies.

Just beyond Maikammer is my favourite wine-village of the Weinstrasse: **St Martin**, entirely devoted to wine and appropriately twinned with Chassagne-Montrachet in Burgundy. Many of the handsome old houses in its narrow streets bear decorative wine motifs, such as ironwork signs of grapes. As in many other such villages, growers tend to use their homes as *Weingüter*, where in a leafy courtyard or old cellar you can drink fresh grapey wine, barely fermented, at minimal prices: I commend especially the Schneider *Weingut* at Maikammerstrasse 5. Beyond dull Edenkoben is another pretty wine-village, Rhodt, where a road leads up the hill to Ludwigshühe castle (closed Dec), built in the style of an Italian villa by Ludwig I of Bavaria in the 1850s. A chair-lift (Easter to Oct) leads from here to the Reitburg summit (550m) for a fine view of the vineyards. **Hainfeld** and **Gleisweiler** are other attractive villages, where old *Weinstuben* with flowery balconies sell their new wine, and elegant gateways lead into the courtyards of prosperous growers – a familiar décor all along the Wine Road.

To the south-west is Annweiler, where a road winds up to ruined **Trifels** castle, high on its lonely hill. This is one of the most startling places in the Pfalz: the very approach is awe-inspiring, past the isolated rock of Asselstein and two more wrecks of hilltop castles, Scharfenberg and Anebos. From the Trifels car park it is then a steep 15-minute walk up to the castle itself (closed Dec), where there's little to see inside: but it is worth the visit, alike for the view and its aura of feudal mystery. The castle was a seat of the Hohenstaufen emperors, and in its royal chapel are copies of their crown jewels. Legend has it that Trifels once held the Holy Grail too; and it's known that Richard the Lion Heart was held prisoner here by Heinrich VI in 1193. Modern history's postscripts: Hitler had the place rebuilt in mock-

---

Gutenberg, the Pioneer of Printing

Johannes Gutenberg (c. 1398–1468), the bastard son of a local patrician, was born and died in Mainz. It is not true that he actually *invented* printing, for the Chinese had been doing it for centuries: but he was the first to pioneer a printing-press using movable metal type. This revolutionised book-making in Europe, which hitherto had been done by scribes; and, amazingly, Gutenberg's invention remained the basis of printing up until this century.

He spent some years in Strasbourg, where he prepared his project: but it was back in Mainz that he set up his workshop and completed his first Bible, in 1455. He used a technique based on the wine-press, with ink made from soot and oil. Soon, however, his local creditors turned against him, he went bankrupt and had to depend on charity. This great inventor died in penury.

Mainz's huge **Gutenberg Museum** (open daily, cl Jan) is utterly fascinating. Here a replica of his original press is set in operation for the public at 10.30 and 12.30, and at other times for guided tours. Here, too, is Gutenberg's actual first Bible, printed on vellum, a priceless treasure: he printed some 180 Bibles, of which 48 still exist, 14 in Germany, 11 in the US, eight in the UK. There is also a map showing the rapid spread of Gutenberg's technique across Europe in the late 15th century.

Romanesque style, and today USAF jets scream by from the big American base at Kaiserslautern.

To the south is **Bad Bergzabern**, whose thermal centre treats rheumatism and migraine. The old part of town has some fine Renaissance houses with protuding corner-windows and Dutch-style stepped façades, e.g. the Gasthof zum Engel (see below) in the Königstrasse. West of the town stretches the fascinating Wasgau, an unspoilt district of forested hills, with trout-streams, rocks in weird shapes, and clifftop castles – notably **Schloss Berwartstein**, a landmark from afar. Once it was a haunt of robber chieftains, whose rooms hewn in the rock can be visited; now it's a restaurant. Further west, the little town of **Dahn** lies in an area of russet rocks eroded into bizarre shapes, some like pinnacles or giant toadstools. A road out of Dahn marked 'Burgruinen' will bring

you to the foot of three ruined 12th-century castles, all within the same outer wall: they are built of the same stones as the reddish rocky bluff on which they stand, so that from below they appear to be part of it (like Les Baux in Provence). It is worth climbing up to this hauntingly romantic spot, where a little museum explains its history; and the view down along the rock-strewn valley is magnificent.

Some way to the West of Dahn is the **SAARLAND**, in population the smallest of the *Länder* apart from Bremen: it has 1.1 million inhabitants and covers 2,571 sq. km. It lies close to France; and though its people are German-speaking and of German culture, it has often belonged to France and was long contested between the two nations. After 1945 it came again under French control. But in 1955 the people voted decisively by referendum to return to Germany, and since 1957 the Saarland has been a Federal Land like any other. Since 1985 its Prime Minister has been Oscar Lafontaine, one of Germany's top socialists and candidate for the Chancellorship in 1990. The Saar is a region of coal-mining and of heavy industry, notably steelworks, engineering and chemicals. But most industry is centred in the south, around Saarbrücken, whereas to the north in the Saar valley and towards the Hünsruck there are lovely rural areas.

The capital, **Saarbrücken** (pop. 200,000), has a university and opera house, and a few interesting buildings, notably the baroque Elector's Palace and the Gothic 13th-century church of St Arnual. The Saarland museum has some modern paintings as well as exhibits relating to local history. A new German–French Park has recently been landscaped by architects from the two countries, and the town has a bilingual Franco-German lycée/Gymnasium – two tokens of today's happy entente between two old enemies.

TOURIST OFFICES

MAINZ: Bahnhofstr. 15, tel (06131) 23 37 41.

WORMS: Neumarkt 14, tel (06241) 85 35 60.

SPEYER: Maximilianstr. 11, tel (06232) 1 43 95.

BAD BERGZABERN: Kurverwaltung, Kurtalstr. 25, tel (06343) 88 11.

SAARBRÜCKEN: Trier Str. 2, tel (0681) 3 51 97.

Accommodation, Eating and Drinking

MAINZ 6500 (tel code 06131):

(H)**Hilton International**, Rheinstr. 68, tel 24 50. All that you'd expect from a huge Hilton, plus a Rhineside setting; three eateries including the agreeable Römische Weinstube for local dishes. Rooms (435) A. Meals A–B (Rheingrill), C (Weinstube).

(H)**Central Hotel Eden**, Bahnhofsplatz 8, tel 67 40 01. A traditional hotel, well modernized, opposite the station. Good French-influenced food. Rooms (64) B–C. Meals (cl Sun) B.

(H)**Hammer**, Bahnhofsplatz 6, tel 61 10 61. Comfortable, cheerful and well run. No restaurant. Rooms (40) C.

(R)**Zum Leininger Hof**, Weintorstr. 6, tel 22 84 84. In an old house with vaulted ceilings; elegant ambience and modern 'creative' cooking. Meals (cl Sun) A–B.

(R)**Rats-und Zunftstuben Heilig Geist**, Rentengasse 2, tel 22 57 57. In a 13th-century house, a large, venerable, rather formal restaurant with antique furnishings. Hearty German bourgeois cooking. Meals (cl Sun dinner) C–D.

(RW)**Doctor Flotte**, Kirschgarten 1, tel 23 41 70. Lovely wine-pub/bistro, elegant and atmospheric, thronged with young people. Tables outside in summer. Good simple food. Meals (cl Sun) D.

(RW)**Löschs Weinstube**, Jakobsbergstr. 9, tel 22 03 83. Cosy, intimate, sympathetic; garden for summer. Short menu. Meals C–D.

(W)**Wilhelm**, Rheinstr. 51, tel 22 49 49. Candlelit wine-tavern in an old house, lively and delightful. Regional snacks.

(There are many other good wine-taverns in the Altstadt, among them Bacchus, Gebert's and Schreiner).

(B)**Eisgrub-Bräu**, Weisliliengasse 1, tel 22 11 04. For this town of wine, quite a daring new venture: an stylish brewery-cum-beer-pub, full of copper vats. Some good simple dishes. Meals D–E.

WORMS 6520:

(H)**Wormser Eck**, Klosterstr. 80, tel (06241) 66 71. Central, comfortable, inexpensive. No restaurant. Rooms E.

DEIDESHEIM 6705:

(H)**Romantik-Hotel Deidesheimer Hof**, Marktplatz, tel (06326) 18 11. A lively, *gemütlich* hostelry run by the Hahn family, leading local wine-growers. Good food and wine. Cl 10 days Jan. Rooms (27) C–D. Meals B–C.

BAD BERGZABERN 6748:

(H)**Pfälzer Wald**, Kurtalstr. 77, tel (06343) 10 56. Welcoming family hotel by a lake, on the edge of town. Good, plain food. Cl Feb. Rooms (25) D. Meals C–D.

(R)**Zum Engel**, Königstr. 45, tel (06343) 49 33. In a lovely 16th-century house; good ambience. Cl Feb and Tue. Meals C–D.

SAARBRÜCKEN 6600:

(H)**Novotel**, Zinzingerstr. 9, tel (0681) 5 86 30. French-owned, convenient and modern, in south-west outskirts. Rooms (100) C. Meals C.

(H)**Meran**, Mainzerstr. 69, tel (0681) 6 53 81. Fairly central, comfortable. No restaurant. Rooms (60) C–D.

(R)**Zum Stiefel**, Am Stiefel 2, tel (0681) 3 12 46. In the Altstadt, an attractive and historic old inn, dating from 1702. Good local specialities; beer garden. Cl Sun. Meals C–D.

CHAPTER FOUR

Baden - Württemberg

THIS LARGE SOUTH-WESTERN *Land* (pop. 9.3 million) is one of Germany's most prosperous, with much high-tech industry; it also has some of its loveliest scenery, including the Black Forest and the Lake of Constance. It epitomizes the picturesque folksiness and warm *Gemütlichkeit* that we associate with southern Germany, but in a gentler manner than Bavaria. Its hilltop castles, glorious wooded hills, mediaeval towns and friendly wine-pubs are travel-brochure material, but also a vivid reality.

The *Land* is in two parts, as its name implies. In 1951 a popular referendum agreed on a merger of the former duchy of Baden, along the Rhine, and the former kingdom of Württemberg, based on Stuttgart (the Württemberg rulers had first been counts, then dukes, then in 1806 their realm was elevated into a kingdom). Today Stuttgart is the *Land* capital, a large, throbbingly industrial but very appealing city; other major towns are Karlsruhe (Baden's former capital), Mannheim, and the old university cities of Heidelberg, Freiburg and Tübingen.

T HE TWO states and their people are rather different, in history and temperament, and the marriage since 1951 has not always been easy. Baden, so near to France, is a largely Catholic region whose people are fun-loving, easy-going, fond of festivals and folklore. Württemberg, by tradition mainly Protestant, forms the main part of an ancient territory known as Swabia – and the Swabians by repute are ponderous, slow, very hard-working, gently humorous but unsophisticated, and somewhat pious and puritanical. It's true that this stereotype has been changing under modern influences (many younger Swabians today are anything but puritanical), but there's still some truth in it. Swabians still use their own strange dialect; and, in all social classes, even when talking standard German they have a rough, rather comic accent that marks them out and is a bit of a joke in Germany. They are lovers of the twee and cosy, for whom even a big mansion is not a *Haus* but a *Häusle* (wee house).

A typical Swabian is Manfred Rommel, Stuttgart's liberal, wrily humorous Lord Mayor. Another is

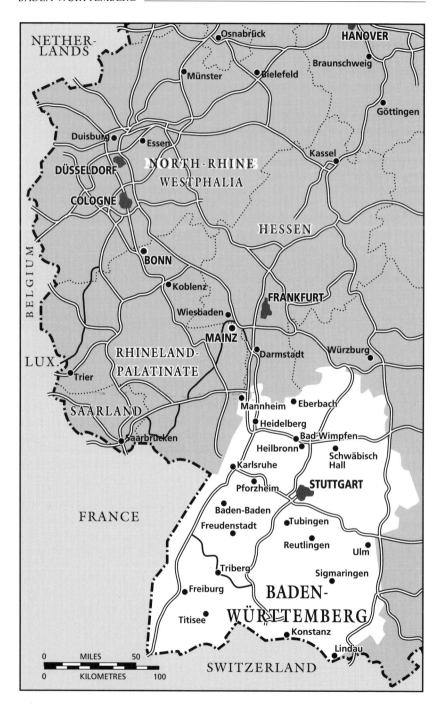

Lothar Späth, the high-profile *Land* Prime Minister (since 1978) and CDU leader, who has has dynamically attracted much new industry. If this state is Germany's richest, it's largely because the Swabians are inventive, resourceful and highly-skilled, and even more hard-working than most Germans. This used to be a poor, ill-served region, and in the 19th century many farmers emigrated, or they set up tiny cottage-industries as the best way of surviving. An old joke goes: 'Come on, children', says a peasant wife, 'clear the supper off the table, father's starting his factory here in the kitchen.' Many small-scale precision industries thus began in modest villages – in watch and clockmaking, textiles, toys, and later in optics, electrical goods, turbines and much else, and they did brilliantly. The star case is that of Gottlieb Daimler, who in 1883–86 invented the motor-car in a Stuttgart garden shed (see p. 115), but there are many others. Today, in parts of Swabia, sophisticated high-tech workshops can be found cheek-by-jowl with antiquated little dairy farms. Today the main larger industries include cars (Stuttgart), electronics, optics and jewellery (Pforzheim). And Baden-Württemberg as much as Bavaria has benefited from the recent tendency of modern German industry to move to the south, attracted by the qualities of the workforce, as well as by climate, scenery and lifestyles. Unemployment is little more than half the West German average.

Agriculture is varied: you will see orchards, wheatfields, tobacco, herds of cattle, cabbage-fields for *Sauerkraut*, and vineyards producing some of Germany's best wines, notably on the western slopes of the Black Forest. The scenery, too, is varied. To the south, the big Lake of Constance (*Bodensee*) has a very mild climate. To the west in Baden is the hilly range of the Black Forest (*Schwarzwald*). In southern Württemberg, the long rocky plateau of the Swabian Jura (*Schwäbische Alb*) is a heartland of the German aristocracy: here three great feudal families, the Hohenstaufen, Hohenzollern and Hohenlohe, built their castles *hohe* on the hills. Today there are more castles here than in any part of Germany save the middle Rhine – along the fringes of the Swabian Jura, in the rolling Hohenlohe coutry to the north, and in the Neckar valley as it flows towards 'romantic' Heidelberg.

Heidelberg, the Neckar Valley and the Hohenlohe

This route begins at Mannheim, Baden-Württemberg's second largest town, then it follows the winding river Neckar upstream, via the old university city of Heidelberg, much loved by foreign tourists. To its east the Neckar is even more densely lined with hilltop castles than the middle Rhine; some are still ruined, but others have been restored as hotels or museums. At first the river is enclosed between steep wooded slopes: but beyond Neckaretz the valley broadens, and is clad with vineyards as you approach industrial Heilbronn and the enchanting little hilltop town of Bad Wimpfen. Here our route turns up the valley of the Jagst, a Neckar tributary, then cuts across a rolling plain where the lords of Hohenlohe still live in their castles; and so it reaches Schwäbisch Hall, one of south Germany's loveliest old towns. An alternative way of seeing the Neckar valley is by regular boat excursion.

MANNHEIM (pop. 305,000), set where the Neckar joins the Rhine, is one of Europe's largest river ports and has long been an important industrial centre (Carl Benz here pioneered the motor-car in 1885, see p. 115). It stands across the Rhine from another industrial city, Ludwigshafen, home of the BASF chemicals firm. Mannheim has been active in culture, too, especially theatre (Schiller's first play, *Die Räuber*, had its première here in 1782) and today it boasts a fine museum of painting, the Kunsthalle, with works by Beckmann and Kokoschka, Corot, Manet and Cézanne, as well as sculptures by Rodin, Brancusi and others. The Reiss museum has details of local history and attractive local porcelain. The central part of the town is built on a grid pattern, each of its 144 blocks being denoted by a letter and number – B2, C3, etc. Between it and the Rhine is the massive Residenzschloss (1720–60), one of the largest baroque palaces in Germany, today housing part of the university: its rococo library and Rittersaal are both ornately decorated and worth a visit.

Schwetzingen (pop. 18,000), on the way to Heidelberg, is a graceful little town whose pink 18th-century château was the summer residence of the Palatine Electors: the rococo theatre in one side-pavilion is still sometimes used for plays. Much more interesting than the château itself is its large and famous park: the front part is formal and French, with fountains and statues, while farther back is a typically 18th-century 'romantic' garden, full of 'follies' and other artifices, but charming in its way – a carefully ruined 'temple of Mercury', a 'temple of Apollo', Pan playing the flute on a mossy grotto, even a mosque with minarets.

'Ich hab mein Herz in Heidelberg verloren' (I've lost my heart in Heidelberg), goes the old song. Few other cities in Europe have inspired so much romantic feeling, real or trite, than **Heidelberg** (pop. 135,000), and it's not hard to see why. The *mise-en-scène* is the apotheosis of German romanticism – the enormous red ruined castle on its green wooded hillside; the Neckar flowing swiftly below, past graceful towers and bridges; and the most warmly traditional and sympathetic of German universities, set right in the heart of the lovely Altstadt, spilling its students into the boisterous pubs and quaint alleyways of a city that was unscathed by wartime bombing. Every vista pleases. In the late 18th century Heidelberg helped to nurture the German Romantic movement, many of whose writers lived and studied there and extolled its charms. And so the romantic image has persisted – down to the operetta *The Student Prince* (1924), by the Hungarian-born American composer Sigmund Romberg, about a rich student's doomed love for a local barmaid. Today the tourist coachloads

The giant, half-ruined castle above the river Neckar at Heidelberg, showpiece of German romanticism.

flood into Heidelberg, but it somehow manages to absorb them and remain itself.

The Prince Electors of the Palatinate (see p. 90) made this their capital in the 13th century. In 1386 Elector Ruprecht I founded the university, Germany's oldest, and around the same time he built the first castle on the hill above, which later was superbly extended in Renaissance style. But in 1689 it was sacked by the French during the Palatinate War, and in 1693 the town was ravaged by fire; soon after, the Electors abandoned their half-wrecked Schloss and moved down to a new palace at Mannheim. The old town was then rebuilt in the sober baroque style that it keeps to this day. At the time of the Romantic movement, the poets Brentano and von Arnim were living and writing at 151 Hauptstrasse (the house still stands), Eichendorff was a student in town, while Hölderlin and Goethe paid many visits. These key Romantics were attracted by the setting, also by the melancholy charm of the castle ruins. But Heidleberg was never more than incidental to their writing, and it would be wrong to look on it as the centre of the Romantic movement – whatever today's tourist brochures may claim.

The university has long been distinguished for the natural sciences, medicine, law and philosophy: the philosopher Karl Jaspers taught here before the war, and Max Weber here pioneered sociology as an academic discipline. Although today it suffers from the general levelling-down of German universities, and is not immune from their malaise, at the student level it does preserve better than most a sense of fun-loving tradition: it has the best student pubs in Germany (see below) and the most colourful fraternities. In this respect, I'd even dare to say that Heidelberg has something of an Oxbridge quality, far more than is usual on the Continent where student life nowadays tends to be solemn and colourless. At Heidelberg, students still know how to enjoy themselves, as in the old days. Maybe it's partly because the local ones are Badeners, with their lively temperament (as compared with the serious Swabians at Tübingen, see p. 121). Or it's due to the cosmopolitan make-up of a student body drawn from 80 nations, including many Americans, who make their easy informality felt: two US universities have branches here. Indeed, the British and Americans have long been drawn to this city. J.M.W.Turner loved it, and has left some characteristic paintings of its varying moods and light patterns. Mark Twain loved it, too, and described it with comic verve in *A Tramp Abroad*. In 1930–32, just when *The Student Prince* had made Heidelberg a household name to American theatre-goers, new university buildings were created with funds donated in the US. So, if this was then one of the very few German cities to be spared the bombs, was it due to the Allies' soft spot for it? Apparently not: the reason was its lack of key industries or transport links. But since the war it has been the US Army headquarters for all Europe: some 15,000 Americans (soldiers plus their families) have lived here. Many are now going back home.

On the first Saturday of June and September and the second Saturday of July, the castle is illuminated, with fireworks and an historical pageant. From late July to late August concerts, plays and operas (including *The Student*

Prince in English) are given in the castle courtyard, or indoors if wet. Fairs on the Karlsplatz include the *Heidelberger Frühling* in June, and the wine festival in September.

The highlight of any sightseeing tour is of course the **Castle**, one of Germany's most impressive buildings. Looming against its backdrop of hilly forest, and built all of local red sandstone, it's a gigantic broad hulk in a hotch-potch of Gothic and Renaissance styles. You can go up by car or cable-car, or on foot, and the grounds and courtyards are free of access at all times (an early morning visit, before the crowds come, can be best): but you must join a guided tour (daily) to see the interiors. These do not contain much, for largely this is just one grandiose ruin, and it has not been overrestored. On the way in, note the graceful Elizabeth Gate which Friedrich V had erected in a single night in 1615, as a surprise for his wife; near it is the Rondell, a former gun-battery now offering a fine view down over the town; and a tree where Goethe dallied adulterously with the poetess Marianne von Willemer (the love-poem she wrote for him is on a tablet on the tree).

The north-western endpiece of the castle proper is the *Dicke Turm* (fat tower, 1533), now just an empty blasted shell. Next to it are the English Wing and the Women's Wing, and then one of the castle's superb Renaissance wings, the Friedrichsbau (1601–07), with its richly ornate façade fronting the central courtyard. On the guided tour, you'll be taken inside to see its moulded ceilings and carved door-frames, and will descend below it to admire the famous Great Vat (late-18th-century), said to be the world's largest wine-barrel, able to hold 50,000 gallons: it supports a platform once used as a dance-floor. Beside it is a statue of the dwarf 'Perkeo', a notorious figure in Heidelberg folk history. He was a Tyrolean who became courtjester and wine-keeper to one Elector in the 18th century: his own consumption of wine was said to be prodigious, up to 18 litres a day, and whenever offered a glass he said, in Italian, *'perchè no?'* ('why not?' – hence his nickname). He died of drinking water – so the story goes.

Beyond the Friedrichsbau is the 14th-century *Glockenturm* (belfry), the castle's tallest tower, close to its other Renaissance glory, the elegant façade of the Ottoheinrichsbau (1557–66), whose interior is totally gutted. In its basement, the guided tour embraces the interesting pharmaceutical museum, including 17th–18th century alchemists' workshops and some hairraising prescriptions of that era. It is also worth looking at the Gothic library building and, at the south-east corner of the castle perimeter, the massive *Gesprengter Turm* (blown-up tower) which was dynamited by the French in 1689 and is now partly subsided, a curious sight. Beyond lie extensive gardens, providing good views of castle, river and town. Even better are the views from the platform of the TV tower (mid-Mar to mid-Oct) on the Königstuhl hill behind the castle: you can get to it by car or cable-car.

Below the castle, the long and narrow **Altstadt** is squeezed between hills and river; down its length goes its traffic-free Hauptstrasse, always packed with students or tourists, or both. The Altstadt is delightful for a stroll, and full of interest. You could begin at the Marktplatz, where a market is held on

Wednesdays and Saturdays. Next to it is the large late-Gothic **Heiligegeist-kirche**, whose tall tower is a leading city landmark: as in mediaeval times, small covered shopping-stalls ply their trade between its buttresses. The oddest fact about this church is that from 1706 to 1936 it was shared between Catholics, who had the choir section, and Protestants who had the rest. Then the Protestants bought out the Catholics and now own it all. The church was one of the few prominent buildings to survive the fire of 1693. Another was the Haus zum Ritter, just opposite and now a hotel, whose stunning Renaissance façade is much photographed.

Traditional student pubs (*Kneipen*) are a feature of this part of the Altstadt: among the best are Schnookeloch, Zum Sepp'l and Roter Ochsen (see p. 109). For centuries these have been haunts of the Verbindungen (fraternities), and their walls are lined with faded photos, swords, trophies and other student flotsam, as well as jokey posters. Today tourists often outnumber students: but in term-time you can still witness, even share in, the old pastime of beer-drinking contests. Each table buys a giant mug of beer in the shape of a glass boot or horn, which is passed round, and the *penultimate* person to finish it must buy the next one. Of course this encourages gargantuan consumption.

In the heart of the Altstadt is the kernel of the **University**: it includes one 18th-century building, a 19th-century festival hall with a painted ceiling, and the American-funded 1930 addition. The huge university library (2.6 million volumes) contains one marvellous star exhibit, the Codex Manesse, a 14th-century collection of 137 illustrated lyrics by troubadours, including the prettily-named Walter von der Vogelweider, greatest of early German poets. The manuscript is shut away in a darkened room, but facsimiles are on display. Close by, in Augustinergasse, is another treasure of old Heidelberg, the former **Students' Gaol** (closed Sun, open Mon), now a protected monument. In the old days, unruly students were handled by the university, not the police, and in 1712–1914 they were put in this building, often for short periods and for minor offences – such as swimming naked in the Neckar, or letting farmers' pigs run loose. Many students regarded it as an honour to be flung in this gaol, and they spent their time inscribing its walls with graffiti, some of which have been restored: 'Here we spent the jolliest time', says one.

The town's most important museum, the **Kurpfälzisches Museum**, is housed in a baroque palace at Hauptstrasse 97. Besides paintings of the Romantic period, it has a superb altarpiece of the twelve apostles (1509) by Riemenschneider, and a cast of the jaw-bone of 'Heidelberg Man' (the original is in the university), believed to date from c. 500,000 BC, one of the oldest human bones ever found. Retrace your steps towards the Markt, and in the Pfaffengasse you'll find the little house, now a museum, where Friedrich Ebert was born in 1871: he was a local saddler who rose to become leader of the German Social Democrats and was President of the Weimar Republic in 1919–25. The history of that period, and of the Right's cruel vendetta against Ebert which led to his early death, are vividly detailed.

Nearby, the Alte Brücke (1788), with its imposing twin-towered gateway, gracefully spans the Neckar. Cross it, and you can climb up the wooded hillside opposite to the **Philosphen Weg** (philosophers' walk) and the Hölderlin memorial, where poets and thinkers have traditionally strolled, mused and debated, inspired maybe by the heartstopping romantic views of the river, town and castle. Today, even non-poets should take this famous Heidelberg walk, to enjoy the same vista, largely unchanged. The swift Neckar used to flood badly, as is shown by the marks inscribed on the bridge. But new locks upstream have now tamed this wild river: the last severe flood was in 1947.

The route up the narrow Neckar valley from Heidelberg passes various hilltop castles, amid striking scenery. At Neckargemünd, a short detour leads to Dilsberg castle, from whose tower there's a fine view down over the winding river; Neckarsteinach, the next town along the valley, lies below four castles, Dilsberg being one; and Schloss Hirschhorn overlooks a dramatic bend in the river. Beyond the busy little town of Eberbach the Neckar enters defiles between pretty wooded hills, but then after Zwingenburg castle the valley becomes built-up and less attractive. Hornberg castle, set high on a hill amid vines, is mainly in ruin: but one wing houses a hotel, and a small museum displays the armour of Götz von Berlichingen (see p. 108) who died here in 1562.

Upstream on the opposite bank is another hilltop Schloss, **Guttenberg**, a most fascinating place. It is the home of the amiable Freiherr von Gemmingen-Guttenberg, a keen bird fancier: in his delightful aviary, every day at 11am and 3pm you can watch his falcons

perform, as they soar and swoop above the valley, then return to their trainer's arm. Also on show are eagles and vultures, and various owls including superb screeching snow-owls from the Arctic. The castle contains an unusual and very eclectic museum, whose star exhibit is an 18th-century herbarium – dried plants concealed in 92 trick wooden boxes that look like books. Other delights include a 1480 altarpiece of the Virgin; instruments of torture that were actually used in the castle until 1860; and big tin-soldier dioramas of local battles, sieges and tournaments. All are explained in hilariously misspelt English.

The superbly picturesque old hilltop town of **BAD WIMPFEN** (pop. 6,000), perched above the river, deserves to be far better known abroad than it is: I much prefer it to Rothenburg. Its alleys are lined with old half-timbered houses in strange shapes – e.g. the very narrow tall one in the Badgasse. Despite its name the town is no spa, but is called 'Bad' because there have long been prosperous saltworks here. The Hohenstaufen kings in the 13th century built a fortress residence here, of which some relics remain: you can climb the 169 steps of its high blue tower for a fine view (its pinnacled neo-feudal top is a tasteless 19th-century addition). The little Steinhaus next door, part Romanesque, part 16th-century, has a museum of local history: behind it, along the terrace above the river, you can see the graceful Romanesque blind arcades with which the kings decorated their palace. At the end of the spur, by the big stone Red Tower, the view downstream takes in giant saltworks and other industry.

This industry lies around **Heilbronn**

(pop. 111,000), a commercial town on the Neckar, centre of a major wine-growing area. It was the setting of von Kleist's classic play, *Käthchen von Heilbronn*, but has little of real interest for the tourist apart from St. Kilian's church with its octagonal Renaissance tower. At Bad Friedrichshall, just to the north, we leave the Neckar to go up the winding Jagst valley, to **Jagsthausen** village where Schloss Götzenburg was the birthplace of the eponymous knight Götz von Berlichingen, of Goethe's racy drama. The old townlet of **Schöntal**, further up the Jagst, is unusual for being set within the grounds of a Cistercian abbey: its church has interesting 17th-century alabaster altars, and its curious *Ordensaal* (orders' room) has wall paintings of the 300 religious and military orders of the 18th century.

A cross-country drive over the rolling plain between Jagsthausen and Schwäbisch Hall will go through the country of the Hohenlohe. This formerly powerful but always liberal dynasty built castles on low hills where some of them still live today: they work quietly as gentleman farmers or civic leaders, in the best tradition of German aristocratic paternalism. Some of their ancestral tombs are in the 15th-century church at Öhringen; Neuenstein has a 16th-century Hohenlohe castle that contains lively souvenirs of the lordly life of that time; and the Schloss of the Hohenlohe-Waldenburgs has a pleasant hilltop setting.

And so to **SCHWÄBISCH HALL** (pop. 31,500), a seductively picturesque old town of half-timbered houses, built in tiers above the river Kocher. The Keckenburg museum in a high Romanesque tower chronicles the town's past as centre for minting silver coins. Many fine old 15th- and 16th-century houses line the Obere and Untere Herrngasse. Down along the river, some modern buildings blemish the urban scenery: but there are good views of the town above from two tiny islands linked to the mainland by charming roofed wooden bridges. Here in the meadows there is folk-dancing in summer, during the well-known drama festival that is held annually in the suitably theatrical Marktplatz. On one side of this sloping square is the baroque Rathaus, sombre but dignified; on the other, wide stone steps lead steeply to the big Romanesque/Gothic church of St Michael, noted for its lofty vaulted ceiling and splendid 16th-century altarpiece.

TOURIST OFFICES

MANNHEIM: Bahnhofplatz 1, tel (0621) 10 10 11.

HEIDELBERG: Hauptbahnhof, tel (06221) 2 13 41.

BAD WIMPFEN: Rathaus, Marktplatz, tel (07063) 70 52.

SCHWÄBISCH HALL: Am Markt 9, tel (0791) 75 12 46.

Accommodation, Eating and Drinking

MANNHEIM 6800:

(H)**Augusta**, Augusta-Anlage 43, tel (0621) 41 80 01. Large, well run, fairly central; restaurants with French and local cuisine. Rooms (105) B. Meals (cl Sun) B–C.

SCHWETZINGEN 6830:

(H)**Romantik-Hotel Löwe**, Schlossstr. 4, tel (06202) 2 60 66. Spruce little hotel opposite castle; cuisine ambitious but uneven. Rooms (20) C. Meals (cl Mon) B–C.

HEIDELBERG 6900 (tel code 06221):

(H)**Alt Heidelberg, Restaurant Graimberg**, Rohrbacherstr. 29, tel 91 50. Central and comfortable; excellent meals in an elegant room. Rooms (80) B. Meals (cl Sat lunch) B–C.
(H)**Zum Ritter**, Haupstr. 178, tel 2 42 72. In the Altstadt, an old 1592 mansion with fine Renaissance façade; lavish period furnishings. Very touristy. Rooms (32) B. Meals B–C.
(H)**Perkeo**, Hauptstr. 75, tel 2 22 55. Central and comfortable. Restaurant owned separately, see below. Rooms (25) C.
(H)**Kohler**, Goethestr. 2, tel 2 43 60. Central, between station and Altstadt. No restaurant. Rooms (43) C–D.
(R)**Zur Herrenmühle**, Hauptstr. 239, tel 1 29 09. 17th-century house with pretty courtyard; superior cuisine. Cl lunch. Meals A.
(R)**Perkeo**, Hauptstr. 75, tel 16 06 13. Traditional and characterful; solid German cooking. Meals C–D.
(BW)**Schnookeloch**, Haspelgasse 8, tel 2 27 33. Historic student pub with nice garden; used by *Verbindungen*. 11 bedrooms, too.
(BW)**Zum Sepp'l**, Hauptstr. 213, tel 2 30 85. Sympathetically boisterous student tavern, dating from 1634.

NECKARGEMÜND 6903:

(H)**Zum Ritter**, Neckarstr. 40, tel (06223) 47 06. Well-modernized old riverside hunting-lodge, built 1579. Folksy décor, terrace, good cooking. Rooms (39) B–C. Meals C.
(H)**Zum Rössl**, Heidelbergerstr. 15, Waldhilsbach, tel (06223) 26 65. 5 km to SW, a modest hotel reputed for its food. Cl 2 weeks Jan–Feb, 2 weeks summer. Rooms (13) D. Meals (cl Mon, Thur) C–D.

EBERBACH-BROMBACH 6930:

(R)**Talblick**, tel (0672) 14 51. Picturesque old half-timbered house with rustic décor; food good value. Cl 2 weeks Jan, 2 weeks July. Meals C. Also 5 rooms, C.

BAD RAPPENAU 6927:

(H)**Schloss Heinsheim**, tel (07264) 10 45. The aristocratic von Racknitz family now run their Schloss as a graceful hotel, where guests are welcomed like friends. Idyllic garden, perfect service. Cl 20 Dec–Jan. Rooms (41) B–C. Meals C.

BAD WIMPFEN 7107:

(H)**Sonne**, Haupstr. 87, tel (07063) 245. Quaint old *Fachwerk* house in the Altstadt, full of warmth and good cheer. Rooms (24) D. Meals C.

HEILBRONN 7100:

(H)**Burkhardt**, Lohtorstr. 7, tel (07131) 6 22 40. Central; informal family ambience; good Swabian cooking. Rooms (57) C. Meals C–D.
(R)**Ratskeller**, Marktplatz 7, tel (07131) 6 22 40. Wine-tavern below Rathaus; garden; Swabian specialities. Meals C.

JAGSTHAUSEN 7109:

(H)**Burghotel Götzenburg**, tel (07943) 22 22. For a Schloss-hotel, unusually inexpensive and unpretentious; antique furnishings, good food. Mar–Oct. Rooms (15) D. Meals C.

SCHWÄBISCH HALL 7170:

(H)**Ratskeller**, Am Markt 12, tel (0791) 61 81. Modernized mediaeval house, with plenty of character. Rooms C. Meals (cl Mon) C.

Stuttgart and its Neighbourhood

Baden-Württemberg's wealthy, go-ahead capital (pop. 560,000) is at once powerfully industrial and cosily bucolic – a stimulating paradox. Its physical setting is much the prettiest of any big German city, for while the others are on plains, central Stuttgart lies in a hollow, cradled by wooded hills: the terraced residential districts rise steeply on either side, and one vineyard slopes down close to the main station. This leafy nest-like frame, almost pastoral, lends a quality of gentleness to this modern high-tech metropolis, most successful industrial city in Europe, home of Bosch, Porsche and Daimler-Benz. It also makes Stuttgart seem smaller than it is, for its manufacturing areas sprawl unseen in other valleys. And it gives a sense of intimacy that fits in well with the character of these cosy Swabians. The economy may be confidently go-ahead, but the people – another paradox – seem slow and provincial, and the tempo is far more easy-going than in showy Munich or busy Frankfurt. Indeed, other German cities tend to look down on 'provincial' Stuttgart. Yet it has world-class culture and Germany's best mayor, Manfred Rommel. For a good picture of Stuttgart, read Fred

Uhlmann's lovely novel *Reunion*, set in the 1930s.

Its name comes from the *Stutengarten* (stud farm) that an Alemannic duke set up here in c. 950: hence the horse on the city coat-of-arms. The counts of Württemberg moved their seat to Stuttgart in 1311: this became a dukedom in 1495, and finally a kingdom in 1806, but during all this time the city's history remained fairly uneventful. Then in the late 19th century the Swabian inventive genius set it on its path to industrial glory. Gottlieb Daimler here pioneered the motor-car, while Robert Bosch founded his electrical firm. Today, greater Stuttgart with its two million people houses the main factories of these two giant companies, and of Porsche, Lorenz, German IBM and many others; the city also has some 200 publishing and 160 printing firms, and others making electronic and optical goods. Above all it is the world's leading producer of luxury high-performance cars. The pale-blue emblem of Daimler's prestigious Mercedes gleams out like a lode-star from dozens of office rooftops, supreme status-symbol of the richest city in Europe.

Another Stuttgart speciality is moderation in politics. Ever since the war the spirit of consensus has been stronger here than in any other big German city – and this is typified by its mayor since 1974, Manfred Rommel (son of the Desert Fox), who is on the liberal wing of the CDU and rules in serene coalition with the SPD. He is the best-known of German mayors and the best-loved, partly for his benign tolerance and pawky Swabian humour. He pours public money into the arts, even into 'alternative' ventures fiercely critical of the CDU. The city has long had a high cultural file, with important modern architecture and good opera; its famous ballet company, if no longer as innovative as when John Cranko ran it, is still one of Europe's best.

Festivals and events in Stuttgart include the spring festival (April); the city centre wine festival (Aug–Sept); the renowned Canstatt folk festival (see feature); and, in mid-December, a colourful pre-Christmas market.

Proud of its many world links, Stuttgart's slogan is *'Partner der Welt'*, yet local temperament and geography make it also just a big village. Within its sprawling borders it produces more wine – light and fruity – than any other German commune. You see vineyards everywhere, even a grape's throw from the main Mercedes factory. Many factory workers still own plots of land and are part-time farmers: in some suburbs you'll still find small unmodernized farms, archaically pastoral. Whereas urbane Munich contrasts sharply with its rural hinterland, here city and country merge as one and there's little difference in spirit between rural Swabia and its capital. True, part of the rebuilt downtown area is the usual concrete jungle of brash office blocks and car showrooms: but even here the vast Schlossplatz, free of traffic, gives a central focus of green and spacious calm.

Next to it is the small and graceful **Schillerplatz**, the city's only old-world square, also traffic-free, and charmingly lit at night with frosted lamps. A food and flower market is held here (Tue, Thur, Sat). In it stands a greenish statue of Schiller, looking pensive, and all around are historic buildings well restored after the bombing. One is the 15th-century **Stiftskirche**, now Protestant: note its octagonal tower and, lining its choir, eleven vivid Renaissance sculptures of mediaeval Württemberg rulers, all in armour. Other buildings are the *Alte Kanzlei* (old chancellery), the *Prinzenbau* (former princes' residence) and, most important, the **Altes Schloss**: in part this is the remains of a 14th-century moated castle, Stuttgart's oldest surviving building, and the rest is a fine Renaissance ducal palace, whose lovely arcaded courtyard is used for classical concerts in summer. The palace houses the **Landesmuseum**, whose important historic collections include the Württemberg crown jewels (note the Gothic playing-cards), many Swabian religious sculptures (note the eight scenes of the Passion by Jorg Syrlin, 1515), and various local Roman and Frankish antiquities.

In 1746 the dukes moved from the Altes to the baroque **Neues Schloss**, which grandly fronts the Schlossplatz. It is now used for major *Land* receptions and its glittering interiors are not open to the public. In the middle of this square is the 60-metre granite Jubilee Column erected in 1841 in honour of Württemberg's King Wilhelm I; beyond it, the pillared neo-classical Königsbau stands on the city's main pedestrian shopping street, the unlovely rebuilt Königstrasse. On the north side of the square, the *Kunstgebäude* (city art gallery) has some notable paintings by Otto Dix, and is used for avant-garde exhibitions which often bemuse the staid Swabian public. Here the pretty Schlossgarten, with its lake full of swans, leads to the glass-and-concrete Landtag building and the turn-of-the-century opera house.

Cross the busy motorway just behind, and you'll come to the city's main cultural 'sight', the *Land*-owned **Staatsgalerie**, a magnficent art museum. It was given a large new wing in the early 1980s by the Scottish architect James Stirling, whose boldly original designs at first caused a local uproar but are now generally admired. I myself don't care hugely for his pink and blue handrails and green window-frames, all a bit too Beaubourg: but his circular courtyard, a mix of Mycaenae and mediaeval castle, is most appealing. The museum begins with 14th to 16th-century old masters, Swabian, Dutch and Italian: but its forte is the more modern era, featuring scores of great names of the past 150 years. It starts with a good range of Impressionists (Renoir, Sisley, etc) and goes on via Nolde, Munch and Kandinsky to Picasso, Léger, Grosz, Ernst and many others. Dix and Beckmann contribute some powerful anti-war canvases. Beuys is present too, and so is the Stuttgart-born artist Oskar Schlemmer (1888–1943), seven of whose lively ballet-figures stand high on pedestals. Unexpectedly, one room contains eight works by Burne-Jones, the cycle of *The Legend of Perseus*. In front of the museum stands a Henry Moore sculpture of a draped woman, which has had an odd Swabian experience. It was commissioned by the *Land* government in 1971 for the terrace of the Landtag: but many citizens denounced as 'ill-minded' this harmless piece, and for 13 years it was hidden away behind bushes. 'Typical!' was one liberal's comment; 'these Swabian culture-snobs, they want to buy the best, then don't like it.' Finally it was reprieved, and put conspicuously beside the also 'shocking' Stirling.

Back downtown, south of the Schillerplatz lies the former Altstadt,

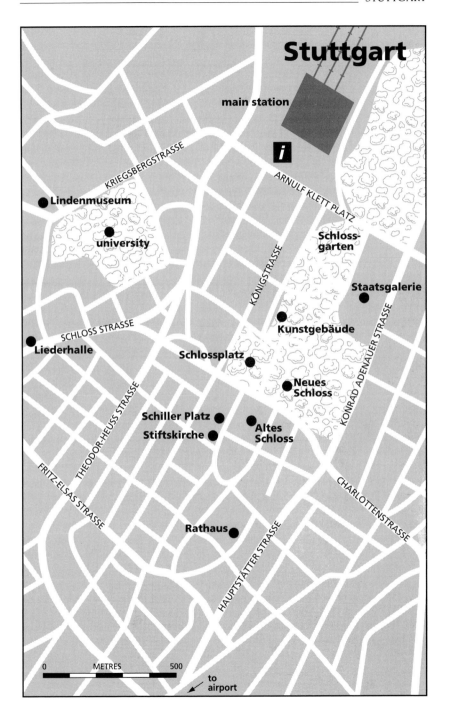

The Stiftskirche fronts a quiet square in the centre of busy Stuttgart.

now rebuilt in modern style. Here is the ugly new Rathaus (its carillon plays folksongs) and, at Eberhardstrasse 53, the modest house where Hegel was born in 1770 (this survived the bombing). Over to the north-west, beyond another ring-road, is another striking modern building, the **Liederhalle** (1956), an ensemble of three concert halls in asymmetrical design. Close to it are the ugly new blocks of the uni-versity, which until recently was a technical college and has little of the character of an older seat of learning such as Tübingen. But you should not miss the adjacent **Lindenmuseum** of ethnology, which has a superb presentation of non-European cultures – Javanese shadow-puppets, African masks and costumes, an Islamic bazaar and much else.

Up on the hill behind, near the big

Daimler Pioneers the Motor-car

Two Baden-Württembergers simultaneously invented the motor car, in the mid-1880s – Karl Benz in Mannheim, and Gottlieb Daimler quite separately in Stuttgart. It was in a greenhouse in his garden at Bad Canstatt that Gottlieb Daimler, a local engineer, produced the world's first moving vehicle to use an internal combustion engine: today this shed, much restored, is a small museum (open Apr–Oct) where you can see his original motor-cycle, just about recognizable as one. The two men were soon producing cars in association, though their firms did not merge until 1926: today no member of either family is directly involved in the huge Daimler-Benz company, owned largely by banks. So who on earth was Mercedes? Answer: when Daimler produced a new model in 1899, his chief salesman named it after his own daughter, Mercedes. Today this producer of heavy trucks and prestigious saloon cars employs some 150,000 workers in Germany alone, mostly in the Stuttgart area and at Bremen. The museum at its HQ in Untertürkheim has a large array of early models, starting with the first Benz car patented in 1886.

Porsche, also a Stuttgart firm, was created in 1931 by an Austrian professor, Ferdinand Porsche, and is still largely owned by the family. Its head factory in the Zuffenhausen district also has a museum (open Mon–Fri), mainly of racing-cars.

---

trade fair grounds, is the delightful **Killesberg park**, very well laid out. It has an open-air theatre and beer-garden, a flamingo pond and miniature railway, and a tower with panoramic views. The nearby **Weissenhof** is a group of houses designed in 1927 by Gropius, Le Corbusier, van de Rohe and other leading architects, as part of the Bauhaus movement; badly hit in the war, it has since been rebuilt, but imperfectly. The Wilhelma park, just to the east, contains botanical gardens and a medium-sized zoo. And if you cross the Neckar here, you'll be in **Bad Canstatt**, an old spa town that is now part of the city; it has a pleasant Kurpark. Stuttgart may not be thought of as a spa: but its mineral springs are said to produce more mineral water (18 million litres a day) than any other European city except Budapest; it supplies three public swimming-pools, where a bathe can be exhilarat-ing. Bad Canstatt is also connected with Daimler and the Volksfest.

Driving upstream from here along the river, you'll come to the Hans-Martin-Schleyer-Halle, a congress and pop-concert hall named after the former Daimler-Benz director who was killed by the Baader-Meinhof terrorists in 1977. It is near to the Daimler-Benz headquarters at Untertürkheim, from where you could recross the river and wind up the hill to the 215-metre **Television Tower**, the first of its kind in the world (1956). The view from its platform is grand – as far as the Alps on a clear day. And from this or any other vantage-point you can see how unusual Stuttgart's lay-out is: its suburbs straggle along winding valleys or clamber up hills to the forests that are the city's lungs. There are no straight lines, only curves. In this garden city, only a quarter of the surface is built over: the rest is woodland, orchard, vineyard, park or pasture. Within the city's borders are many small farms, notably to the south near the airport: they are dairy-farms, or they grow cabbage for *Sauerkraut*, which can produce an acrid rotten smell at harvest-time in October.

Several excursions can be made to places of interest around Stuttgart. First, you could visit the vineyard areas to the east. From Untertürkheim and its Mercedes factories, country lanes lead up to the village of **Rotenburg**, where an ugly mausoleum stands on a hilltop: King Wilhelm I of Württemberg built it in 1820 for his Russian wife Katharina, and it has a Russian Orthodox chapel. The view from its terrace is amazing, half pastoral, half heavy-industrial – giant power-stations beside the Neckar, and rows of vines climbing with Swabian neatness over the crests of small rounded hills, like well-combed hair. Nearby, the pretty wine-village of Uhlbach has a wine museum. **Esslingen**, to the south, is an industrial town whose attractive old *Fachwerk* buildings relate to its past as a Free Imperial City: notable are the 15th-century former Rathaus, and the Gothic Stadtkirche and Liebfrauen-kirche.

To the north-east, amid hilly vineyards, you'll find the most picturesque of the local wine-villages: **Strümpfel-bach**. Its main street is lined with 17th-century half-timbered houses, notably a tiny quaint Rathaus in the middle of the road. Vineyards climb the slopes all round, sometimes covered in blue plastic wrappings (not so pretty) to protect the young grapes from the birds. The whole area around here, between Weinstadt and the Aich and Schur forests, is extremely pretty: not only vines, but also orchards of peaches, apples and cherries, lovely in blossom-time, cover the gentle hill-slopes. To the east, industrial **Schorn-dorf** (pop. 34,000) was Württemberg's capital for a while before the Thirty Years' War. The best of its many half-timbered houses are in and around the broad Marktplatz, with its rococo fountain. On the rear wall of the modern Rathaus, a frieze relates how the women of the town once defended it against attackers when the pacifist mayor and council had refused to do so. And at Höllgasse 7 is the house where Gottlieb Daimler was born in 1834: it is now a small museum (open Tue, Thur pm). It is in a street closed to cars!

A second excursion could take you to the lakes and rolling woodlands due west of Stuttgart, around the village-suburbs of Botnang and Busnau. Stuttgarters like to go hiking here, even cross-country skiing in winter. Here you can walk beside the Pfaffen and Bären lakes (there's a good pub at the Bärensee). To the north is famous **Schloss Solitude**, an elegant little cream-coloured, oval-shaped pavilion, set on a plateau facing north towards Ludwigsburg castle (see below). Built in Hellenic style in the 1760s, it has interior decor part neo-classical, part rococo. The Duke of Württemberg created the Schloss as a home for his mistress, siting it so that he could see it on its hilltop from his own palace at Ludwigsburg, 15 km to the north.

This, the largest baroque palace in Germany (452 rooms), stands near the centre of industrial **LUDWIGSBURG** (pop. 76,000) and is the object of our third excursion. More-or-less modelled on Versailles, it was built in 1704–33 by Duke Eberhardt of

---

Volksfest and 'Broom-Pubs'

Swabians may not be as boisterously fun-loving as Bavarians, but they have their own merry drinking-habits. The late-September *Volksfest* in the Stuttgart suburb of Canstatt is Germany's biggest annual beer-festival (five million visitors) after Munich's *Oktoberfest*. Begun in 1818 as a harvest festival, it takes place in four giant beer-tents with adjacent fun-fair, around a tall priapic 'fruit-pillar' stacked with fruit and veg. Applying themselves to jollity with due solemnity of purpose, the locals down 1.5 million litres of beer, some miles of pretzels and 300,000 chickens, and belt out the usual songs with arms linked, swaying to-and-fro. The beer is all local: but Stuttgarters have had to sink their pride and borrow from the Bavarians some accoutrements of jollity and folksiness, for lack of their own. The men, from Lord Mayor Rommel downwards, wear pointed green Bavarian hats with feathers, the waitresses have Bavarian *Dirndls* with high-busted white puffy bodices; and the beer-tent orchestras, their musicians clad in *Lederhosen*, are mostly imported from Bavaria. But the food consumed is Swabian, such as blood-sausage and *Magenbrot* (stomach-bread); and sturdy Swabian steeds, gaudily caparisoned, pull wagonloads of beer from local breweries.

A thoroughly homegrown Swabian tradition is that of the delightful *Besenwirtschaften* (broom-pubs): by old custom, vine-growers in the Stuttgart area put a broom outside their house in November, to show that their new wine is ready, and until March they can use their home as an impromptu pub, just for selling this vintage. Some of these places have grown large and commercialized: but in others you really do sit in rough farmhouses or peasant parlours, in a matey ambience, drinking glasses of sweetish half-fermented wine at well below pub prices. Simple food is served too. It's a good way to make friends with the locals.

Württemberg, and its grandeur illustrates the wealth and ambition of that ruling family. It now belongs to the *Land*: but the present duke has use of some rooms. Take the guided tour (daily) to see the State rooms with their tapestries and porcelain, the rococo chapel and royal bedrooms, and little theatre still sometimes used for plays; in the vault are 90,000-litre wine-barrels. The formal gardens are best seen in spring when the tulips and roses bloom; its 'fairy-tale park', with mechanical tableaux of Grimm tales, will please children. In summer the palace has a major festival, with fireworks, plays and high-quality concerts. Marbach, to the north-east, was the birthplace of Schiller (see feature). From here you could return to Stuttgart along the attractive Neckar valley, via Remseck.

TOURIST OFFICES

STUTTGART: Klett-Passage, main station, tel (0711) 222 82 40.

LUDWIGSBURG: Wilhelmstr. 12, tel (07141) 91 02 52.

Accommodation, Eating and Drinking

STUTTGART 7000 (tel code 0711):

Downtown hotels tend to be expensive; much cheaper ones can be found on the outskirts, some of them semi-rural inns. Good Swabian restaurants are numerous, many of them inexpensive; also wine taverns serving simple local dishes, and *Besenwirtschaften* (see feature), notably in the suburbs and surrounding villages.

(H)**Am Schlossgarten**, Schillerstr. 23, tel 202 60. Luxurious, and nicely situated, looking onto the park and opposite main station. Food average. Rooms (125) A. Meals A–B.

(H)**Royal**, Sophienstr. 35, tel 62 50 50. Modern, stylish and fairly central. Good food, not too pricey. Rooms (100) A. Meals B–C.

(H)**Park-Hotel**, Villastr. 21, tel 28 01 61. Near a hilly park and the TV and radio studios, 2km from centre; quiet. Good cooking. Rooms (75) A. Meals B; C–D in **Radiostüble**, cl Sun and lunch.

(H)**Azenberg**, Seestrasse 116, tel 22 10 51. On hillside, with views, but fairly central; indoor pool. No lunches, dinner for residents only. Rooms B.

(H)**Ketterer**, Marienstr. 3, tel 203 90. Central, on traffic-free street. Rooms (107) B–C.

(H)**Waldhotel Degerloch**, Guts-Muths-Weg 18, tel 76 50 17. On a quiet hill in suburbs, 3km S of centre. Nice views, garden; good food. Rooms (50) B–C. Meals B–D.

(H)**Hirsch**, Eltingerstr. 2, Botnang, tel 69 29 17. Pleasant traditional hotel in W suburbs, near forests. Excellent food. Rooms (40) C–D. Meals (cl Sun dinner, Mon) B–D.

(H)**Rotenberg**, Stettenerstr. 87, tel 33 12 93. Secluded on a hill in E suburbs, just above vineyards, with lovely views. Cl 24 Dec–15 Jan. Rooms (23) C–D.

(H)**Muckestüble**, Solitudestr. 25, Weilimdorf. Unassuming rural inn just below Schloss Solitude, 10km W of city centre. Garden. Excellent Swabian cooking. Rooms (25) D. Meals (cl Tue) C–D.

(R)**Alte Post**, Friedrichstr. 43, tel 29 30 79. The best restaurant in town: stylish traditional décor, superb Swabian cooking with a modern touch. Cl Sat, Mon lunch, Sun, early Aug. Meals A–B.

(R)**Lamm**, Mühlstr. 24, tel 85 36 15. In Feuerbach suburb: attractive Swabian décor and excellent cooking. Cl Sun, Sat lunch, Christmas period. Meals A–B.

(R)**Mövenpick**, Kleine Schlossplatz 11, tel 22 00 34. Well-known Swiss chain restaurant, best for beef, fish and Swiss dishes. Stylish service. In several sections: **Baron de la Mouette**, A–B; **Chesa**, B–C; Red Spot and **Möpi**, D.

(R)**Zeppelin-Stüble**, Lautenschlagerstr. 2, tel 22 40 13. In huge Hotel Graf Zeppelin. Good authentic Swabian food. Meals C–D.

(R)**Weinstube Paule**, Augsburgerstr. 643, tel 32 14 71. In Obertürkheim suburb. Simple wine-tavern with first-rate Swabian cooking. Cl Christmas, 3 weeks Aug, Thurs. Meals C.

(R)**Weinstube Schellenturm**, Weberstr. 22, tel 23 48 88. Central, in an old tower, lots of atmosphere and good local food. Cl lunch, Sun. Meals C–D.

(R)**Bäcka-Metzger**, Aachenerstr. 20, Bad Canstatt, tel 54 41 08. Intimate with lively ambience and high-quality Swabian cuisine. Cl lunch, Sun, Mon, 3 weeks June. Meals C–D.

(R)**Alte Zunft**, Herdweg 19, tel 22 57 78. Honest, classic Swabian local restaurant; friendly, good food. Meals D.

(W)**Weinstube Zur Kiste**, Kanalstr. 2, tel 24 40 02. Best-known of the downtown taverns, crowded and a full of local yuppies. Good wines and adequate local food (D). Cl lunch, Sat dinner, Sun.

Environs of Stuttgart

STETTEN IM REMSTAL 7053:

(H)**Weinstube Idler**, Dinkelstr. 1, tel (07151) 420 18. In a wine-village east of Stuttgart: elegant but cosy old inn with sound local cooking. Cl Mon. Rooms D. Meals C.

(R)**Zum Ochsen**, Kirschstr. 15, tel (07151) 420 15. An 18th-century house, stylishly furnished and *gemütlich*. Excellent local cooking. Cl Wed, 3 weeks Feb–Mar. Meals C.

STRÜMPFELBACH 7056:

(R)**Lamm**, Hindenburgstr. 16, tel (05171) 623 31. In a picturesque wine-village: friendly, unpretentious inn, with fine authentic Swabian food. Cl Mon, Thur, 2 weeks Jan, 3 weeks Aug. Meals C.

ESSLINGEN 7300:

(H)**Jägerhaus**, Röomerstr. 1, tel (0711) 37 12 69. Friendly inn just E of town, with garden and rural views. Rooms (38) D. Meals C–D.

LUDWIGSBURG 7140:

(H)**Heim**, Schillerstr. 19, tel (07141) 261 44. Near station, pleasant. No restaurant. Rooms (42) C–D.

(R)**Post-Cantz**, Eberhardtstr. 6, tel (07141) 235 63. Reliable fair-priced cooking. Cl Wed, Thur, 3 weeks July. Meals C.

ASPERG 7144:

(H)**Adler**, Stuttgarterstr. 2, tel (07141) 630 01. Half-timbered old hostelry, a bit too ornate and formal, but food excellent. Rooms (63) B–C. Meals (cl Mon, 3 weeks summer) BC; **Stube** (cl lunch, Sun) C–D.

Tübingen, Ulm and the Swabian Jura

The long limestone plateau of the *Schwäbische Alb* (Swabian Jura) stretches slantwise between the Neckar valley on its north side and the upper Danube to its south. Beside the Neckar is the old university city of Tübingen, while on the Danube is another city just as fine: Ulm. Nowhere is the plateau very high or wild, but like France's Jura it is cut in places by deep rocky valleys. The mediaeval lords of this part of Swabia, notably the great dynastic families of Hohenstaufen and Hohenzollern, once built defensive bastions on these hills – and today, set on spurs or outcrops of the range, you will see many feudal castles, some in ruins, others restored to good condition such as the mighty Schloss Hohenzollern. If you use the Stuttgart–Munich *Autobahn*, you will cross the Swabian Jura where the road divides in two and describes a sweeping curve up the wooded hillside. But to explore the massif in more detail you could follow the scenic Schwäbische Albstrasse along its northern side. In the plain below, the winding Neckar valley is beautiful in places.

This sinuous itinerary first skirts the north-eastern fringe of the Black Forest. It begins at **Maulbronn**, whose renowned Cistercian monastery is one of Germany's oldest and is well preserved. Its 12th-century church exemplifies the transition from Romanesque to Gothic in Germany. The cloister, the chapter-house and the monks' refectory with its low vaulted ceiling are all attractive. To the south, on the edge of the Black Forest, is industrial **Pforzheim** (pop. 105,000), a major production centre for jewellery, watches and gold ornaments: all this can be studied in the town's jewellery museum.

To the south-east, the Wurm valley winds to **Tiefenbronn**, where the parish church contains marvellous 15th- and 16th-century altarpieces, notably one by Lucas Moser in the south aisle. **Weil der Stadt** (pop. 14,000), up amid open rolling countryside, is a remarkable old rampart-girt town and a focus of Fasching tradition, being a Catholic enclave in mostly Protestant Swabia: a merry costumed pageant is held on the 'Elfte Elfte Elfte Elfte' (i.e. 11.11 am on 11 November) at the start of the pre-carnival period. A small museum honours a famous local son, the 17th-century astronomer Johannes Kepler. In the Gothic church of St Peter and St Paul is a modern stained-glass window of Christ being tempted in the desert, with the Devil looking exactly like Hitler: this was the work of the wartime curé, himself an artist, and very anti-Nazi. He got into trouble with the Gestapo for it.

A road through the woods leads down to the Nagold valley – to **Bad Liebenzell**, a fairly elegant spa whose mineral springs supply its large and popular swimming-pool complex. To the south, on the outskirts of **Hirsau**, are the magnificent reddish sandstone ruins of an old Benedictine abbey, dating from 830. They are free of access, and a stroll at dusk or by moonlight can be a haunting experience. Only the Gothic chapel of St Mary, still used as a church, closes at night. Note the stately Romanesque *Eulenturm* (owl tower), with its frieze of human and animal figures, and the stark ruin of the *Saalbau* (reception hall). In one corner, an octagonal tower is still actively used as a church tower. **Calw**, further along the

Nagold, is an old market and industrial town with many fine half-timbered houses, beside the river and in and around the Lederstrasse and wide traffic-free Marktplatz: here no. 6 was the birthplace of the novelist Hermann Hesse who spent much of his youth in the town (the Heimatmuseum has souvenirs).

TÜBINGEN (pop. 78,000), one of Europe best-known university cities, is charmingly situated on the Neckar where old gabled houses in pastel shades stand terraced on the steep slope above the river, below the ancient Schloss. The university, founded in 1477, has traditionally been strong on philosophy, theology and medicine: it has had many famous students, including the philosopher Hegel and Kepler the astronomer, while post-war teachers have included the philosopher Ernst Bloch and the Catholic theologian Hans Küng. Today the university suffers like others from the malaise afflicting all German higher education: yet this lively student-filled city still retains the flavour of a venerable place of learning. Of its total population, as many as 30,000 are students and teaching staff – 'You see, we have a town on our campus,' quipped one professor.

Today the university is in three parts – the huge new science campus on the hill north of the town; the main faculty area around the downtown Wilhelmstrasse; and the ancient nucleus above the Neckar where the pink Bursa, part 15th-century, is still in use for lectures. By the river below is the Hölderlin tower. The hilltop Schloss has 11th-century foundations but was rebuilt during the Renaissance: the sign on its imposing gateway, *'Honi soit qui mal y*

pense', recalls an honour given to the Duke of Württemberg by Queen Elizabeth in 1597. In the nearby Am Markt square, farmers mix with students on market days, around the fountain in front of the 15th-century Rathaus: its much-restored façade has *trompe-l'oeil* paintings added in 1876, and a monument to the university's founder, Eberhardt the Bearded. In the Holzmarkt, a venue for left-wing students and *Alternative*, the 15th-century Stiftskirche has a fine canopied pulpit, and in its cellar some tombs of Württemberg princes. Nearby in a decorated cellar is the former student prison. All around here, the fascinating alleys of the old town are full of antique shops, bookshops and Greenish eco-shops, while on fine days the little squares are busy with buskers and street orators. In summer the banks of the Neckar, overhung with weeping-willows, and the leafy Platanenallee promenade beside it, are crammed with students, strolling, debating, flirting, sitting in the sun. Some go drifting in punts, as on the Cam or Cherwell; and rowing races are some times held between the *Verbindungen* (student fraternities).

North of the city, in Schönbuch forest, is the Cistercian abbey of **Bebenhausen**, dating from the 12th century. Un-Cistercian later additions, such as baroque ornaments, frescoes and timbered outbuildings, have disguised its original purity: but the cloister and chapterhouse are rather beautiful.

East of Tübingen, **Reutlingen** (pop. 100,000) is a brashly prosperous modern industrial town (textiles, engineering) that does also have an old quarter with pretty fountains and a museum of local history. A road south leads up into the Swabian Jura, which is full of interest. The **Bärenhöhle** (bear cave), near Erpfingen, is one of several caves in this area with impressive stalactites; **Lichtenstein**, in a rocky hilltop setting with a fine view, is an old castle rebuilt in 1842 in mock-mediaeval style; **Bad Urach**, a little spa town in a cleft of the hills, has lovely old half-timbered houses in its Marktplatz; and **Hohenneuffen** is a ruined, unrestored hill-fortress also offering good views. Just beyond Owen, yet another feudal ruin stands on a wooded spur. This is **Teck**, which has links with the British royals: the father of George V's queen, Mary of Teck, was the Herzog von Teck, a member of the House of Württemberg that once owned this castle. The walk up to it through the woods is dull, and at the top there's little to see apart from the view, for the castle is a total ruin. The high tower that looks so grand from the valley below is a modern addition. Could not clever Germans do better with high-Teck?

From the papermill town of Ober-Lenningen, a road through a rocky gorge winds back up onto the main plateau. Here you will find the small ruined 14th-century fortress of **Reussenstein,** set superbly on a lonely rock high above the valley: its position must have been impregnable, and today the sheer rockface is giddily used by climbers. The tower offers a good view of the wooded cliffs and the villages far below. Back down in the valley, at **Holzmaden**, is the remarkable Hauff Museum, displaying fossilized skeletons of ichthyosaurs 160–180 million years old. For over a century the Hauff family have owned stone quarries in the area, and thus they found the skeletons buried in layers of schist. Their private museum now superbly displays these crocodile-like creatures. One saurian mother has five embryos in her womb and a baby beside her. You can also see big fossilized sea-lilies, like sea-urchins, more animal than vegetable.

From here the *Autobahn* to Munich

Swabia's Poets: Schiller and Hölderlin

As well as inventors, Swabia has produced many great writers, among them Hegel, Brecht, and the poets Schiller and Hölderlin. Hegel was born in Stuttgart, Brecht in Augsburg (Bavarian Swabia); and Friedrich Schiller was born in 1759 in Marbach, north of Stuttgart, in a modest house that is now a tiny museum (open daily). Also in Marbach and open daily, and much larger and more interesting, is the **Schiller Nationalmuseum**, the foremost German literary archive. Besides portraits and manuscripts, it has costumed figures and tableaux that evoke Schiller's best-known plays: in Germany this stirring radical poet-dramatist is the most-performed of all playwrights – except for Shakespeare!

Schiller was a great dramatist: but his contemporary Hölderlin, born near Heilbronn in 1770, was the better poet – indeed, one of Germany's greatest. He studied at Tübingen, where Hegel and Schelling were amongst his friends. Later Hölderlin went gently mad, and spent his last 36 years in the care of a local carpenter's family, in a tower-house by the river at Tübingen that is now a museum devoted to him, the Hölderlinturm.

winds back over the Swabian Jura, to the wonderful city of **ULM** (pop. 101,000), on the upper Danube. Much of it is new since wartime bombing: but the old fishermen's and craftsmen's quarter, astride the narrow river Blau, has been nicely restored (note the bulky half-timbered Schiefes Haus, c. 1500). And from the river-walk on the far side of the Danube (here you are in the suburb of Neu-Ulm, in Bavaria) there are lovely views of the soaring cathedral and the old gabled houses along the banks: here the Metzgerturm (butchers' tower) is the one surviving gateway of the old ramparts.

The cathedral spire (161m) is the tallest of any church in the world, and this is Ulm's main claim to fame. The spire was not erected until 1890, though the great Gothic building itself dates from 1377. It has a lovely porch, a high interior with fan-vaulting, and exceptional wood-carved choir-stalls (1469–74) by Jörg Syrlin. Energetic spirits can climb the 768 steps to the top of the spire, for a stunning view over town, river and mountains, even as far as the Alps on a clear day. The graceful Rathaus (Gothic/Renaissance) has an astronomic clock on its west front; in the nearby Marktplatz is the vividly-coloured 15th-century *Fischkasten* (fish-crate) fountain, also by Syrlin; and the Ulmer Museum has Picassos and Klees as well as works by Syrlin and other early Ulm masters. The city's greatest son however was not Syrlin but a certain Albert Einstein, born here in 1879.

West of Ulm, near the village of **Blaubeuren**, a mysterious deep blue pool is set idyllically amid trees and rocks; close by, amid a group of charming old half-timbered buildings, is an old abbey with a distinguished 15th-century altarpiece. Rejoin the Danube at Ehingen and you'll come to **Obermarchtal** where there's another fine old abbey and church, 17th-century, formerly a monastery of the Premonstratensians. From here the flat Danube valley leads up to **Sigmaringen** (pop. 15,000), where a mighty Hohenzollern castle looms on a high rock above town and river. Originally the major feudal stronghold of the Catholic branch of the Hohenzollerns (see below), it has since been rebuilt in a jumble of styles, and its ornate interior lacks elegance. But it teems with history: the walls of the big banqueting-hall are hung with portraits of past Hohenzollerns, who provided kings for Portugal and Romania (the grandfather of the present ex-king Michael). In other rooms are old boots and banners from the Thirty Years' War, also suits of armour, blunderbusses, hunting trophies. The castle has even played a part in recent French history, for the Nazis took Pétain here in August 1944. Outside its walls is a rococo church, and a museum with primitive Swabian paintings.

West of here the upper Danube valley becomes more beautiful. In some places it is gently pastoral, in others the stripling river curves through defiles between rocky cliffs, topped by ruined castles. The stately Benedictine abbey of **Beuron** has specialized in Gregorian chant since the Middle Ages, and any day you can enjoy it by attending Mass or vespers in its fine baroque church (the abbey itself is closed to the public). Upstream, the Knopfmacherfelsen belvedere affords a fine view of the curving river and of Bronnen castle on its crag. Then turn north up over the Heuberg plateau, the southern arm of the Swabian Jura, where the Lochenstein rock provides another excellent view.

Beyond Balingen, a side-road winds up to **Hohenzollern**, the grandest castle in all Swabia, high on a wooded spur and visible from afar across the plain. With its numerous grey pinnacles, it has a bit of a 'fairy-tale' look as if, like Neuschwanstein, it is not to be taken too seriously. Indeed, little of it is very old, for it was largely rebuilt in this neo-Gothic style after an earthquake in 1867. But it oozes history, and is still lived in by the Hohenzollerns, greatest of German lordly families. These one-time rulers of Swabia later acquired a domain in Brandenburg – and thus in 1701 they became kings of Prussia, and of a unified Germany after 1871. But the Sigmaringen branch of the family remained in Swabia, and they still own this castle. The guided tour takes in the former bedrooms of the Wilhelmine kings and other living rooms, most quite small and cosy; the Festsaal, now sometimes used for public concerts; the tomb of Frederick the Great in the Protestant chapel; and the larger Catholic chapel, one of the few remaining mediaeval bits of the castle (lovely stained glass). A small museum contains the crown jewels. From the ramparts you get a view over the wooded massif and the plain towards Stuttgart. To the west, the old town of **Haigerloch** is strikingly situated in deep wooded gorge, astride two loops of the river Eyach. From here it's a short drive back to Tübingen.

TOURIST OFFICES

TÜBINGEN: Eberhardsbrücke, tel (07071) 3 50 11.

ULM: Münsterplatz, tel (0731) 6 41 61.

Accommodation, Eating and Drinking

PFORZHEIM 7530:

(H)**Ruf**, Bahnhofplatz 5, tel (07231). Tradition and modern comfort; good local dishes. Rooms (53) C. Meals B–C.

TIEFENBRONN 7533:

(H)**Ochsen Post**, Franz-Josef Gall-Str. 13, tel (07234) 80 30. Fine old 17th-century inn with ornately folksy décor, a shade pretentious, but cosy and welcoming; superb food. Cl Jan. Rooms (19) C–D. Meals (cl Sun) B.

TÜBINGEN 7400 (tel code 07071):

(H)**Krone**, Uhlandstr. 1, tel 3 10 36. The town's main hotel, a bit dull, but dependable. Cl Christmas. Rooms (48) B. Meals B–C.
(H)**Hospiz**, Neckarhalde 2, tel 2 60 02. Central, near Schloss, with nice view; simple comfort. Rooms (52) C–D. Meals C–D.

(R)**Waldhorn**, in Bebenhausen, Schönbuchstr. 49, tel 6 12 70. Elegant rustic décor, notable wines and superior cooking, e.g. lobster lasagne. Cl Thur, 3 weeks summer. Meals A–B.

(R)**Forelle**, Kronenstr. 8, tel 2 29 38. Classic *Weinstube* serving good game and trout dishes. Cl mid-Aug to mid-Sept, Tue. Meals D.

(R)**Mauke Neschtle**, Bergsteige. Near the Schloss, lively and popular; serves 26 types of *Maultaschen*. Much recommended.

REUTLINGEN 7410:

(H)**Achalm**, 4km to east, tel (07121) 1 70 11. Pleasant modern hotel in a hilltop setting, with fine views; restaurant (tel 4 26 01) with rustic décor and terrace, noted for its lamb dishes. Rooms (43) C. Meals B–C.

ULM 7900 (tel code 0731):

(H)**Goldener Bock**, Bockgasse 25, tel 2 80 79. Former brewery, now a tiny, comfortable hotel, quite central; good food, too. Rooms (11) C. Meals (cl Sun in summer) B–C.

(H)**Ulmer Spatz**, Münsterplatz 27, tel 6 80 81. Opposite cathedral; small garden and terrace. Rooms (40) D. Meals C–D.

(R)**Pflugmerzler**, Pfluggasse 6, tel 6 80 61. Old wine-tavern with good local cooking. Cl Sun. Meals C.

(R)**Zur Forelle**, Fischergasse 26, tel 6 39 24. An old fisherman's house by the Blau river, full of character; excellent for fish and Swabian dishes. Cl Sun. Meals B–C.

(R)**Zunfthaus der Schifferleute**, Fischergasse 31, tel 6 44 11. Former fishermen's guildhall; very popular, good value. Meals D.

SIGMARINGEN 7480:

(H)**Gästehaus Schmautz**, Im Mucketäle 33, tel (07571) 5 15 54. Simple guesthouse in pleasant setting by the Danube, just outside town. Rooms (15) E. Meals residents only.

STARZACH 7245:

(H)**Schloss Weitenburg**, 7 km to north, tel (07457) 80 51. For those with lordly tastes: a large 16th-century hilltop castle, still lived in by its charming owner, Baron Rassler, but now also a stylish yet not expensive hotel; pool, sauna, golf, riding school. Rooms (35) C. Meals B–C.

Baden-Baden, Freiburg and the Black Forest

The Black Forest is one of Germany's most popular holiday areas. It has hundreds of excellent small hotels with real local character, and superb tourist facilities: but it gets crowded in summer. Stretching for some 170 kilometres, it is a long range of wooded hills with rounded tops, none of them rising above 1,500 metres. All the scenery is lovely. The trees are mostly conifers, and the name 'black' comes from the dark look of the forest in some lights. But this is anything but a gloomy area. The valleys and upland meadows are pastorally serene, the air is clear and the views uplifting. Many trees have been affected by the 'acid rain' sickness, but this is not too noticeable to the visitor.

Everywhere the hiking is excellent. Some tourist packages enable you to hike from hotel to hotel each day, and your luggage is taken ahead for you by car. You can swim in some lakes, or go trout-fishing. Cross-country skiing is a Black Forest speciality, with some long well-marked trails. Downhill skiing is feasible until mid or late March in the area south of Freiburg, while some resorts have nursery slopes for beginners.

This is not a wealthy area, and most buildings are quite simple. But the living sense of rural tradition is as strong as anywhere in Germany. Older farmhouses have low thatched roofs and wooden walls; on some, rows of corncobs hang up. Some traditional industries still exist in the valleys: glassblowing, and of course the making of cuckoo-clocks, mostly for sale to tourists. Many areas have their own special local costume (*Tracht*), still worn for

Sunday church and festivals – but seldom for daily use. Girls will often have black bodices with puffy white sleeves, brocaded aprons and pleated skirts; men will wear a black costume with red lapels and linings, flowery waistcoats and small round broad-brimmed black hats. It is all most fetching. Girls in the Triberg area used to wear coloured top hats; in the Gutach valley, they had hats with big red pompons of velvet or wool; and a bride would don a wedding-hat decorated with coloured beads, straw flowers and baubles, looking like a gaudy bird's nest. Alas you seldom see these hats nowadays. Nor, except as a tourist gimmick, will you often come across one of the old clock-pedlars, with his black breeches, red waistcoat, black stockings, and clocks on a board that he carried on his back.

This long itinerary begins north of the forest, in the ducal city of Karlsruhe. It takes in Baden-Baden,'queen of spas', and part of the Baden 'wine-road' in the Rhine valley, then strikes up into the scenic heights of the Black Forest, around the big resorts of Baiersbronn and Freudenstadt. It traverses the most typical part of the region, around fascinating Triberg, heartland of its folk tradition, then comes to the delightful university city of Freiburg. It takes in more big resorts, Hinterzarten, Titisee and Badenweiler, in the southern sector of the range which has its highest summits, Belchen and Feldberg.

KARLSRUHE (pop. 267,000), close to the Rhine but not quite on it, is today an important industrial and legal centre: but its ducal palace survives as a reminder of its past as the capital of Baden. The Margrave Karl Wilhelm began to build his new palace here in 1715; it was completed later in the century, in neo-classical style, and in 1806 the city became the capital of the Grand Duchy of Baden. The palace stands in a pleasant formal park, and the central streets radiate from it fanwise – an unusual geometric pattern that gives the town originality. Otherwise it is today rather a dull, workaday place, though it does have some good museums. The Badisches Landesmuseum, housed in part of the palace, has a large collection of Greek and Roman antiquities, as well as some trophies brought back from Turkey by one Margrave in 1683–92. The Orangerie contains a fine selection of works by the 19th-century German landscape artist Hans Thoma, who died in Karlsruhe. And the Staatliche Kunsthalle has paintings ranging from German primitives (Grünewald, etc) via Holbein and a Rembrandt self-portrait to Monet and Cézanne.

The town's industries include a Michelin tyre plant, and large refineries linked to the oil pipeline from the Rhone delta. It contains the main German nuclear research centre and Germany's oldest school of technology, where Hertz discovered electro-magnetic waves in 1888. Since the war, the city has been the seat of the Federal Republic's Appeal Court and Constitutional Court – typical examples of the decentralized German system.

Rastatt (pop. 37,000), to the south, has a big reddish baroque castle built in c. 1700 by a Margrave called Ludwig the Turk (today it houses a large military museum). And it was for his widow, the Margravine Sibylla Augusta, that the much smaller and more elegant **Schloss Favorite** was built in 1711 as a summer residence, amid fields south-east of the town. From the outside this baroque château looks a bit dull, but the interior is ornate, with mosaics, imitation marble floors, and much porcelain. Beside the Autobahn to the south-west, near the Baden-Oos service station, is one of those modern motorway churches that the Germans have built as 'symbols of man's solidarity': this one, pyramid-shaped and very striking, has lovely stained glass by a Karlsruhe artist, Emil Wachter.

And so to **BADEN-BADEN** (pop. 50,000), still the world's most fashionable spa-resort (along with Montecatini Terme). Its countless visitors are attracted by its glamorous reputation and its programme of smart events, also by its very mild climate (it lies secluded in the green valley of the little river Oos) and, of course, by its healing waters. It was these that drew the Emperor Caracalla who came to ease his rheumatism (there are vestiges of Roman baths opposite the modern ones). The Margraves of Baden located their feudal seat here in the 12th century, and in the 16th the great physician Paracelsus came to treat one of these princes. Then in the mid-19th century Baden-Baden was a pioneer of the new craze for casinos, just ahead of Monte Carlo, and it became the leisure capital of European royalty in summer, just as Monte was in winter. Napoleon III, Bismarck and Queen Victoria were among those who rode along the elegant Lichtentaler Allee, a leafy walk in a park beside the Oos, where Edward Prince of Wales once went dressed in sheets to attend a 'ghost party'.

Where are those ghosts today? Inevitably, there are now far fewer of the royals and other grandees who used to stay for weeks with their large retinues. Hence the total of hotel beds has dropped from 15,000 to 4,000 since 1900: the mighty Kaiserhof hotel is now a supermarket. Even so, over 40 per cent of overnight visitors are foreign, many of them wealthy Americans and Arabs; senior businessmen, German and other, come on anti-stress cures; and the spa does a thriving convention and seminar trade. Whereas most German spas rely mainly on routine *Kurgäste* paid for by national insurance, at Baden-Baden some 95 per cent come privately, and most are well-to-do. All summer there are smart concerts in the elegant white-colonnaded Kurhaus, where charity galas and society balls are held too; in August the racing week at nearby Iffezheim, by the Rhine, is Germany's answer to Ascot.

This Kurhaus, built in 1821, also houses the casino. On one side is the *Trinkhalle* (pump room), with murals of local legends; in front are stylish outdoor cafés, flower-gardens, and arcades with expensive boutiques. Nearby is the Lichtentaler Allee. All the town's through-traffic is now diverted down a newly opened tunnel, and the central area is a pedestrian zone. Next to it is the majestic thermal centre, whose warm springs are radioactive and rich in chloride: here the new ultra-modern Caracalla-Therme, glass-walled and circular in shape, complements the much older Friedrichsbad, that grandiose temple where you can still enjoy the spa's exhilarating speciality, the 'Roman-Irish bath'. This complicated sauna-cum-Turkish-bath ritual, where at one point men and women frisk in the nude together in a big pool, is so called because in Roman days this technique of alternating warm water and hot air treatment had been imported from Ireland.

Above the baths on a low hill is the Neues Schloss, a 14th-century fortress rebuilt later in Renaissance style by the Margraves, whose summer palace it was until 1918; today it houses the Zähringer local history museum. Just north of the town, and easily reached by car, are two ruined mediaeval castles: the Altes Schloss (Hehnbaden), with fine views over town and valley, and Ebersteinburg, whose panorama embraces the Black Forest Hills.

South-west of the town, dominating the Rhine plain, stands yet another ruined hilltop fortress – 13th-century **Yburg**. The top of its tower (free access) offers a splendid view as far north as Karlsruhe, and south to Strasbourg, even to the Vosges on a clear day. In the foreground, the bright-green Baden vines go right up the slopes to a line where the dark-green pine-forest begins – a symphony of greens. The vineyards roll tidily, cut by little roads where the grape-carts can pass – all amazingly neat. The *Badische Weinstrasse* (Baden wine-road, clearly singposted) begins just here, at Steinach, and leads south through a number of picturesque wine-villages, such as Neuweier and Altschweier. Beyond Bühl it winds up to Altwindeck, another ruined hill-castle with a good view, then down to the plain again, to Sasbach where the French general Henri de Turenne was killed in battle in 1675 (a stele marks the spot). Just up the slope is the show-village resort of **Sasbachwalden**, full of neat flower-decked half-timbered houses – all a bit too prettified.

Leaving the plain and its vineyards, the road winds up past cherry orchards, rural inns and old farm-houses, to reach the **Schwarzwald-hochstrasse**, the tourist highway that runs south from Baden-Baden along the crest of the northern Black Forest: at several points there are car parks and belvederes, with wide views over the plain. One very popular beauty-spot is the **Mummelsee**, a little dark lake amid trees by the road, whence it's an easy drive or walk to the top of the Hornisgrinde, highest hill in the area (1,160m: splendid panorama). A ghost lived in the lake, says a local legend – and in summer a 'ghost' with a white beard and costume of seaweed duly struts around on stilts to amuse the trippers. More salutary is the adjacent triangular shaped Catholic church, built in 1971: its red-and-blue stained glass by Emil Wachter is especially impressive.

The scenic crest road reaches Ruhestein, where it's worth making a detour to **Allerheiligen**, a romantic and unusual place down a wooded comb off the road: the ruins of a 13th-century pink sandstone church stand next to three 18th-century ornamental fish-ponds, not far from a waterfall amid rocks. A private boarding-school has been added more recently. Back at Ruhestein, you can get to Freudenstadt either along B500 over a plateau via the resort of Kneibis (good hiking coun-try), or else along the wooded upper Murg valley via **Baiersbronn**, a large, straggling all-year resort in a lovely open setting, good for walking as well as skiing. It has some very fashionable hotels.

Just to the south, amid rolling hills, is **Freudenstadt** (pop. 20,000), another major resort and also an old historic town. It was built in the early 17th-century to house local silver-miners, on the orders of the Duke of Württem-berg; then near the end of World War II it was badly damaged by fire, but has since been carefully rebuilt on its origi-nal grid pattern, with a criss-cross of streets around a broad arcaded main square. The unusual 17th-century Stadtkirche has two aisles set at right-angles, each with its own green-domed tower; inside is a 12th-century carved lectern, borne by coloured figures of the evangelists.

The road south along the eastern edge of the Black Forest comes to **Alpirsbach**, whose glass-blowing fac-tory is open to visits. The town is best known for its beautiful Romanesque abbey church, whose ascetically simple nave contains faded 12th-cen-tury frescoes; the much-restored clois-ter is flamboyant Gothic. South along the Kinzig valley is **Wolfach**, an old town with a castle and some prettily painted houses; it, too, is a traditional glass-blowing centre, whose factory can be visited. Just south-east of Hausach, by the railway, is the Black Forest's hugely popular Freilicht-museum, called the **Vogtsbauernhof** because its main building is a large handsome wooden farmhouse of that name, with thatched roof, and bee-hives on its flowery balconies. The house was built here in 1570, and now the outdoor museum's other buildings have been grouped around it, brought from other parts of the region. Some contain old furniture and tools, includ-ing plenty of cuckoo-clocks, inevitably. There's an old smithy, an oil-mill and bakery, and a museum of the local wood industry. One house is a single room that the peasants shared with their animals.

We are now in a strongly traditional part of the Black Forest where many old customs survive. In and around the pretty village of **Gutach**, some girls on festive days wear hats with large black or red pompons of wool or velvet, and these are still made locally. Just to the south, a road to the right winds up through a beautiful forest of thick trees, then provides glorious distant hilly views to the north before descending to Oberprechtal. Turn south here into the idyllic **Prechtal**, a pastoral vale of little farms, still surprisingly free of mass tourism. At its far end, a road climbs up east through high forests to reach the little ski-resort of **Schonach**, best known for 'the world's biggest cuckoo-clock': a local clockmaker has built a clock so large that it forms one entire façade of a small chalet. You can go inside, and thus be tempted to buy one of his small cuckoo-clocks – a cunning sales-stunt that of course draws the crowds.

Busloads of Americans intent on buying cuckoo-clocks flood also to **Triberg** (pop. 5,500), the most interesting town of the central Black Forest. It straggles for over a mile down a steep wooded hill, to the clock factories deep in the valley. One main attraction is the Schwarzwaldmuseum, with its splendid array of local *Tracht*, such as Gutach festive hats; also on show are other local products such as wood-carvings, straw boots and, of course, cuckoo-clocks. There's a working model of the remarkable Black Forest railway, built in the 1870s over the hills from Villingen to Offenburg, in a series of loops, and still in service today. The reason for the display of local radios is that the well-known Saba radio-making firm was founded in Triberg. In a pine-forest at the top end of town is the also remarkable Triberg waterfall, floodlit at night, which cascades in sec-

tions down a total of 162m. You can walk beside it, up or down a steep zig-zag path: the round trip takes about an hour, and there are car-parks at either end. I would not advise walking back on foot along the main road. Also along this Schönwald road is the pilgrimage church of Maria in der Tannen (*Tannen* means 'fir-trees'), with baroque carvings.

Beyond the skiing and hiking resort of Schönwald is the industrial clockmaking town of **Furtwangen** (pop. 10,000). It has a technical school that teaches this craft, alongside an impressive modern museum that displays clocks of all kinds, old and new, local and foreign, as well as details of clockmaking and its history. Note the elaborate monumental clock made in the 1880s at nearby Villingen: it has 23 functions, some of them wilfully comic, but is set in motion only for guided tours.

South of the town, a side-road off B500 leads into the beguiling **Hexenloch** (witches' hole), a deep wooded valley where an old watermill still turns. The road climbs back onto the spacious rolling plateau, to reach St Märgen, a village with a fine baroque church. Even more attractive is nearby **St Peter**, whose large baroque church (1727) has tall onion-dome towers of reddish sandstone. Here one Sunday we stumbled upon a special Mass, with everyone in colourful local *Tracht* – the girls in green skirts, the old ladies in flowery aprons and black-and-white bonnets, the widows all on one side of the aisle, the old men on the other. The acoustics of this bright, ornate church were superb, and we savoured the feeling of authentic local tradition. From here you can drive to Freiburg along the pastoral **Glottertal** valley,

The 16th-century Haus zum Walfisch (whale house), one of the loveliest buildings of old Freiburg. Kaufhaus

busy with timber-cutting and wine-producing.

Cradled on three sides by green hills, at the point where the Black Forest meets the Rhine plain, the old university city of **FREIBURG IM BREISGAU** (pop. 176,000) has a lovely setting, and enjoys a specially sunny climate. It's the kind of place where foreigners like to live: many visitors count it as their favourite of all German towns, even above Munich. The university, stronger on the arts than on science, lies right downtown and its 25,000 students provide plenty of animation; but even outside term-time it's a youthful,

lively place, with lots of culture and outdoor festivals, and an easy-going ambience that seems more Latin than Germanic. Vineyards lie close to the town centre; the cathedral's soaring spire unites earth and sky. What explains Freiburg's charm? Is it the sunshine? The wine? The cultural tradition? The youthful population? The proximity to France? Or some Viennese influence, for it was under Habsburg rule for over 400 years? Maybe a mixture of all these things.

'The happiest women, like the happiest nations, have no history', wrote George Eliot. Maybe Freiburg is in that league, for it largely escaped the turmoil of the Middle Ages and the religious wars. Founded by local dukes in the 12th century, it was ruled by Austria from 1368 to 1805, then became part of Baden. It is still a key centre of Rhenish Catholicism. Its big Altstadt suffered badly from wartime bombing (an *un*happy interlude) but has been well rebuilt and remains the focus of local life, full of alleyways, small shops and wine-taverns (the Zum Roten Bären, see p. 137, is claimed to be Germany's oldest inn, dating from 1311). Some special features have been preserved. One is the mosiac paving of some streets, using pebbles from the Rhine – an expensive process dating from the 19th century. Another is the network of tiny streams (*Bächle*) that run down many narrow Alstadt streets. From mediaeval times they were used for essential water supply; now they are purely decorative. But they are fed by mountain rivers, and in rainy times these gullies can soak your shoes and trousers – watch out!

Among Freiburg's **festivals** are the orchestra festival in March, the tent music festival (jazz, rock and classical) in early June, the wine festival at the end of June, and the Schlossberg festival in August.

A tour of the Altstadt on foot could begin at the **Münster**, one of Germany's finest cathedrals and the town's major landmark, with its towering grey lacework steeple (116m). The transept is Romanesque (c. 1200) but the main building is Gothic. It is deliberately kept dimly-lit inside, so as to preserve the magical glow of the sunlight shining through the superb stained glass, mostly 13th to 16th century (this was kept hidden during the war, and so escaped the heavy damage to the building itself). Among the other works of art are paintings by Cranach and Holbein the Younger, and a superb high-altar triptych by Hans Baldung Grien (1516). Best of all are the expressive 13th-century sculptures on the west porch, of processions of Wise and Foolish Virgins. Note, on the left wall, the grotesque parable of Satan, disguised as a glamorous knight, with his victim, a half-naked woman. You can climb the tower, for wide views as far as the Vosges.

A busy outdoor market, where farmers sell fresh produce, is held daily round the cathedral. The buildings on the north side of this Münsterplatz were flattened in the war, but three notable ones on the south have survived: the baroque archbishop's palace (1756); the reddish Kafhaus, late-Gothic, with first-floor statues of Habsburg monarchs (civic receptions and concerts are held inside); and the house that the painter Christian Wenzinger built for himself in 1761. *Clochemerle* fans please note that the 18th-century guardhouse beside the Münster is now a public urinal and the only one in Germany to be a protected historic monument.

The most delightful part of old Freiburg lies just south of the Münster, between it and the picturesque 13th-century Swabian Gate (*Schwabentor*), part of the old ramparts. Near it is the best of Freiburg's museums, the **Augustiner**, in a former monastery: this provides an ideal setting for its superb display of 13th to 15th-century religious art from the Upper Rhine area, notably Grünewald's altar painting *The Foundation of Santa Maria Maggiore in Rome* (1517), from a church in Aschaffenburg. You'll also find early choirbooks, porcelain, etc. The nearby modern art museum (Neue Kunst) has some attractive Otto Dix, e.g. his allegorical *Christophorus* (1941), but little else of note. Here you are in the quiet and charming area called Insel, where the picturesque former cottages of fishermen line a canal. North of the Schwabentor is the narrow cobbled Konviktstrasse, whose 17th-century houses have just been trendily restored and are now full of smart boutiques and rich flats. A footpath here leads over the main ring-road and up onto the Schlossberg, the once-fortified hill that affords a good view down over the city.

The Altstadt's wide, traffic-free main street, the Kaiser-Joseph-Strasse, used once to be lined with arcades, but lost them in the 19th century; now, smashed up in the war, it has been rebuilt in its old arcaded style. To its west is a fine ensemble of buildings around the Rathausplatz – the Gothic Franciscan church of St Martin; the elegant Haus zum Walfisch (1516) with its red-and-gold façade, a patrician mansion where Erasmus, fleeing the Reformation in Basle, took refuge in 1529–31; and the Neues Rathaus, partly Renaissance 16th-century, i.e. about as *neu* as New College, Oxford. Freiburg's university, whose main campus is just south-west of the Neues Rathaus, is one of Germany's oldest, founded in 1467: it has two rococo courtyards and a *Jugendstil* lecture-hall, but most of its buildings are quite new, including the vast Library, housing two million volumes. On its north side, in the Colombipark, is the tiny Schloss Colombi, neo-Gothic, now housing a museum of archaeology.

On the edge of Freiburg are two places worth a visit. To the south, the Black Forest high-point of Schauins-land (1,286m), reachable from the city by road or by tram and cable-car, affords a majestic panorama. And to the west are the large Eugen Keidel thermal baths, opened only ten years ago: they are used for treating rheumatism and heart complaints, but are also packed out with ordinary healthy bathers and fitness fanatics.

North-west of Freiburg, the low **Kaiserstuhl** hill produces some of the finest Baden wines on its slopes, thanks to its warm dry micro-climate. Nearby, the old fortified town of **Breisach** stands on a promontory beside the Rhine, crowned by a massive Romanesque/Gothic church whose frescoes and high altar are remarkable. Breisach used to be a key defensive post along this war-torn frontier, today so peaceful and open. From Kaiserstuhl you can follow the southern stretch of the Baden Wine Road, to go south to **Staufen**, a market town with a painted 16th-century Rathaus, and a ruined castle above the vineyards. The wine road goes on via Müllheim to the large spa resort of **Badenweiler**, the most fashionable in south Germany after Baden-Baden. Anton Chekhov used to be a *Kurgast*, and he died here in 1904 while staying at the Park-Hotel. This lovely hillside resort has a graceful Kurpark and smart new Kurhaus, as well as a very elegant modern glass-roofed thermal *piscine*, used for treating chest and blood disorders. Next door are the well-preserved vestiges of baths built by the Emperor Vespasian in the 1st century AD.

East of Badenweiler you can drive up into the glorious highlands of the southern Black Forest. Via the pastoral upper Münstertal, where St Trudpert monastery stands amid meadows, you can reach the broad, easy mountain road that leads to the summit of the **Belchen** (1,414m): this gently rounded height offers majestic views over the Black Forest and Vosges, with the Bernese Oberland and even Mont Blanc visible on a clear day. Down in the Wiese valley you'll come to **Todtnau**, which has a glass-blowing factory; above it, spread across an upland valley, is the isolated hill-resort of **Todtnauberg** (fine views). The main road east from Todtnau leads up to the Feldberg pass, just below the **Feldberg** (1,493m), highest point of the whole Black Forest: a short walk and a chair-lift will bring you to the Bismarck statue close to its summit, where as well as the expected wide panorama there's a more intimate view over the little Feldsee, just below.

Further east, the large and trippery resort of **Titisee** is set beside a lovely clear lake of that name, amid wooded hills. It has traditional wooden houses with wide eaves. **Hinterzarten**, just off the Freiburg road, is smaller but much more stylish, one of the most fashionable of Black Forest resorts. Ideal for skiing or hiking, it has a lovely pastoral upland setting: its posh hotels are set beside ponds where swans and ducks swim, meadows where horses graze, and a deer park. Hinterzarten has deliberately eschewed mass-tourism and large new high-rise buildings. Yet it swings with the times, for outside the post office is a most curious Beuys-like 'action-sculpture' – a table, chair, rucksack, telephone, books and other items loosely scattered around. It certainly makes a contrast with the scenery.

TOURIST OFFICES

KARLSRUHE: Bahnhofplatz 6, tel (0721) 3 55 30; Karl-Friedrich-Str. 14, tel (0721) 1 33 34 55.

BADEN-BADEN: Kurdirektion, Augustaplatz 8, tel (07221) 27 52 00.

FREUDENSTADT: Promenadeplatz 1, tel (07441) 86 40.

TRIBERG: Kurhaus, tel (07722) 8 12 30.

FREIBURG IM BREISGAU: Rotteckring 14, tel (0761) 2 16 32 89.

BADENWEILER: Ernst-Eisenlohr Str. 4, tel (07632) 7 21 10.

Accommodation, Eating and Drinking

KARLSRUHE 7500 (tel code 0721):

(H)**Schlosshotel**, Bahnhofplatz 2, tel 35 40. Newly renovated in '1900' style; two good restaurants. Rooms (96) B. Meals B–C.
(H)**Käbler**, Bismarckstr. 39, tel 2 26 11. Comfortable and central; no restaurant. Rooms (97) C.

(HW)**Goldene Krone**, Langestr. 1, tel 3 02 19. In the southern suburb of Rüppurr, a Viennese-style wine-pub (Heuriger): lively ambience, good simple dishes, low prices. Rooms (12) E. Meals E.

(R)**Unter Den Linden**, Kaiserallee 71, tel 84 91 85. A smart place, but fine value; good Baden dishes. Cl 2 weeks Feb. Meals B–C.

(R)**Dudelsack**, Waldstr. 79, tel 2 21 66. A charming courtyard-terrace and good Baden cooking make this lively place very popular. Cl Sun. Meals B–C.

(B)**Harmonie**, Kaiserstr. 57, tel 37 42 09. Beer pub with live music; dishes include salad buffet. Meals C–D.

ETTLINGEN:

(H)**Erbprinz**, Rheinstr. 1, tel (07243) 1 20 71. Sleek and luxurious, this 'Crown Prince'; garden terrace; wood-panelled gourmet restaurant, highly reputed. Rooms (49) B. Meals A–B; cheaper *Weinstube*, too, C.

BAD HERRENALB 7506:

(H)**Mönchs Posthotel**, Doblerstr. 2, tel (07083) 74 40. Graceful half-timbered posthouse, full of charm; in centre of town, but with big garden; indoor pool. Panelled dining-room serves good *nouvelle*-ish food. Rooms (50) B. Meals B.

BADEN-BADEN 7570 (tel code 07221):

(H)**Brenner's Park**, Schillerstr. 6, tel 35 30. One of the world's grandest, most famous hotels: Queen Victoria *et al.* stayed here. Discreet opulence, tactful service, vast suites, conventional upper-class food. Beauty farm, pool, etc. Rooms (100) A. Meals A.

(H)**Romantik-Hotel Der Kleine Prinz**, Lichtentalerstr.36, tel 34 64. The charming Rademacher family run this stylish and intimate hotel with real warmth; light, original décor, lovely rooms, excellent cuisine. Rooms (28) B. Meals (cl Mon, Jan) B.

(H)**Greiner**, Lichtentaler Allee 88, tel 7 11 35. Simple but comfortable; no restaurant. Cl 2 weeks Nov. Rooms (33) D.

(R)**Molkenkur**, Quettigstr. 19, tel 3 32 57. Popular with local radio journalists; fair prices; pretty garden. Cl Sun. Meals C–D.

BÜHL 7580:

(H)**Grüne Bettlad**, Blumenstr. 4, tel (07223) 2 42 38. Distinguished picturesque 17th-century inn; good local cuisine. Rooms (8) C. Meals (cl 2 weeks summer, 2 weeks Christmas, Sun dinner, Mon) B.

(R)**Burg Windeck**, Kappelwindeckstr. 104, tel (07223) 2 36 71. Next to a ruined hilltop fortress, an opulent gourmet venue with panoramic views. Cl Mon, Tue. Meals A.

SASBACHWALDEN 7595:

(H)**Talmühle**, Talstr. 36, tel (07841) 10 01. Notable cooking at this idyllic hotel beside a stream; lovely garden, too. Cl Dec. Rooms (33) B–C. Meals B–C.

SCHWARZWALDHOCHSTRASSE:

(H)**Schlosshotel Bühlerhohe**, 7580 Bühl, tel (07226) 5 51 00. By the crest road, with fine views, an incredibly opulent luxury hotel, popular with Arab oil sheikhs. Park, indoor pool, health clinic. Rooms (90) A. Meals A–B.

(H)**Unterstmatt**, 7580 Bühl, tel (07226) 2 04. Delightfully informal ski-hotel, family-run, with real Baden ambience; rustic-style bedrooms, jolly cellar *Stube*, excellent Baden dishes (e.g. local smoked ham). Own ski-slope for beginners. Cl 2 weeks April, mid-Nov to mid-Dec. Rooms (16) C. Meals (cl Mon dinner, Tue) B–C.

BAIERSBRONN 7292:

(H)**Mitteltal**, Gärtenbühlweg 14, tel (07442) 470. The Bareiss family's big, beautiful modern hotel, with its south-facing balconies, elegant sun-terraces and bright modern décor, has more than a touch of the Riviera. Super comfort, stunningly good food and wines in the **Bareiss** restaurant. Rooms (176) A. Meals A (Bareiss cl Mon, Tue, mid-May to mid-June, Dec).

(H)**Zum Engel**, Rechtmurgstr. 28, Mitteltal, tel (07449) 28. Friendly, quiet and traditional. Indoor pool; massage. Rooms (68) B–C. Meals C.

FREUDENSTADT 7290:

(H)**Gut Lauterbad**, Dietrichstr. 5, Lauterbad, tel (07441) 74 96. Comfortable, friendly modern hotel on edge of town, amid streams and meadows; hearty cooking. Cl 2 weeks Jan, mid-Nov to mid-Dec. Rooms (20) D. Meals (cl. Wed) C–D.

TRIBERG 7740:

(H)**Parkhotel Wehrle**, Gartenstr. 24, tel (07722) 8 60 20. Warmly civilized and richly furnished old hostelry, run by the Wehrle/Blum family since 1707. In town centre: garden rooms quietest. Superb food. Indoor pool. Rooms (56) B–C. Meals B.

(H)**Staude**, Obertal 20, at Gremmelsbach, 9km to north, tel (07722) 48 02. Up a quiet valley, simple but pleasant; meals excellent value. Cl mid-Nov to mid-Dec. Rooms (9) E. Meals (cl. Tue) D.

SCHÖNWALD 7741:

(H)**Zum Ochsen**, Ludwig-Uhland-Str. 18, tel (07722) 10 45. Set amid woods and meadows, an elegantly rustic little chalet-style hotel, family-run, folksy yet sophisticated; local décor, very good French-influenced cooking. Cl 2 weeks Nov. Rooms (39) C–D. Meals (cl Tue, Wed, 2 weeks Dec) B–C.

ST PETER 7811:

(H)**Zur Sonne**, Zähringerstr. 2, tel (07660) 203. Ideal village inn, simple and charming; excellent Baden cooking. Cl mid-Jan to mid-Feb. Rooms (14) D. Meals (cl Wed) C–D.

(H)**Zum Hirschen**, Bertholdsplatz 1, tel (07660) 204. On main square, also simple and charming. Cl mid-Nov to mid-Dec. Rooms (25) E. Meals (cl Thur) C.

GLOTTERTAL 7804:

(H)**Zum Goldenen Engel**, Friedhofstr. 2, tel (07684) 250. Another typical village pub, lively and *gemütlich*. Big helpings. Cl 2 Jan to mid-Feb. Rooms (9) E. Meals (cl Wed) C–D.

FREIBURG IM BREISGAU 7800 (tel code 0761):

(H)**Colombi**, Rotteckring 16, tel 3 14 15. Much the best hotel in town, sleekly elegant; smooth, courteous service; refined high-class cooking and splendid Baden wines. Rooms (101) A. Meals A–B.

(H)**Zum Roten Bären**, Oberlinden 12, tel 3 69 13. 12th-century house with painted façade, said to be Germany's oldest inn (1311); now comfortably modern and well-run. Staff in Baden *Tracht* serve good traditional food. Rooms (25) C. Meals B.

(H)**Rappen**, Münsterplatz 13, tel 3 13 53. Characterful inn facing cathedral; some rooms have Baden country furnishings. Cosy restaurant, good for game, wild pig, etc. Rooms (19) C. Meals C.

(H)**Am Rathaus**, Rathausgasse 6, tel 3 11 29. In Altstadt, well-run and comfortable. No restaurant. Rooms (40) C.

(R)**Dattler**, on the Schlossberg hill, tel 3 17 29. Panoramic view of the city and fairly good food. Cl Tue and Jan. Meals C.

(R)**Kühler Krug**, Torplatz 1, in Günterstal, S of town, tel 2 91 03. Serious bourgeois cooking in a rural setting; good value. Pleasant bedrooms, too. Cl 3 weeks June. Rooms (7) D. Meals B–C.

(R)**Grosser Mayerhof**, Grünwaldstr. 7, tel 2 25 52. In Altstadt; popular and unpretentious, with good Black Forest dishes. Cl Tue. Meals C–D.

(W)**Zur Sichelschmiede**, Insel. In the Altstadt, a wine-tavern in an old house, with a small garden; popular with students. Snacks.

MÜNSTERTAL 7816:

(H)**Romantik-Hotel Spielweg**, Spielweg 61, tel (07636) 618. Delightful old rural inn with local ambience plus modern comfort; fine cooking. Rooms (33) B–C. Meals (cl Mon) B.

BADENWEILER 7847:

(H)**Romantik-Hotel Sonne**, Moltkestr. 4, tel (07632) 50 53. Appealing old family-run inn dating from 1620; central but quiet; *Weinstube* and good Baden cooking. Cl mid-Nov to Jan. Rooms (40) C. Meals (cl Wed) B–C.

(H)**Hochblauen**, 8km to SW on Blauen hilltop, tel (07632) 388. Friendly, unassuming hostelry with panoramic views. Cl Nov–Feb. Rooms (15) D–E. Restaurant for residents only, cl Wed, Thur.

TODTNAUBERG 7868:

(H)**Sonnenalm**, Hornweg 21, tel (07671) 18 00. Sweeping vistas as far as the Alps from this simple but pleasant little upland hotel. Cl mid-Nov to mid-Dec. Rooms (13) D. Restaurant for residents only.

TITISEE 7820:

(H)**Josen**, Jostalstr. 90, tel (07651) 56 50. Quietly located 6km N of Titisee: old Gasthof with good French and local dishes. Cl mid-Nov to mid-Dec. Rooms (30) C. Meals (cl Thur) C.

HINTERZARTEN 7824:

(H)**Park-Hotel Adler**, Adlerplatz 3, tel (07652) 12 70. One of Germany's loveliest hotels, very elegant and luxurious, in a rural setting; indoor pool, tennis, garden. Owned by Riesterer family since 1446! Rooms (76) A. Meals A–B.
(H)**Sassenhof**, Adlerweg 17, tel (07652) 15 15. Stylishly superior but very friendly little pension; no restaurant, but garden, sauna and lovely indoor pool. Cl 2 weeks Dec. Rooms (24) C.

BREITNAU 7821:

(H)**Kaiser's Tanne-Wirtshus**, Am Wirbstein 27, tel (07652) 15 51. Secluded amid pastoral country, a folksily *gemütlich* and welcoming chalet-style hotel; very good food. Cl mid-Nov to mid-Dec. Rooms (29) C. Meals (cl Mon) B.

The Lake of Constance (Bodensee)

The Rhine flows into Lake Constance (*Bodensee*) at its eastern end, and out at the west. Bordered by Germany to the north, Switzerland to the south, and Austria to the east, this is much the biggest of the lakes that touch German soil and has been nicknamed 'the Swabian ocean'. It is Germany's Midi, or Deep South, with a mild climate that permits sub-tropical plants and trees; and the north shore is what passes for a German Riviera, lined with small, picturesque resorts. Happily, they have so far been preserved from big package hotels or high-rise horrors. The gentle hillsides are clad with vines; onion-domed churches and half-timbered houses stand near the landing-jetties where wind-surfers and sailboats carve their patterns against the backdrop of Swiss pre-Alps to the south. The road along the north shore is always dense with traffic, and no *Autobahn* has yet been built, owing to local farmers' opposition: but at least the main towns and resorts, such as enchanting Meersburg, are set off the road, down by the water. One way to see the lake is by excursion boat; or by hiking along panoramic paths in the hills. The lake extends westward in two arms – the Überlingersee with steep wooded banks, and the Zellersee, a kind of broadening of the Rhine.

The Bodensee's main town is **KONSTANZ** (Constance, pop. 70,000) which lies astride the Rhine at the point where it leaves the lake. It has pleasant waterside parks and some interesting buildings, witness to its historic past. The cathedral, large and a bit austere, was built in stages between the 11th and 16th centuries and thus is in a mixture of styles; note the decorated panels on its main doorway. The Rathaus, a Renaissance building with a lovely courtyard, is far more attractive. The Rosgarten museum gives insights into local history. And the Steigenberger-Insel Hotel by the lake is quite an historical monument: built in 1525 as a Dominican monastery (its cloister survives intact), it later became a textile factory, then a hotel in 1875. The Zeppelin family once owned it, and the Graf von Zeppelin who invented airships was born here in 1838.

On a hill in the northern suburbs is the ugly new university, whose main distinction is that Ralf Dahrendorf was its professor of sociology, both before and after his LSE days. Further on, across a causeway, lies the tiny but celebrated offshore island of **Mainau**, whose elaborate floral park attracts endless coachloads of visitors. Its giant veteran sequoias are claimed to be Germany's largest trees, its massed dahlias number 20,000, its banana palms and orange groves add further exoticism, while some flower-banks are arranged topiary-style in the shapes of rabbits, peacocks and owls. The appeal of Mainau depends also on the fame of its charismatic Swedish owner, Count Lennart Bernadotte, who in 1989 celebrated his 80th birthday there, in his yellow 18th-century château (built by a Bavarian king), with his nephew King Carl Gustav of Sweden and his five younger children, then aged six to 14 (he had married his secretary). The count is an avid publicist: beaming photos of him and his young German wife fill the pages of his glossy brochures of Mainau, welcoming foreign potentates or joking with Japanese schoolgirls. And when reports spread that the Bodensee had become too polluted for bathing, the worried Count at once rang up the TV networks and got himself filmed wading into the lake and drinking from it!

On the larger low-lying island of **Reichenau**, to the west, two superb old churches survive as reminders of its glory as a key monastic centre in the tenth–11th centuries. The large abbey at Mitelzell has ancient frescoes and a Romanesque tower, as well as some fine modern stained-glass. In the tiny church at Oberzell, the wonderfully vivid frescoes of Christ's miracles (AD c. 1000) look as if just painted – as they were, in a sense, for the church was totally restored in 1982. Reichenau today has grown prosperous on market-gardening and tourism.

At **Allensbach** on the mainland is Germany's foremost public opinion institute, created and run by the German 'Dr Gallup', the redoubtable Professor Elisabeth Noelle-Neumann. Over by the northern arm of the lake, the Überlingersee, you come to **Bodman**, where two old castles stand beside neolithic and Roman remains. And on the lake's far shore is **Überlingen**, a handsome old ramparted town where stately patrician houses line the pleasant waterside promenades, against a backdrop of wooded hills. Its Münster has five aisles, with Gothic fan vaulting; its 15th-century Rathaus has fine woodcarving in its Gothic council chamber; another 15th-century building houses the local museum, which has more carvings, also cribs. Further east, the delightful little pilgrimage church of **Birnau** (1746–50) stands splendidly isolated by the lake; its rococo interior contains the famous statuette of the Honigschlecker (honey-sucker) – a cherub sucking his finger. Another curiosity by the lake is the museum of German pre-history at **Unteruhldingen**, where recent excavations have brought to light a primitive lake settlement. The museum gives details; you can also visit the lake-village of wooden huts on stilts that has now been artfully constructed offshore. To the north is Salem Abbey, seat of the Margrave of Baden, and worth visiting for its fine library and baroque Kaisersaal. The Monastery buildings house Germany's most famous private boarding school, founded in the 1920s by Dr Kurt Hahn who later founded Gordonstoun in Scotland.

The prettiest town along the entire lake is **Meersburg** (pop. 5,300), which celebrated its 1,000th birthday in 1988. Above its pleasant promenade, old alleys lined with half-timbered houses curve up to the quaint old Marktplatz; the hall of mirrors of the baroque Neues Schloss is a venue for concerts in summer; and the nearby Känzle terrace affords a fine view over the lake. Best of all is the Altes Schloss, said to be Germany's oldest fortress: it is a fearsome feudal hulk, with secret *oubliettes* and dark stone walls towering on a cliff in the centre of town. Inside you can inspect the modest bedroom where Annette von Droste-Hülshoff (see p. 49), Germany's greatest poetess, died in 1848 of consumption and a broken heart, as she gazed over the lake and lamented her unrequited love for the novelist Levin Schücking, 18 years her junior. All is unchanged since her day – the décor and furniture, and her bed. The white lilies, freshly renewed, were her favourite flowers. Poetic melancholy reigns supreme.

A string of pleasant little resorts, notably Immenstaad and Hagnau, line the lake between Meersburg and industrial **Friedrichshafen** (pop. 52,000), famous in aviation history. Its excellent Zeppelin museum tells the saga of how, around 1900, Graf Ferdinand von Zeppelin here built and tested the first of the giant dirigible airships that were given his name; here too they began their first flights to America. Later Claude Dornier, an engineer working for Zeppelin, built his flying-boats here in the 1920s and tested them on the lake. Dornier created his own firm, which built military aircraft here in both world wars; the factory still exists, now part of the Daimler-owned MBB company. As well as industry, the town has pleasant lakeside promenades.

Lindau, the next well-known town along the lake, is just inside Bavaria (see p. 147). Inland you will find some impressive old towns – first **Ravensburg** (pop. 43,000), formerly a Guelph bastion, which has towers and painted gateways, notably the high Mehlsack (sack of flour) tower. In the Liebfraukirche, 14th-century but since modernized is a copy of the superb 15th-century *Virgin of Ravensburg* sculpture, whose original is in the Dahlem Museum in Berlin. **Weingarten** (pop. 22,000), another old Guelph town, contains a famous abbey, whose basilica is the second biggest baroque church in Germany: note the vast ornate organ (1750) in its elaborate interior.

Wangen im Allgäu is one of my favourite Swabian towns. Two 17th-century gateways with painted façades, the St Martin-Tor and the Frauentor, enclose its busy traffic-free Altstadt, where one half-timbered house contains a folk museum devoted mainly to local Allgäu cheeses. And Wangen's picturesqueness is now enhanced by some of those modern outdoor sculptures so much in vogue in German towns. In the main Herrnstrasse, bronze pigeons peck on the pavement's edge and a drinking-fountain has elaborate groups of figurines with donkeys. In the Saumarkt, where a pig market is held every Wednesday, seven bronze piglets are scattered in lifelike poses. One is talking to St Anthony, who sits on a bench with a bible.

TOURIST OFFICES

KONSTANZ: Bahnhofplatz 13, tel (07531) 28 43 76.

MEERSBURG: Kirschstr. 4, tel (07532) 8 23 83.

Accommodation, Eating and Drinking

KONSTANZ 7750 (tel code 07531):

(H)**Steigenberger-Insel Hotel**, Auf der Insel, tel 2 50 11. Ex-monastery (see p. 000), now a fairly grand and formal hotel, by the lake. Regional and fish dishes. Rooms (100) A–B. Meals B–C.

(H)**Buchner Hof**, Buchnerstr. 6, tel 5 10 35. In quiet street near lake; spruce and friendly. No restaurant. Cl Dec 20-Jan 10. Rooms (13) C.

(R)**Seehotel Siber**, Seestr. 25, tel 6 30 44. Superb food in an elegant lakeside setting. Cl 3 weeks Feb. Meals A. Rooms (11) B.

(R)**Zum Nicolai-Torkel**, Eichhornstr. 83, tel. 6 48 02. Classic fish dishes, terrace with view. Cl late Feb and end Oct. Meals B-C. Rooms (5) C.

(R)**Konzil**, Hafenstr. 2, tel 2 12 21. Nice terrace with lake view. Cl mid-Dec to mid-Jan. Meals C.

REICHENAU (island) 7752:

(H)**Romantik-Hotel Seechau**, Schifflände 8, tel (07534) 257. By the lake, spruce and friendly; good local fish dishes. Cl Nov, Dec. Rooms (11) B–C. Meals (cl Sun dinner, Mon) B.

ÜBERLINGEN 7770:

(R)**Romantik-Hotel Hecht**, Münsterstr. 8, tel (07551) 6 33 33. Old *Weinstube* serving local and French-influenced dishes; excellent value. Cl 2 week Feb, Sun dinner, Mon. Meals B–C. Also 9 rooms, C.

MEERSBURG 7758:

(H)**Bären**, Marktplatz 11, tel (07532) 60 44. Very picturesque old 17th-century inn, run by a friendly family. Cl mid-Nov to mid-Mar. Rooms (16) D. Meals (cl Mon) C–D.

Above the shimmering Bodensee (Lake of Constance), the Alte Schloss in Meersburg.

HAGNAU 7759:

(H)**Erbguth's Landhaus**, Neugartenstr. 39, tel (07532) 62 02. Elegantly converted private house, run with warmth and style by a young couple; lovely food served by candlelight. Cl Jan to mid-Mar. Rooms (22) B–C. Meals (cl Tue) B–C.

IMMENSTAAD 7997:

(H)**Strandcafe Heinzler**, Strandbadstr. 10, tel (07545) 768. Family-run friendly chalet-style hotel; good food (lakeside terrace). Cl Jan. Rooms (16) D. Meals C.

RAVENSBURG 7980:

(H)**Romantik-Hotel Waldhorn**, Marienplatz 15, tel (0751) 1 60 21. Characterful, cosy and family-run; classy French cooking. Rooms (40) B–C. Meals (cl Sun) A–B.

WANGEN IM ALLGÄU 7988:

(H)**Romantik-Hotel Alte Post**, Postplatz 2, tel (07522) 40 14. 15th-century coaching-inn; cosy rooms (four-posters); good Swabian food. Rooms (28) C. Meals B–C.

CHAPTER FIVE

Bavaria
(Bayern)

BAVARIA, WHICH HAD its own king until 1918, is the largest of the *Länder*, the second most populous (11 million), and the one with much the strongest sense of its own nationhood. Its people feel as separate from other Germans as Scots do from English, and I have met some who say, 'My first loyalty is to Bavaria, my second to Europe, and only my third to Germany.' Jovially self-confident, fond of gregarious beer-drinking, sometimes rough and coarse but generally warm and humorous, they like to assert themselves – and can get resented for it by other Germans. Politically this *Land* today has no more or less autonomy than any other: but everywhere you will see the blue-and-white chequered flag and colours of *Freistaat Bayern*, the Bavarian 'Free State'.

A ll this is the product of history. Under the Wittelsbach dynasty who ruled it without a break for over 700 years, 1180 to 1918, Bavaria was one of the first German duchies, with Regensburg as its capital until 1255, then Munich. The Dukes became Electors in 1623, and in the 18th century they were bidding to rival Austria. In 1805 Napoleon elevated the duchy to a kingdom, and under Ludwig I it became a major centre of the arts. These 19th-century Wittelsbachs were liberal and benign monarchs, but not without their darker side: Ludwig II (1864–86), the patron of Wagner, became an unstable, over-poetic megalomaniac, built Neuschwanstein and other extravagant castles, retreated

into madness, and drowned himself just after he was deposed.

In 1871 he agreed to the inclusion of Bavaria in the Kaiser's new German Empire, but with the retention of many privileges: it still kept its own embassies abroad and its own army. Then the ousting of the monarchy in 1918 was followed by brief months of extreme-Left government, and later by Hitler's choice of Bavaria as the prime sanctuary of his power ideology – witness the abortive Munich *Putsch* of 1923, the Nuremberg rallies and the building of his alpine eyrie at Berchtesgaden. In today's happier times, the spirit of the Wittelsbachs is still amazingly alive in the hearts of their people, who are proud of their

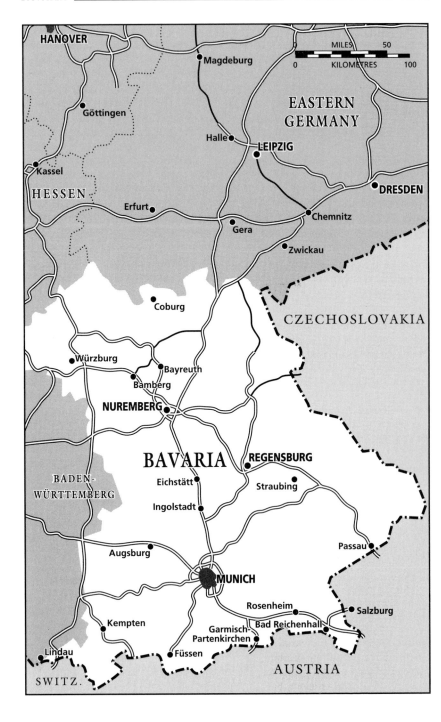

royal legacy. The present Duke, who lives near Munich, is still treated with ceremony as a kind of unofficial head of state: he is addressed as 'your Royal Highness', and has the right to hold parties in the monarchy's former palace of Nymphemburg (see page 176).

Bavarians love father-figures: that helps to explain the popularity of the emperor-like Franz Josef Strauss, who failed in his ambition to be Federal Chancellor, but was *Land* Prime Minister from 1978 until his death in 1988. He was unquestioned king of the Christian Social Union (CSU), the Right-wing Catholic party that has ruled Bavaria since the war. Especially in rural areas and smaller towns (the larger ones tend to be SPD), this mainly Catholic *Land* is deeply conservative; and Strauss, a local butcher's son, world-class statesman and demagogic demon, cleverly exploited his hold over them, wooing the farmers with speeches in broad Bavarian. Today he has no potent successor within the CSU. Some of the local support for him has now transferred to the new extreme-Right Republikaner, whose leader for all Germany is also a Bavarian, the former SS officer Franz Schönhüber!

However, there's much more to Bavaria than beery Right-wing bluster. Its economy has developed hugely since the war, becoming much more industrial, and like Baden-Württemberg it is benefiting from modern industry's preference for the south. Audi cars are made at Ingolstadt, BMWs at Munich and near Regensburg; Nuremberg and Augsburg are also big industrial centres. Agriculture is still important too: cereal-growing on the plains tends to be large-scale and efficient, but many

of the dairy farms are still small and backward. Yet they form a potent political lobby, which lends the CSU much of its support, and has often obstructed the EC in Brussels, in its bid to cut inefficiency and reduce surpluses.

The landscape varies greatly – and so do the people. In the south, high Alps rocky or snow-covered run along the border with Austria: the stunning scenery, good skiing, pretty villages and spectacular castles make this Germany's foremost tourist region. And here in Upper Bavaria you are most likely to find the archetypes of men in *Lederhosen*, beer-festivals, and flower-decked wooden houses. The rest of the *Land* consists of wide rolling spaces, partly forested, cut by the valleys of the Danube, Isar, Lech and other rivers. The area in the south-west, around Augsburg, is part of Swabia (see p. 180), and the people have the temperament, cuisine and dialect, not of Bavarians but of their fellow-Swabians in Württemberg. Over to the east, along the Czech border, are the long wooded hills of the *Bayerischer Wald* (Bavarian Forest) and Oberpfalz, where the villages are still rather poor, remote and backward. Lastly, the whole of the north is the historic region known as Franconia (*Franken*): this was not even part of Bavaria until 1803, and its people still do not consider themselves fully Bavarian. And even within Franconia, there are big differences between Nuremberg, the capital, and Würzburg, centre of a wine-growing district in the pretty Main valley. Würzburgers, merry and easy-going like so many wine-growers, tend to consider Nürnbergers dour and taciturn, and they may be right – while both in turn resent Munich and the south. Parts of Franconia around

Bayreuth are Lutheran enclaves. Such is the Bavarian patchwork. But all its historic cities are fascinating – not only Munich and Nuremberg, Würzburg and Augsburg, but also Regensburg, Bamberg, Passau and others.

Bavaria has much in common with Austria, even parts of North Italy, alike in its Catholic tradition and its baroque architecture. The profusion of fine baroque building is striking, even down to village churches with their coloured onion-domes. Many old churches, abbeys or castles were built originally in Gothic or Romanesque style, then in the 18th or early 19th century their interiors were re-modelled in the ornate baroque or rococo style that the Wittelsbachs favoured. As for older vernacular buildings, there is less half-timbering than in most German regions; instead, most rural houses have white-painted lower floors, and upper floors of slatted wood with flower-decked balconies and wide overhanging eaves. Notably this is so in sub-alpine Upper Bavaria, where some house-façades carry elaborate paintings.

The people in rural areas tend to be stocky and fresh-faced, close to one's image of an Alpine peasant. Many a small town or village has its annual beer-festival: it will first be blessed by the local priest, followed by days on end of the old Bavarian drinking-songs, arms linked, swaying together. Many villages also have a traditional May Day festival, when they dance around a maypole, decorated with local scenes and characters. And, notably in Upper Bavaria, traditional clothes and costumes (*Tracht*) are still in wide daily use, not put on just for special occasions. This is an aspect of Bavarian national feeling. In country areas, some women can still be seen in brocaded *Dirndls,* and men in *Lederhosen* and felt hats with feathers. The exact style varies from area to area. In Munich and other towns, it is chic to wear jackets, suits or capes made of thick *Loden* cloth, usually green, sometimes stylishly designed by top couturiers. And a printed invitation to a smart society wedding in Munich may even stipulate that the wearing of Bavarian *Tracht* is obligatory!

The Bavarian Alps

The 'German Alpine Road' winds for some 480km along the foothills of the Bavarian and Allgäu Alps from Lindau on the Bodensee in the west to Berchtesgaden in the east. It is a marvellous trip to make, not only for the majestic mountain scenery, but for the many remarkable places along the way – 'fairytale' Neuschwanstein and the other Royal Castles, old towns such as Mittenwald and Oberammergau (scene of the famous passion play). It is a well engineered road, but not quite finished, so that you must make detours into Austria or down onto the plain: this itinerary descends to the lowlands to visit the Tegernsee, Chiemsee and other lakes (the little Fraueninsel on the Chiemsee is not to be missed).

There is good skiing in many places, notably around Garmisch. And at many points you'll find chair-lifts or cog-railways that will take you to the Alpine summits for roof-of-the-world views. In the picturesque sub-Alpine villages, many houses are still in traditional style – a whitewashed ground floor and wooden upper floor, with flower-filled balcony. Some houses have façades elaborately painted with bucolic or religious scenes. And some farmers still keep up the old custom of piling logs in front of their house for winter fuel. This used to be a token of prosperity: a girl from a family with high-piled wood was considered to merit a handsome dowry. From this the term *Holz-vor-der-Hütten* (wood-before-the-house) has come colloquially to mean 'a girl with lots in front'.

LINDAU (pop. 25,000), a Free Imperial City from 1275 to 1802, is set strikingly on a small offshore island reached along a causeway. It's a lovely and fascinating old town, but deluged with visitors all summer. A tall tower and the statue of a lion guard the entrance to the picturesque harbour, where the 13th-century fortified Mang tower stands by the promenade; nearby, from the terrace of the Römerschanze gardens, you get a sparkling view across the lake to the Austrian and Swiss pre-Alps. Among Lindau's many beautiful old buildings are the *Diebsturm* (brigands' tower) with its watchtowers and battlements; the 15th-century Altes Rathaus, finely frescoed; and the baroque Cavazzen House, now containing the civic museum (historical documents, some paintings). Lindau's suburbs, over on the mainland, include the smart new bathing resort of Bad Schachen.

East of Lindau, and north of the Austrian border, lies the rolling pastoral country of the **Allgäu**, whose dairy-farms produce some of Germany's best cheeses. As the B308 winds up into the foothills of the Allgäu Alps, it passes the hat-making town of Lindenberg, the ski-resort of Oberstaufen below the high Hochgrat, and Immenstadt with its 17th-century castle. To the south is the large Alpine resort of **Oberstdorf**, ringed by lime-stone heights and popular alike for summer hiking, winter skiing, and rock-climbing. From here you can drive into the Kleinwalsertal, a quaint Austrian enclave accessible only from Germany; or go by cable-car up the 2,250m Nebelhorn for superbly panoramic mountain views; or hike to the Breitachklamm gorges, seen at their best in winter when the ice hangs in drapes.

From Immenstadt a detour will bring you to **Kempten** (pop. 58,000), the Allgäu's capital, where the ancient Rathaus has a Renaissance staircase and the Heimat Museum is strong on local history. From here it's worth making a further big detour north to visit the huge baroque abbey of **Ottobeuren**, superbly ornate. It dates from the eighth century, but was rebuilt in the 18th by Johann-Michael Fischer and others: the organ and the carved choir-stalls are especially remarkable.

Back on the Alpenstrasse at Sonthofen, a very scenic mountain route leads to the resort of Hindelang, where the looping 'road of 106 bends', with fine views down into the Tyrol, climbs up to another resort, Oberjoch. To the north-east, beyond another Austrian enclave, is the scattered ski-resort of Pfronten: towering above it, on the crest of the Falkenstein, stands a mighty ruined castle that Ludwig II planned to restore *à la* Neuschwanstein. You can go by chair-lift up the nearby Hochalp (1,600m), or by cable-car up the Breitenberg (1,870m), for mountain walks amid majestic scenery. Further east, in a region of pretty lakes at the foot of high peaks, **Füssen** is a pleasant old alpine town in a gorge of the river Lech, close to an impressive waterfall by the Austrian border.

Füssen's old castle is less interesting than the strange 'Dance of Death' painting (c. 1600) in St Anne's chapel.

And so, via the village of Schwangau, you come to the two major tourist sights of this region – the extravagant royal castles of **Hohenschwangau** and **Neuschwanstein** (both open daily). The former, on a forested hill, was built in neo-Gothic style from the ruins of a feudal fortress, by Maximilian II in the 1830s. The eccentric Ludwig II spent much of his youth here: you are shown the music room that evokes his love of Wagner, and his bedroom whose ceiling was made to look like the sky at night (the stars could light up). Other rooms contain Biedermeier furniture and murals on chivalrous themes. For all its neo-Gothic blatancy, the castle does feel like a place that was once someone's home – unlike Neuschwanstein, which Ludwig built in the 1870s to please his romantic fantasy but then lived in for only six months. This absurd high-pinnacled pile, archetype of a German 'fairy-tale' castle, stands in a setting of snow-peaks, deep woods and a clear blue lake. Inside as well as outside, it resembles an operatic stage-set. The tourist hordes climb to it up a steep path, and are then escorted through rooms decked with chandeliers, marble and gilt panelling, and drenched in Wagnerian symbolism – the singers' hall that recalls *Tannhaüser*, the Great Chamber with its *Lohengrin* décor, the grotto full of stalactites and the neo-Byzantine throne-room.

At Steingaden, to the north-east, the Klosterkirche is interesting: this church, originally Romanesque, was remodelled in baroque style in the 18th century – like so many in Bavaria. Further east, set alone amid fields, is the even more remarkable **Wies** church, one of Germany's finest examples of rococo art. Built c. 1750 by Dominikus Zimmermann as a pilgrimage church, it is quite small and outwardly simple, but marvellously rich and light inside: above the frescoes and stuccoes is a splendidly ornate dome, symbolizing Christ in heaven.

East again, a signpost on B23 points to the splendidly-named spa of Bad Kohlgrub, evoking visions of inferior official hospitality in Bonn. Further south, the world-famous village of **OBERAMMERGAU** (pop. 5,000), set below wooded alpine foothills, evokes something entirely different. Its passion play stems from a vow made by the villagers after they narrowly escaped a plague epidemic in 1633. The play is presented every ten years (next in AD 2000) in May to September, with some 100 performances drawing audiences of over 500,000; it takes all day, with a break for lunch, and its cast of over 1,000 are all local villagers. The men grow suitably biblical beards. Usually an unwed girl plays the Virgin, and when a married mother-of-two in her thirties was picked for the part for 1990, there were some protests. But a far worse scandal that year was the fraudulent sale of some 70,000 fake tickets for the play, some 20,000 of them to British visitors. In any year, the village is worth a visit for its pretty painted houses – but not for its religious kitsch, aimed at the tourist trade. Woodcarving, on folksy or Christian subjects, is the main regular activity, but little of what you see in the shops is of much quality. However, some better products in a more modern style are displayed at the Pilatushaus co-operative, where sometimes you can watch bearded woodcarvers at work.

At **Ettal**, further along B23, a huge white abbey stands by the main road. Founded by Benedictines in 1330, it was – typically – rebuilt in baroque style in the 18th century, and has a fine cupola painted by Johann-Jakob Zeiller. To the west is **Schloss Linderhof** (open daily), another of Ludwig II's bizarre follies, but less ludicrously grandiose than Neuschwanstein. He built it in the 1870s in a mix of baroque and Renaissance styles, with imitation tapestries, ornate suites and French statues. More entertaining than the house itself is its park – waterfalls and terraces in the Florentine manner, a Moorish pavilion with bronze peacocks, a blue grotto imitating Capri's, and much else.

GARMISCH-PARTENKIRCHEN

(pop. 27,000), lying in a flat valley with mountains all round, is Germany's leading ski resort and the main town of the Bavarian Alps, also a major US Army centre. It's really two adjacent towns, with the railway between: Garmisch is the smart resort, Partenkirchen is older and more interesting. The Heimatmuseum in Partenkirchen is worth a visit: Bavarian carnival masks, ceramic ovens, painted cupboards and illuminated cribs, plus many historic photos and souvenirs of mountaineering in the area. Garmisch parish church has mediaeval murals and 16th-century Gothic vaulting. The composer Richard Strauss lived in Garmisch from 1908 until his death in 1949.

Skiing on the nearby heights is good from November to May, while many big annual events are held in the two giant Olympic ice and skiing stadia, built for the 1936 Winter Olympics. And there are enjoyable excursions to be made in the area. You can go up by cable-car to the summit of the Wank (1,780m), for fine views of the Wettenstein range to the south; and you can go by cable-car and on foot to the striking Partnachklamm gorge, south-east of Garmisch. But the star local attraction is the mighty **Zugspitze** (2,966m), claimed as Germany's highest peak though in fact it's astride the Austrian border. A road west from Garmisch leads to the charming dark-blue Eibsee, below the Zugspitze's towering rock wall; and either from here or from Garmisch a cog-railway will take you up as far as the Schneefernerhaus, where you board a cable-car from the mountain's summit. Here the wide views over the Austrian and Swiss Alps are sensational.

At Klais, east of Garmisch, a toll-road leads through the pinewoods to **Schloss Elmau**, a huge gabled mansion in a lovely secluded pastoral valley. It's an unusual kind of private-hotel-cum-cultural-centre (300 beds: see p. 156), worth a visit even if you don't plan to stay there. It was built during the 1914–18 War by the idealistic Johannes Müller, as a new kind of harmonious and informal community; and though his religious intentions are today less in evidence, in what has become a lay venture, it is still owned and run by his family. The conviviality is genuine, and meals are taken communally; the staff tend to be educated young ladies who mix with the guests as equals. Activities include lectures, painting, music and dancing classes, and concerts and music weeks where Yehudi Menuhin is sometimes present. The huge halls and long corridors give Elmau something of a boarding-school feel: but there's plenty of comfort.

Nearby is **Mittenwald** (pop. 8,000), a picturesque old town noted for the overhanging eaves and richly painted façades (rural scenes, etc) of many houses – quintessentially Bavarian. The best are in the Obermarkt and the Im Gries quarter. Inside the baroque church are fine frescoes; and outside is a monument to the town's local hero, Mathias Klotz (1653–1743), who imported violin-making to Bavaria after working in Cremona. The little Geigenbau- und Heimatmuseum (closed Nov, Dec, weekends) has a collection of old violins and other string instruments, and details of their history. Violins are still made by hand in Mittenwald and a technical school teaches the craft. Some of these violins are on sale – and so, in souvenir shops, are marzipan violins, or local liqueur in violin-shaped bottles. Indeed it's a very touristy town, and thick with traffic.

Mountains with rocky peaks – the Karwendel and Wetterstein – rise sheer above the town. A cable-car will take you up to near the summit of the Karwendel, for a stunning view. This is also a region of lovely blue-green alpine lakes. To the north, beyond the pretty village of Wallgau, is the Isar waterfall, which was made by diverting part of the water of the river Isar so as to fuel the Walchensee hydro-electric station. On the west side of this lake, a chair-lift leads up to the Herzogstand summit where the panoramic view of lakes, valley and high Alps is marvellous – even as far as the Grossglockner on a clear day.

The next lake to the north is the dark-blue Kochelsee, set between mountains and quiet pastures. On its south shore is a big power station and on the north is **Kochel**, a small resort where Franz Marc, the Expressionist painter, used to live (his home is now a

museum). The farms and villages in this part of Bavaria are so picturesque (flower-filled balconies, white lower walls, wooden slatted upper walls) that there seems less need than in northern Germany for an open-air museum of rural heritage and conservation. But just west of Kochel is the Freilichtmuseum of Upper Bavaria, where some 30 rural buildings have been regrouped by a stream. One handsome manor was moved here from the Chiemsee as recently as 1987. There's also a decorated maypole, an old watermill still turning, a flock of sheep, and a fine display of old cribs and *tableaux vivants*, most of them from a church at Bad Tölz. Craftsmen come sometimes to work in the museum – crib-carvers, saddlers, weavers, etc – to show visitors how these crafts used to be practised.

At **Benediktbeuern**, north of Kochel, a huge and stately abbey stands alone amid fields, its twin onion-domes visible from afar. Dating from the eighth century, it was once Benedictine: but since 1930 the buildings have been occupied by Salesian fathers who run a theology school there. The big 17th-century church and the little chapel of St Anastasia both have splendid frescoes. Curiously, in summer the abbey mounts an exhibition of models of fairy-tales which is even in the Guinness Book of Records. To the northeast is handsome **Bad Tölz** (pop. 13,000), still a living centre of Bavarian tradition: you'll see many people wearing *Tracht* in its streets, notably in the graceful traffic-free Marktstrasse which slopes to the Isar and is lined with lovely painted house-façades. On a hill high above the town stands an 18th-century chapel. And across the Isar is the modern spa, whose iodized

The delightful little Fraueninsel (women's island) on the Chiemsee.

waters are used in treating heart complaints.

East of Bad Tolz lies the **Tegernsee**, most popular of all the lakes south of Munich. Its shores are one string of busy resorts: but its clear sail-studded waters are still beautiful, with their backdrop of wooded hills and far peaks. On its west shore, the biggish spa of **Bad Wiessee** has sulphur and iodized springs that relieve rheumatism and blood and heart complaints. A larger and smarter resort, set round a beautiful bay at the lake's southern tip, is **Rottach-Egern**. It is in two parts. Egern, with its neat chalet-hotels by the water, is fairly quiet and residential; Rottach is trendier, full of bars, bou-

tiques and chic visitors – yet I have seen cows strolling down its main street as if they owned it. That's Bavaria. The Wallberg peak to the south (1,722 m) can be reached by cable-car – or indeed on foot. The main resort on the east shore bears the lake's name, Tegernsee: its Benedictine monastery, dating from the eighth century, was turned into a summer home by Maximilian I and now serves beer.

To the east, beyond the lake resort of Schliersee, a detour leads up to the remote and lovely little Spitzingsee, amid alps. East again, the skiing and hiking resort of **Bayrischzell** lies in a pretty valley, below the mighty Wendelstein (1,838m). This rocky peak can be reached either by new cable-car, or by a slow cable-railway up the north side from near Degerndorf, an old town with charming wood houses. From the upper cable station, to reach the very summit where the views are superb, you must take a steep walk up a path in the rock. The chapel here dates from 1718; the church lower down is popular for weddings.

Strike north-east across country into the plain and you'll come to the largest of Bavarian lakes, the **Chiemsee**. This is not an alpine lake, but its low wooded north and west shores are pretty, with the far peaks as a backdrop. Its main resorts are Prien, Gstadt and Seebruck, all popular for sailing and windsurfing, while writers and artists from Munich frequent the old village of Breitbrunn. But the lake's main attraction is its two little islands, the **Herreninsel** and **Fraueninsel** (there are frequent boat services to both, from Prien and Gstadt). The former was for Ludwig II and his court, the latter for nuns: hence the names of 'men's isle' and 'ladies' isle'. In the 1880s Ludwig built a kind of imitation Versailles on Herreninsel – a palace with formal French gardens, now open daily to visitors. It has a magnificent hall of mirrors, and a state room where in summer classical concerts are held by candlelight.

The intimate and beguiling Fraueninsel, all suffused with religious peace and feminine grace, is a total contrast – and I can think of few places in all Germany that enchanted me more. Benedictines have had a monastery here since AD 780, and their nuns (one of them is English) still live here. They run a girls' boarding school: and they still brew their traditional *Klostergeist*

('convent spirit') liqueur, that you can drink in their Klostercafé. The convent is closed to the public (it is often used for religious retreats), but you can visit its tiny 13th-century church, restored in Gothic style. Behind its elaborate altar are some charmingly naïve ex-votos, some by local fishermen giving thanks to St Irmengard, the island's saint. Visitors can inscribe their own appeals to the saint in a little book, where I read: 'Please help Granny to die soon, that she may not have to suffer', 'Please help my friendship with Helge to endure', 'Please help all AIDS victims' . . . and so on. Even a cynic might be touched. It is a lushly fertile island, and along its shore you will pass cottage gardens full of apple-trees and sun-flowers. Fishing-nets hang up to dry, birds sing, a violin plays gently.

The Chiemgau Alps south of the lake extend as far as Ruhpolding, a busy resort with charming old wooden houses. Here a cable-car ascends the Rauschberg (1,671m: superb views). The Alpine Road then leads through pastoral scenery to the icefield of *Gletschergarten* ('garden of glaciers') where you can study glacial erosion. The road winds along the deep Weissbach valley, to reach the major resort town of **Bad Reichenhall** (pop. 18,500), full of hotels: its main promenade, the Ludwigstrasse, is quite smart. The saline springs, used for treating pneumonia, are the largest and most powerful in Europe. You can take a guided tour (daily Apr–Oct, winter Tue, Thur only) of the old salt works that Ludwig I built in 1834 in grandiose 'mediaeval' style (the original machinery is still there). Also worth a visit is the stately white church of St Zeno, originally Romanesque, then remodelled as baroque. Note the gilt sculpture of the

Coronation of the Virgin on the sumptuous high altar.

The best scenic route from here to Berchtesgaden goes over the Schwarzbachwacht pass to the charming village of Ramsau; to its west, the Hintersee lies amid meadows backed by rocky peaks – a glorious setting. Finally the Alpine Road ends at renowned **Berchtesgaden** (pop. 8,000), set in a valley amid more high peaks. Few small German towns are more swamped by tourists, which is no surprise for it has so much to offer – superb skiing and scenery, intriguing salt-mines, splendid castle and museum, and not least the grisly appeal of its Hitlerian ghosts. The castle, for centuries an important Augustinian priory, was in 1810 acquired and secularized by the Wittelsbachs: Crown Prince Rupert, son of the last Bavarian king, lived here from 1923 till his death in 1955. He collected many of the treasures now displayed in its fine Renaissance rooms (cl Sat, open Mon): porcelain, tapestries, oriental art, and beautiful early German wood-carvings. The Gothic dormitory and 13th-century cloister are also impressive.

A guided tour (open Mon; cl Sun in winter) of the famous salt-mines is a mind-boggling experience – a didactic version of a Magical Mystery Tour. These mines, exploited since 1515, have always belonged to the Bavarian State: they yield some 500,000 cubic m of brine a year, which is refined at Bad Reichenhall into 150,000 tonnes of salt. First you have to put on grey traditional miners' clothes, plus a black felt hat and a leather pad for your bottom; women are given white trousers and blue hats. Then, sitting tight together, you ride on a little open train deep into the mine, where you hurtle down deep chutes. Your guide, a real miner, explains the old mining equipment (e.g. a brass pump used 1817–1930) and shows you a film of the mines' history which ends as a commercial for the best-known German brand of table-salt, mined here. Next you board a wooden boat and, as if crossing the Styx, are towed across an eerily-lit underground lake of black water. All in all, very clever PR – and great fun.

One notable excursion from the town is to Königsee village, where a boat will take you – and hordes of other trippers – along the long, thin **Königsee**, dramatically enclosed between the towering heights of the Kahlersberg and Watzmann. On the west bank you visit the remote 18th-century chapel of St Bartholomä. However, the classic local excursion is up to **Obersalzberg**, where Hitler built his grandiose mountain retreat. He first settled in a chalet here after his abortive *Putsch* in 1923, then had it much enlarged; here he welcomed many top-rank visitors, including Neville Chamberlain in 1938. The complex was smashed in an air raid in April 1945, and what was left the Allied forces then razed to the ground. A US army leisure centre now occupies the nearby Plattenhof, once a Nazi 'people's hotel'. But of Hitler's home, the infamous Berghof, only some overgrown slabs of masonry remain, and it is not signposted: today's authorities do not want neo-Nazi pilgrims to use it as a shrine, so they avoid publicizing it. However, the sign 'Cafe Türken' will lead you to a shabby hotel of that name, where a Turkish general once lived. Its owners were evicted by Hitler, but now they are again running it. They have made part of it into a little museum where you can climb down into part of the Berghof's derelict air-raid shelter; the foyer displays souvenirs and photos of the Berghof in its heyday, with Adolf and Eva enjoying domestic bliss. This tasteless venture is not featured in the local tourist brochures: but in a free society, I suppose it has to be allowed.

The scenery around Obersalzberg is stupendous. You can make a round-trip along the Rossfeld-Ringstrasse, Germany's second highest road: it offers grandiose views down over the Salzburg plain, and of the Hoher Goll and other peaks. For other stunning panoramas, you can also take a special bus to the Kehlstein summit (1,834m), along a road closed to cars, that Hitler had blasted in the cliffside. The pub on its summit is called 'Eagle's Nest', but Hitler never lived here.

TOURIST OFFICES

LINDAU: Hauptbahnhof, tel (08382) 50 22.

OBERSTDORF: Schlossstr. 8, tel (08386) 20 24.

OBERAMMERGAU: Eugen-Pabst Str. 9a, tel (08822) 49 21.

GARMISCH-PARTENKIRCHEN: Bahnhofstr. 34, tel (08821) 1 80 22.

MITTENWALD: Dammkarstr. 3, tel (08823) 10 51.

ROTTACH-EGERN: Rathaus, Nordliche Hauptstr. 9, tel (08022) 2 67 40.

BAYRISCHZELL: Kirchplatz 2, tel (08023) 648.

PRIEN AM CHIEMSEE: Rathausstr. 11, tel (08051) 30 31.

BAD REICHENHALL: Wittelsbacher Str. 15, tel (08651) 30 03.

BERCHTESGADEN: Königseerstr. 2, tel (08652) 50 11.

Accommodation, Eating and Drinking

LINDAU 8990 (tel code 08382):

(H)**Bayerischer Hof**, Seepromenade, tel 50 55: Smart hotel on the seafront, yet quiet; lake views, heated pool, flowery terrace; good fish dishes. Cl Nov–Easter. Rooms (95) B. Meals B–C.
(H)**Strand-Hotel Tannhof**, Oeschländer Weg 24, tel 60 44. On mainland at Bad Schachen; charming and intimate, with lakeside garden, heated pool. Cl mid-Mar to Oct. Rooms (29) B–C. Meals B–C.
(H)**Brugger**, Heidenmauer, tel 60 86. On the island, near car parks; useful overnight stop. No restaurant. Rooms (20) C–D.
(R)**Zum Sünfzen**, Maximilianstr. 1, tel 58 65. 14th-century house in the old town; good Swabian cooking. Cl Feb. Meals C–D.

OBERSTDORF 8980:

(H)**Wiese**, Stillachstr. 4a, tel (08322) 30 30. Best of the resort's many medium-price hotels: family-run, friendly and flowery; sun-terrace. No restaurant. Rooms (13) C.
(H)**Waldesruhe**, Stillachstr. 20, tel (08322) 40 61. Peacefully secluded, with Alpine views. Cl mid-Oct to mid-Dec. Rooms (40) C. Meals (cl Tue) C–D.
(R)**7 Schwaben**, Pfarrstr. 9, tel (08322) 38 70. Lots of Swabian ambience, good Swabian fare. Cl 4 weeks after Easter. Meals C–D.

SONTHOFEN 8972:

(H)**Kurhotel Sonnenalp**, tel (08321) 720. Large and luxurious, with health centre and all sports amenities (golf, riding, tennis, etc); lovely upland setting and superb breakfast buffet. Rooms (230) A. Demi-pension terms only.

OY-MITTELBERG 8967:

(H)**Mittelburg**, tel (08366) 180. Stylish rustic charm and *Gemütlichkeit*, in a health and skiing resort. Very good value. Rooms (31) D. Demi-pension terms only.

SEEG 8959:

(H)**Pension Heim**, Aufmberg 8, tel (08364) 258. Plain cooking but good Alpine views at this quiet and friendly family-run pension in a rural setting. Cl Nov–20 Dec. Rooms (18) C.

HOPFEN AM SEE 8958:

(H)**Alpenblick**, Uferstr. 10, tel (08362). Spruce and flowery, in the local style; lakeside setting and fine Alpine views. Good cooking. Rooms (46) C. Meals C.

FÜSSEN-WEISSENSEE 8958:

(H)**Weissensee**, on B 310, tel (08362) 70 95. Again, a lakeside setting and mountain views; alpine décor, cordial staff; good fish dishes. Cl mid-Jan to mid-Feb, mid-Nov to Christmas. Rooms (22) C–D. Meals C–D.

SCHWANGAU 8959:

(H)**Schlosshotel Lisl und Jägerhaus**, Neuschwansteinstrasse 1–3, tel (08362) 8 10 06. Romantic views of the floodlit Royal Castles, plus courtesy, comfort and fine food. Cl Jan to mid-Mar. Rooms (56) C–D. Meals C.

OBERAMMERGAU 8103:

(H)**Zur Rose**, Dedlerstr. 9, tel (08822) 47 06. Simple but very hospitable and *gemütlich* little inn; honest, copious cooking. Cl Nov to mid-Dec. Rooms (24) E. Meals D.

ETTAL 8107:

(H)**Benediktenhof**, Zieglerstr. 1, tel (08822) 46 37. Beamed 15th-century farmstead with rustic and baroque furniture; good food. Cl Nov to mid-Dec. Rooms (18) D. Meals C.

GRAINAU 8104:

(H)**Alpenhof**, Alpspitzstr. 22, tel (08821) 80 71. Quiet and charming, in local chalet style; garden, indoor pool, alpine views; decent Bavarian cooking. Cl Apr, mid-Nov to mid-Dec. Rooms (37) B–C. Meals C.

GARMISCH-PARTENKIRCHEN 8100:

(H)**Posthotel Partenkirchen**, Ludwigstr. 49, tel (08821) 5 10 67. Historic coaching-inn with lavish Bavarian décor; food good. Rooms (61) B–C. Meals B–C.

(H)**Buchenhof**, Brauhausstr. 3, tel (08821) 5 21 21. Central, in the old part of town; indoor pool, small garden. Cl mid-Nov to mid-Dec. No restaurant. Rooms (15) C–D.

(R)**Alpenhof**, Bahnhofstr. 74, tel (08821) 5 90 55. In the modern Spielbank (casino), but traditional in style; excellent food, very good value. Meals B–D.

KLAIS 8101:

(H)**Schloss Elmau**, tel (08823) 10 21. Large private hotel cum cultural centre, in secluded pastoral setting (see p. 149). Cl mid-Nov to mid-Dec. Rooms (300 beds) D. Full pension terms.

MITTENWALD 8102:

(H)**Alpenrose**, Obermarkt 1, tel (08823) 50 55. Mediaeval house with Bavarian décor but mod cons (indoor pool etc). Local cuisine, musical ambience. Rooms (44) C. Meals C–D.

(R)**Arnspitze**, Innsbrucker Str. 68, tel (08823) 24 25. Mountain views and excellent regional cooking. Cl 3 weeks spring, mid-Oct to mid-Dec. Meals C.

KOCHEL 8113:

(H)**Schmied von Kochel**, Schlehdorfer Str. 6, tel (08851) 216. Picturesque old inn with true Bavarian cooking and ambience; zither music. Rooms (34) C. Meals C.

BAD TOLZ 8170:

(H)**Hiedl**, Ludwigstr. 8, tel (08041) 90 21. Friendly and unassuming; good food in its Bürgerstuben. Rooms (16) D. Meals C–D.

(R)**Zum Alten Fährhaus**, An der Isarlust 1, tel (08041) 60 30. Old ferryboat station by the Isar, now elegantly done up in Bavarian style with excellent local cuisine to match. Cl Mon, Tue lunch. Meals B. Also 5 rooms, C.

BAD WIESSEE 8182:

(H)**Lederer am See**, Bodenschneiderstr. 9, tel (08022) 82 91. Sedate but fairly smart hotel by the lake; indoor pool. Cl Nov to mid-Dec. Rooms (98) B: demi-pension terms only.

(R)**Freihaus Brenner**, Freihaus 4, tel (08022) 8 20 04. Old farmhouse high above the lake, with fine views; atmospheric, very popular; some Bavarian specialities. Meals B–C.

ROTTACH-EGERN 8183:

(H)**Seehotel Überfahrt**, Überfahrtstr. 7, tel (08022) 66 90. Excellent, fairly sophisticated hotel by the lake; indoor pool, health centre. Rooms (124) B. Meals B.

TEGERNSEE 8180:

(H)**Fischerstüberl am See**, Seestr. 51, tel (08022) 46 72. Lovely lakeside setting, pretty terrace; good food, especially fish. Cl mid-Nov to mid-Dec. Rooms (20) D. Meals C–D.

BAYRISCHZELL 8163:

(H)**Romantik-Hotel Meindelei**, Michael-Meindlstr. 13, tel (08023) 318. Cosy, stylish and family-run; Bavarian décor a bit *too* heavily folksy. First-class food, elegantly presented; indoor pool. Cl 2 weeks spring, mid-Oct to mid-Dec. Rooms (17) C. Meals (lunch only) C.

SEEBRUCK 8221:

(H)**Malerwinkel**, tel (08667) 488. Attractive lakeside hotel with view of lake and Alps. Good, very popular restaurant. Rooms (23) D. Meals C.

CHIEMING-ISING 8224:

(H)**Zum Goldenen Pflug**, Kirchberg 3, tel (08664) 790. Set amid fields and meadows, a handsome rustic-style hotel with Bavarian furnishings; riding-school, sailing, golf, etc. Six restaurants. Rooms (55) C. Meals C.

BAD REICHENHALL 8230 (tel code 08651):

(H)**Kurhotel Luisenbad**, Ludwigstr. 33, tel 50 11. Classic, well-run spa-hotel, with large bedrooms, indoor pool, fitness centre, etc. Cl Nov to mid-Dec. Rooms (83) A–B. Meals B–C.

(H)**Hofwirt**, Salzburgerstr. 21, tel 6 20 21. In a quiet residential area; very good food. Cl mid-Jan to mid-Feb. Rooms (20) C. Meals (cl Mon) C.

(H)**Haus Seeblick**, Thumsee, tel 29 10. In a lovely isolated lakeside setting W of town; garden, nice views. Cl Nov to mid-Dec. Restaurant for residents only. Rooms (54) C–D.

(R)**Bürgerbräu**, Rathausplatz, tel 24 11. Typical old pub-cum-brewery; reliable Bavarian dishes. Meals D.

RAMSAU 8423:

(H)**Seehotel Gamsbock**, Am See 75, tel (08657). Beside the lovely Hintersee, good views, quiet simplicity; restaurant best for game. Cl Nov to mid-Dec. Rooms (26) D–E. Meals C–D.

BERCHTESGADEN 8240:

(H)**Krone**, Am Rad 5, tel (08652) 6 20 51. On a hill in the outskirts: charming family-run hotel with Bavarian painted furniture and good home cooking. Cl Nov to mid-Dec. Restaurant for residents only, cl lunch. Rooms (28) C.

(H)**Bavaria**, Sunklergäschen 11, tel (08652) 26 20. Snug and central, with mountain views. Cl Nov to mid-Dec. Restaurant for residents only, cl lunch. Rooms (29) D.

Regensburg, Passau and the Danube

The Danube, Europe's longest river after the Volga, rises on the edge of the Black Forest, then winds across south Germany to Austria, on its way to the Black Sea. This itinerary follows two bits of the middle Danube valley, around the graceful old cities of Passau and Regensburg, where the river traverses a broad, fertile plain, rich in livestock-breeding and wheat-growing. One pleasant way of seeing the Danube is by regular excursion boat. Or, as an alternative to following this valley, our route proposes a detour up into the Bavarian Forest (*Bayerischer Wald*), a long stretch of wooded upland near the Czech border (unlike the GDR's to the north, this frontier has never had a real defensive system, and since November 1989 it is open and friendly: but you should stick to the official crossing-points and avoid straying across accidentally in the forest). Nowhere very high, but often beautiful, the Bayerischer Wald is too wild and vast to have been spoilt by its mass of summer holiday-makers. It is

an area whose quaint old towns have preserved their folklore traditions – costumed pageants, etc – better than most in Germany.

West of Regensburg, the Danube thrusts its way dramatically through a gorge. Here we leave this river, to go up its charming tributary, the Altmühl, lined by rocky escarpments.

PASSAU (pop. 52,000), right on the Austrian border, is a bit like a smaller Salzburg. It stands on a narrow strip of land where two rivers, the broad Inn and the lesser Ilz, flow into the Danube between wooded hills. Today it is a key centre of Bavarian Right-wing Catholicism, and its citizens tend to be very conservative. In the Middle Ages it was a powerful bishopric, later a Free Imperial City, and these glories have bequeathed many fine buildings – notably the lofty green-cupola'd cathedral, whose spacious interior holds some notable paintings and a huge organ (17,000 pipes). This is played daily at noon in summer. Though later rebuilt in baroque style, the building was originally late-Gothic: for the best view of its noble

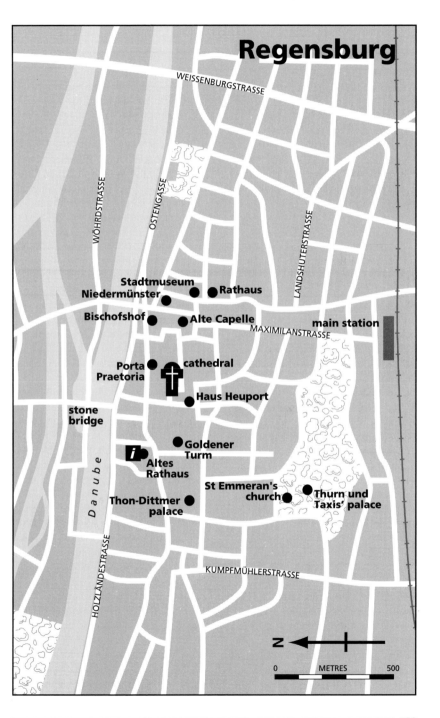

Regensburg

WEISSENBURGSTRASSE

WÖHRDSTRASSE

OSTENGASSE

LANDSHUTERSTRASSE

Stadtmuseum

Niedermünster ● ● Rathaus

Bischofshof ● ● Alte Capelle

MAXIMILANSTRASSE

main station

Porta ● cathedral
Praetoria

Haus Heuport

stone
bridge

Danube

● Goldener
Turm

Altes
Rathaus

St Emmeran's
church ● ● Thurn und
Taxis' palace

Thon-Dittmer ●
palace

HOLZLÄNDESTRASSE

KUMPFMÜHLERSTRASSE

N ←

0   METRES   500

east façade, in flamboyant Gothic, go to the lovely old Residenzplatz, flanked by handsome Renaissance mansions, one of them housing a little museum of toys. In the Rathausplatz by the Danube is a large museum of glass, opposite the ornately painted façade of the 14th-century Rathaus whose main halls are lined with frescoes of Nibelungen sagas. The big white hilltop fortress across the river, the Veste Oberhaus, was built by the local Prince Bishops in the 13th century, copying the fortress at Salzburg. From its terrace or tower you get a fine view of the old town, with its narrow streets and quiet river promenades, ideal for a stroll.

From Passau you could strike up into the Bavarian Forest – to Regen, where a lovely valley winds up to **Bodenmais**, a big, assertively Bavarian resort (flowery balconies, shops selling *Tracht*, etc): it has a museum of precious stones and a disused mineshaft open to visitors. The scenery of green meadows and pine-forests is glorious. Just to the north, near the Czech border, is the highest point of these hills, the Grosser Arber, where a chair-lift will take you to the summit (1,458m) for a sweeping panorama. The main road below it passes an impressive dark lake amid woods, the Arbersee. This road winds north-west through fine open country, via the pretty village of Lohberg and the busy upland resort of Lam, to reach one of the most fascinating places in Bavaria, the old walled town of **Furth Im Wald** (pop. 10,000). On the second Saturday of August a famous pageant is performed in its streets, the 'Drachenstich' ('dragon-sticking'), based on a mediaeval mystery play about St George and the Dragon: a young man and girl are

elected each year as the *Ritterpaar*, and the man has to slay the fearsome green monster, amid much mirth, music, and parading of bizarre floats. The 18-metre dragon, with engine and wheels inside, can be inspected all year; and the museum next to its hideout gives details of the pageant's history. It also has a room given over to the Czech area just across the border: this was seized by Hitler in 1938, and then after 1945 the Czech government in reprisal expelled its large Germanic minority, many of whom settled in the Furth area. For decades there was bitterness. But now the border is open, and new links are being formed.

Drive south from Furth and you'll reach the Danube at **Straubing** (pop. 42,000), another interesting old town. It is the market centre of a rich cattle-breeding and wheat-growing plain, and every August it hosts the boisterous *Gauboden* (fertile plain) festival, Bavaria's largest folk event after Munich's *Oktoberfest*. In the Stadtplatz is a fine Renaissance fountain and a 13th-century tower. And the cemetery of St Peter's church holds the tombstone of the tragic folk-heroine Agnes Bernauer, a Bavarian girl who was charged with sorcery and then cast into the Danube at Straubing in 1435, on the orders of a cruel Duke of Bavaria, her father-in-law. Her life has inspired many poems, operas and plays: one play, by Friedrich Hebbel, is staged every four years (e.g. 1993, 1997) in the ducal palace.

Some miles up the Danube is an unexpected sight – the Doric temple of **Walhalla**, on a hill above a bend in the river. Ludwig I had it built in 1842 to honour Germany's greatest men, and inside are some 200 busts and plaques of these soldiers, artists, scientists, etc.

More appetizing, to my mind, is the view upstream of ruined Donaustauf castle and Regensburg's spires.

REGENSBURG (pop. 128,000) is one of the loveliest of old German cities, radiating mellow warmth. Its mediaeval centre was undamaged in the war and has since been tastefully redecorated and smartened up, without loss of character; some of its narrow streets are now closed to traffic and delightful for a stroll, past the façades of the old houses, a mix of pinks, browns and yellows. Above soar the cathedral's twin spires, while the Danube floats by, beneath a mediaeval bridge. In the 13th century this was the largest and richest city in south Germany, and it has left a heritage not of grandiose buildings but of artistic intimacy and grace: it has a human scale, and along with the Bavarian cosiness its ambience seems in some ways Italian, too. Most un-Italian, though, is the **beer festival** known as *'Dult'*, held for two weeks in May, and two weeks in August/September.

Regensburg (also once known as Ratisbon) was colonized by the Romans as a fortress town on the Danube, and some relics of that time remain. From the sixth century it was a seat of the Dukes of Bavaria, and by the time it became a Free Imperial City, in 1245, it was immensely prosperous as a trading centre, where the culture of the high Middle Ages found full expression. Its merchants did much trade with Venice, over the Brenner Pass, and so they became influenced by Italian domestic architecture: many of them built themselves town mansions with towers, of the kind you still see in San Gimignano. The height of the tower was a symbol of wealth.

Regensburg used to have 60 of these patrician towers, and 20 survive in some form: they are unique north of the Alps.

In the 14th century, overtaken by the rise of Nuremberg and Augsburg, the city began a slow decline in prosperity (as a result, there was little new building, which has brought the benefit of preserving the mediaeval centre intact). But it remained politically important. It had long been occasionally the venue of the Holy Roman Empire's Imperial Diet; and when in 1663 this Diet became permanent – the first German parliament – its seat was the Regensburg Rathaus, as it remained until 1803. Then in 1810 the city was incorporated into Bavaria. Today it is a booming industrial centre, with new BMW, Siemens and Toshiba factories, amongst others. Its new university, opened in 1967, has 20,000 students, more than it can cope with. And the city's cultural attractions include the cathedral's famous boys' choir, the *Domspatzen* ('cathedral sparrows'), that often tours abroad. That name 'sparrows' gives some hint of the spirit of cosy whimsy that permeates this very *gemütlich* town – as you can see also from its ubiquitous jokey sculptures, both ancient and modern.

Even the **cathedral** has its share. This majestic but odd building is regarded as the finest Gothic church in south Germany: but it took 600 years to complete, for its high spires (105m) were not finished until the 19th century. Its west front has fine statues, while the lofty interior contains superb 14th-century stained glass (some was destroyed by bomb blast and has been replaced by decent modern glass). The baroque high altar is 17th-century; and near the transept is the famous 'laughing angel of Regensburg', a smiling statue that fits in with the tradition of whimsy. The lovely cloisters lead to the Allerheiligenkapelle (Romanesque) that has traces of frescoes. And, up on the roof, a comic statue of a man with a jug is said to be that of the building's first architect who threw himself off the tower after losing a bet. Not so whimsical blackbirds, homing in from the hills, swirl noisily round the cathedral at dusk every evening, then spend the night in the warmth of the steeples.

On the cathedral's north side is the Bischofshof, which from the 11th century was the bishop's home and is now a hotel (see p. 166). It faces a pretty patio containing the 'goose fountain', a modern comic sculpture of a fox disguised as a priest luring innocent geese (at a festival in September, beer flows from this fountain for all to buy, and the proceeds go to charity). An even quirkier sculpture, dating from the 14th century, stands in the porch of the handsome old Haus Heuport, facing the Dom's west front: it depicts the seduction of an imprudent virgin (note the snake, symbolizing evil, emerging from the seducer's back). The courtyard of this old fortified merchant's house has 14th-century hoists up near the roof, and a baroque 17th-century stairway.

Just to the west in the heart of the Altstadt are some of the old patrician tower-mansions with loggias, notably the Baumburger Turm and, highest of those still extant, the nine-storey Goldener Turm, with a wine-bar on its top floor. Close by, in a picturesque little square, is one of the city's finest buildings, the Gothic **Altes Rathaus** (1530). Inside you can visit (daily) the 16th-century electoral chamber, with a fine panelled ceiling, and the magnifi

cent *Reichssaal* (imperial hall) where the Diet met: it too has a lovely ceiling, also a 13th-century minstrels' balcony. In the basement were the prison and torture-chamber, and the latter is now a museum of torture: you can inspect gruesome old instruments such as stretching-machines, 'Spanish donkey' and 'Spanish block' (the cruellest torture devices came from Spain). The judges sat behind a screen, waiting for victims to confess.

In the attractive Haidplatz to the west is the recently restored Thon-Dittmer palace, whose lovely arcaded Renaissance courtyard is used for concerts in summer. A fish market is held daily in the little Fischmarkt near the river, and from here it's a short walk along the banks to Germany's oldest sausage-house (see p. 166), and to the equally famous 12th-century stone bridge over the Danube, quite a feat of mediaeval engineering: from it there's a good view over the town. Back in the cathedral quarter, take a look at the massive stone slabs of the Porta Praetoria, built by the Romans in AD 179 as part of their defences against the wild tribes beyond the Danube. There are several fine old churches round here – the Niedermünster, where excavations have recently unearthed the house altar of a Roman emperor; the baroque Carmelite church; and the Alte Capelle, an early Romanesque building (1002) later lavishly revamped in rococo style. The huge **Stadtmuseum**, in a nearby former monastery, has room upon room devoted to the town's history and culture, including a number of works by the great Albrecht Altdorfer, who in the early 16th century was a member of the city council. Among the museum's many local Roman finds are

Regensburg's Gothic cathedral, and its mediaeval bridge across the Danube.

some fourth-century Christian tomb-stones. Roman relics are still being dug up in this part of Bavaria: in 1989 some people working on a canal came across a platter full of some 170 Roman gold and silver coins.

After the Dom itself, probably the most interesting of the city's churches is **St Emmeran's**, which dates in part from the 8th century and has some of Germany's oldest Romanesque carv-ings, as well as a lavish baroque inte-rior; among its tombstone effigies is that of the understandably sad-looking Queen Emma who was executed in 1280. The church is part of a former abbey that since 1812 has been the res-idential palace of the Princes of **Thurn**

und Taxis: this famous family pio-neered the European mail service in the 15th century, and then held the monopoly of German postal services right up until 1867. This made their fortune, to such an extent that the pres-ent Fürst von Thurn und Taxis is said to be the richest man in Germany, worth some five billion DM. He owns many Bavarian timber forests, the largest Bavarian private brewery, and 17 per cent of all Regensburg's build-ings. He and his family spend part of each year in this abbey-turned-palace, which at other times is open to visits – and is worth a look for its Gothic clois-ter, Brussels tapestries in the state rooms, and museum of vintage cars.

The T und Ts come mainly in the hunting season, to shoot deer in their woods: one frequent guest was Franz Josef Strauss, and it was on a visit in 1988 that he suddenly collapsed, and then died in a local hospital. The present Fürst's wife Gloria, more than 30 years his junior, is a racy PR-conscious lady known as 'the punk princess'. The famous coffee-house-cum-confectioner opposite the Alte Rathaus, the Café Prinzess, founded in 1686, is now doing a nice line in luxury chocolates which it calls *'Kesse Gloria'* ('saucy Gloria'). The café's more traditional *'Barbara-Küsse'* ('Barbara's kisses') chocolates are named after a saucy local lady of the 16th century, Barbara Bromberg, mistress of Charles V. What with all this, the old sausage-house, a dumpling-inn and lots of student wine-taverns, you can see that Regensburg is quite a fun place.

Up the Danube from Regensburg is the little town of Kelheim, where on a hill above the river there stands an ugly yellowish rotunda, looking a bit like a gasworks. This is the **Befreiungshalle** (liberation hall), another of Ludwig I's pompous follies in honour of the new German nationalism. He had it built in 1842–63 to celebrate 'liberation' from Napoleon's rule, and within its high-domed interior are plaques of generals and female statues marking the German victories of 1813–15. The inscription reads, 'May the Germans never forget what made the struggle for freedom necessary.' Two world wars later, that sounds a shade ironic.

West of Kelheim, the Danube goes through the **Donaudurchbruch**, a spectacular defile that curves between limestone cliffs; beyond it, in a fine secluded setting, is the old Benedictine abbey of **Weltenburg**. You can visit both gorge and abbey by excursion boat from Kelheim (in summer), or go on foot through the woods, or by car to Weltenburg village. 'The Danube in Flames', a floodlit illumination of the gorge, takes place on the first Saturday of July. In the abbey's graceful baroque church (1718) is a striking statue of St George, above the high altar.

The little river **Altmühl** flows into the Danube at Kelheim. Its winding valley, prettily pastoral and lined with charming villages, is still undiscovered by mass tourism: a journey up it from Kelheim to Eichstätt is delightful. At **Prunn**, a small white castle (open to visits) stands theatrically atop one of the rocky cliffs that line parts of the valley. There are other hilltop castles further west, at Riedenburg and Kipfenberg, and at Arnsberg where the river curves between gentle meadows backed by cliffs. **Eichstätt** (pop. 14,000), an architectural showpiece, is a superior little episcopal city of classic elegance. The 14th-century cathedral, a mix of Romanesque, Gothic and baroque, contains the famous Pappenheim altar. Rococo mansions, neatly painted pale blue or yellow, line the Residenzplatz, crowned by a gilded statue of the Virgin. All is aesthetically impressive, but a bit like a stage set, with the Willibad fortress looming on a hill above. The town has a small private Catholic university. To the south-east, back on the Danube, the larger town of **Ingolstadt** (pop. 93,000) is closer to modern reality, with its oil refineries and Audi car factory. But it has remains of old ramparts, too, an attractive *Altstadt*, and several fine churches, notably the 15th-century Liebfrauenmünster.

TOURIST OFFICES

PASSAU: Höllgasse 2, tel (0851) 3 34 21.

FURTH IM WALD: Schlossplatz 1, tel (09973) 38 13.

STRAUBING: Theresienplatz 20, tel (09421)1 63 07.

REGENSBURG: Altes Rathaus, tel (0941) 5 07 21 41.

EICHSTÄTT: Domplatz 18, tel (08421) 79 77.

INGOLSTADT: Hallstr. 5, tel (0841) 30 54 15.

Accommodation, Eating and Drinking

PASSAU 8390:

(H)**Wilder Mann**, Schrottgasse 2, tel (0851) 3 50 71. Modernized 11th-century nobleman's mansion facing Danube; very good food in its **Kaiserin Sissi** restaurant (tel 3 50 75). Rooms (60) B–C. Meals B.

(H)**Laubenwirt**, Bräugasse 27, tel (0851) 3 34 51. Attractively set where the 3 rivers meet; terrace restaurant. Rooms C. Meals C.

(R)**Heilig-Geist-Stift-Schenke**, Heiliggeistgasse 4, tel (0851) 26 07. Picturesque house dating from 1358; garden. Cl Wed and 3 weeks Jan. Meals C–D.

HOHENAU 8351:

(H)**Romantik-Hotel Bierhütte**, tel (08558) 315. Up in the hills, a former brewery and glassworks, modernized in a folksy style; views and cooking both good. Rooms (43) C. Meals C.

GRAFENAU 8352:

(R)**Säumerhof**, Steinberg 32, tel (08552) 24 01. Superb sophisticated cooking and a personal welcome from the owner/chef. Cl lunch Mon–Wed. Meals B. 11 rooms, too, C.

FURTH IM WALD 8492:

(H)**Hohenbogen**, Bahnhofstr. 25, tel (09973) 15 09. Lively and unpretentious; café with dancing; cooking above average. Rooms (45) E. Meals C–D.

CHAM 8490:

(R)**Ratskeller**, Am Kirchplatz, tel (09971) 14 41. Rustic décor, friendly ambience, excellent local dishes. Cl Sun dinner, Mon, 3 weeks Jan. Meals C–D. 11 rooms too, D.

RETTENBACH 8449, near St-Englmar:

(H)**Gut Schmelmerhof**, tel (09965) 517. Chalet-style holiday hotel secluded in the hills; accent on sport and health (heated and outdoor pools, kids' playground); good food amid rustic décor. Rooms (32) C. Meals C.

STRAUBING 8440:

(H)**Seethaler**, Theresienplatz 25, tel (09421) 1 20 22. Central; good local dishes. Rooms (25) D. Meals (cl Mon) C–D.

REGENSBURG 8400 (tel code 0941):

(H)**Arch**, Am Haidplatz 4, tel 50 20 60. Charming hotel in an old building tastefully restored. No restaurant. Rooms (40) C.

(H)**Bischofshof am Dom**, Kräuterermarkt 3, tel 5 90 86. Former bishops' residence, now a *gemütlich* old inn. Good food, and so it should be: licensee/chef was private chef of Thurn und Taxis for 13 years. Patio/beer-garden. Rooms (67) D. Meals B–D.

(H)**Münchner Hof**, Tändlergasse 9, tel 5 82 62. Well-run and friendly, very central; cooking good. Rooms (40) D. Meals D.

(R)**Zum Krebs**, Krebsgasse 6, tel 5 58 03. In a mediaeval Altstadt house; small, cosy and stylish. Dinner only; Cl Sat, end Aug. Meals B.

(R)**Ratskeller**, Rathausplatz, tel 5 17 77. In historic building; reliable local cooking. Cl Sun dinner, Mon. Meals C.

(R)**Dampfnudel-Uli**, Am Watmarkt 4, tel 5 32 97. Former private chapel of Baumburger tower, now a quirky little dumpling-inn, run with whimsical panache by Uli Deutzer. Mainly steamed dumplings; some other simple dishes. Cl Sun, Mon, after 6 pm. Meals E.

(R)**Historische Wurstküche**, Weisse-Lamm-Gasse 3, tel 5 90 98. Tiny famous folksy place by the river, said to be Germany's oldest sausage-house (c. 1140). Till 7pm. Just sausages: E.

(B)**Bräuerei Kneitinger**, Arnulfsplatz 3, tel 5 24 55. Lively old wood-panelled beer-tavern, popular with locals; simple Bavarian dishes, well cooked. Cl Sun in summer. Meals E.

ESSING 8421:

(H)**Schneider**, Altmühlgasse 10, tel (09447) 354. Charming old riverside village inn, simple but friendly. Rooms (13) E. Meals (cl Mon) C–D.

INGOLSTADT 8070:

(H)**Bavaria**, Feldkirchener Str. 67, tel (0841) 5 60 01. Quiet residential setting; indoor pool. Rooms (58) D. Meals (dinner only; cl Sun, Christmas period). C.

Munich (München)

Stately baroque capital, glamorous centre of modern fashion, earthily extrovert city of thigh-slapping beer-drinkers – Bavaria's *Hauptstadt* (pop. 1,291,000) is all these things, and more.

The Wittelsbachs who ruled here have left it with a legacy of great palaces, museums and churches without parallel in Germany; despite wartime devastation, it remains a supremely elegant town. And against this baroque backdrop it plays out its pantomime as

Germany's capital of high-society sophistication, and of its showbiz, fashion and advertising worlds. It is the smartest German city, also the most exuberant, hedonistic, self-confident – and self-congratulatory. Müncheners, like other Bavarians, proclaim constantly that *they* are the best and have the best – the best beer, the best music and the best football team, Bayern München.

Munich has dubbed itself *'Weltstadt mit Herz'* ('world-class city with heart'), and certainly it is full of fun and feeling, even kitschy sentimentality. Whether it is truly world-class is a matter of opinion. The massive growth of new industry (Siemens, BMW, etc) has made it a key business centre, and its daily life has a fast, nervous tempo not unlike that of Paris: it's by far the most Paris-like of German cities – but without the true metropolitan touch of Paris. Beneath all the glamour and diversity, old hard-core Munich still has a certain parochialism, as witness the in-jokes in the cabarets. But it has been swamped by new arrivals and is very cosmopolitan: most inhabitants today were not born there. According to the surveys, this is the city that most Germans would prefer to live in if they left their own; and it is the prime destination of the upwardly-mobile middle classes. They are drawn in part by the delights of the nearby Alps and lakes – but less so by the climate, often marred by the *Föhn*, a dry, sultry headache-producing wind from the mountains.

Munich originated in the ninth century near a monastic settlement: hence the child dressed like a monk that is today its ubiquitous emblem. It became a trade centre under Henry the Lion in 1156. Then in 1180 it came under the Wittelsbachs: from 1255 it was their ducal residence, and from 1503 the capital of all Bavaria. During the Thirty Years' War the Wittelsbachs made it the stronghold of German Catholicism. In the 17th and 18th centuries they began to endow it with the palaces still surviving from that period, the Residenz and Nymphenburg. But it was in the 19th century that the city reached its artistic prime: Ludwig I (1825–48) first turned it into a magnificent European cultural capital, drawing artists and architects to his court, until his scandalous liaison with the Spanish dancer Lola Montez accelerated his abdication. After the death of 'mad' Ludwig II in 1886, the regent, Prince Luitpold, continued the work of grandiose construction (the new Rathaus, the Deutsches Museum, etc).

After 1918, when the Bavarian monarchy ended, the city entered a troubled period. In 1918–19 it was briefly taken over by a Bolshevik revolution under Kurt Eisner, which was put down by force. This episode made a great impression on the young Adolf Hitler, who was in Munich. The newly formed National Socialist (Nazi) party set up its headquarters here in 1919, and he became its leader; here in 1923 he staged his abortive *Putsch*. Hitler loved Munich, and though after 1933 he ruled from Berlin, he continued to hold major parades here, and he erected some hideous buildings, in one of which Chamberlain and Daladier signed away the Sudetenland in 1938. Some visible traces of this Nazi past survive today (see pp. 172–3). Müncheners are not too pleased with this legacy. But they take pride in the fact that their city was also a key centre of the anti-Nazi resistance: the brave 'White Rose' movement was active here in 1943, until its leaders,

Hans Scholl and his sister Sophie, both young students, were caught and executed. In the 71 Allied air-raids, some 10,000 buildings were destroyed. Some central streets were then hurriedly rebuilt in graceless style: but luckily most of the fine baroque churches and mansions were spared the bombs, or have been tactfully restored. In general, post-war planning has been intelligent, with few high-rise horrors. And the Olympic Games of 1972 gave the city the incentive to build a superb modern transport infrastructure, including three concentric ring-motorways and a gleaming super-efficient Metro. Sadly, the Games themselves were marred by a ghastly Arab terrorist outrage against the Israeli athletes' quarters, in which 16 people died.

Munich today is a major industrial centre. It used not to be so, but after the war Siemens and some other big firms moved their headquarters here from Berlin; BMW is here too, and MBB the aerospace firm, and these and other giants have created a spin-off effect, so that Munich has been expanding fast in electronics and other advanced industries. Chemicals, optics and publishing are also important. Politically, the city is to the Left of its Bavarian hinterland, and is ruled by a moderate SPD-led coalition. After the extremism of the inter-war years, it has returned to its old liberal tradition, and is remarkably permissive: witness the nude sun-bathing allowed in the parks (see p. 173).

Culturally, Munich ranks equal with Berlin as the main German centre of the arts: Berlin, like Frankfurt, is stronger on the avant-garde, while Munich's forte is more showy and conventional. It has an excellent opera, and one of Germany's top civic theatre companies, the Kammerspiele, as well as many fringe theatres. The range of good museums is finer even than a united Berlin's. In the early part of the century, the Schwabing district was a distinguished European intellectual forum – Brecht and Mann, Trotsky and Spengler, Klee and Kandinsky all lived there. Today that glory has faded. But many leading German writers, artists, musicians, etc, still choose to live in Munich; it has arguably Germany's best daily paper, the liberal *Süddeutsche Zeitung*, and two universities. It is also Germany's film-making capital, with major studios, and the leading centre of fashion and advertising, with a glossy and snobby social scene.

And it loves fun. The other side of the coin from the fashion shows and exclusive society balls is the great popular tradition of carnival and beer-drinking. This is not just laid on for tourists but belongs vibrantly to local life. There are scores of beer-gardens, and here in summer the Münchener go in big family parties to spread their picnics on the tables: some of these alfresco pubs are small and idyllic, some large and boisterous, such as the one at the Chinese pagoda in the Englischer Garten. Then in winter some make for the beer-halls, where thighs are slapped and brass-bands deafen, as sturdy pink-faced citizens roar out the choruses, arms linked, swaying together – '*In München steht ein Hofbräuhaus, Eins, Zwei, Gsuffa . . .*' But this unsophisticated image is perhaps more typical of small-town Bavaria than of the capital – save during the mighty annual *Oktoberfest* (see p. 175) when all inhibitions are cast aside. The other great annual spree is *Fasching*, as the pre-Lenten carnival is called in

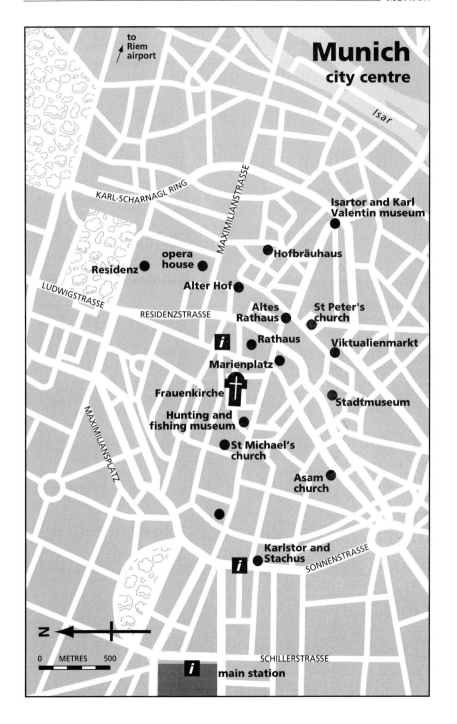

Munich
city centre

to Riem airport

Isar

KARL-SCHARNAGL RING

MAXIMILIANSTRASSE

Isartor and Karl Valentin museum

Hofbräuhaus

opera house

Residenz

LUDWIGSTRASSE

Alter Hof

RESIDENZSTRASSE

Altes Rathaus

St Peter's church

i Rathaus

Viktualienmarkt

Marienplatz

Frauenkirche

Stadtmuseum

MAXIMILIANSPLATZ

Hunting and fishing museum

St Michael's church

Asam church

Karlstor and **i** Stachus

SONNENSTRASSE

N

0 METRES 500

SCHILLERSTRASSE

i main station

south Germany. A young 'prince' and 'princess' are elected, and the fun goes on all night for several days, with hundreds of local masked balls as well as big processions.

Festivals and events in Munich include *Fasching* (early January to Shrove Tuesday); *Auer Dult*, a popular market and fair on Mariahilfplatz, held at the end of April, end of July and end of October; the opera festival, mid-July to mid-August (classical concerts are also held in summer in Schloss Nymphenburg, Schloss Schleissheim, Blutenburg, etc, and there's a music biennale every even year). From mid-September to the first Sunday in October is the celebrated **Oktoberfest**; and from the end of November to Christmas Eve the pre-Christmas market on Marienplatz.

Central Munich lies on the left bank of the Isar, a dull tributary of the Danube that offers little in the way of pretty city vistas or pleasant river walks. To the north are the major museums, the bohemian/intellectual/night-life district of Schwabing, and the Englischer Garten, a huge park. To the west is Nymphenburg palace; to the east and south, the Landtag, the Deutsches Museum, the zoo and the film studios. In the centre is the **Altstadt**, bounded by a ring-road where three of the old city gates still exist. Parts of this compact Altstadt are now a pedestrian zone, pleasant for strolling. Very little of it is mediaeval and much is modern: but many splendid classical buildings survive, such as the Residenz palace and a clutch of churches whose pealing bells at evensong make a stirring sound.

The Altstadt
The mighty **Residenz**, former home of the Wittelsbach rulers, is a vast complex of buildings erected between the 16th and 19th centuries, with seven inner courts; parts are Renaissance, parts rococo, parts neo-classical. Though it was badly bombed, many of its sumptuous furnishings were spared, and it has been well restored; you must buy separate tickets for the different guided tours of its various parts. In the oldest part is the Antiquarium (1571), a magnificent vaulted chamber, very long, its ceiling covered with lively frescoes. Adjoining it are State rooms in lavish rococo style, and halls hung with paintings of the Nibelungen. A highlight not to be missed is the former court theatre (1751), a jewel of rococo art by the Walloon architect Francois Cuvillies. In the Königsbau is the Schatzkammer (treasury) whose amazingly rich collection includes an 11th-century cross made for Queen Gisela of Hungary, a marvellous jewelled gold statuette of St George and the dragon, made in Munich in c. 1590, and exotic works from Persia and Turkey. The Residenzmuseum has rooms full of Meissen porcelain and portraits of Wittelsbach ancestors, including Charlemagne. The Festsaalbau and the 17th-century *Hofkapelle* (court chapel) are also notable.

On the north side of the Residenz is the former royal park, the pleasant and flowery Hofgarten, which leads to the grandiose bombed-out hulk of the former Bavarian Army Museum: this was long left as an anti-war memorial but is now being refurbished as a museum of Bavarian history. Just opposite the Residenz is another grim souvenir, the Feldherrnhalle portico where Hitler's 1923 *Putsch* was nipped in the bud, in a shoot-out that left 14 Nazis dead.

Behind it rise the yellowish towers of a stately church, the 17th-century Theatinerkirche, with a baroque 18th-century façade by Cuvillies. The episcopal palace down a side-street behind it is also the work of Cuvillies.

On its south side the Residenz abuts the State Opera House, at the top of **Maximilianstrasse**. This is the city's smartest street, lined with exclusive galleries and fashion boutiques: on its way to the river, it leads past Munich's premier luxury hotel, the Vier Jahreszeiten; the main civic theatre, the Kammerspiele; and a modest museum of non-European ethnography (Völkerkunde). Maximilianstrasse, Theatinerstrasse and Maffeistrasse are the focus of Munich's wealth and glamour, where you will see the most chic women, and the most opulent cafés, stores and banks. But turn off Maximilianstrasse into the network of little streets to its south, and at once you're in a different world, that of the raucous populist beer-halls. On the Platzl square is the largest and most famous of them, the **Hofbräuhaus** (see p. 179), where (*inter multa alia*) Hitler in January 1923 launched his political programme. Nearby, quite a contrast, is the Alter Hof, a tall, appealing 13th-century building (restored) around a nice courtyard: here the Wittelsbachs resided from 1253 to 1474.

The smallish **Marienplatz** has for centuries been the hub of the city's life, and in a way it still is. Here the great pre-Christmas market is held. And all year round you'll find an impromptu carnivalesque scene, full of buskers, street-musicians, political demonstrators – and of course tourists, who come mainly to look at the Glockenspiel that performs daily at 11 am (also 5 pm in summer) on the façade of the grandi-

ose neo-Gothic **Rathaus** (1867–1908): the girating copper figures of this two-tier carillon depict, above, a ducal wedding of 1568 and, below, a coopers' dance of 1517, aimed at cheering up citizens during a plague. The tower of the Rathaus affords a good view over the town. The marble column in the square, bearing aloft a Madonna, was erected in 1638 to commemorate the sparing of the city in the Thirty Years' War. On the eastern side is the romantic silhouette of the Altes Rathaus – a stepped-gable façade and a pinnacled Gothic tower, both rebuilt in 15th-century style. They stand opposite the Gothic church of St Peter, Munich's oldest (superb view from its tower). The broad Tal shopping-street leads from here to the stocky Isartor (1337), best preserved of the old city gates. This contains a notable curiosity, the **Karl Valentin Museum**, devoted to the life, jokes and political crusades of this famous Munich comedian and folk-hero (1882–1948) who has been called 'the German Chaplin'. Whimsical exhibits include 'a jar of Berlin air', also many vivid souvenirs of pre-war Munich.

Not far away is the **Viktualienmarkt**, for the past 200 years the city's main outdoor food-market, known for its excellent fresh produce (not cheap), its cheeky saleswomen and its cafés and pubs loud with gossip. Beyond it you'll find the remarkable **Stadtmuseum**, which besides Munich history has sections dealing with cinema, brewing and puppets: note the set of ten carved wooden Morris Dancers (1480) by Erasmus Grasser. The museum puts on brilliant special exhibitions, too. To its west, in Sendlingerstrasse, is the delightful **Asamkirche** (1733), a rococo marvel of frescoes, sculptures and stuccowork, harmoniously designed by the Asam brothers. Back nearer the Marienplatz, the Kaufingerstrasse is the city's main pedestrian shopping mall, rather down-market (Wool-worths, etc); and just beyond it is the late-Gothic cathedral, **Frauenkirche** (1468), whose tall twin onion-domed towers are almost as much a symbol of Munich as the Eiffel Tower is of Paris. Its exterior of worn red brick is sombre; inside, the lofty nave is white and bright. The modern pulpit and altar (war damage was heavy) contrast with surviving ancient works, such as the 17th-century mausoleum of Emperor Ludwig, 24 carved 15th-century busts of the Apostles by Grasser, and the 14th-century stained glass in the north chapel.

On Kaufingerstrasse, a disused baroque church contains the German Hunting and Fishing Museum (*Jagd und Fischereimuseum*), full of stuffed fish, stags' heads, old guns, and other objects of doubtful interest. Next door, the handsome and spacious church of **St Michael** (1583), with its Renaissance façade and huge barrel vault, holds in its crypt the tombs of Wittelsbachs, including poor Ludwig II. Going down Neuhauserstrasse, you will pass the Richard Strauss fountain (he was born in Munich), decorated with scenes from his opera *Salome*. At no 48, the church oddly named Bürgersaal holds the tomb of Father Mayer, a bravely outspoken anti-Nazi who was its parish priest during the war and narrowly escaped execution. And so you will come to the Karlstor, another old city gate, where the wide Karlsplatz (also called Stachus) is one of Munich's main meeting-points.

North of the Altstadt:
the Museums and Schwabing:

Five of the city's art museums are just north-west of the Altstadt. Three of them stand around the Königsplatz, a broad square that Ludwig I lined with colonnaded neo-classical buildings looking like Greek temples. One of these, the **Glyptothek**, houses Ludwig's collection of Greek and Roman statues, some of them removed from the Temple of Aphaia on Aegina (c. 500 BC). The **Antikensammlung**, just opposite, is a collection of classical Greek vases, some for domestic use, others for funeral worship; there is also some lovely jewellery from the ancient world. Entirely different from these two museums is the **Lenbach-haus**, a graceful Florentine-style villa that was the home of the Bavarian painter Franz von Lenbach (1836–1904); it now houses his rather dull paintings, and better work from the so-called Blauer Reiter (Blue Knight) group that included Kandinsky, Marc and later Klee. Contemporary stuff includes some provocative collages by Beuys. This is not my favourite Munich museum. Nor am I enamoured of the Music School on nearby Arcisstrasse, but for other reasons: this gloomy edifice was built by Hitler as his Munich headquarters, and from its balcony he reviewed parades. Here too the notorious 'Munich' summit of September 1938 was held. It seems curious that the city has not pulled it down.

Up the street is the huge **Alte Pinakothek**, one of Germany's two or three greatest art museums, notable for its marvellous collection of German Old Masters. It was built in 1826–36 in Venetian Renaissance style, to house the paintings collected by the Wittels-bachs since the 16th century. Altdorfer's majestic crowd-scene, *The Battle of Alexander* (1525), and his more intimate and colourful *Suzannah in the Bath*, are two of its most striking works. Note also Dürer's *Self-Portrait* and *Four Apostles*, and works by Grünewald, Cranach, Grien, and the Tyrolean Michael Pacher. The Dutch and Flemish schools are well represented (Rubens, Van Dyck, Rembrandt, Franz Hals, etc); from Italy there are works by Raphael, da Vinci and Tiepolo; not much from France, but some fine El Grecos and Murillos from Spain. The smaller **Neue Pinakothek**, in a new building replacing one wrecked in the war, has mainly 19th-century works, Romantic, Neo-classical or Impressionist. Friedrich's dreamy landscapes, and Carl Spitzweg's affectionate scenes of daily life (he was a Münchner) are the best of the German works; Monet and Manet, Gauguin, van Gogh and Klimt are also all in good form.

Two other art museums are northeast of the Residenz, on Prinzregentenstrasse. The **Bayerisches Nationalmuseum**, in a large gloomy building, was founded in 1855 to house Bavarian art treasures. Folk art, including cribs, is on the ground floor; upstairs is an array of tapestries, porcelain, jewellery, icons, of interest mainly to specialists. Notable are the 15th to 16th-century wood sculptures, by Riemenschneider and others. There is also an Italian Renaissance section. The **Staatsgalerie Moderner Kunst** is in a building erected by Hitler to enshrine Nazi principles of art. There he derisively put on a show of the 'degenerate' modern art that he loathed – just the kind of art that today this museum proudly displays! Its 'degenerates' include Ernst and Nolde, Dix and

Beckmann, also Picasso, Dali and Magritte; plus 'pop art' moderns (Warhol, etc) that Hitler might have equally loathed.

From the Odeonsplatz near the Residenz, the Ludwigstrasse, a stately neo-classical boulevard, leads past the State Library to the central buildings of the huge University. Just beyond is **Schwabing**, the famous district that corresponds roughly to Chelsea-plus-Soho or St-Germain-des-Prés. As an intellectual centre it is past its prime, and Munich's true avant-garde has left it for Haidhausen (see below). But many writers and film-makers such as Hans Magnus Enzensberger still live here, in high 19th-century town houses looking slightly seedy. And Schwabing still teems with students, and has scores of little fringe theatres, art cinemas, arty pubs and bistros. The Leopoldstrasse, its main avenue, can be magical on a summer evening, in its gaudy way – milling crowds, art-students hawking their wares, and French-style terrace-cafés. The Soho-like nightlife sector is east of Leopoldstrasse: Alt-Schwabing, Schwabinger Brettl and Mutti Bräu are among its most typical pubs. Here the once-famous political cabaret *'Lach und Schiessgesellschaft'* ('Laugh and Shoot Society') just about survives.

The **Englischer Garten** to the east of Schwabing, created in 1793 by an American-Briton, Count Rumford, claims to be Europe's largest city park, four miles long. It has a Chinese pagoda, a small Greek temple (the Monopteros), boating lakes, several beer-gardens, and woodland walks where you might be in deep country. On its lawns in summer, Munich youth besports itself in the style of the St Tropez beaches: this is tolerated, save

The baroque spires of old Munich, backed by the Bavarian Alps.

when girls step naked out of the park into city trams, as has been known to happen. North-west of Schwabing is the **Olympiapark**, built for the 1972 Olympics and now a mammoth sports and leisure complex: open-air pop and rock concerts are held here on summer weekends. Its main stadium has a curious seven-hectare curly roof of acrylic glass, looking like some giant fish-net hung out to dry. The 290 metre Olympiaturm, now a TV tower, is worth ascending (open daily) for a stupendous view as far as the Alps; the

Olympic Village built to house the athletes is now blocks of flats; and the grassy hill to one side was made out of rubble collected from the war bombing. Nearby, the strange modern tower in the shape of four linked cylinders is the **BMW headquarters**: the equally odd bowl-shaped building below it houses a museum (open daily) of BMW cars and motor-bikes, with the accent on modern high-tech.

At Oberschleissheim, in the northern outer suburbs, the two Schleissheim châteaux are worth visiting. The smaller Altes Schloss contains a surprise: a newly-opened museum of Christian folk-art from 60 countries, including decorated Polish Easter eggs, Provençal *santons*, vivacious religious paintings from Latin America, even Tibet, all collected over the years by Professor Gertrud Weinhold. Some if this art is kitschy, some truly lovely, and all is fascinating. The larger and more conventional Neues Schloss is by comparison a bit dull – a long white palace (1701–27) whose ornate State rooms are hung with Rubens, Velasquez, Breughel, etc, not at their best. Concerts of baroque music are held here in summer. The hunting-lodge at the far end of the gardens holds a notable collection of Meissen porcelain.

East and South of the Altstadt

Above the east bank of the Isar stand a number of imposing edifices. The 19th-century Friedensengel, a golden 'angel of peace' on a high monumental pillar, towers up on the Prinzregentenstrasse. The grandiose palace to its south, the Maximilianeum, was built for Maximilian II in the 1850s and now houses the Bavarian parliament. South again, it's the turn of a modern building, the huge red-brick Gasteig

Kulturzentrum, erected in the mid-1980s as a multi-purpose cultural centre: it contains a concert hall, library, theatre, etc. Just to its east is **Haidhausen**, a former working-class district that has been taking over much of Schwabing's role as the true centre of the avant-garde and the 'Alternative': it has filled up with arty bars and trendy galleries, jazz-clubs, health stores and craft-shops.

On an island in the river is Munich's largest museum and the foremost in Germany for science and technology: the **Deutsches Museum** (open daily), dating from 1925. Its titanic hangar-like rooms contain every kind of train, carriage, boat and aeroplane, including a real Starfighter. There are reconstructions of 16th-century chemists' workshops, coal-mines, Lascaux caves, etc. Some of the exhibits look dated: but a new Telecomm section has been added. All is very well laid out. Five km upstream is the city's large zoo, **Hellabrunn**, where many of the animals live in liberty in a spacious park. And further south again, at Geiselgasteig, are Germany's biggest film studios, Bavaria Filmstadt (guided tours daily, Apr–Oct). Here you have almost reached the smart suburb of **Grünwald**, where many rich Münchners have villas; there are pleasant woodland walks here beside the Isar.

West of the Altstadt: Nymphenburg

The Theresienwiese, a big park and fairground south-west of the main station, is the site of the world's largest and best-known beer-festival, the **Oktoberfest**, held from mid-September to the first Sunday in October. Dating from 1810, when the engagement of Prince Ludwig (later Ludwig I) to Princess Theresa was celebrated here, it has since swollen into a massive annual jamboree, commercialized and vulgar in some ways, yet exhilarating, and hugely popular with Bavarians (hordes of tourists come too, and you need to book a hotel well ahead). On the opening day, great horse-drawn wagons of the local breweries arrive amid brass-bands and much pomp; next day there's a big folklore procession from the town centre. During the 16 days, some four million litres of beer are consumed, two oxen are roasted daily; and by the end of each night, *Bierleichen* ('beer-corpses') lie totally sozzled on the floors of the giant beer-tents. In the afternoon, when family parties come, the scene is more salubrious – but always raucous. And over it all looms the 35-metre statue of Bavaria.

A contrast indeed is provided by serene and elegant **Nymphenburg**, one of Germany's loveliest formal palaces and parks. Begun in 1664 in the Italian style, then expanded over the next 100 years, this was the Wittelsbachs' summer residence. The principal building has a splendid rococo banqueting hall, all gold, white and green, with lively frescoes; in the south wing is a Chinese laquer room, a museum with handsome old royal horse-carriages and sleighs, and a gallery of portraits of beautiful women of Ludwig I's time, including his mistress, Lola Montez. Concerts are often held in the palace. Nymphenburg's supreme jewel however is the Amalienburg hunting-lodge designed by Cuvillies: outwardly modest looking, it has sumptuous interior decoration, notably in the hall of mirrors and the panelled central room with its ken-

nels for hunting-dogs. The park itself is in parts very formal, like Versailles, with Grecian statues and waterways (Resnais filmed *Last Year in Marienbad* here): but other parts are wild and romantic, with woods and lakes. Here you'll find the octagonal Chinese-style Pagodenburg, the ornately ceilinged *Badenburg* (bathing pavilion) and fine botanical gardens (open daily).

On the city's western fringe, in Obermenzing, is the charming church and ex-monastery of **Blutenburg**, set amid fields by the river Würm: today it houses an international youth library, and summer concerts are held in its courtyard. Lastly, out to the south-west of Munich are two pleasant lakes, the **Starnbergersee** and **Ammersee**, lined with bathing-resorts and popular with day-trippers from the city – 'Summer surprised us, coming over the Starnbergersee with a shower of rain', wrote one visitor, T.S. Eliot, in *The Waste Land*. In 1886, King Ludwig II was due to be interned in his lakeside castle at Berg, after being deposed: but instead he mysteriously drowned himself, and it has never been clear whether this was suicide or an accident; the site is marked by a cross in the water near Berg. Starnberg, the leading resort, has its own Wittelsbach castle, and a museum of local history. The north part of the shore is built up, but beyond Tutzing it becomes pleasantly pastoral. East of the Ammersee stands the Benedictine priory of **Andechs**, once a major pilgrimage centre. Its pink Gothic church, later remodelled in rococo style, has a sumptuous rococo interior; concerts are held here in summer. The monks who still inhabit Andechs brew a famous strong beer, which you can enjoy in the priory's pub and beer-garden.

Dachau Concentration-Camp

Of all the former Nazi prison camps in Germany that are now museums and memorials to those who suffered and died there, this is perhaps the most moving – after Buchenwald, in Saxony. It is north-west of Munich, on the edge of the pleasant town of Dachau (follow the discreet signs 'KZ', *Konzentrationslager*). Whereas Belsen camp (see p. 239) was razed to the ground, here many of the buildings still exist, and some have been reconstructed so as to give a harrowing picture of camp life. You can inspect two barrack-huts, which by 1945 were each housing 400 prisoners in rooms intended for 40. You can see the crematorium and its ovens, and the gas-chamber that the Nazis disguised as a shower-room, as at Auschwitz: but it was never used for extermination, for though Dachau was the first concentration camp that Himmler opened, in 1933, it was used mainly for non-Jewish political prisoners and so was not essentially a 'death camp'. Its offices are now a museum that vividly traces the rise of Nazism and the torture methods used in the camp. In the grounds are Catholic and Protestant chapels and a Jewish memorial.

TOURIST OFFICES

Main station, tel 239 12 56; Rathaus, tel 239 12 72; airport, tel 239 12 66.

Accommodation, Eating and Drinking (Post code 8000, tel code 089)

The huge concentration of hotels in or near the centre includes some inexpensive *pensions* in the Schwabing area or by the station, but these tend to get booked out well ahead. There are some delightful hotels in such outer suburbs as Obermenzing, Grünwald and Ismaning. Restaurants of all nationalities abound. Of those with a Bavarian flavour, many of the best are also in the suburbs, in a garden setting. If you want to eat cheaply in the local manner, in a lively ambience, try one of the countless beer-houses or beer-gardens: most of these serve snacks or simple food as well as great tankards of beer, and at many beer-gardens you can bring your own picnic and eat it on the long trestle tables, while chatting with your neighbours. This is a hugely popular pastime with Münchener in summer. Some of the best beer-gardens are around the Englischer Garten, or in the suburbs.

(H)**Vier Jahreszeiten Kempinksi**, Maximilianstr. 17, Munich 22, tel 23 03 90. Munich's premier hotel, very palatial, used by many top visitors. Rooftop pool; several restaurants. Rooms (344) A. Meals (cl Aug) A; Bistro Eck C.

(H)**Bayerischer Hof**, Promenadeplatz 6, Munich 2, tel 212 00. Elegant period furnishings in its adjacent **Palais Montgelas** annexe. Heated rooftop pool, sauna. Rooms (442) A. Three restaurants (Palais Keller is cheapest), A–D.

(H)**Trustee Parkhotel**, Parkstr. 31, Munich 2, tel 51 99 50. Efficient little modern hotel west of centre, near station and Theresien Wiese. Courtyard. Cl Christmas. Rooms (36) A. Meals C.

(H)**Romantik-Hotel Insel Mühle**, Von-Kahrstr. 87, Munich 50-Untermenzing. Restored 16th-century mill by a stream in western suburbs, stylish and idyllic. Good local cooking; beer-garden. Rooms (37) A–B. Meals (cl Sun) B–C.

(H)**Schloss-Hotel Grünwald**, Zeillerstr. 1, 8022 Grünwald, tel 641 79 35. Just S of Munich, a former ducal hunting-lodge, now a smart inn by the Isar; antiques, nice views. Cl 2 weeks Jan. Rooms (16) B–C. Meals B–C.

(H)**Forsthaus Wörnbrunn**, in Grünwald forest, 8022 Grünwald, tel 641 78 85. Woodland setting, rustic décor; beer-garden. Good food. Rooms (17) B–C. Meals B–C.

(H)**An der Oper**, Falkenturmstr. 10, Munich 2, tel 290 02 70. In side-street near opera; friendly and personal. No restaurant. Rooms (55) B–C.

(H)**Reinbold**, Adolf-Kolpingstr. 11, Munich 2, tel 59 79 45. Near station but not noisy. No restaurant. Rooms (61) B–C.

(H)**Biederstein**, Keferstr. 18, Munich 40, tel 39 50 72. Modern and spruce, in quiet part of Schwabing. No restaurant. Rooms (31) C.

(H)**Gästehaus Englischer Garten**, Liebergesellstr. 8, Munich 40, tel 39 20 34. Creeper-covered millhouse by a stream in Schwabing. Annexe rooms less comfortable. No restaurant. Rooms (14) C.

(H)**Marienbad**, Barerstr. 11, Munich 2, tel 59 55 85. Central but quiet, near Alte Pinakothek. No restaurant. Rooms (27) C.

(H)**Fischerwirt**, Schlossstr. 17, 8045 Ismaning, tel 96 48 53. 14 km N of city centre: friendly modern inn with small garden. Rooms (44) C–D.

(H)**Am Sendlinger Tor**, Blumenstr. 40, Munich 2, tel 23 18 80. Modern, central and comfortable. No restaurant. Room (33) C–D.

(H)**Gästehaus Monopteros**, Oettingerstr. 35, Munich 22, tel 29 23 48. Friendly little *pension* near Englischer Garten. Rooms (11) D.

(H)**Pension Erika**, Landwehrstr. 8, Munich 2, tel 55 43 27. Simple *pension* west of centre, near station. Rooms (20) D.

(R)**Aubergine**, Maximiliansplatz 5, tel 59 81 71. Munich's top restaurant, intimate and elegant: distinguished modern cooking, clientele to match. Cl 2 weeks Aug, Christmas, Sun, Mon. Meals A.

(R)**Bogenhauser Hof**, Ismaningerstr. 85, tel 98 55 86. Small and fashionable; excellent cooking. Cl Sun, Christmas. Meals A–B.

(R)**Käferschenke**, Prinzregentenstr. 73, tel 41 681. Also in Bogenhausen and trendy; fine food; delicatessen and café, too. Cl Sun. Meals A–B.

(R)**Halali**, Schönfeldstr. 22, tel 28 59 09. Near Hofgarten. Pretty rustic décor; modern and local cooking. Cl Sun, 2 weeks May. Meals B–C.

(R)**Seehaus**, Kleinhesselohe 3, tel 39 70 72. Charming lakeside setting in Englischer Garten; outdoor terrace. Meals B–C.

(R)**Ratskeller**, Marienplatz 8, tel 22 03 13. In cellars of Rathaus; full of Bavarians tucking into huge platefuls. Meals C.

(R)**Schlosswirtschaft zur Schwaige**, at Schloss Nymphenburg, tel 17 44 21. Most sympathetic: pretty décor, elegant beer-garden, sound local cooking. Meals C.

(R)**Franziskaner**, Perusastr. 5, tel 22 50 02. Large, popular, typically Munich, and central. Sound Bavarian cooking. Meals C–D.

(R)**Spatenhaus**, Residenzstr. 12, tel 22 78 41. Like Franziskaner but smaller; warm ambience, good Bavarian food. Meals C–D.

(R)**St Emmeramsmühle**, St Emmeram 41, tel 95 39 71. By the Isar in Unterfohring: Bavarian décor, trendy lively clientele, good local cooking, and a big beer-garden for summer. Super. Meals C–D.

(R)**Weichandhof**, Betzenweg 81, Obermenzing, tel 81116 21. In western suburbs: idyllic riverside setting, pretty garden, cosy décor, good local cuisine. Super place: best forget it was Hitler's favourite local restaurant. Cl Aug, Sat. Meals C–D.

(R)**Nürnberger Bratwurstglöckl**, Frauenplatz 9, tel 22 03 85. Next to the Frauenkirche; atmospheric, folksy décor; Bratwurst and other Franconian dishes. Meals C–D.

(R)**Café Extrablatt**, Leopoldstr. 7, tel 33 33 33. In Schwabing, very fashionable, with '20s décor; a slick café serving beer, wine, light meals. Owner a gossip columnist. Meals D.

(B)**Augustiner-Keller**, Arnulfstr. 52, tel 59 43 93. In an ugly area behind the station, a large, shady beer-garden very popular with Münchener.

(B)**Aumeister**, Sondermeierstr. 1. Attractive beer-garden at N end of Englischer Garten. Some food served.

(B)**Chinesischer Turm**, tel 39 50 28. Huge popular place in middle of Englischer Garten, teeming and touristy but fun. Some food.

(B)**Waldwirtschaft Grosshesselohe**, Georg-Kalbstr. 3, tel 79 50 88. By the Isar in S suburbs, near Grünwald, a large, lovely beer-garden with good simple pub food; live jazz sometimes.

(P)**Hofbräuhaus**, Platzl 9, tel 22 08 59. Huge, famous beer-hall near Rathaus; touristy but fun, sometimes rowdy. Brass band, dancing, courtyard garden; good serious restaurant upstairs.

(P)**Café Giesing**, Bergstr. 5. Utterly different: a smallish pub/café in Haidhausen, owned by a pop singer, frequented by artists, intellectuals; live music.

(P)**Heiliggeiststuberl**, Heiliggeiststr. Tiny, atmospheric pub near Viktualienmarkt.

(W)**Weinkrüger**, Maximilianstr. 21, tel 22 92 95. Wine tavern near opera and main theatre; very popular.

(C)**Luitpold**, Briennerstr. 11. Elegant café near Residenz; bourgeois clientele. Light meals.

Augsburg, Würzburg and the Romantic Road

This itinerary takes in two of Bavaria's main historic cities, Augsburg and Würzburg, also the so-called 'Romantic Road' (*Romantische Strasse*) that runs between them. This is a modern touristic term that links several mediaeval towns typifying picturesque old-time Germany. The best known is picture-postcardy Rothenburg ob der Tauber, always swamped with visitors: others such as Dinkelsbühl or Weikersheim are quieter but almost equally rewarding. The route traverses pleasant if unexciting scenery, past feudal castles, ramparts, baroque palaces and churches. At Bad Mergentheim it crosses briefly into Baden-Württemberg.

AUGSBURG (pop. 250,000) is the third largest city of Bavaria but not typically Bavarian: it is the capital of the Swabian part of the *Land*, and its architecture, cuisine and dialect are all distinctly Swabian. It's an impressive place, with many fine churches and palaces, and hidden curiosities. From the Emperor Augustus via Fugger the Rich to Diesel and Bertolt Brecht, it's had a distinguished and somewhat unusual history.

The city, now over 2,000 years old, was founded in 15 BC by the family of Augustus (hence its name). The Romans made it a trading centre on the route to Italy: but almost nothing remains of what they built, for the stones were later plundered for other buildings. Augsburg became a Free Imperial City in the 13th century; and by the late 15th it was just about the richest town in Europe, with colossal financial influence. This was due largely to two powerful local merchant families, Fugger and Welser. The Welsers at one time owned the whole of Venezuela, and the Fuggers were mightier still. Jakob Fugger 'the Rich' (1459–1525), king of the copper and silver trade, was said to be 'five times as rich as the Medicis': he ran the Papal Mint in Rome, was the financier of the Habsburgs, and provided Augsburg with some of its fine buildings. What's more, he was a devout philanthropist, who created one of the world's earliest social-welfare settlements, the Fuggerei, still in use today. Augsburg also played a part in the Reformation:

Luther visited it several times, and here in 1518 he defended his reform plans. Then in 1555, under a treaty known as the Religious Peace of Augsburg, the Catholic and Lutheran member princes of the Holy Roman Empire agreed to allow both creeds to co-exist officially. Later, local Catholics and Lutherans agreed on full parity, as a result of which two Lutheran churches were built against the walls of existing Catholic ones – and you can still see these unusual 'double churches' today. It has taken the rest of Germany 300 years to catch up with such ecumenical intimacy! However, in our own time, Augsburg's long tradition of tolerance has hardly extended to its treatment of its most famous modern son, Bertolt Brecht, born in 1898. He called his home town *'Scheiss-stadt'* ('city of shit'), finding it far too bourgeois – and the civic worthies, seldom men of the Left, replied by ignoring and outlawing him – at least till very recently (see below).

Hans Holbein the Younger was also born in Augsburg, which has close connections, too, with Rudolf Diesel and Willi Messerschmidt. Here in 1893 Diesel invented his fuel engine, in the MAN engineering factory in the northern suburbs: the factory's small museum displays the prototype. Messerschmidt had aircraft factories here during the war: but he was condemned at the Nuremberg trials, and Augsburg today does not commemorate him (the airstrip for his fighters is now a university site). The town has many big engineering and textile firms. The rebuilding of its historic centre, badly bombed in the war, has not been quite as inspired as in some German towns, for the new brown and grey façades, though carefully done, wear a severe look. This is true even of the mansions in the famous main street, the Maximilianstrasse, built during the Renaissance. Augsburg is a stately and absorbing town, but to my mind it lacks cosy charm.

The most intriguing place, just east of the centre, is the **Fuggerei**, founded in 1519: here Fugger the Rich housed virtually free some of the city's poor with their teeming families. It is a walled enclosure of some 65 little three-storey ochre houses: their neat design, with stairways and kitchens, must have been ultra-modern in 1519 and puts to shame much Victorian housing in Britain. Today some 300 elderly or widowed people still live here, behind outer gates still locked each night at ten pm. They still pay the original 1.72-mark nominal annual rent; their only obligation is to be good Catholics and to 'pray for the souls of the founders'. The Fugger family still run the settlement; they also still own a bank in the city, and live in a Schloss to the south. But they are *not* five times as rich as Paul Getty.

The few narrow streets just to the south-west, such as the Vorderer Lech, lined with boutiques and antique shops, are a kind of Altstadt. The nearby square-fronted, onion-domed **Rathaus**, a massive work of Renaissance monumentalism by Elias Holl, faces a big square with a fountain-statue of Augustus. The Rathaus was badly smashed by British bombs in 1944; and its famous *Goldener Saal* (golden hall), a symphony of gold and brown with an elaborate painted ceiling, was restored and reopened only in 1985 (free access during office hours). Near the Rathaus, down a narrow cobbled street, Auf dem Rain, is the **Brecht Museum**, in the neat grey house where he was born, son of a paper-factory owner. He lived in Augsburg till he was 20, and remained proud of being Swabian and fond of Augsburg in a way, but also sharply critical (even Fugger's charity he called 'an insult to the working-class'). Finally the city seems to have forgiven him for the insults: now it stages his plays at its festivals, and the municipality created the museum, in 1985. This has photos of his early days and of old Augsburg; best of all, it screens a superbly evocative video of his life, with some of his songs and poems.

The tall white red-roofed **cathedral**, first Romanesque, then rebuilt in Gothic style, is a bit of a jumble but has much worth admiring – outside, the 11th-century Romanesque bronze door and the Gothic sculptures on the south portal; inside, the paintings by Holbein the Elder and the 12th-century stained-glass windows, among the world's oldest. The quiet streets to its east, full of clerical institutes and girls' convent schools, have the authentic air of a cathedral town. To the north is the little red house where Mozart's father was born, now a Mozart museum. Even today, Mozart is a common name in Augsburg.

Back in the city centre, the 14th-century **church of St Anne** typifies local ecumenicism. It is a Protestant church that three times a year holds a Catholic mass for the Fuggers, as it has since the 16th century. Its grandiose Fugger funeral chapel, regarded as the earliest main Renaissance work in Germany, has tombs of some Fuggers and a famous portrait of Luther by Cranach. It also has three cheeky little sculptures of plump *putti*, naked, and half asleep. Close by is the broad, majestic Maximilianstrasse with its three bronze Renaissance fountains; its south end is the least spoilt by the rebuilding. Here the beautiful Renaissance courtyard of the Fugger family palace is sometimes used for concerts. The **Schaezler Palace** (1770), also very fine, was until recently the home of a well-to-do local family of silversmiths, the Schaezlers; now it is a civic art museum. You pass through its huge and magnificent Festsaal, all a-glitter with chandeliers, gilt-framed mirrors and rococo frescoes, to reach the painting galleries: note the Holbeins, and the famous portrait of Fugger the Rich by Dürer. The Roman Museum, in a former church, has some local Roman fragments; the Maximilian Museum, devoted to the history of the town's golden age, I found disappointing. To the south is one of the city's two 'double churches', **St Ulric and St Afra**. The Lutheran one is rather small and dull, but the adjacent high-towered Catholic one, much larger and older, is magnificent. It has a lofty light interior, an elaborate sculpted nativity scene by Hans Degler (c. 1604) above the altar, and a pulpit with a canopy. To the south-east is the Rotes Tor, a group of fortified 16th-century buildings.

Going north from Augsburg across the plain, the Romantic Road comes first to **Donauwörth**, an old walled town above the Danube: its baroque *Heiligkreuz* (Holy Cross) church is interesting. **Harburg**, on the banks of the Wörnitz, is dominated by its big fortified castle, dating from the 13th century but enlarged in the 18th: its collection of gold, silver, ivory and tapestries is impressive. **Nördlingen**,

an old town with circular ramparts, has a number of fine buildings, such as the 14th-century Rathaus, the Salvator (Saviour's) church (13th-century frescoes) and the Georgkirche (flamboyant Gothic tower). From here you can go straight to Dinkelsbühl over the wheat-plain, or make a scenic detour via Wassertrüdingen. **Dinkelsbühl**, with its watchtowers and ramparts, is an unspoilt mediaeval/Renaissance town of much character: the *Hetzelhof* (galleried courtyard), the Deutsches Haus (richly painted façade) and St George's church (unusual fan-vaulted aisles) are the best buildings. In the Thirty Years' War, the town's children appealed to the attackers and thus saved it from destruction: this happy event is marked by a week of pageantry, music and drama every mid-July. The pleasant town of **Feuchtwangen**, further north, has a museum of Franconian folklore and a delightful Romanesque cloister.

The Romantic Road now enters the Tauber valley and comes to **ROTHENBURG OB DER TAUBER** (pop. 12,500), one of the best-known small towns in Germany, finely sited on cliff above the curving river. In mediaeval times an important town flourished here, but it never recovered from the aftermath of the Thirty Years' War. Thus it stayed poor, without further building – and so it has survived as Germany's purest example of a mediaeval ramparted town – 'a fairy-tale city', as the gushing brochures put it. Carefully rebuilt after wartime bombing, it is often used for location work on films set in mediaeval times. In the

The Herkules Fountain in the centre of Augsburg.

ultra-picturesque Marktplatz, the 14th-century Rathaus has a museum in its Gothic imperial hall; one part of the building is Renaissance. Handsome mansions line the Herrngasse, which runs from here to the Burg-garten (fine views over the river). Also worth a look are the old hospital at the southern end of the ramparts; the Baumeisterhaus with its statues of the seven deadly sins and seven virtues; and St Jacob's church (superb 1504 altarpiece by Riemenschneider).

A feat of drinking saved Rothenburg from destruction during the Thirty Years' War: the Imperial Army had seized this Protestant town and was about to destroy it, but the general then said he would relent if a leading citizen could down in one draught a 3-litre mug of local wine, which one ex-mayor managed to do. The story is enacted daily at 11 am, noon, and one, two, three, nine and ten pm, by an animated clock on the Ratstrinkstube, near the Rathaus; and there is a pageant on the same theme at Whitsun and on the second Sundays of July and September. Shepherds' dances and comic plays are staged one Sunday each month in summer. All great fun: but Rothenburg's charm is tarnished by the endless coachloads of camera-clicking tourists that throng it all year through. If by quaffing three litres of Bocksbeutel I could persuade them all to depart, I'd happily have a go.

The Tauber valley above Rothenburg is especially pretty, as the river winds between woods and orchards. At **Creglingen** there's another Riemenschneider altar, in the *Herrgottskirche* (Chapel of Our Lord). And **Weikersheim** boasts a stately castle by the river, built in 1580–1680 by the Hohenlohe princes. It has a pleasant formal park, a fine collection of glass, furniture and tapestries, and a superb Rittersaal with painted coffered ceiling. **Bad Mergentheim** (pop. 20,000), an attractive old town with half-timbered houses, is where the Order of the Teutonic Knights founded their castle, and their crest still adorns its gateway. The local museum gives details of the strange history of this Order, which was founded in 1190 and was long both military and religious. The town is now a leading spa centre, whose salty springs are used for treating gastric disorders. The village of **Stuppach**, to the southwest, is well worth a visit for Grünewald's superb *Virgin and Child* painting (1519) in its church. And, on the way to Würzburg, **Tauberbischofsheim** has numerous half-timbered and baroque buildings.

The distinguished old city of **WÜRZBURG** (pop. 124,000) has a pleasant setting on the river Main, amid vineclad hills. It is the second largest town of Franconia (after Nuremberg) and the province's wine capital. As in so many wine-producing areas, the people tend to be jovial, open-minded and welcoming – more so than in the Nuremberg area, which grows no wine. Würzburg is dominated by two grandiosely magnificent buildings, the Marienburg hilltop fortress and the Residenz palace, both of them the legacy of the Prince-Bishops who for more than six centuries ruled this major episcopal city. They were men of taste who hired great artists to design or beautify their buildings – notably, the mediaeval sculptor Riemenscheider, and in the 18th century the architect Neumann and the Venetian painter Tiepolo. And today much of this work survives, in a city of fine churches where baroque and rococo hold pride of place.

Würzburg was christianized in the seventh century by the Irish missionary, St Kilian, 'the Apostle of the Franks'. He was put to death in 689 (and is today still venerated locally): but his work was not in vain, for by 758 Würzburg was a bishopric and some 20 churches were built in 1000–1200. The Emperor Barbarossa honoured the town by celebrating there in 1156 his marriage with Beatrice of Burgundy; he also promoted the bishop to the rank of Duke of Franconia. This dynasty of Prince-Bishops resided in the Marienberg fortress from then until the early 18th century, when they moved down to their newly-built Residenz across the river; it was three Prince-Bishops of the Schönborn family who in this period endowed the city with most of its lovely buildings, and they ruled it till 1803. In 1815 it became part of Bavaria. In March 1945 it was devastated in an Allied air raid: the major edifices have since been well restored, but the Altstadt has been rebuilt in a dull modern style. Würzburg, despite its baroque and its wine-taverns, is thus a less cosily picturesque town for a stroll than, say, Heidelberg. But its 15,000 students (the old university is strong on medicine) enhance its ambience. **Festivals** in Würzburg include the Mozart festival in June, in the gardens and halls of the Residenz; and the Kiliani pilgrimage and festival, in early July.

The best place, historically, to begin a tour of the city is the hilltop **Festung Marienberg**, a fine sight at night when floodlit: you can walk up to it across the Mainbrücke, or drive up from the back. It's an impressively massive hulk, thick-walled, built between the 12th and 16th centuries. Its chief interest for the visitor is the Mainfränkisches Museum in the former arsenal, containing Franconian popular art and craftwork, fine old furniture and – above all – a marvellous collection of sculptures in stone and wood by the great **Tilman Riemenschneider** (1460–1531): note the wonderfully expressive faces and hands of his creations, e.g. a Madonna in mourning. He was born in the Harz but spent most of his life in Würzburg, where he became a city councillor – and a radical one, for in 1525 he sided with the peasants during their great revolt. For this he was imprisoned for some months in the Festung's dungeon, below its tall 13th-century tower. Next to this is a 105-metre well that was dug down through the rock in c. 1200; and a tiny fortified church built just after the Kilian era (706), one of Germany's oldest. From the Festung's terrace you get a fine view across to the town and vineclad slopes behind.

Across the Main in the town centre is the **Residenz**, one of the largest and most splendid baroque palaces in Germany, built in 1720–44 to the designs of the great Balthazar Neumann. It was intended to symbolize the wealth and power of the Prince Bishops, just as Versailles did for Louis XIV. It was badly burned in the 1945 raid, but most of its finest treasures escaped grave damage – notably the Grand Staircase, whose ceiling is covered with a giant fresco by Tiepolo representing the Four Continents. The grandeur and the colour are breaktaking. Almost equally fine is the oval Kaisersaal upstairs, where another huge Tiepolo ceiling-fresco illustrates the marriage of Barbarossa and other events of local history: note the artist's clever use of *trompe-l'oeil* in blending stucco and painting. Today this room is used as the stunning setting for concerts and banquets. The guided tour also takes in a succession of smaller chambers, all sumptuous, many of them recreated since 1945 in careful detail. To one side of the palace is the elegant Hofgarten, while in front is the ornate Franconia Fountain. The palace chapel, the **Hofkirche**, is another Neumann masterpiece of dazzling baroque fantasy.

Nearly all the other city sights can be reached on foot from here. The lofty **Cathedral of St Kilian** is basically Romanesque but with later additions, and has been much rebuilt since 1945. Its modern altar harmonizes well with the baroque stuccowork, and with the lovely Riemenschneider sculptures: best is one of a monk with a happy, dreamy face. The **Neumünster**, just opposite, also originally Romanesque, was rebuilt as baroque in the 18th century and has a superb baroque façade; it was built over the graves of St Kilian and two fellow apostles. Its fine and fascinating crypt contains a modern (1986) reliquary above the tombs of these three martyrs; a seventh-century font where the saint is believed to have baptized people; and a modern tomb, too – that of Bishop Ehrenfried who was imprisoned for daring to speak out against the Nazis. His splendidly appropriate name means 'honour, peace'.

The **Marktplatz**, a lively focus of the local scene, with a big daily food market, is adjoined by two very fine buildings – the Marienkapelle, a late-Gothic hall-church; and the picturesque rococo Haus Zum Falken, now housing the tourist office. Not far away are the Bürgerspital and the huge Julius-spital, founded as almshouses in respectively the 14th and 16th centuries; today they still shelter some old people, and also own vast vine-growing estates. Both serve as wine-taverns, too (see p. 188). Spanning the river is the graceful 15th-century Alt Mainbrücke, adorned with baroque statues of bishops and saints. Beyond it, on a hill opposite the Festung, is the **Käppele**, a curious double church: one part was built in 1680 as a tiny pilgrimage chapel, then B. Neumann (him again!) added a larger and ornate baroque wing, with fine frescoes by Matthias Günther. Pilgrims still climb the steep steps to it. Agnostics too can enjoy the ravishing view.

In the **Main valley** north-west of the city, at Veitshöchheim, is a lovely formal rococo garden laid out by the Prince-Bishops. The valley upstream from Würzburg, lined with vineyards, has some charming old riverside townlets: among them, Ochsenfurt with its ramparts and half-timbered houses, and Marktbreit whose Renaissance ensemble include a fine gateway.

Away to the west is **Aschaffenburg** (pop. 60,000), also on the Main. Its massive pink Schloss Johannisburg, built in Renaissance style in 1605–14 for the Bishops of Mainz, has a graceful inner courtyard with feudal keep; by the river at the end of its garden is the curious Pompeianum, built by Ludwig I of Bavaria in imitation of the Castor and Pollux house in Pompeii. Art of a more serious kind – a superb painting of Christ by Grünewald (1525) – is in the Gothic Stiftskirche, which has an attractive Romanesque cloister, too. On the castle's south side, above the river, is a quiet quarter of old *Fachwerk* houses down narrow alleys – surprisingly unspoilt.

TOURIST OFFICES

AUGSBURG 8900: Bahnhofstr. 7, tel (0821) 50 20 70.

ROTHENBURG 8803: Rathaus, tel (09861) 4 04 92.

BAD MERGENTHEIM 6990: Marktplatz 3, tel (07931) 5 71 35.

WÜRZBURG 8700: main station, tel (0931) 3 74 36; congress centre, tel (0931) 3 73 35.

ASCHAFFENBURG 8750: Dalbergstr. 6, tel (06021) 3 04 26.

Accommodation eating and drinking

AUGSBURG 8900 (tel code 0821):

(H)**Steigenberger Drei Mohren**, Maximilianstr. 40, tel 51 00 31. Tsars and dukes once stayed in this slightly sombre but superior hotel; fine Swabian cooking in its **Fuggerkeller** basement restaurant. Rooms (110) A. Meals (Fuggerkeller) C.

(H)**Riegele**, Viktoriastr. 4, tel 30 90 39. Opposite station, well run, good Swabian dishes. Rooms (37) C. Meals C.

(H)**Dom**, Frauentorstr. 8, tel 15 30 31. Near cathedral, quiet, pleasant. No restaurant. Rooms (44) C–D.

(H)**Gästehaus Iris**, Gartenstr. 4, tel 51 09 81. Fairly central, good service. No restaurant. Cl Aug. Rooms (10) D.

(R)**Zum Alten Fischertor**, Pfärrle 14, tel 51 86 62. In the old town; sophisticated, with ambitious variations on Swabian cuisine. Cl Sun, Mon, Christmas, 3 weeks Aug. Meals A.

(R)**Welser Küche**, Maximilianstr. 83, tel 3 39 30. Gimmicky, but not vulgar: banquets served nightly in 16th-century style, with music and merriment, in an old patrician house, using the 16th-century recipes of the rich Welser family. Meals A–B.

(R)**Fuggerei-Stube**, Jakoberstr. 26, tel 3 08 70. Inside the Fuggerei, family-run, very popular. Cl Mon, Sun dinner. Meals C.

(R)**7-Schwaben-Stuben**, Bürgermeister-Fischer-Str. 12, tel 31 45 63. Very Swabian in food and folksy ambience. Meals C–D.

NÖRDLINGEN 8860:

(H)**Zum Engel**, Wemdingerstr. 4, tel (09081) 31 67. Simple, pleasant old brewery-inn, near ramparts. Cl 3 weeks Sept–Oct. Rooms (9) E. Meals (cl Sat) D.

DINKELSBÜHL 8804:

(H)**Deutsches Haus**, Weinmarkt 3, tel (09851) 23 46. 15th-century half-timbered house; décor and local cooking both delectable. Cl 2 weeks Feb. Rooms (11) C. Meals C–D.

FEUCHTWANGEN 8805:

(H)**Romantik-Hotel Greifen-Post**, Marktplatz 8, tel (09852) 20 02. Solid family-run coaching-inn, dating from 1450; modern comfort, good Franconian cooking; pool in style of Roman baths. Rooms (35) B–C. Meals (cl Jan) B–C.

ROTHENBURG 8803:

(H)**Goldener Hirsch**, tel (09861) 20 51. Full of grace and character, built over ramparts; terrace with fine view; food a little dull. Cl mid-Dec to Jan. Rooms (80) B–C. Meals B.

(H)**Glocke**, Am Plönlein 1, tel (09861) 30 25. Sympathetic tavern, popular with locals more than tourists. Rooms (28) C. Meals C–D.

WEIKERSHEIM 6992:

(H)**Laurentius**, Marktplatz 5, tel (07934) 70 07. New hotel in old building where Goethe's forebears lived; good food in vaulted cellar. Cl 2 weeks Feb. Rooms (12) D. Meals C.

BAD MERGENTHEIM 6990:

(H)**Bundschu**, Cronbergstr. 15, tel (07931) 30 43. Not elegant but spacious and cosily inviting, run by a friendly family; excellent Swabian cooking. Cl mid-Jan to mid-Feb. Rooms (50) C. Meals (cl Mon) C.

WÜRZBURG 8700 (tel code 0931):

(H)**Maritim**, Pleichertorstr. 5, tel 5 08 31. Modern and practical; indoor pool, two restaurants. Rooms (293) A–B. Meals A–C.

(H)**Walfisch**, Am Pleidenturm 5, tel 5 00 55. Lovely rooms, some with view of Festung. Excellent Franconian cooking. Rooms (41) B–C. Meals C.

(H)**Zur Stadt Mainz**, Semmelstr. 39, tel 5 31 55. Comfortable old inn, rooms recently renovated. good Franconian restaurant, rather touristy. Rooms (22) C. Meals (cl Sun dinner, Mon) C.

(H)**Russ**, Wolfhardtgasse 1, tel 5 00 16. Quiet hotel run by charming lady. Serious cooking (restaurant separately owned). Rooms (30) D. Meals (tel 5 91 29) C–D.

(R)**Ratskeller**, Langgasse 1, tel 1 30 21. The Rathaus' former chapel; an above-average Ratskeller, smart and select. Also a simpler Bierstube. Cl 2 weeks Jan, Tue in winter. Meals C.

(R)**Backöfele**, Ursulinergasse 2, tel 5 90 59. Lively, rustic, full of local atmosphere; patio; good local dishes. Meals C–D.

(R)**Zum Stachel**, Gressengasse 1, tel 5 27 70. Historic wine-tavern with pretty courtyard. Cl lunch, mid-Aug to early Sept. Meals C.

(R)**Nikolaushof**, Am Käppele, tel 7 26 82. On a hill above the town – a delightful place, romantic but modest. Panoramic garden for summer, candlelight for winter. Simple dishes. Meals D.

Bürgerspital, Theatrestr. 19, tel 1 38 61. Historic old hospice, serving good food and wine, popular locally. Cl Tue. Meals D.

MARKTHEIDENFELD 8772:

(H)**Anker**, Obertorstr. 6, tel (09391) 40 41. Modern, stylish and welcoming; family-run by vine-growers whose superb and elegant Weinhaus restaurant is opposite. Rooms (36) B–C. Meals at **Weinhaus** (cl 2 weeks Dec, Mon) A–B.

ASCHAFFENBURG 8750:

(H)**Romantik-Hotel Post**, Goldbacherstr. 198, tel (06021) 2 13 33. Busy inn, excellent food, bedrooms ordinary. Indoor pool. Rooms (71) C. Meals B–C.

Nuremberg (Nürnberg)

For many people outside Germany, Bavaria's second city (pop. 465,000) evokes above all the Nazis' pre-war mass rallies and the 1945–46 trials that sent ten of their leaders to the gallows (see page 193). But Nuremberg's more important place in history lies much further back – in the Middle Ages, when it was a major seat of the Holy Roman Emperors, and one of the key artistic and scientific centres of Europe. Its great mediaeval ensemble within the ramparts survived intact until the bombing raid of 2 January 1945 that wiped out 90 per cent of this Altstadt. Parts have since been rebuilt in a modern style: but the street lay-out has been preserved, and many old buildings such as Albrecht Dürer's house have been meticulously restored, with the dormer windows, red roofs or stepped gables that are typical of Nuremberg. So the city still retains much of its former graceful quality.

It's a fiercely impressive place: few other German towns convey so vividly the sense of a long-ago history rich in culture. And its modern ambience is very civilized too. The Altstadt, though picturesque, is spacious and never too crowded; unusual fountains play in its squares, the old houses beside its little river are gently floodlit, and its streets are lined with galleries, bookshops and lovely old pubs, patronized by locals as much as tourists. Nürnbergers have a keen sense of local patriotism: some 5,000 of them belong to a club that puts private money into restoring old houses. But these Franconians can be reserved, even gruff, not as jovial and outgoing as southern Bavarians.

Nuremberg dates from the 11th century when two emperors built castles on the slopes above the Pegnitz. It was later favoured by the Holy Roman Emperors as one of their main residences, and from 1356 each new emperor was expected to hold his first diet here in the Kaiserburg fortress: so it was a kind of German capital. It also grew into a wealthy commercial centre at a crossroads of European north–south and east–west trade routes – and it was this, along with the intellect and artistic skills of its citizens, that led to its amazing golden age of innovative culture and science in the 15th–16th centuries. Gold-beating and bronze-casting flourished, as did music and poetry. Peter Vischer pioneered brass-founding; Adam Kraft excelled in stone sculpture; the Nuremberg school of painting produced Michael

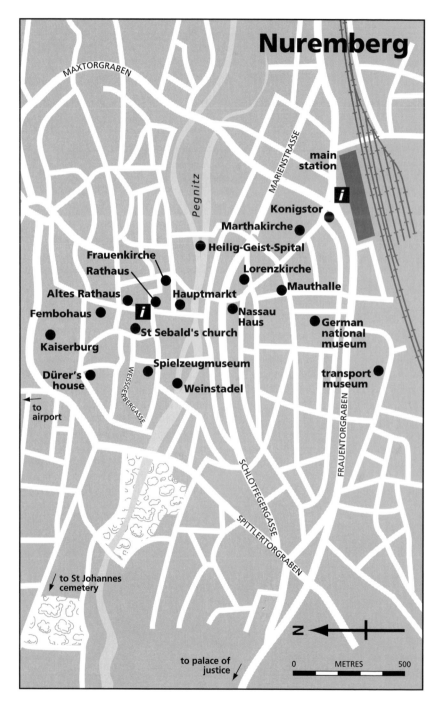

Nuremberg

MAXTORGRABEN

Pegnitz

MARIENSTRASSE

main station

Konigstor

Marthakirche

Heilig-Geist-Spital

Frauenkirche

Rathaus

Lorenzkirche

Altes Rathaus

Hauptmarkt

Mauthalle

Fembohaus

Nassau Haus

St Sebald's church

German national museum

Kaiserburg

Spielzeugmuseum

Dürer's house

Weinstadel

transport museum

WEISSERGERGASSE

to airport

FRAUENTORGRABEN

to St Johannes cemetery

SCHLOTFEGERGASSE

SPITTLERTORGRABEN

N

to palace of justice

0   METRES   500

Wolgemut and his renowned pupil Albrecht Dürer (1471–1528); the cobbler-turned-songwriter Hans Sachs (1494–1576) was born and died in the city, which was the home of his *Meistersinger*. In the field of science, the explosion of genius was just as remarkable. Peter Henlein here produced the first pocket watch, and the cosmographer Martin Behaim made the first globe, in 1490, just before Columbus discovered America. Mechanical toys, the clarinet and the gunlock were among Nuremberg's many other inventions, and in 1526 the first German science university was founded here. The city is still a centre of toy-making; and as a tribute to Nuremberg the German inventors hold their annual exhibition here.

The tradition of technology has since continued: Germany's first railway was built here in 1835, between Nuremberg and nearby Fürth. And today this is still an important industrial centre, producing typewriters (Adler), electronic and engineering goods (Siemens, AEG, etc), lorries, motor cycles and much else.

Nuremberg's principal **festivals and events** are the toy fair (February); the organ festival in late June; the international bardic meeting of singers and songwriters, with free open-air concerts (early August); the inventors' fair and the Altstadt popular festival, both in September; and in December, the **Christkindlesmarkt** in the Marktplatz: the oldest and largest of all German pre-Christmas fairs, a lavish and colourful display of all kinds of local handmade goods (not just kitsch), such as toys, brass and glassware – and the famous Nuremberg gingerbread cakes (*Lebkuchen*), which come in all shapes and sizes.

Nearly everything worth seeing is within the **Altstadt** (except for Hitler's sports arenas, to the south). It is a big Altstadt, about a mile across, but best visited on foot. Across it runs the delightful river Pegnitz: most older buildings are to the north, while the modern rebuilt streets are to the south, many of them traffic-free and full of big stores. To get an idea of the Altstadt's scale, you should drive or walk around the outside of the massive 15th-century ramparts, to admire the 46 towers, the four huge gateways, and the moats now grassed over.

A tour of the Altstadt on foot could well start on its north side at the **Kaiserburg** (open daily), the vast and ancient castle where the kings held court in 1050–1571. It's a mighty rambling hotch-potch built at various periods, well restored after wartime damage, and awesomely grandiose. The oldest bit is the high Pentagonal Tower, c. 1040, relic of a Hohenzollern castle long destroyed; other parts were added by the Hohenstaufens a century later, and others are 14th–15th-century. The Imperial Chapel, 12th-century, is on two levels: the airy upper gallery was for the emperor's use, the gloomy lower part was for his courtiers. The Knights' Hall (*Rittersaal*), now decked out with 16th-century paintings, is used for concerts by candlelight. And the Imperial Stables, built in 1495 as a granary, are now a youth hostel. From several rooms and towers there are fine views down over the town; and the various small galleried inner courtyards are most appealing. In one of these is the Deep Well, that supplied the castle with its drinking-water from springs in the rock 60 metres below.

Directly below the castle is the most

picturesque part of the old town, huddling against the ramparts. Here is the 15th-century gabled house that **Dürer** bought in 1509 and lived in till his death in 1528. Remarkably, it was little damaged in the war, and its beautiful interiors are largely authentic, though 19th-century repro furniture has been added. It is now a museum of the work of this great artist/writer/scientist politician: there are some originals of his woodcuts, copies of his other works, first editions of his treatises, and curious pastiches done as homage to him by modern artists. The charming square outside the house, and all the little streets nearby, are full of quaint half-timbered houses, artfully rebuilt, many of them historic pubs and restaurants: this is the most atmospheric quarter of 'Alt Nürnberg'. The Hausbrauerei Altstadthof, in Bergstrasse, is a brewery/pub/museum where you can walk through the sandstone rock under the castle. This used to be an area of rich merchants' mansions, but few have been rebuilt since 1945, save the pink gabled Renaissance **Fembohaus** in Burgstrasse, now a museum of city history, with some rather odd décor. The patrician trading families that held sway in Nuremberg during its heyday have now largely vanished from the limelight, though they do still exist.

Just south of the Fembohaus is the **Altes Rathaus**, a handsome Renaissance building on the model of a Venetian *palazzo*: it has fine doorways, underground dungeons and a torture chamber. Beside it you'll see one of Nuremberg's most popular fountains, the bronze Goose Fountain (1555), depicting a farmer carrying to market two geese that spout water. Opposite the Rathaus soar the twin towers of St

Sebald's, Nuremberg's oldest church (13th century) and one of its two finest: it marks the transition from late Romanesque to Gothic. Today it is Protestant, in a largely Catholic city. Of its many artworks, the best is the bronze shrine (1519) of St Sebald, the city's patron saint, by Peter Vischer: as well as a silver sarcophagus, it has a striking bronze figurine of the artist himself, in apron and skullcap. The church also has a sculptured tomb by Adam Kraft and a crucifixion by a third great local artist of that period, Veit Stoss. Just west of the church is the Weissgerbergasse, a delightful old cobbled street lined with *Fachwerk* houses, many of them pubs full of young people (I liked the one advertising 'polizeifreundlich', i.e. 'police-friendly', low-alcohol, drinks); and the **Spielzeugmuseum** (toy museum), which has dolls' houses, model trains and other toys across the ages to intrigue adults as well as kids.

The central focus of the Altstadt is the broad **Hauptmarkt**, which has a big daily food and flower market as well as the pre-Christmas one. Most of the buildings around it are new and dull, but the Gothic Frauenkirche survives, with its elaborate façade: it has an early mechanical clock (1509) that performs at noon (on the theme of seven Electors coming to honour Karl IV in 1356), while inside are tombstones by Kraft and the beautiful 15th-century Tucher-Altar. This church faces across to the city's most famous fountain, the 14th-century **Schöner Brunnen**, an 18-metre spire-like pillar adorned with 40 figures including those seven Electors again. Nearby, bridging an arm of the Pegnitz, is the pink 14th/15th-century **Heilig-Geist-Spital**, one of the biggest hospitals built in mediaeval times: it

Nazi Mass Rallies and Nuremberg Trials

This city, to its intense annoyance today, is more closely identified with the Nazis than any other, except maybe Berlin. Here in 1933–38 Hitler held his mass rallies and parades, with fanatical crowds of up to 250,000 yelling 'Sieg Heil!'. So why did he choose Nuremberg for this? Not because it was especially pro-Nazi (quite the reverse, before 1933 it had a Socialist mayor and its Nazi vote was almost nil). He picked it for its central position between Berlin and Munich; for its role as the 'treasure chest' of early German history; *and*, before 1933, to help the local police chief, a keen Nazi, in his conflicts with local government.

The buildings put up for the rallies still exist, in the south-east suburbs, and are awesome places to visit. The city council reluctantly preserves them as grim memorials, and school groups are taken there. But most guidebooks, including *Baedeker*, *Michelin* and *Fodor*, disgracefully fail to mention them.

In the **Luitpoldhain** park the Nazi rallies began back in 1927, and Hitler later used it for SS and SA parades; it is now again a recreation park, nicely grassed over. Nearby is the huge round **Congresshalle**, modelled on the Colosseum in Rome and even bigger, which the Nazis half-built and never completed: now suitably derelict-looking, it is used for storage and sometimes for pop concerts. The major setpiece, designed by Hitler's architect Albert Speer, is the **Zeppelin Tribune** where the mass rallies were held every September in the stadium below; special trains brought the faithful. These rallies were the major display of Nazi power, with Hitler's speeches as their climax. Partly dismantled, the vast concrete tribune now holds a small museum, where old newsreels on video show a ranting Hitler at his maddest and the marching Nazis at their ugliest: to see these films *in situ* is sobering indeed. The stadium is now used for sports by the US Army.

The Palace of Justice, where the trials were held in 1945–46, is just west of the Altstadt. This large pinkish building is still in use as the city's lawcourts, so is not open to visits – a pity. Here in 1935 the Nazis passed the infamous laws that deprived Jews of German citizenship, etc. So the victorious Allies found this lawcourt a fitting place for trying the guilty. Ten leading Nazis, including Streicher, were hanged here on 16 October 1946; Göring managed to commit suicide first.

has graceful galleried courtyards and stands opposite a memorial to Hans Sachs. From here it is agreeable to walk west along the river banks, to the most idyllically pretty spot in Nuremberg: this is the **Weinstadel**, an old half-timbered wine storehouse next to a 14th-century water-tower and a quaint covered walkway across the river, the **Henkersteg** (hangman's bridge). Weeping willows, and soft floodlighting at night, complete the picture.

The part of the Altstadt south of the river, though mostly modern, has a few notable old buildings – and the star among them is the **Lorenzkirche**, 13th–15th-century Gothic, the town's largest church and possibly its loveliest. It has a superb rose window, and three amazing artworks in the nave – a polychrome wood *Annunciation* by Veit Stoss, suspended from the vaulting; a lively clay group (1420) of the 12 Apostles; and a stone tabernacle by Kraft who has included a sculpted portrait of himself, crouching, with staring eyes. On one of the 19 altars, note the realistic sculpture of St Rochus showing his pest boils to an angel.

Outside the church is another startling fountain, the **Tugendbrunnen**, with a statue of a lady whose breasts sometimes spout water. Opposite is the Nassau House, a 13th-century tower-shaped patrician dwelling. Going south-east down Königstrasse you will pass the curious Mauthalle with its six tiers of tiny dormer windows: it was built as a granary in c. 1500. And so you'll come to the Konigstor gate in the ramparts, where a courtyard has been reconstructed as a 'mediaeval craftsmen's village' (*Handwerkerhof*): here tourists can watch toymakers, blacksmiths and the like at work, and be regaled with *Bratwurst* and/or gingerbread. Deeper insights into local cultural tradition are to be obtained at the nearby **Marthakirche**, where the Meistersingers, led by Sachs (in his spare time from shoemaking) held their singing school in 1578–1620 – as related by Wagner in his famous opera.

As if all this historic richness were not enough, you have only to walk 400 metres westward to find one of the country's greatest museums, the **German National Museum**. This was founded in 1852, at a time of political ferment, and was intended to give cultural backing to the movement for German unity, by offering a panoramic display of Germanic arts across the ages. This it does. Housed partly in a former 14th-century Carthusian monastery, it is a huge, rambling museum of great diversity. There are collections of old weapons and of peasant folk-art, also of ceramics, glasswork, Nuremberg gold and silver work, and other decorative arts. Behaim's first globe of the earth is one star exhibit. But best of all are the carvings and sculptures by Kraft, Stoss, Riemenschmeider and other Franconian masters of the 15th–16th centuries; and the superb collections of paintings of the same period, by Altdorfer, Cranach, Wolgemut, and of course Dürer. Note his imaginary portrait of Charlemagne. Nearby, next to the rebuilt opera house, is the **Transport Museum** (open daily), devoted mainly to the early history of railways.

Just west of the Altstadt, the **St Johannes cemetery** is one of Germany's oldest and most famous, dating from the 13th century. Dürer, Stoss, Sachs and other great sons of the city lie buried here. Many of the 16th- and 17th-century tombs have elaborate bronze decorations, depicting the life of the dead person.

TOURIST OFFICE

Main station, tel 23 36 32; Rathaus, tel 23 36 35.

Accommodation, Eating and Drinking (Postcode 8500, tel code 0911)

Hotels and restaurants are less expensive than in many big German cities. The Altstadt has a wide range of inexpensive taverns and eating-places in local style, full of atmosphere. Nuremberg *Bratwurst* sausages are one speciality.

In the heart of Nuremberg, the 14th-century Heilig-Geist-Spital (hospital) straddles the river Pegnitz.

(H)**Atrium-Hotel**, Münchenerstr. 25, tel 4 74 80. Large very modern hotel in Meistersingerhalle park, 3 km SE of centre. Pool, sauna, sun-terrace, beer-garden, etc. Rooms (200) A–B. Meals B.

(H)**Burghotel**, Lammsgasse 3, tel 20 44 14. In Altstadt, below Burg; cosy, *gemütlich* and characterful, with Bavarian décor; pool, too. Rooms (44) B–C. No restaurant.

(H)**Am Jakobsmarkt**, Schottengasse 3, tel 24 14 37. In SW corner of Altstadt, cheerful and modern; no restaurant. Rooms (70) C.

(H)**Marienbad**, Eilgutstr. 5, tel 20 31 47. Near main station; efficiently run. Rooms (55) C. No restaurant.

(H)**Bayerischer Hof**, Gleissbühlstr. 15, tel 2 32 10. Near main station, well modernized. No restaurant. Rooms (80) C.

(H)**Urbis**, Könogstr. 74. tel 23 20 00. Inside Altstadt, but near main station; modern and well run. No restaurant. Rooms (53) C.

(H)**Am Schönen Brunnen**, Haupmarkt 17, tel 22 42 25. On main square, facing famous fountain. No restaurant. Rooms (25) C–D.

(H)**Weinhaus Steichele**, Knorrstr. 2, tel 20 43 78. Characterful old wine-tavern and hotel in Altstadt; good Franconian cooking. Rooms (56) C–D. Meals (cl lunch Sun, Mon) C–D.

(R)**Gasthof Bammes**, Bucher Haupstr. 63, tel 38 13 03. In suburb of Buch: an old local tavern, now smart and stylish, with excellent Franconian cuisine. Cl Sun, public hols. Meals A–B.

(R)**Goldenes Posthorn**, An der Sebalduskirche, tel 22 51 53. Lovely old tavern founded 1498 (Dürer was an habitué), now chic and romantic. Good local cooking. Cl Sun. Meals B–C.

(R)**Zum Sudhaus**, Bergstr. 20, tel 20 43 14. Traditional, nicely furnished, intimate; local and international dishes. Cl Sun. Meals B–C.

(R)**Böhms Herrenkeller**, Theatergasse 19, tel 22 44 65. Small, old and traditional; Franconian dishes. Cl Sun. Meals C.

(R)**Alte Küche**, Albrecht-Dürerstr. 3, tel 20 38 26. Panelled 15th-century cellar below Burg, full of atmosphere. Cl Sat. Meals C–D.

(R)**Schlenkerla**, beim Tiergärtnertor 3, tel 22 54 74. Famous old Altstadt pub below Burg; some local dishes. Meals D–E.

(R)**Bratwurst-Glöcklein**, Im Handwerkerhof, tel 22 76 25. Lively *Bratwurst* eatery in old courtyard; touristy. Cl Sun. Meals D–E. Another branch at Rathausplatz 1, tel 22 76 95.

(W)**Weinkrüger**, Wespennest 6–8, tel 23 28 95. Large old wine pub by river; serves food too (C–D).

(J)**Schmelztiegel**, Bergstr. 21, tel 20 39 82. Lively Altstadt cellar with live jazz twice weekly. Drinks and snacks.

(C)**Confiserie Neef**, Winklerstrasse 29, tel 22 51 79. Elegant café with superb cakes, chocolates, gingerbread, strudels. Cl Sun.

Northern Franconia: Bayreuth, Coburg and Bamberg

This itinerary takes in the northern part of Franconia, between Nuremberg and the Czech and former GDR borders. It passes through pleasant rolling countryside, and it takes in several old towns of great interest, notably Bayreuth with its Wagner associations, Coburg with its British royal links, and the beautiful city of Bamberg.

Out in the undulating Oberpfalz region, east of Nuremberg, is the charming old town of **Amberg** (pop. 46,000). It has ramparts and some notable churches, such as the rococo Schulkirche; old houses line the banks of the gently-flowing river Vils. The Vils valley used to have major iron-ore deposits, whose mining can be dated back to the eighth century BC: but the mines have now been exhausted, or undercut by cheaper imported ore, and the last active pit in the area, at Auerbach, closed in 1988. However, some foundries and smelting-works are still active, using imported ore. And the area's industrial heritage is today being meticulously conserved, for visitors to study: notably, in the former mining town of **Theuern**, south of Amberg, an old mansion has just been converted into an excellent museum of local mining and industry, the Bergbau- und Industriemuseum Ostbayern. The best exhibits, in outbuildings, are some ancient machinery and industrial tools still in working order: as well as grinding-mills and mirror-polishers, they include some 16th-century wooden hammers and a giant pair of antique bellows, actually in use at Auerbach up until 1953 – 'Technology here', I was told, 'remained unchanged from the 16th to the mid-20th century.'

North-west of Auerbach is so-called **Fränkische Schweiz** (Swiss Franconia) – a misnomer, for its landscape is hardly sub-alpine and its hills are not high. But there is much of interest in this curious wooded district of winding valleys, strewn with oddly-shaped rocks and punctured with caves full of stalactites. **Tüchersfeld** and **Pottenstein** are two typical villages: finger-like crags tower up in the middle of the former, while the latter is built partly on a cliff, partly in the valley below, and has a tenth-century castle. Nearby is the **Teufelshöhle** (devil's cave), a suite of large, damp caves in the hillside: of its many stalactites, some have been given comic names such as 'Barbarossa's Chamber' or 'The Pope'. In some corners you can see the dry bones of bears that are believed to have been trapped here and died of starvation 30,000 years ago. The little market town and resort of **Gössweinstein**, to the west, stands high above the curving river Wiesent, in a dramatic landscape: the best view is from the castle rock. From here, follow the pretty Wiesent valley north to **Schloss Zwernitz**, a fortified castle that was remodelled by Wilhelmina of Bayreuth (see below): she also devised its intriguing Sanspareil rock-garden, filling its rock-strewn beechwood with baroque follies.

Wilhelmina, sister of Frederick the Great, married a ruling Margrave of **BAYREUTH** in 1731. She was a gifted and versatile lady of culture, who instigated the creation of the elegant Margrave Opera House and other fine baroque and rococo buildings that today still adorn this elegant town (pop. 72,000). So it was that Bayreuth became a vigorous centre of art and music, long before Richard Wagner thereby chose it in 1872 (with Ludwig II's backing) as the best place for staging his operas. He designed the Festspielhaus, which opened with *The Ring* in 1876. Set on a hill in the outskirts, amid streets with such names as Parsifalstrasse and Nibelungenstrasse, this lofty red-brick festival theatre is outwardly no beauty but has superb special acoustics. The famous and fashionable opera festival, devoted solely to the Meister's works, is still held here annually. Prices in the town tend to double during its season.

Wagner, his wife Cosima and her father Franz Liszt all spent some years in Bayreuth. The Wagners lie buried in the garden behind their former home, the Villa Wahnfried: rebuilt after wartime bombing, this is now a museum (open daily), with many photos of the Wagner family and of opera productions. Recitals are held in its library in summer. The attractive park behind the house leads to the Neues Schloss, one of Wilhelmina's creations. She adored romantic extravaganza – as you can see by visiting her delectable **Eremitage** (hermitage) park and castle just east of the town. Here the *Schloss* has cells where her guests could pretend they were hermits; the garden includes a temple covered with mythological scenes, a decorative pool full of winged horses and cherubs, a theatre built as an artificial ruin, and a curved summerhouse made of stripes of multicoloured quartz. In creating the Eremitage, Wilhelmina was one of the first in Europe to indulge in the 18th-century vogue for whimsical romantic 'follies' (witness the slightly later Peacock Island in Berlin).

North-east of Bayreuth is the pineclad **Fichtelgebirge** massif, where it is well worth visiting the **Luisenberg**, a vast labyrinth of high granite rocks eroded into bizarre shapes: amid this drama of nature, a drama festival is held each summer. To the north is **Selb**, home of the Rosenthal porcelain factory. And over to the west is **Kulmbach** (pop. 29,000) whose large breweries are known for their bitter dark beers and strong, sharp Pils. Towering above its Marktplatz is the impressive fortress of Plassenburg, whose austere exterior gives no hint of the gentle elegance of its inner Renaissance courtyard, lined with ornate tiered galleries. The castle contains an unexpected collection of some 300,000 tin soldiers and other figures, grouped into dioramas of famous battles and other scenes. Further north-west you'll come to the old fortress town of **Kronach**, birthplace of Cranach; and then to **Neustadt** whose museum of some 1,000 dolls in folk costume bears witness to the town's long tradition of doll-making. North of Kronach, the wild wooded hills of the Frankenwald, fine country for camping or hiking, stretch to the GDR border. Until November 1989 this was a sadly isolated area: Ludwigsstadt, in a strip of Bavaria enclosed on three sides by the GDR, struck me on my visit in 1985 as an exceptionally gloomy little town. But now, with the opening of the border, lively normality has returned.

COBURG (pop. 44,000), with its royal associations, was for centuries the seat of that so-called 'royal stud farm', the Saxe-Coburg Gotha family, who provided brides and grooms for so many European monarchies: one of them, Prince Albert, was born at Schloss Rosenau north-east of the town and spent his childhood in Coburg. Queen Victoria was also related, but more distantly. She came to stay six times at Schloss Ehrenburg, the grey, formal Renaissance palace in the town centre where the family lived till 1918. The guided tour takes in her modest bedroom, also the Giants' Hall with its painted ceiling, and the neo-baroque Throne Room. Most rooms however are smallish, with an intimate, lived-in feel; plays and concerts are often held here. There's a statue of Prince Albert in the nearby Marktplatz, facing the Renaissance **Rathaus**. The Saxe-Coburg Gothas lived till 1945 in the Veste, a massive fortress with a double ring of ramparts, on a hill above the town: it was built in the 12th century, then rebuilt in the 16th. Its stark exterior contrasts with the charming inner courtyard, prettily half-timbered. In the castle museum are paintings by Dürer and Cranach, also horse-carriages and old weapons; the Fürstenbau has souvenirs of Luther's visit in 1530. A natural history museum (open daily) stands on the slope below the castle.

Lichtenfels, to the south, is the leading centre of basket-making in Germany. A few miles downstream along the upper Main, two remarkable buildings face each other on hillsides above this gentle valley. On the north slope is the vast former Benedictine abbey of **Banz**, founded in the 11th century and rebuilt in the 18th to the design of

The Gothic courtyard of the Alte Hofhaltung (old residence) in Bamberg.

Johann Dientzenhofer. The main buildings are now a conference centre; but you can visit the church, with its magnificent baroque painted ceiling. On the south side, more splendid still, is the pilgrimage church of **Vierzehn-heiligen**, dedicated to the 'fourteen saints' who help people in trouble. On this spot a shepherd boy in 1445–46 had visions of Christ among these saints: so a chapel was built, then in the 18th century a rococo church designed by that master of baroque, Balthazar Neumann. Its yellowish exterior looks dull: but the light, bright interior, all gold, blue and white with multi-coloured marble pillars, is breath-taking. In its middle is the altar of the 14 saints of intercession, an ornate rococo pyramid beneath a canopy. Here the statues of the saints still draw a stream of pilgrims, for one saint may help you find a husband, another helps if you fail your exams, a third is for tummy upsets – and so on. The out-buildings house a diocesan centre. The bazaar-like shops at the entrance asser-tively sell religious kitsch.

The valley leads down to **BAMBERG** (pop. 71,000), which for my money is as lovely an old town as any in Germany – and, being quite a big and busy place, it is not a mere tourist museum-piece like little Rothenburg. It lies astride the rushing river Regnitz which from the 12th century divided the episcopal city on the hill from the burghers below – and they were incessantly in conflict (the bishops finally won, in the 16th century). This dichotomy is one reason why the quaint old Altes Rathaus, with its painted façades, was built on a tiny islet in the river, where it was best able to serve the town's two parts. The river banks are lined with charming old gabled cottages, while narrow ancient streets wind up to the high **cathedral** with its four green spires.

This superb building, Romanesque with Gothic additions, dates from the 11th century. It has richly sculpted doorways and, inside, some renowned artistic treasures – in the nave, the tomb of Heinrich II and his queen Kunigunde, sculpted by the great Riemenschneider; and the Bamberger Reiter (1230), a stone statue of horse and rider, typifying the mediaeval ideal of knighthood. The 14th-century choir-stalls, and the sumptuous royal and episcopal costumes in the diocesan museum, are also worth noting. Next to the cathedral, on the broad, cobbled traffic-free Domplatz, is the **Alte Hofhaltung**, the prince-bishops' old residence, now housing a local history museum: Gothic half-timbered buildings with wooden balconies line its delightful courtyard, where outdoor plays are staged in summer. Next door is the huge **Neue Residenz**, part Renaissance, part baroque: its state rooms contain some fine allegorical frescoes and Gobelin tapestries. The rose-garden at the back offers a good view over the town.

In the more modern part of town, the main curiosity is the former home of E.T.A. Hoffmann, artist, musician and writer of satiric fantasies (Offenbach used some for his opera). This little house, where he lived in 1809–13, is now a Hoffmann museum: one room has a hole in the floor, through which this intriguing eccentric would joke and quarrel with his wife in the room below.

TOURIST OFFICES

BAYREUTH: Luitpoldplatz 9, tel (0921) 8 85 88.

COBURG: Herrngasse 4, tel 7 41 80.

BAMBERG: Hauptwachstr 16, tel 2 10 40.

Accommodation, Eating and Drinking

AMBERG 8450:

(H)**Goldene Krone**, Waisenhausgasse 2, tel (09621) 2 29 94. Characterful old inn (1598), very modest but friendly; good local cooking. Rooms (24) E. Meals C–D.

AUERBACH 8572:

(H)**Romantik-Hotel Goldener Löwe**, Unterer Markt 9, tel (09643) 17 65. Very spruce and comfortable, in a former iron-mining town. Original 'mining' décor, friendly service, good food. Rooms (23) C–D. Meals B–C.

PEGNITZ 8570:

(H)**Pflaums Posthotel**, Nürnbergerstr. 14, tel (09241) 72 50. One of Bavaria's best hotels, run by the charming Pflaum family since 1707; beautiful, stylish and hospitable. Excellent food. Much frequented by top musicians. Rooms (58) B–C. 2 restaurants, A and B–C.

WIESENTHAL 8551:

(H)**Feiler**, Oberer Markt 4, Muggendorf, tel (09196) 322. Delightful old inn with pretty courtyard. Excellent Franconian cooking. Cl Jan. Rooms (12) C. Meals A–B.

BAYREUTH 8580:

(H)**Bayerischer Hof**, Bahnhofstr. 14, tel (0921) 2 20 81. Excellent modern hotel near station; heated pool, rooftop restaurant (local dishes). Rooms (62) B–C. Meals (cl Sun) B–C.
(H)**Schlosshotel Tiergarten**, in Thiergarten suburb, tel (09209) 13 14. Converted Schloss, now a smart restaurant with rooms; local and French dishes. Rooms (8) B. Meals (cl Sun dinner, Mon) A.
(H)**Am Hofgarten**, Lisztstr. 6, tel (0921) 6 90 06. Near park and Wagner museum; sauna, etc. No restaurant. Rooms (17) C.
(H)**Fränkischer Hof**, Rathenaustr. 28, tel (0921) 6 42 14. Fairly central, small, well run; good French restaurant. Rooms (12) C–D. Meals (cl Wed) B–C.
(R)**Annecy**, Gabelsbergerstr. 11, tel (0921) 2 62 79. Good French cooking, sympatheic bistro ambience. Cl Sun dinner. Meals B–C.

SEULBITZ 8580:

(H)**Waldhotel Stein**, tel (0921) 90 01. In a village just east of Bayreuth; quiet and comfortable, family-run; good food. Cl Dec. Rooms (59) B–D. Meals C.

WUNSIEDEL 8592:

(H)**Kronprinz von Bayern**, Maximilianstr. 27, tel (09232) 35 09. Near the Felsen rocks. Comfortable, good food. Rooms (27) D. Meals C–D.

KRONACH 8640:

(H)**Bauer**, Kulmbacherstr. 7, tel (09261) 9 40 58. Friendly and classic; cooking above average. Cl 2 weeks Jan, 2 weeks Aug. Rooms (18) D. Meals C–D.

COBURG 8630:

(H)**Stadt Coburg**, Lossaustr. 12, tel (09561) 77 81. Near station. Fine restaurant with 'rustic' ambience. Rooms (44) C. Meals (cl Sun) C–D.

(H)**Coburger Tor**, Ketschendorfer Str. 22, tel (09561) 2 50 74. Solidly comfortable; its excellent but pricey **Schaller** restaurant (cl Fri, Sat lunch) serves regional and *nouvelle* dishes. Rooms (17) C–D. Meals A–B.

(H)**Goldener Anker**, Rosengasse 14, tel (09561) 9 50 27. Central, friendly; roof terrace, indoor pool. Rooms (60) C–D. Meals (cl Sun) C.

BAMBERG 8600:

(H)**Gästehaus Steinmühle**, Obere Mühlbrücke 5, tel (0951) 5 40 74. Old millhouse, stylishly converted. Its adjacent **Böttingerhaus** restaurant, in a beautiful baroque mansion, is excellent. Rooms (28) B–C. Meals B–C.

(H)**Sankt Nepomuk**, Obere Mühlbrücke 9, tel (0951) 2 51 83. Picturesque old house on stilts on the river, finely converted. Very good food and service. Rooms (12) C. Meals B–C.

(H)**Romantik-Hotel Weinhaus Messerschmitt**, Langestr. 41, tel (0951) 2 78 66. Solid family-run hostelry, very central. Notable cooking. Rooms (14) C. Meals B–C.

(H)**Weierich**, Lugnak 5, tel (0951) 5 40 04. Central, homely; Franconian restaurant with rustic décor. Rooms (23) D. Meals C–D.

(B)**Zum Schenkerla**, Dominikanerstr. 6, tel (0951) 56060. Famous 17th-century tavern, picturesque and animated; good place for drinking the local smoked beer. Light meals too.

CHAPTER SIX

Hessen

HESSEN (HESSE IN English; pop. 5.6 million) is the most centrally situated of all the *Länder*, and one of the richest. But it lacks distinctive character, perhaps because its historical identity is so sketchy. Its present area was long split up between various local rulers, such as the Dukes of Nassau who reigned in Wiesbaden. The major part of Hessen became a Prussian province in 1866, and the *Land* was created in 1949. Its political capital is Wiesbaden, largest and grandest of the many spa towns of the hilly Taunus area, in the west. But the biggest town by far is Frankfurt, Germany's banking and commercial capital: this is where Hessen's wealth comes from, also from the heavy industry of the Frankfurt area and in Kassel, in the north. Since 1986 the *Land* has been ruled by the CDU, under the liberal-minded Walter Wallmann, a former lord mayor of Frankfurt and federal minister for the environment. Before that it was SPD-ruled; and in 1985, when the SPD lost its working majority, it was here in Hessen that the Greens first entered a Land coalition. But this so-called 'Red-Green coalition' soon broke down, when the two parties came to blows on the issue of nuclear power. The Greens wanted all nuclear stations closed down, and the SPD refused.

Hessen embraces a stretch of the Rhine's east bank, around Rüdesheim, where the Rheingau vineyards produce some of Germany's best wine. To the north are the attractive wooded Taunus hills, and the scenic Lahr valley: this river flows past several interesting towns, including Limburg (hilltop cathedral), Wetzlar (Goethe associations) and Marburg (famous old university). Other Hessen towns are Darmstadt, a cradle of the *Jugendstil* movement, and Kassel, with its exuberant Wilhelmshöhe park.

Frankfurt-am-Main

The skyscrapers of central **Frankfurt** (pop. 617,000) soar up near the river Main, giving this city its nickname of 'Mainhattan': none other in Europe has so many tall office tower-blocks so close together in the centre. They are symbols of its role as Germany's banking and commercial capital, and have helped foster its reputation as a brash, soulless, over-materialistic place. But this is an unfair image. Of course Frankfurt is highly commercial – but that gives it the money to be highly cultural too: it has good theatre and opera, excellent museums, and a famous Book Fair that unites commerce and literature. Goethe's home town has played a key role in German history, and has a less provincial ambience than most in Germany. Moreover, its banking scene is countered by an assertive Left-wing and 'alternative' scene, making this an exciting city, full of creative tensions.

Centrally located between north and south Germany, it has been a trade centre since Roman times – and then a political capital too. Starting with Barbarossa in 1152, many mediaeval German kings were elected here; then in 1562 Frankfurt replaced Aachen as the place where the Holy Roman Emperors were crowned, a role it held until 1806. Goethe called it 'Germany's secret capital'. In 1848–49 the first pan-German parliament met here, but the city then failed in its bid against Berlin to become the capital of the new united Germany. Across the centuries its financial role was developing, too. In the 16th century it won the right to mint money, and in 1585 its Stock Exchange was founded. In the 19th century it became a major world banking centre, thanks to Rothschild and other local financiers, many of them Jewish. Few of the great Jewish bankers have returned since the Nazi period: but the banking goes on. After 1945 many people urged that Frankfurt, not Bonn, should be chosen as the federal capital: but Adenauer's wishes prevailed (see p. 66). In many ways it was a pity, for Frankfurt would have made a much less artificial Hauptstadt.

But if money rules, then Frankfurt since the war has lived up to Goethe's claim for it. It is the site of the all-powerful Bundesbank, and headquarters of most leading German banks and of many insurance and advertising firms; some 388 world banks are represented here, many of them housed in those skyscrapers. Frankfurt also has Germany's major international airport, and along with Hanover is its leading trade fair venue. It is a large inland port, and an industrial centre for chemicals (Hoechst), machine tools and much else. The welter of high-level international activity gives it a metropolitan flavour quite out of scale with its modest population: 'It's a very open, modern society,' said one cultivated Berlin banker who settled here, 'much less cliquey than, say, Munich. People are competitive, even ruthlessly so, but also hospitable and outward-looking.'

The city lavishes its wealth on culture: the proportion of its budget spent on the arts, eight per cent, is the highest in Europe. And not all of it is 'safe' culture for the moneyed classes. The opera under Michael Gielen was recently the most avant-garde in Germany; rebels such as the late Rainer Werner Fassbinder have been active in local drama; fringe theatres and 'alternative' art centres abound. Major serious publishers such as Suhrkamp are here, too, supporting the Book Fair. And Frankfurt possesses two of the three most prestigious German daily papers, the *Allgemeine* and the *Rundschau*.

The huge and famous university, with 45,000 students, has long been a powerhouse of new ideas; key radical philosophers such as Adorno and Habermas have worked here. Since the war this campus has been seen as a

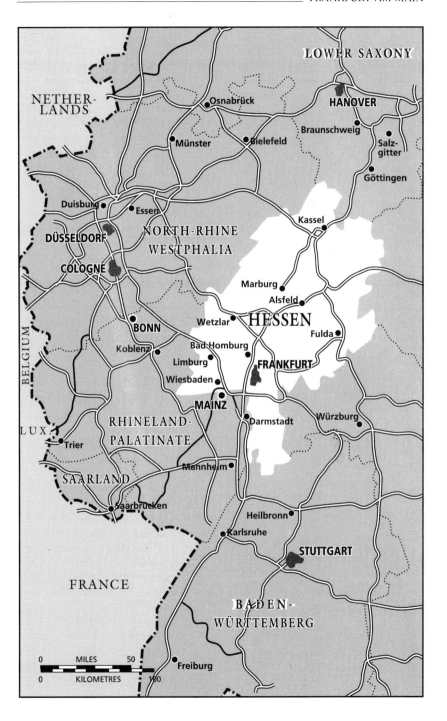

hotbed of Leftism, and this has helped to give Frankfurt its reputation for noisy political polarization – can it be that the banks' blatant and successful capitalism has provided the Left with a sitting target and led to a sharpening of its knives? Certainly Left-wing and Green protest has been stronger here than anywhere except West Berlin, culminating in the violent campaign of the early 1980s against the extension of the airport. The city council was then in CDU hands, but today it is ruled by an SPD/Green coalition, and meanwhile extreme-Left militancy has died down. It is ironical that Greens should be helping to run this city of bankers. One of their councillors is none other than Danny Cohn-Bendit, the May '68 rebel leader, who for years has been working quietly in the local Green scene. He is now in charge of relations with the huge local immigrant worker population, 22 per cent of the total: they add colourfully to Frankfurt's diversity. Drugs and crime are also at the highest German level. Quite a metropolis.

The two most notables **festivals** are Main river festival in early August, and, later the same month, the Sachsenhausen fountain festival. **Trade fairs** include international fairs in March and August; the Easter fur fair; and the world's largest book fair in early October.

Central Frankfurt is in three main parts. First, to the west around the station and trade fair ground (*Messe*) is the new business district with its skyscrapers. Few of these are individually attractive, but their harmonious grouping is impressive, especially seen from across the river. South of the river is Sachsenhausen, known for its lively pubs and night-life, also for the six fine museums along the south bank of the

Main. Thirdly, on the north bank is what remains of the old town centre, within the semi-circle of the former ramparts, now a strip of parkland. Before the bombing, Frankfurt had the largest mediaeval Altstadt of any German town: but only a small corner of it, around the cathedral and the Römer, has been restored in the old style: the rest is modern, mostly ugly. More than most German cities, Frankfurt has changed almost beyond recognition.

The **Römer**, a tight knot of 15th-century houses, was the main city hall from 1405 onwards, though a big newer Rathaus now stands next door. The inner court has an elegant Renaissance stairway, leading up to the *Kaisersaal* (open daily) where the coronation banquets were held; now lined with 19th-century portraits of the 52 emperors, it is still used for civic receptions. The cobbled square outside, the **Römerberg**, was for centuries the city's focus, for markets and festivals as well as royal occasions: today it is visited mainly by tourists, but its handsome half-timbered houses give some idea of what old Frankfurt used to look like. In its centre is the Justice Fountain (1611) and the tiny Gothic red-sandstone Nikolaikirche, formerly a court chapel. Among the various rebuilt 15th- to 17th-century houses round the square, note the Wertheim Haus on the west side, and the stone Steinernes Haus on the east. The **History Museum**, on the south side, has industrial as well as religious exhibits, also replicas of crown jewels, and some remarkable scale models of the Altstadt as it used to be, plus vivid details of the wartime devastation. The Saalhof chapel (1175), beside the museum, is all that remains of an imperial palace once standing on this site.

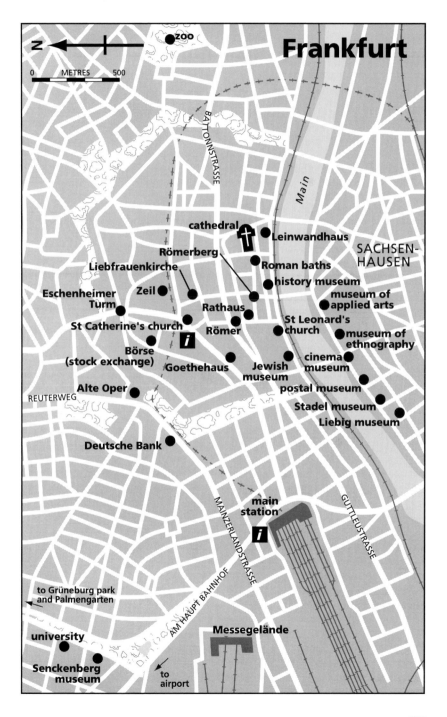

Frankfurt

ZOO

N

0   METRES   500

BATTONNSTRASSE

Main

cathedral

Leinwandhaus

Römerberg

SACHSEN-
HAUSEN

Liebfrauenkirche

Roman baths

history museum

Eschenheimer
Turm

Zeil

museum of
applied arts

Rathaus

St Catherine's church

Römer

St Leonard's
church

museum of
ethnography

Börse
(stock exchange)

Goethehaus

Jewish
museum

cinema
museum

Alte Oper

postal museum

REUTERWEG

Stadel museum

Liebig museum

Deutsche Bank

main
station

GUTTLEUSTRASSE

MAINZERLANDSTRASSE

to Grüneburg park
and Palmengarten

AM HAUPT BAHNHOF

Messegelände

university

Senckenberg
museum

to
airport

Goethe's Youth in Frankfurt

Wolfgang von Goethe (1789–1832), revered by Germans as the greatest of their writers, was born and brought up in Frankfurt, where the handsome family house is now a museum. His father, a retired lawyer of North German origin, was a cultured but solemnly serious man; his mother, from a patrician Frankfurt family, was much livelier. Indeed, Goethe's own writing combined the moral and intellectual rigour of the north with a southerly life-loving artistic hedonism – and he often said that he derived these contrasting qualities from his parents. At 15 he fell in love with a local barmaid, Gretchen (the first of his innumerable loves!) who became the model for Marguerite in *Faust*. Later he went to Leipzig University, spent periods in Wetzlar (see p. 216) and Strasbourg where there were more love-affairs, and finally settled in Weimar (see p. 321).

The **Goethehaus** (open daily), dating from 1590, was badly damaged in the war but has been well restored. Part is a museum, with letters and portraits including a copy of the famous Tischbein of a dreamy Goethe in Italy, the land he loved best. The rest of the house, refurnished in the style of the period, includes Goethe's bedroom and library, with the puppet theatre that fascinated him. Goethe described the house as 'spacious, light and gay': it is certainly elegant and cultured, though by today's standards it seems cramped.

Just east of Römerberg, some modernistic buildings have been placed next to ancient ones, to create a contrast. The latter include the Kultur-Schirn, a glass-walled culture-centre, and the Ostzeile, a row of new gabled town houses. They give straight on to the remains of Roman baths of c. AD 75–110 and of a Carolingian palace: these were unearthed here after the bombing. Right next to them, in this intriguing hotch-potch of an area, is the **Cathedral of St Bartholomew**, with its high 15th-century Gothic tower (worth the climb, for a fabulous view of the city). In this severe reddish sandstone church the emperors were crowned: its somewhat gloomy interior has attractive 14th-century choirstalls and 15th-century murals. To the right of the choir is the simple chapel (**Wahlkapelle**) where the seven electors of the Holy Roman Empire made their final choice of king. The orna-

ments they wore, and other treasures, can be inspected in the cathedral's museum. On its south side is the 14th-century Leinwandhaus, a former cloth hall, now also a small museum.

Back near the Römer, St Leonard's church by the river is 15th-century Gothic, with some Romanesque features from an earlier basilica; inside is some fine stained glass. At Untermainkai 14–15 is the new **Jewish Museum**, highly impressive: it traces the history of the Jewish colony in Frankfurt, once so large, and gives details of Jewish life. Its treasures include a part of the Rothschild library. The Nazi period is treated with great restraint. Turning north, you will pass the city theatre and the BfG skyscraper, and come to the Goethehaus. The Hauptwache, an 18th-century baroque building, stands at one end of Zeil, the city's hideous main shopping mall, typical of the hurried early post-war rebuilding. Two nearby churches are worth noting: St Catherine's, where Goethe was baptised, and the 15th-century Liebfrauenkirche, with an unusual altar. The Börse (stock exchange), open to visits 11.30am to 1.30pm weekdays, will give you insights into Frankfurt money-making. Beyond it is the tall 15th-century Eschenheimer Turm, a survivor from the 42 towers that once ringed the city. Fronting the broad Opernplatz to the west is the massive neo-classical **Alte Oper** (opera house), built in the 1880s and newly reopened after wartime damage: however, it is now used for conventions and some concerts, not for operas (these are performed in the big city theatre).

The financial district between here and the station is dominated by the most elegant of the city's skyscrapers, the 24-floor twin-towered Deutsche Bank building, with its gleaming blue-grey façade of glass and steel. The quiet residential streets behind it, the Westend district, form a pleasant contrast to the brash surrounding gigantism, most noticeable at the huge **Messegelände** (Trade Fairground) on Friedrich-Ebert-Anlage, where the tallest office building in Europe (254 metres) has just been completed. The new SPD-Green city council are dubious about this honour, but when they came to power it was too late to cancel the project. North of the Messe is the university, also the Senckenberg natural history museum (open daily: notable collection of ancient animals such as dinosaurs). The nearby Grüneburg Park is the only large stretch of green in the city proper, and includes a botanical garden and tropical garden (Palmengarten). Over on the east side of town, the **Zoo** (open daily) is one of the best in Germany: notable features include the darkened Grzimek-Haus for nocturnal creatures (bats, dormice, etc), and the Exotarium which has beautiful rare fish. The hideous apes are charming.

Sachsenhausen on the south bank of the Main, is a large residential district now again becoming fashionable; it was little bombed, and some 16th–17th-century houses survive. This is the best place to go to find old Frankfurt cider-pubs and other night entertainment. A group of narrow streets at the eastern end, off Elisabethenstrasse, are largely given over to pubs, discos and cheap eateries: they look picturesque, but have gone tackily down-market and at the weekend are crammed with US soldiers getting drunk.

You might be more edified by the row of six remarkable **museums** along the Main bank at Sachsenhausen, some newly opened or rebuilt, and evidence of the city's go-ahead cultural policy. From east to west they are: (1) The **Museum of Applied Arts** (*Kunsthandwerk*), a gleaming white modern building designed by the American Richard Meier. Its glories include baroque glass, Meissen porcelain, *Jugendstil* furniture, and a fine Islamic and oriental section. (2) The **Museum of Ethnography** (*Völkerkunde*), with masks and other cult objects from native tribes. (3) The **Cinema Museum**: mainly technical, with exhibits of early inventions by Melies and others; some displays of how films are made, but not much about directors or actors. (4) **Postal Museum**: lots about early mail-coaches, postage stamps, also telephones. (5) **Stadel Museum**, one of Germany's major art collections. There's a lot in it, from the 15th to 20th centuries, but all somewhat muddled up together. The earlier period includes a fine altarpiece by Holbein the Elder, also works by Bosch, Altdorfer and Cranach. There's a splendid Tintoretto, *Moses strikes water from the cliff*; also a lovely Vermeer, several Rembrandts, a superb Renoir, *La fin du déjeuner*, and Monet, *Le déjeuner*. Moderns such as Picasso and Matisse are not in their top form. But German painting of the past 200 years is vividly represented, starting with Tischbein's famous portrait of a pensive Goethe reclining in the Roman countryside (1787). There are many pleasing works by the German impressionist Max Liebermann; other Germans on display include Thoma, Beckmann, Kirchner and Nolde. All in all, a rich collection. The huge contemporary canvases on the second floor may not please everyone. Lastly (6) the **Liebig Museum** is devoted to sculpture, mostly classical: it ranges from Egypt via Greece and Rome to the Renaissance and baroque.

Ten km west of the city centre is the old mediaeval town of **Höchst**, now part of Frankfurt. Not bombed in the war, its little Altstadt of timbered houses survives intact and is worth a visit. The town is also the home of the huge Hoechst chemicals firm, employing 38,000 locally, which produces many special dyes and drugs. One building of note is the Justiniuskirche, of Carolingian origin with later additions; another is the baroque Bolongaro palace, former home of Italian snuff-makers. The red-brick Renaissance castle, partly ruined, has a high round white tower and contains two small museums, one of local history, the other devoted to the Hoechst firm. Höchst was a famous porcelain-producing centre in the 18th century, and today this industry is being revived, at the Dalbergerhaus: here you can inspect the historic porcelain collection and also, if you wish, buy new porcelain. It is not cheap. Between Höchst and Frankfurt is the Main-Taubus-Zentrum, said to be Europe's largest shopping-centre, very imposing. Just east of the city, the industrial town of **Offenbach** is the main centre of the German leather industry and has a famous leather museum (open daily), with displays of shoes and handbags dating from mediaeval times.

TOURIST OFFICES
Main station, tel 212 8849; Römer, tel 212 87 08; airport, hall B, tel 69 31 53.

Accommodation, Eating and Drinking (Postcode 6000, tel code 069)
Hotels in Frankfurt are expensive, as you might expect. Those in the medium range tend to be utilitarian, and small hotels of character are very few. Restaurants of the expense-account kind are also highly-priced, and very numerous. However, there are plenty of cheaper, lively eating places and taverns, mainly in Sachsenhausen, and in the Bornheim district. In some of these they serve not wine or beer but the dry cider, *Äppelwoi*, that is a Frankfurt speciality.

Modern Frankfurt beside the river Main (its nickname is 'Mainhattan').

(H)**Hessischer Hof**, Friedrich-Ebert-Anlage 40, Frankfurt 97, tel 754 00. Near station and Messe, a converted town house with elegant décor and antiques. Rooms (134) A. Meals A–B.

(H)**Pullman Savigny**, Savignystr. 14, Frankfurt 1, tel 753 30. In a quiet street near station. Modern and elegant. Rooms (124) A. Meals B (dinner), B–C (lunch).

(H)**Mozart**, Parkstr. 17, Frankfurt 1, tel 55 08 31. Near Gruneberg park. Unusual décor. Cl Christmas. No restaurant. Rooms (35) B.

(H)**Am Dom**, Kannengiessergasse 3, Frankfurt 1, tel 28 21 41. Behind cathedral. No restaurant. Rooms (32) B–C.

(H)**Westend**, Westendstr. 15, Frankfurt 1, tel 74 67 02. Small and personal with old-world service. Snacks only. Rooms (20) B–C.

(H)**Alte Scheune**, Alt Erlenbach 44, tel (06101) 445 51. In Erlenbach, 14 km to N. Converted farm building with rustic décor; good food. Rooms (25) C. Meals (cl Sat dinner, Sun Mon) B–C.

(H)**Am Zoo**, Alfred-Brehm-Platz 6, Frankfurt 1, tel 49 07 71. Facing zoo. Cl Christmas, New Year. Rooms (85) C.

(H)**Maingau**, Schifferstr. 38, tel 61 70 01. In Sachsenhausen, quite near river. Dull but useful. Rooms (100) C. Meals C.

(H)**Arcade**, Speicherstr. 3, Frankfurt 1, tel 27 30 30. Near station. Rooms (193) C–D. Meals (cl Sat Sun, mid-Jul to mid-Aug) C.

(R)**Weinhaus Brückenkeller**, Schützenstr. 6, tel 28 42 38. Famous and luxurious old vaulted tavern, full of antiques. Splendid cooking in wine, fine wines. Cl lunch, Sun. Meals A.

(R)**Gargantua**, Friesengasse 3, tel 77 64 42. Popular bistro with *nouvelle cuisine*. Cl lunch, Sun Mon, 3 weeks summer. Meals A.

(R)**Mövenpick: Baron de la Mouette**, Opernplatz 2, tel 206 80. Reliable Swiss luxury chain-restaurant, good for beef. Meals B; **Orangerie** C.

(R)**Neuer Haferkasten**, Löwengasse , tel 353 29. In Neu-Isenburg, 7km S of city. Good Italian cooking; outdoor summer dining. Cl Sun, mid-Jul to mid-Aug. Meals B.

(R)**Henninger Turm**, Hainer Weg 60, tel 606 36 00. In Sachsenhausen, two revolving restaurants in a tower; fine views over the city. Cl Mon. Meals B–C.

(R)**Gerbermühle**, Deutschherrnufer 105, tel 65 50 91. Beer-garden by Main in Sachsenhausen, former haunt of Goethe. Meals C.

(R)**Zum Bären**, Schlossplatz 8, Höchst, tel 30 15 24. Old Höchst inn with good home cooking. Outdoor terrace. Cl Mon. Meals C.

(R)**Zum Böckchen**, Grosse Rittergasse 52, tel 62 67 81. Typical Alt Sachsenhausen eatery; good local dishes. Music. Meals C–D.

(R)**Zum Gemalten Haus**, Schweizerstr. 67, tel 61 45 59. Old Sachsenhausen cider tavern always crowded. Simple dishes. Cl Mon Tue. Meals D. **Wagner**, next door, tel 61 25 65, is similar.

(P)**Zur Sonne**, Bergerstr. 312, Bornheim, tel 45 14 20. Ancient friendly cider-pub with garden; some snacks. Meals.

(W)**Blaubart**, Kaiserhofstr. 18, tel 28 22 29. Traditional wine-cellar in city centre; pub food and grills.

(W)**Dünker**, Bergerstr. 265, Bornheim. Crowded, bohemian wine-tavern in very old building. Atmospheric. Cl Sun.

(W)**Abstkeller**, Abstgasse 7, tel 62 68 32. Delightful romantic candlelit wine-pub in Alt Sachsenhausen. No food.

(P)**Brotfabrik**, Bachmannstr. 2, tel 789 43 40. In NW suburb of Hausen, an old bakery, now a large, lively 'alternative' cultural centre with music, theatre, garden, pub, some food including American dishes. Most attractive.

(W)**Fidelio**, Opernplatz, tel 72 57 58. Trendy wine-tavern near Opera, popular with yuppies. Classical music.

(C)**Cafe Schwille**, Gr. Bockenheimerstr. 50, tel 28 41 83. Large fashionable café/tearoom on main shopping-street.

Wiesbaden, the Rheingau and the Taunus Hills

The western part of Hesse, to the north-west of Frankfurt, is dissected by the long, low range of the Taunus hills, gloriously forested, ideal terrain for hiking. There are many mineral spas in the area, including two large and famous ones, Bad Homburg and Wiesbaden, the *Land* capital. To the north, in the winding Lahr valley, are the historic cathedral towns of Limburg and Wetzlar. And west from Wiesbaden, along the right bank of the Rhine, there stretches one of Germany's leading wine regions: the Rheingau.

WIESBADEN (pop. 269,000), Hesse's capital, former seat of the dukes of Nassau, sits pleasantly in the wooded foothills of the Taunus. Its abundant mineral springs led to its development in the 19th century as a fashionable spa. Today a town of *nouveau riche* opulence, it strives to renew its old reputation.

The Romans first used its healing waters, and built a forum; just one arch now survives from their time. Obscure in the Middle Ages, Wiesbaden did not really develop until 1744 when Prince Karl of Nassau set up residence in his new palace of Biebrich. From 1816 the town was the capital of the new Duchy of Nassau; the Nassaus, who held court in high style, endowed it with stately public buildings, and encouraged its growth as a leading German spa. Then in the years before 1914 Wiesbaden was the favourite summer resort of Kaiser Wilhelm II: this was its heyday.

Today, rich Arabs and Americans have replaced 19th-century Russian princes as the spa's principal foreign patrons. It is also a town of well-to-do retired people, many of whom frequent the scores of private clinics in the suburbs. There are 26 warm springs (c. 20°C), helpful against rheumatism: some are in the spa hotels, some in the big public thermal baths. Expensive boutiques and antique shops line the main boulevard, the Wilhelmstrasse, and some other streets. Because of its past grandeur, Wiesbaden in 1946 was chosen as *Land* capital, rather than its much larger neighbour, Frankfurt. And – a feature of Germany's decentralization – it is also the site of two major federal agencies that have huge headquarters in the suburbs: the Federal Statistical Office and the Federal Criminal Department.

The **May Festival**, a smart international affair, offers opera, ballet and theatre at night, horse-racing by day; the Rheingau Wine Week is held in early August.

There's not so very much to see in Wiesbaden: but its central area does have elegance. In a small park by the Wilhelmstrasse are two stately porticos built in the 1820s, the Brunnenkolonnade and Theaterkolonnade, adjoining the grandiose opera house (1894). Behind is the amazing **Kurhaus**, first built in the 1920s as a thermal centre, then remodelled in 1907 as a concert hall, and today mostly hired out for trade fairs, conventions and galas. It also houses the casino. Its décor, in the extravagant style typical of the Wilhelmine period, is a bizarre mix of neo-byzantine, neo-classical, neo-baroque and art nouveau – notably in the main Friedrich von Thierschsaal and the Muschelsaal. All weirdly impressive: but it is not open normally to the public, so to take a look you must gatecrash one of the trade fairs.

The Kurpark at the back is pleasant. The city museum has little of note save some paintings by the 'Blauer Reiter' artist Alexei Jawlensky. In the small and unremarkable Altstadt is the Nassaus' second sumptuous ducal palace, today the home of the Landtag. And in nearby Kranzplatz you'll find the Kochbrunnen, a public outdoor mineral spring where locals come to drink the hot salty water or bottle it, free. Out in the suburbs are two relics of Wiesbaden's past grandeur. On the wooded Neroberg hill, to the west, is a Greek Orthodox chapel (open Apr–Oct) with five gilded onion-domes: it was built in 1855 as the mausoleum of a Russian princess who married a duke of Nassau. And over by the Rhine in a pleasant park is the Nassaus' baroque Schloss Biebrich (1744), now the home of the German Film Industry Federation.

Going west from Wiesbaden along the Rhine, you can turn up right to the village of **Kiedrich**, whose 15th-century pilgrim church has flamboyant décor and carved coloured pews. Further on is lovely **Eberbach Abbey** (open daily), founded by the Cistercians in 1135 as a companion to Clairvaux. Its secluded setting, up a green vale, is typically Cistercian, and so is the architecture – the fine *Fachwerk* cloister, the 14th-century monks' dormitory with ribbed vaulted ceiling, the plain Romanesque church now used for concerts. The abbey was secularized in 1803, and together with its adjacent vineyards is now owned by the *Land* which uses it for wine-tastings and wine-auctions. In the lay brothers' refectory is an impressive array of old

wine-presses dating from 1668 (the Cistercians produced wine, but never drank it themselves). On a hillside further west, the handsome yellowish **Schloss Johannisberg** also has vineyards, and a shop that sells its distinguished wines. This 18th-century castle was given to Prince Metternich in 1816 and still belongs to his family; from its terrace there's a fine view.

Back by the river you'll come to **Rüdesheim** (pop. 10,000), the Rheingau's wine capital. It has some picturesque old houses, but today has become vulgarly touristy – especially its famous alley, the Drosselgasse. Lined with old wine-pubs dating from the 18th century, this must once have been charming, but the area has now moved brashly down-market and is awash with Chinese take-aways, McDonalds, kitschy souvenir-shops, and noisy German bandsmen in red coats. Escape it, and visit two 13th-century castles both housing interesting museums – the Brömserhof (early mechanical musical instruments), and on the edge of town the square fortified Brömserburg (open Mar to mid-Nov), with a display of old wine-presses and other vinous objects, some very ancient.

To the west, high on a hill above the Rhine, is another 13th-century castle, **Ehrenfels**, this one very ruined. Nearby is a centre for breeding and training eagles and falcons (open for visits all year); and the huge **Niederwald** memorial, erected after 1871 to celebrate France's defeat and German unification. The Rhine then curves past the smart resort of Assmannshausen, to reach the old village of **Lorch**, which has a notable Gothic church and a gabled Renaissance mansion, the Hilchenhaus.

The castle at Bad Homburg, once a fashionable spa.

At Lorch, you should leave the Rhine and drive up through the pretty Wisper valley to Bad Schwalbach, a sizeable spa in the Taunus hills. To the north is the picturesque old town of **LIMBURG** (pop. 29,000), whose unusual red-and-white cathedral stands on a rocky spur above the river Lahn. Begun in 1235, this building illustrates the transition in Germany from Romanesque to Gothic: its façade, with its curious red, black and yellow stripes, is Romanesque, but the lofty vaulted interior is Gothic, with black pillars, galleries and fine stained glass. The nearby diocesan museum has interesting mediaeval religious art.

Limburg also contains a delightful ensemble of very old *Fachwerk* houses, notably in the pedestrian zone around the Römer and Fischmarkt: those at 2, 4 and 6 Römer are said to be Germany's oldest of this kind, dating from c. 1290. Some of these rickety buildings now lean over precariously, almost touching others across the narrow alleys, and have to be propped up with buttresses.

The wooded Lahn valley winds upstream from Limburg to Wetzlar. There's no road along the river, so you must make detours to get to the interesting places on its banks. First comes **Runkel**, an unspoilt old village with a graceful bridge, below a severe feudal fortress. At **Weilburg** (pop. 13,000), the dukes of Nassau built a handsome Renaissance *Schloss* on a cliff above the river, and the town then grew up around it. This château has a cobbled courtyard whose elegant twin-columned gallery is topped by red-and-white half-timbered buildings; the ornate interiors are attractive, too, and so is the terraced garden. Further east, the mediaeval village of **Braunfels** lies below a hilltop castle far older than Weilburg's and very different: its massive battlements and pointed towers look quite dramatic. The small museum imside (open Apr–Sept) has details of the former feudal owners.

WETZLAR (pop. 50,000), until 1806 a seat of the tribunals of the Holy Roman, is rather gloomy to my mind: but it has some historic interest, and there are fine old *Fachwerk* houses around the Kornmarkt and Eisenmarkt. Like Limburg's, its soaring hilltop cathedral is somewhat curious, with a high red limestone tower and a 14th-century Gothic façade that was never finished. Wetzlar has long made cameras, and even played a part in the 19th-century pioneering of photography. But above all it is known for its links with Goethe. As a young lawyer he came to work there in 1772 (the house where he lived, now in part a Greek restaurant, is in in the Kornmarkt). He fell in love with a local girl, Charlotte Buff, whose fiancé, the diplomat Kestner, then committed suicide: this profoundly affected the poet and provided inspiration for *The Sufferings of Young Werther*, where Charlotte is 'Lotte'. The Buffs' home is now a museum (*Lottehaus*) with Goethe souvenirs; next door is a museum of local history, in a former commandery of the Teutonic Order.

Some way south-east of Wetzlar is the sizeable spa of **Bad Nauheim**, whose warm carbonic springs help to relieve heart and blood disorders. It has an elegant Kurpark with a lake. Further south, in the Taunus foothills, a detour will lead to **Saalburg**, a 2nd-century fort that the Romans built on the defence line (*limes*) along the northern border of their realm. Little but its foundations now remain: however, under Kaiser Wilhelm II the fort was ambitiously reconstructed, with battlements, gateways, colonnades and statues, to give an impression of what it might have been like. This is very phoney – typical of that tasteless epoch. But the museum has many genuine Roman relics found on the spot – even children's shoes! And whether or not the walled camp is open, you can always inspect the stone foundations that are just in front: wells, living quarters, a Roman heating system.

Further south is **BAD HOMBURG** (pop. 52,000), once one of Europe's leading spas and a famous gambling centre: one of Germany's first casinos was opened here, in 1841, and Dostoevsky used Bad Homburg as the setting for his novel *The Gambler*. Edward Prince of Wales was a frequent visitor in the 1890s, as was Kaiser Wilhelm. But today, unlike Baden-Baden, Bad Homburg has failed to retain its glamour: none of its hotels is fashionable, and its Kurhaus and main street have been rebuilt since the war in tawdry style. However, the big Kurpark is pleasant, with its unusual fountains and (curiously) a Thai temple and Russian chapel, two souvenirs of royal visitors from those lands. The stately 17th/18th-century castle, with its high round white tower, was in 1866–1918 a summer home of the Kaisers; its well-kept garden has gigantic wide-spreading cedars of Lebanon.

From here you can drive west into the Taunus, along a road that winds up through gorgeous forests of beech and oak to the Grosser Feldberg (880m), highest point of the range: its viewing tower offers wide views over the Frankfurt plain and the Westerwald hills. The road then descends to **Königstein**, set below the ruins of a mighty feudal fortress – and so back to Wiesbaden.

TOURIST OFFICES

WIESBADEN: Rheinstr. 15, tel (06121) 31 28 47; Hauptbahnhof, tel (06121) 31 28 48.

RÜDESHEIM: Rheinstr. 16, tel (06722) 29 62.

LIMBURG: Hospitalstr. 2, tel (06431) 20 32.

WETZLAR: Domplatz 8, tel (06441) 40 53 38.

BAD HOMBURG: Kurhaus, Louisenstr. 58, tel (06172) 12 13 10.

Accommodation, Eating and Drinking

WIESBADEN 6200 (tel code 06121)

(H)**Nassauer Hof**, Kaiser-Friedrich-Platz 3, tel 13 30. Classically elegant and luxurious, rather like the Crillon in Paris; frequented by wealthy Arabs, showbiz stars, etc; Mayo health clinic, indoor pool. Rooms (210) A. Two excellent restaurants, Ente vom Lehel, A; Orangerie, B.

(H)**Schwarzer Bock**, Kranzplatz 12, tel 1 55 0. Classy hostelry dating from 1486, redone in art nouveau style; roof garden, thermal pool, spa treatment. Rooms (135) B. 4 restaurants, A–D.

(H)**Central**, Bahnhofstr. 65, tel 37 20 01. Comfortable, near station. No restaurant. Rooms (70) C–D.

(R)**La Belle Epoque**, in Kurhaus, tel 52 69 37. Elegantly restored in *belle époque* style, a haunt of the *beau monde*, but food not outstanding. Cl Mon, 4 weeks July–Aug. Meals A. No lunches: but the Kurhaus' cheaper **Le Bistrot** (B–C), also '1900' style, *is* open for lunch.

(R)**Alt Prag**, Taunusstr. 41, tel 52 04 02. Cosy Czech restaurant, less full of homesick exiles since Prague embraced democracy. Good Bohemian dishes (goose, wild pig, etc). Cl Mon. Meals B–C.

(R)**Weihenstephan**, Armenruhstr. 6, tel 6 11 34. In suburb of Biebrich; good Bavarian dishes, fine value. Cl Sat, 3 weeks July, Aug. Meals B–C.

(W)**Caspari**, Einer, Zur Weinzunft are good wine-taverns in Wagemannstr., Altstadt. Some food, too.

OESTRICH 6227:

(H)**Romantik-Hotel Schwan**, Rheinallee 5, tel (06723) 30 01. Facing the river; owned by a leading local wine-grower; fairly smart but a bit charmless. Mar to mid-Nov. Rooms (66) B–C. Meals B–C.

RÜDESHEIM 6220:

(H)**Rheinstein**, Rheinsteinstr. 20, tel (06722) 20 04. By river, good view. Apr–Nov. Rooms (43) C–D. Meals C–D.

ASSMANNSHAUSEN 6220:

(H)**Krone**, Rheinuferstr. 10, tel (06722) 20 36. Famous old riverside hostelry, long frequented by writers (Hoffmann von Fallersleben wrote *Deutschland über Alles* here in 1841); modern comfort plus heavy Victorian furnishings; lovely pool, good food served on river terrace. Cl Jan, Feb. Rooms (79) B–C. Meals B.

(H)**Altes Haus**, Lorcherstr. 8, tel (06722) 20 51. 16th-century *Fachwerk* house; good cooking. Cl Jan Feb. Rooms (26) D. Meals (cl Wed) C–D.

LIMBURG 6250:

(H)**Romantik-Hotel Zimmermann**, Blumenröder Str. 1, tel (06431) 46 11. Modern hotel with lavish antique furnishings; friendly owner. Rooms (55) B–D; meals for residents only.

WETZLAR 6330:

(H)**Bürgerhof**, Konrad-Adenauer-Promenade 20, tel (06441) 4 40 68. 18th-century coaching-inn, well modernized. Rooms (44) C. Meals (cl 3 weeks July–Aug) C.

BAD HOMBURG 3588:

(H)**Haus Daheim**, Elisabethenstr. 42, tel (06172) 2 00 98. Pleasant and central; no restaurant. Rooms (18) C.

KÖNIGSTEIN IM TAUNUS 6240:

(H)**Sonnenhof**, Falkensteinerstr. 9, tel (06174) 2 90 80. Baron Rothschild's former hunting-lodge, in its own big park; elegant décor, nice pool. Rooms (44) B–C. Meals B.

Fulda, Marburg and Kassel

The northern part of Hesse is hilly and wooded and has some interesting towns – episcopal Fulda, studenty Marburg, and Kassel with its Wilhelmshöhe park. Around Alsfeld you are in Grimm fairy-tale country.

FULDA (pop. 56,000) is a city whose religious past has left it with a legacy of baroque buildings and ornaments. In the 8th century St Boniface, an English missionary sent to christianize the Germans, ordered the foundation here of a monastery that became highly influential and was centre of early German literature. His tomb lies in a crypt below the high altar of the baroque cathedral that was built in 1704–12 by the Prince-Bishops; the adjacent Dom Museum (cl mid-Nov–mid-Dec) holds the relics of the saint – his head and sword, and the book that he used to try to ward off the assassins who martyred him.

The Prince-Bishops endowed the city centre with other fine baroque buildings too – among them, the Stadt-schloss, a white stucco palace now housing the town hall, and the Orangerie, now a congress centre. By contrast, tiny St Michael's church, next to the cathedral, is 9th-century Caro-lingian. Outside the town, it is worth visiting the huge baroque Schloss Fasanerie (pheasant castle), built in 1756, now housing a museum; and the hilltop Petersberg church which has 9th-century frescoes in its crypt. Fulda today is still a religious centre, host to an annual conference of Catholic bish-ops. It is also known to NATO strate-gists, for it lies close to the old GDR border, and the so-called 'Fulda Gap' where Warsaw Pact tanks were thought likely to attempt a break-through, in the event of war. But that was in another era, that ended in 1989.

To the north-west is **Alsfeld** (pop. 17,000), a picturesque old town with half-timbered Renaissance buildings: in the Marktplatz, the Hochzeithaus (1565), built for weddings, stands opposite the twee little Rathaus (1516), set on arcades where markets were held. Alsfeld is the centre of the Schwalm country, whose folk tradi-tions fascinated the brothers Grimm: the girls' red folk-dresses are still worn at summer festivals.

The old university town of **MAR-BURG** (pop. 79,000) is well worth exploring. Pilgrims crowded here in the Middle Ages to the shrine of St Elisabeth, a daughter of the King of Hungary who devoted herself to the town's sick and poor after her husband had died of the plague; in 1231 she then herself died, of exhaustion, aged 24. **St Elisabeth's**, Germany's first Gothic church, today Protestant, was then built above her tomb; it's a superb building, with pink spires that domi-nate the town, and some fine stained glass. Its sacristy (open daily) holds the saint's shrine, wrought magnificently of gold in 1250; on its panels are scenes from her life. Another famous figure, Field Marshal von Hindenburg (d. 1934) is also buried in the church.

Marburg's other landmark is the bulky Schloss on a nearby hill; former residence of the Landgraves of Hesse, it has a handsome Knights' Hall, a museum of regional art and history, and a park with pleasant views. Tiered on the hillside below is Marburg's pic-turesque Altstadt of narrow streets and *Fachwerk* houses: here the Gothic Rathaus (1524) has a curious statuette of Elisabeth carved on its tower. The fountain in the Marktplatz is today still a meeting-place for students: this old quarter has a studenty ambience and the university, long a centre of Protestant theology, is one of Germany's oldest (1527) and most venerable.

Going north, you will reach the attractive Eder valley at **Frankenburg**, a handsome town with a turreted Rathaus and wooden 16th-century houses. In the woods near Haina to the east is a Cistercian abbey that became a mental hospital in 1533; today, still a hospital, it is closed to visitors save for its beautiful Gothic church. The spa town of **Bad Wildungen** (pop. 16,000), treating kidney and gall-bladder complaints, also has a notable church, with a lovely altarpiece (1403). From here a scenic road winds north to **Waldeck** (pop. 7,000), surmounted by the former castle of the Waldeck princes: this today is part hotel, part museum (Apr–Oct), and has a Witches' Tower with three prison cells. The castle terrace offers a view over the artificial Eder lake, created by the huge Eder Dam: this was built c. 1910, then blown up in 1943 by a four-ton RAF bomb which caused fearsome flooding, and has since been repaired. The countryside around Waldeck is most attractive.

Industrial **KASSEL** (pop. 197,000), the chief city of north Hesse, has varied associations in German minds – among them, the romantic-fantastic Wilhelmshöhe park, the brothers Grimm, the Documenta modern art exhibition, and the colloquial phrase *'Ab nach Kassel'* which means 'Off we go!'. The town was developed in the 17th and 18th centuries by the Landgraves of Hesse who built the Wilhelmshöhe and also attracted industry: the Frenchman Denis Papin, an inventor of steam power, worked here around 1706. Kassel was badly bombed in 1943 and has been rebuilt without much imagination: its Altstadt is no more. Dependent on engineering, chemicals and other heavy industries, it is a town without much character, but it does have redeeming features. And its setting is pleasant.

The Landgraves were great art collectors, as you can see in the Wilhelmshöhe museum (opposite); this tradition continues with the **Documenta**, an international exhibition that began in 1955 and is now held every five years (i.e. 1992, 1997), lasting all summer. Avant-garde and multi-media, it was much patronized by the late Joseph Beuys, one of whose 'action sculptures' was the planting of 7,000 oak-trees in the city, each marked by a basalt block.

Of the downtown museums, much the best is the **Landesmuseum**. This has a collection of early scientific and astronomical instruments, such as 16th-century planetary clocks; also globes dating from 1585. The prehistoric section includes local pottery from c. 5000 BC, and displays of early farming settlements. The wallpaper museum upstairs, said to be the only one of its kind, has wall-hangings as old as the 16th century. The **Neue Galerie** is devoted to 19th- and 20th-century art. Little of it is first-rate, though there are pleasing works by Tischbein, best known of North Hesse artists; the roomful of Beuys includes a minibus drawing sleighs. Next door is the Grimm museum. Kassel's main square, the Friedrichsplatz, is lined with a few eye-catching buildings: the stately white Neo-classical Fridericianum, main venue of the Documenta (this also spreads around the town); the oddly-shaped Ottoneum, Germany's oldest theatre (1606), now

The Brothers Grimm

Northern Hesse, around Kassel, is the heartland of the folk-tales collected locally by the brothers Jacob and Wilhelm Grimm – and today, for tourist purposes, a route running through it is designated the *Deutsche Märchenstrasse* (German Fairy-Tale Road). The Grimms were born at Hanau, near Frankfurt, and studied law at Marburg University. They then spent their early careers (1805–30) as court librarians at Kassel, where they conceived a passion for folklore and were the first to research it scientifically. Jacob was the scholar, Wilhelm the poet who could put the folk-tales into readable form for a wide public. They scoured the region, collecting their material orally from country people: for example, at Alsfeld, where the girls wore red cloaks, they heard the story of *Little Red Riding-Hood*.

The Grimm museum in Kassel has details of how they did their work, and illustrated editions of their collected tales in many languages. One later rewritten version, by Janosch, was an attempt to make the tales less frightening to small children. At Sababurg above the Weser valley (see p. 224), the feudal castle where the Grimms went for hunting-parties is now a smart hotel where fairy-tale plays are staged. It claims to have been the castle that inspired *The Sleeping Beauty*.

housing a natural history museum; the new opera house; various avant-garde outdoor sculptures, a Documenta legacy; and, next to a church, a sex-shop with unusually blatant window-displays.

On a hillside in the western outskirts is Kassel's greatest glory – the majestic **Wilhelmshöhe Schlosspark** and its monuments. Initiated by Landgrave Karl in 1701, this is one of Europe's finest Romantic landscaped parks. At its top end is a huge 70m grey granite monument crowned by a Hercules statue, copy of the Farnese Hercules in Naples: you should drive up to it from the west side (clearly signposted) for a grandiose vista down over park and town. Below the Hercules are waterfalls and fountains (they play Wed and Sat only, Whit to Oct). And below these are various delectable 18th-century follies – the Devil's Bridge, Pluto's Grotto, some baroque temples and, facing them, the amazing Löwenburg

castle. With its fortress walls and grey pinnacles, this looks like some vast mediaeval pile, but is pure Romantic fantasy (1793–97). Farther down is the pink-granite Schloss Höhenlohe itself (1786–1801), where Jerome Bonaparte, King of Westphalia, held court stylishly in 1807–13: Napoleon III was interned here after his 1870 defeat at Sedan, and as he went through Aachen the people jeered at him, '*Ab nach Kassel!*' – the original of the catchphrase that I quoted. Today the palace holds an enormous museum, whose Greek, Roman and Egyptian antiquities are less notable than its superb painting collection, strong on Dutch and Flemish masters (Van Dyck, Franz Hals, Jordaens, Rembrandt and especially Teniers, e.g. his *Peasants' Dance*). The best view is from the back of the Schloss up towards the Hercules. Just below the park, a lavish modern bathing centre, the Kurhessen Therme, has a range of amenities including

Japanese restaurant and salt-water cures for rheumatism. Just north of Kassel is the charming rococo Schloss Wilhelmsthal, designed by Cuvillies; its ornate interior features Tischbein portraits of lovely ladies.

TOURIST OFFICES

FULDA: Schlossstr. 1, tel (0661) 10 23 46.

MARBURG: Neue Kasseler Str. 1, tel (06421) 20 12 49.

KASSEL: Main station, tel (0561) 1 34 43; Königsplatz, tel (0561) 1 71 59.

Accommodation, Eating and Drinking

FULDA 6400:

(H)**Zum Kurfürsten**, Schlossstr. 2, tel (0661) 7 00 01. 18th-century palace of prince-bishops (Queen Victoria, Bismarck, etc stayed here), now modestly reincarnated as a classic middle-range hotel; good food. Rooms (69) C–D. Meals C.
(H)**Backmühle**, Känzeller Str. 133, tel (0661) 7 78 00. In south suburbs; modest, pleasant. Rooms (19) D. Meals C–D.
(R)**Felsenkeller**, Leipzigerstr. 12, tel (0661) 727 84. Large characterful pub with garden. Meals C–D.

MARBURG 06421:

(H)**Europäischer Hof**, Elisabethstr. 12, tel (06421) 6 40 44. Old hotel well modernized, near station; **Atelier** restaurant (tel 6 22 55) also good. Rooms (95) C. Meals C.
(H)**Zur Sonne**, Markt 14, tel (06421) 2 60 36. Tiny, cosy hotel in old half-timbered house; genuine German cooking. Rooms (11) D. Meals (cl Mon) C–D.

WALDECK 3544:

(H)**Burghotel Schloss Waldeck**, tel (05623) 53 24. Converted feudal hilltop castle; fine views. Cl Jan–Mar. Rooms (14) C. Meals B–C.

KASSEL 3500:

(H)**Schlosshotel Wilhelmshöhe**, Schlosspark 2, tel (0561) 3 08 80. Near the park, spacious and modern, with garden terrace; pool, sauna, etc. Food so-so. Rooms (105) B. Meals B–C.
(H)**Waldhotel Schäferberg**, in Espenau-Schäferberg 3501, tel (05673) 79 71. In a village 10km to north; modern, family-run, with a garden. Good local dishes. Rooms (95) C. Meals C.
(H)**Westend**, Friedrich-Ebert Str. 135, tel (0561) 10 38 21. Between town and Wilhelmshöhe. No restaurant. Cl Dec 23–Jan 5. Rooms (43) C–D.
(R)**Kropfwirt**, Opernplatz, tel (0561) 77 27 64. Central, down-to-earth and locally popular. Meals D.
(R)**Weinhaus Boos**, Wilhelmshöher Allee 97, tel (0561) 2 22 09. Lively tavern on way to park. Cl lunch. Meals C.

CHAPTER SEVEN

Lower Saxony
(Niedersachsen)

LOWER SAXONY IS the largest *Land* in area, after Bavaria, and the least thickly populated. It was created as a *Land* in 1946, out of the old Prussian province of Hanover (once a kingdom) and the duchies of Brunswick (Braunschweig) and Oldenburg; Hanover is its capital. In Roman times and the Dark Ages it was inhabited by the Saxon tribes: but they later migrated up the Elbe to settle in present-day Saxony, around Leipzig and Dresden. Lower Saxony is thus quite separate from Saxony proper, especially in its people: the true Saxons are exuberant and fun-loving, the Lower Saxons are reserved and a bit solemn. Politically, they are evenly balanced between CDU and SPD: in the 1990 *Land* elections the CDU lost power to the SPD.

Many of the *Land*'s small and middle-sized towns are every bit as picturesque and full of interest as those of south Germany – notably Goslar, an enchanting place, also Wolfenbüttel, Celle, Lüneburg and Stade. The traditional architecture is mostly red-brick with much half-timbering – graceful, if a bit monotonous. The *Land* is West Germany's main agricultural producer after Bavaria, notably for livestock, cereals, sugar-beet and potatoes. Huge modern farms sprawl over the rolling plains, interspersed with forests; the only uplands are the Harz mountains in the south-east, but they barely rise above 1,100 metres. The main resort areas are the Harz (skiing, hiking), the Lüneburg Heath (walking, riding) and the East Friesland islands (bathing, etc). Modern industry is set in and around the larger towns, Hanover, Brunswick, Wolfsburg (home of Volkswagen) and Wilhelmshaven, most of them badly bombed in the war. Hanover, not just a modern trade-fair city, is packed with varied interest.

Hameln and the Upper Weser Valley

Broad and majestic, yet also gently pastoral, the winding river valley of the middle Weser, from Münden to Hameln, is one of the loveliest in Germany. First it flows between forested uplands as far as Bad Karlshafen, then enters a plain. The villages are quiet and unspoilt, and the traffic on the main B 80 along the valley is far from heavy. Studded with romantic castles, the region is a heartland of German folklore, rich terrain for the brothers

Grimm (see p. 221). This is not to forget the Pied Piper of Hameln, nor the tall stories of Baron von Münchhausen who lived at Bodenwerder.

The attractive old town of **Münden** (pop. 28,000) stands 'where Werra and Fulda kiss each other' (as a well-known German poem goes), for here these rivers meet, and jointly become the Weser: the spot is marked by a stone monument on a headland, the Weserstein. Münden's narrow traffic-free streets are lined with black-and-white *Fachwerk* houses; the Renaissance façade of its Rathaus faces a square where an annual pantomime tells of the life and work of Johann Eisenbart (1661–1727), an eccentric local doctor whose provocative methods of treatment were oddly effective.

The Weser valley winds down from Münden to Veckerhagen. Here you could drive up onto the broad plateau to the west, where the hilly vistas are wonderfully spacious. You would come to the romantic Schloss Sababurg with its Grimm assocations, now a hotel (see p. 227): its adjacent zoo, Germany's oldest (1571), has bears, buffaloes, penguins, etc. A woodland road will lead you back down to the Weser at Gieselwerder, where the broad valley has a serene pastoral beauty, as the river flows between meadows where cows graze, against a backdrop of wooded hills. **Bad Karlshafen**, farther downstream, was founded in 1699 by Landgraf Karl of Hessen who settled it with Huguenots: it is a notable example of baroque town planning, symmetrically graceful, with monumental white buildings by the river: today it's a small spa. Further on, near Beverungen, the pastoral idyll is modified by a large factory plus cooling tower. But northwards the valley again becomes attractive around the hilltop village of **Fürstenberg**, famous for its white porcelain. The factory, in an old castle, has been making it since 1747 and has a porcelain museum (open daily Mar–Oct). The village shops are full of its wares, but they are not cheap, and not always attractive.

At **Höxter**, back on the left bank of the Weser, the Altstadt is somewhat overrun with traffic but does have some pretty half-timbered façades. Note the fine Renaissance pulpit in St Kilian's church. In the eastern outskirts is the massive white rectangle of **Corvey Abbey**, founded in 822 by Benedictine monks from Corbie Abbey near Amiens (this link is still kept up, through a town-twinning). Its foundations date from that time. It remained a monastery until 1803, and was later turned into a château by the Duke of Ratibor, whose descendants still own it today. This grandiose building today hosts a museum (open Apr–Oct) of local history and folklore; its main interest is the large library, which in 1860–74 was in the charge of the poet Hoffmann von Fallersleben, author of *Deutschland, Deutschland über Alles*. In May and June, concerts are given in the banqueting hall. The tall church, part ninth-century, part later baroque, adjoins a pleasant cloister with a painted ceiling.

Bodenwerder, further downstream, was the home town of that raconteur of improbable tales, Baron von Münchhausen (1720–97). A small museum devoted to him is next to his birthplace, now the Rathaus; the statuette in front, of a man sitting on half a horse, relates to one of his taller stories. Some of these are performed here as plays on the first Sunday of the month, May to

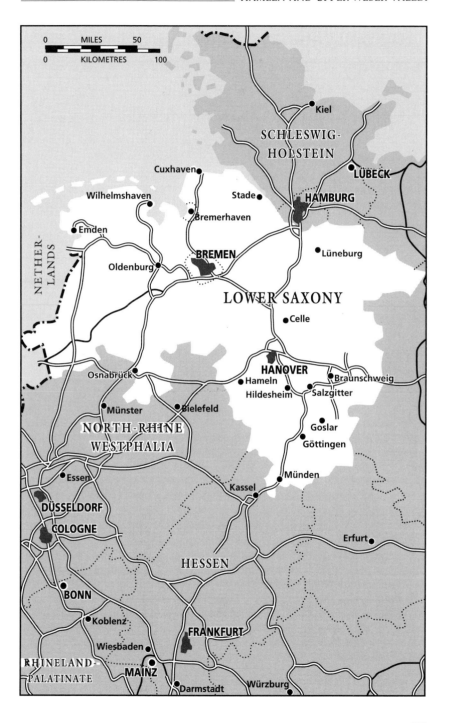

Sept. Due west of Bodenwerder, across country, is the fairly smart spa town of **Bad Pyrmont**, set amid forested hills; it has an elegant white Kurhaus, prettily lit at night, and a Kurpark with palm trees. Goethe was a frequent visitor.

HAMELN on the Weser (pop. 60,000), the Pied Piper's town, I found rather disappointing: its central traffic-free area was gracelessly rebuilt after the wartime bombing and has also become over-commercialized. Of its more picturesque old buildings, the Dempter House (1607) is now a bank and the Canons' House (c. 1550) a café; I preferred the Marriage House (1610) and the charming pink Leisthaus. Many of these houses have very elaborate façades, in 'Weser Renaissance' style, i.e. their gables have ram's-horm scrollwork and pinnacles. Pied Piper souvenirs are everywhere, appealing to tourists – e.g. the modern bronze statue of him outside the Rathaus, and the many shops selling sweets and toys in rat shapes. The Germans call him *Der Rattenfänger von Hameln* – the ratcatcher. The so-called Rattenfänger-haus, typically Weser Renaissance, is now a restaurant: one dish it serves is *Rattsteller!* I did not dare try it. Every summer Sunday at noon, by the Marriage House, there's a dramatized performance of the famous legend (told by Goethe and Browning) about the piper in motley who in 1284 enticed the town's rats to a watery death in the Weser, then lured away all the children when he was not given his promised reward. The probable historical reality behind this folk-tale is that, at a time of over-population, young people were being brutally deported to colonize areas in the east.

At **Fischbeck**, north-west of Hameln, is a fine old abbey dating from the tenth-century, whose church, crypt and cloister are all 12th-century Romanesque. Today, like Wienhausen, it is a home for elderly Protestant ladies. **Bückeburg** has a fine Renaissance castle (open daily) with a majestic façade and lovely courtyard. From here it is an easy drive to Minden or to Hanover.

TOURIST OFFICES

MÜNDEN: Rathaus, tel (05541) 7 53 13.

BAD PYRMONT: Arkaden 14, tel (05281) 46 27.

HAMELN: Deisterallee, tel (05151) 20 25 17.

MINDEN: Grosser Domhof 3, tel (0571) 8 93 85.

Accommodation, Eating and Drinking

MÜNDEN 3510:

(H)**Jagdhaus Heede**, Hermannshägerstr. 81, tel (05541) 23 95. In eastern outskirts, peaceful and pleasant. Cl Nov. Rooms (20) D. Meals (cl Mon) D.

SABABURG 3520 Hofgeismar:

(H)**Burghotel Sababurg,** tel (05678) 10 52. Self-consciously romantic: a converted 14th-century Schloss with Grimm associations, now a stylish hotel with canopied beds; lovely views, good game dishes in season. Grimm fairy-tales are sometimes read aloud during meals; in summer, outdoor concerts and fairy-plays in the feudal courtyard. Cl Jan Feb. Rooms (19) B–B. Meals B–C.

BAD KARLSHAFEN 3522:

(H)**Zum Schwan,** Conradistr. 3, tel (05672) 0721. Old hunting-lodge (1780) with a rococo balcony, near thermal baths; garden; game dishes in season. Cl Jan–mid-Feb. Rooms (32) C. Meals C.

HOLZMINDEN 3450:

(R)**Hellers Krug,** Altendorfer Str. 19, tel (05531) 21 15. Friendly ambience and excellent ambitious cooking, fairly priced. Cl Sun. Meals B–C. 10 modest bedrooms, E.

BAD PYRMONT 3280:

(H)**Brunnenstr. 32,** tel (05281) 60 93 03. Discreet, much used by cure visitors. Rooms (45) C–D. Meals for residents only.

HAMELN 3250:

(H)**Dorint,** 164er Ring 3, tel (05151) 79 20. Set quietly by a garden; modern and enterprising, with morning jazz sessions, good cooking. Rooms (103) B. Meals B–C.

BÜCKEBURG 3062:

(R)**Grosse Klus,** Am Klusbrink 19, 5km west of town, in Röcke, tel (05722). Delightful old half-timbered manor with cosy décor; fish dishes highly reputed. Cl Thur. Meals C–D.

Göttingen, the Harz Mountains and Brunswick

The south-eastern part of Lower Saxony includes Göttingen, a rather dull city with a famous university; Goslar, a delightful little town; and the industrial centres of Brunswick and Wolfsburg, the latter the home of Volkswagen. South of Goslar lie the Harz mountains, astride the former GDR border.

Until the Revolution of 1989, this whole border had become a tourist attraction for West German sightseers and for busloads of schoolchildren who were dutifully taken to observe what had happened to the *Vaterland*:

---

the Federal border police had at some points erected placards giving details of the GDR's deadly weaponry, and you could even peer through field-glasses at life in the 'other Germany' (but you wouldn't see much, for GDR citizens were not allowed within five km of this border, without a special pass). However, already by about 1987 the Honecker regime was modifying the fortifications, in the interests of détente with the West: the minefields and the sinister shrapnel-scattering guns were removed, and the guard-dogs howled less often at night. Then the border was suddenly thrown open, and in 1990 work was due to begin on dismantling the grim watchtowers on stilts, the barbed wire and the steel fences.

The university at **GÖTTINGEN** (pop. 133,000) has long been one of Germany's most distinguished. Founded in 1737 by King George II of Great Britain, in his role as Elector of Hanover, it rapidly became fashionable with young men of good family, Hanoverian, English and Russian. Many of them were less interested in their studies than in duelling, drinking, womanizing and horse-riding. But later the university grew into a major centre of scientific learning, with the appointment in 1807 of the mathematical genius Karl-Friedrich Gauss as professor of astronomy (his name has been given to a unit of the field of magnetic intensity). Göttingen became strong also in law and philology, and it developed a more liberal, free-thinking climate than was usual in Germany.

The great Max Planck, creator of the quantum theory in radiation, spent his final years in the town and is buried

there. In his honour, since 1945 the university has been the headquarters of the Max-Planck-Institut which groups some 50 high-level scientific research bodies all over Germany. So Göttingen's tradition continues. And yet, with the general post-war levelling of German universities, it now stands out less eminently than it used. Students come mainly from the local catchment area, they work doggedly and go back home at weekends. Of course there are student taverns: but the town's student ambience is less vivacious than, say, at Freiburg or Heidelberg – perhaps because these are stolid Lower Saxons, not jolly wine-drinking southerners. And the town itself is of no great charm or interest, though it does have a 14th-century Rathaus and some pleasant old *Fachwerk* houses. The best of these are in or near the Marktplatz, where students gather round the modern fountain/statue of a goosegirl, and are supposed to kiss it when they pass their finals. None of the museums are of any special note; but in June there is a renowned **music festival** devoted to Händel.

North-east of Göttingen, the pineclad Harz astride the GDR border are North Germany's only mountain range, and not a high one. They are good for hiking, in some places for skiing too, and contain several resorts; some of the villages have painted wooden houses. You will come first to **Herzberg**, at the edge of the plain; its handsome half-timbered Schloss holds a big collection of those tin model figures that Germans love. Here a road winds up into the Harz – to **St Andreasberg**, an odd place: once a silver-mining centre, it is now a neat resort, and its streets of painted houses descend the slope of a very steep hill. At the bottom, the Samson mine-head is now a small museum of local mining (cl mid-Nov to mid-Dec). The mine closed in 1910, undercut by cheaper imported silver from Mexico, like others in the Harz. A plaque tells that Goethe went down this mine in 1777, and then recorded in his diary that it upset him a lot.

Braunlage, to the east, is a biggish winter and summer resort with a splendid skating-rink. Here a cable-car will take you up to the Wurmberg (971m), right by the former GDR border: from the tower on top you get a sweeping view of what's left of the old Iron Curtain fortifications, right at your feet, forging their way over the heights. The road north leads to the resort of Torthaus, just across the border from the Harz's highest point, the famous **Brocken** (1,142m) where – as Goethe relates in *Faust* – witches once held sabbath. From Torthaus a scenic road winds westward over the hills to **Clausthal-Zellerfeld** where there's another mining museum: this shows details of the curious mining methods used here until the last local mine closed in 1931.

The Gose valley winds down to **GOSLAR** (pop. 49,000), for me the loveliest old town in North Germany. This former Free Imperial City, a seat of the Salian emperors in the 11th century, owes its architectural glories to its prosperity as a centre of lead and silver mining in mediaeval times. But after 1550 it began to decline, owing to religious feuding between the Free City and the Dukes of Brunswick, owners of the mines (some of these, in the Rammelsberg hills to the south, are still worked today). Goslar's intimate charm rests on its variety of beautiful

buildings of different epochs and styles – Gothic, Renaissance, baroque – all close together in an area of narrow streets, much of it closed to traffic. The façades are not the ubiquitous red brick found further north, but black-and-white half-timbering or plain stone.

On one side of the picturesque Marktplatz, with its bronze fountain, is the 15th-century Gothic Kaiserworth, now a hotel (see below): on one corner gable, note the saucy statue of a boy ejecting a coin from his rear (a symbol of Goslar's ancient right to mint coins). Opposite is the old arcaded Rathaus, whose famous Huldigungssaal (open daily) is lined from floor to ceiling with gorgeous coloured frescoes, by an unknown artist of c. 1500; it also contains the Goslar Gospel (1230) and, in a tiny chapel, an arm-reliquary of c. 1300. On the west side of the Rathaus, around the Marktkirche, Am Schuhhof and the narrow Münzstrasse, are many lovely buildings. Also of note in the central area: St Anne's chapel with its wooden galleries; the Frankenberg and Neuwerk churches; the Siemenhaus (1639), built by an ancestor of the Siemens industrial family; the 11th-century royal palace, rebuilt in the 1870s; and the Goslar museum of local history (cl Sun). From the terrace by the Bismarck statue, beyond the railway, you get a good view of the town and its green encircling hills.

The East European Revolution of 1989–90 can be studied at a local level by visiting the former GDR border at the village of Lochtum, east of Goslar. Lochtum and adjacent Abbenrode, across the border, had close links in the old days and many families were related. Then until November 1989 they were totally cut off: people working in the fields could see each other, but the GDR citizens were forbidden even to wave, and Lochtumers could make visits only when relatives were dying. Now, amid rejoicing, normal contacts have resumed. The sinister watch-towers and electrified fence were likely to be dismantled in 1990.

To the north is **Wolfenbüttel** (pop. 50,000), a distinguished and historic old town of *Fachwerk* houses, the best being in the Holzmarkt and Stadt-markt. Its big white Schloss, with a fine Renaissance tower, dates from the 12th century and was later rebuilt in baroque style. Close by is the Herzog-August-Bibliothek, which in the 17th-century was the major library in Europe: its six million volumes include rare mediaeval illuminated manu-scripts. Next to it is the former home of the playwright G. E. Lessing, who was the duke's librarian in 1770–81: it has souvenirs of his life and work.

BRAUNSCHWEIG (Brunswick in English; pop. 252,000), the *Land*'s sec-ond largest city, was very badly bombed in the last war and then rebuilt without much grace: so it is hard today to get much sense of what it was like in its mighty prime. But some notable buildings survive. In the 12th century it was the chosen seat of the powerful Guelph prince, Henry the Lion, Duke of Saxony and Bavaria. His symbol is the masterly bronze lion statue, built in his own day (1166), that still adorns the central square, the Burgplatz. Henry endowed his city with other fine works of art, too – notably the Romanesque **cathedral**, which con-tains a huge seven-branch candela-brum donated by him, the magnificent Imervard Crucifix (1150), and the finely carved tomb of Henry and his wife Mathilda of England. Another bit

of the old city centre that has been restored after the bombing is the Altstadtmarkt, lined with half-tim-bered Gothic and Renaissance build-ings, including the 13th–15th-century Altstadtrathaus, the *Gewandhaus* (linen hall) and St Martin's church. St Michael's and the Magnikirche are other fine old churches. Best of the town's four museums is that of Herzog Anton Ulrich, with paintings by Rem-brandt, Rubens, Vermeer, Cranach and others. The city was an important com-mercial centre in the Middle Ages, and from 1753 to 1918 was the residence of the Dukes of Brunswick. Today it's mainly an industrial centre (machin-ery, lorries, food canning, etc).

Brunswick in fact is the centre of an important industrial region: to its north-east is Wolfsburg, home of Volkswagen, and to the south-west is Salzgitter with its steelworks. Further west you will come to **HILDESHEIM** (pop. 100,000), an historic city whose ensemble of Romanesque buildings suffered badly in the war and has been only partly rebuilt. In the Marktplatz, the 15th-century Templarhaus is the only original structure to have sur-vived; the Gothic Rathaus is a recon-struction. St Michael's, also much restored, is the best of the town's churches – 11th-century Romanesque Ottonian, with two apses and a painted wooden ceiling. The 11th-century cathedral, likewise rebuilt, contains some interesting art works that escaped the bombs – a carved 13th-century font; and a large round chan-delier and a bronze column carved with scenes from the life of Christ. Both are 11th-century. In the cloister garden is a famous rose-tree that, according to legend, dates from the time of Ludwig the Debonair in 815.

The picturesque main square of Goslar, in the Harz.

Certainly it is very old, if not that old. Although badly burned in the 1945 air raid, soon afterwards it suddenly burst into bloom: this has increased its symbolic importance in local eyes. Hinterer Brühl, a street just south of the cathedral, is picturesque and not yet touristy.

From Hildesheim you can drive to Hanover or return to Göttingen by a scenic road that will take you via **Einbeck** (pop. 29,000), a picturesque town with *Fachwerk* houses around its cobbled Marktplatz. In the Middle Ages it had no less than 700 breweries; though today only one remains, it still produces a well-known and potent beer.

TOURIST OFFICES

GÖTTINGEN: Altes Rathaus, Markt 9, tel (0551) 5 40 00.

GOSLAR: Markt 7, tel (05321) 28 46.

WOLFENBÜTTEL: Stadtmarkt 8, tel (05331) 2 75 93.

BRUNSWICK: main station, tel (0531) 7 92 37; Bohlweg, tel (0531) 4 64 19.

HILDESHEIM: Am Ratsbauhof 1c, tel (05121) 1 59 95.

Accommodation, Eating and Drinking

GÖTTINGEN 3400 (tel code 0551):

(H)**Gebhards**, Goetheallee 22, tel 5 61 33. Central, near station; garden, indoor pool. Rooms (61) B–C. Meals (cl Sun) B.

(H)**Zur Sonne**, Pauliner Str. 10, tel 5 67 38. Central, pleasant; beds softer than hard German average. No restaurant. Cl Christmas period. Rooms (41) D.

(H)**Hainholzhof-Kehr**, Borheckstr. 66, tel 7 50 08. Half-timbered house in a forest in the suburbs; simple, with good cooking. Rooms (12) D–E. Meals (cl Mon) C–D.

(R)**Junkernschänke**, Barfüsserstr. 5, tel 5 73 20. 14th-century tavern, lots of atmosphere. Meals (cl Mon) B–C.

(R)**Zum Schwarzen Bären**, Kurzestr. 12, tel 5 82 84. Another old *Fachwerk* house in city centre, a student haunt. Meals (cl Mon) C.

(B)**Zum Altdeutschen**, Prinzenstr. 16, and **Marktstübchen**, Weenderstr. 13, are among the most popular student taverns.

BRAUNLAGE 3389:

(H)**Romantik-Hotel Tanne**, Herzog-Wilhelm Str. 8, tel (05520) 10 34. Flowery green façade, cosy local-style décor, warm welcome, very good food. Rooms (22) C–D. Meals B–C.

GOSLAR 3380:

(H)**Kaiserworth**, Markt 3, tel (05321) 2 11 11. Old guildhall (1494), now cosy hotel; terrace. Rooms (56) C. Meals C.

(H)**Schwarzer Adler**, Rosentorstr. 25, tel (05321) 2 40 01. Near station; fine cooking. Rooms (27) C–D. Meals (cl Sun dinner, Mon, Aug) C.

(R)**Weisser Schwan**, Münzerstr. 11, tel (05321) 2 57 37. Good Yugoslav dishes in an old coaching-inn. Meals C–D.

BAD HARZBURG 3388:

(H)**Braunschweiger Hof**, Herzog-Wilhemls Str. 54, tel (05322) 78 80. In a Harz spa town, a classic 19th-century spa hotel, well modernized; quiet woodland setting, indoor pool, reliable cooking. Rooms (78) B–C. Meals B–C.

BRAUNSCHWEIG 3300:

(H)**Mövenpick-Hotel**, Welfenhof, tel (0531) 4 81 70. Central, Swiss-owned, very smoothly run; indoor pool, solarium; usual slick Mövenpick cuisine. Rooms (132) B. Meals B–C.

(H)**Pension Wienecke**, Kuhstr. 14, tel (0531) 4 64 76. Convenient, quiet; no restaurant. Rooms (17) D–E.

(R)**Gewandhauskeller**, Altstadtmarkt 1, tel (0531) 4 44 41. Fine old 12th-century guildhouse, elegantly cosy décor; reliable cooking. Cl Sun dinner. Meals B–C.

(R)**Neustadt-Rathaus**, Küchenstr. 1, tel (0531) 4 19 04. Atmospheric and candlelit, in 13th-century house. Some 'mediaeval' recipes. Meals C.

SALZGITTER 3320:

(R)**Reinhardt's Höhe**, Thiestr. 18, Lebenstedt, tel (05341) 4 44 47. Dull location but attractive interior; sophisticated cooking, highly reputed. Cl Mon, 3 weeks July; dinner only. Meals C.

HILDESHEIM 3200:

(R)**Ratskeller**, Markt 2, tel (05121) 1 44 41. Above-average Ratskeller. Meals C.

EINBECK 3352:

(H)**Zum Schwan**, Tiedexer Str. 1, tel (05561) 46 09. Elegant little restaurant-with-rooms in *Fachwerk* house; *soigné* cooking. Rooms (9) D. Meals (cl Fri, Sat, Sun lunch) B–C.

Hanover

This big commercial city (pop. 510,000; conurbation, 1.1 million), home of Europe's leading annual trade fair, exudes prosperous self-confidence and a dynamic business spirit. At first sight it might seem a dull place for the tourist: but it turns out to be full of interesting things: important museums, some of the finest classical gardens in Germany, and a curious and unusual Altstadt that has been pieced together since the bombing that destroyed 80 per cent of the town centre. As befits a city that gave a Royal House to Britain, it breathes tradition. Its people are reserved and may lack sparkle: but they are very well-mannered, and they speak the most pure and accentless German, with formal clarity and correctness.

Hanover did not have much history until the mid-17th century, when a branch of the House of Brunswick moved its princely residence there, and built a palace at Herrenhausen. In 1679–98, under the ambitious Elector Ernst August and his cultured wife Sophie, the city saw a flowering of the arts: Handel came to give concerts, and the philosopher Gottfried Leibnitz became court librarian. So how did Hanover later make its 'take-over' of the British throne? Well, Sophie was a Stuart, grand-daughter of James I, and

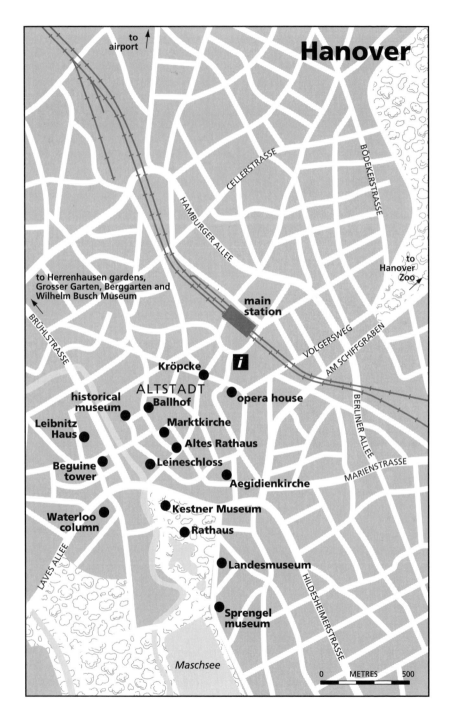

Hanover

to airport

CELLERSTRASSE

BÖDEKERSTRASSE

HAMBURGER ALLEE

to Herrenhausen gardens,
Grosser Garten, Berggarten and
Wilhelm Busch Museum

to Hanover Zoo

BRÜHLSTRASSE

main station

VOLGERSWEG

AM SCHIFFGRABEN

Kröpcke

i

ALTSTADT

opera house

historical museum

Ballhof

BERLINER ALLEE

Leibnitz Haus

Marktkirche

MARIENSTRASSE

Altes Rathaus

Beguine tower

Leineschloss

Aegidienkirche

Waterloo column

Kestner Museum

Rathaus

LAVES ALLEE

Landesmuseum

HILDESHEIMERSTRASSE

Sprengel museum

Maschsee

0   METRES   500

Hanover's neo-classical Rathäus, reflected in the waters of the Maschsee.

the British parliament chose her as successor to Queen Anne; she died just before that queen, in 1714, and so it was her son Georg Ludwig who became King George I. Britain and Hanover (by then a kingdom too) thus came under the same monarch, and the court divided its time between Herrenhausen and London (but George I never learned English!). However, when in 1837 William IV died childless, this union came to an end: Victoria ascended the British throne, but Hanover was under a Salic law that barred women from succession, so Victoria's uncle Ernst August became its king. He employed the architect Friedrich Laves to create some fine neo-classical buildings. But then in 1866 Hanover was annexed by Prussia and ceased to be a separate kingdom. Today it is a centre for automobile, rubber and audio-visual industries, amongst others, but is known above all for the trade fairs held in its massive Messegelände to the south-east: up to 37 international ones a year, and over 100 purely German.

Hanover's principal **fairs and festivals** are the main trade fair in late April; a major archery festival (*Schützenfest*) in early July, claimed to be the world's largest, including fireworks, parades, floats, etc; and between June and August, plays and concerts in the Herrenhausen gardens.

The main downtown area between the station and the Altstadt has been well rebuilt since the war, on a spacious pattern with touches of modern elegance: it has broad traffic-free shopping streets and a smart new shopping-arcade, the Galerie Luise. The hub of this district is the big **Kröpcke**-piazza, whose neat outdoor cafés have coloured parasols. Some of the new buildings are quite striking. From here you can make a tour on foot of the city's main points of interest (but you will need a car or tram to get out to Herrenhausen). Near Kröpcke is Laves' stately Opera House (1852), now rebuilt. The Georgstrasse, lined with smart boutiques, leads south from here towards the fascinating Gothic blue-towered **Aegidienkirche**, carefully kept in ruins as a war memorial – like the Gedächtniskirche in Berlin. Below its gutted belfry is the 'peace bell', a gift in 1985 from Hiroshima, Hanover's twin-town. I found it all rather moving.

Across the ringway to the south is the huge neo-Gothic **Neues Rathaus** (1901–13), typical of Wilhelmine grandiosity. Inside, the scale models of Hanover in 1689 and 1939 give a good idea of what the city used to look like; and for a view of it today you could ascend the high central dome by lift (Apr–Oct). Next door is the Kestner Museum, founded by August Kestner, a son of Goethe's 'Charlotte Buff' (see p. 216). The star exhibit of its mediaeval art collection is a 12th-century bronze head-reliquary of a saint. There are also Greek, Roman and Egyptian relics, notably a bust of the Pharaoh Akhenaten (c. 1350 BC). The museum is known as 'the house of 5,000 windows', because of the modern concrete lattice-work that has been wrapped over the original 1889 façade in order to preserve it.

Just south of the Rathaus are two other major museums. The **Landesmuseum** has sections on archaeology and natural history, but its main interest is its varied collection of paintings – from Florentine primitives and Cranach altarpieces, via 17th-century Flemish masters, to recent times. The German late-19th century is well represented – Corinth, Liebermann, Paula Modersohn-Becker, and romantic woodland scenes by Hans Thoma. The adjacent **Sprengel Museum** (named after a chocolate tycoon who donated many of its best works) is one of the finest in Germany for modern art – it has whole roomfuls of Klee, Leger and Picasso (the latter in somewhat sombre mood); some attractive Munchs; Dali and Magritte, Kokoschka and Kandinsky; and numerous Germans such as Beckmann, Dix, Macke and

Nolde. Several rooms are devoted to the Hanover-born surrealist Kurt Schwitters, whose work is not to my own taste. Post-war photo-realism and conceptual art also feature.

This museum faces Hanover's largest lake, the man-made **Maschsee**, which was created in the Strength Through Joy era, 1934–36, and is still a major recreation centre (sailing, rowing, bathing, etc). There are pleasant walks along its banks, where you'll find a casino and a training centre for Olympic swimmers. To the west is the tall Waterloo Column, honouring the key role played by Hanoverian troops in Napoleon's final defeat. A walk from here along Lavesallee will lead to the old **Leineschloss**, remodelled by Laves in stately Neo-Classical style and now housing the Landtag; it is close to the round mediaeval Beguine Tower, a relic of the old city ramparts. Here flows the river Leine, on whose banks are three cheeky pop-art sculptures, the 'Nanas' (the word means 'wench' in French) by the French artist Niki de St-Phalle: these rotund multi-coloured oddities caused a local outcry when they were first put up, but are now easily accepted in a city that prides itself on its many outdoor modern sculptures. A flea-market is held by the Leine on Saturdays.

Behind the Leineschloss lies the **Altstadt**, not as large or as obviously 'picturesque' as many in Germany, but full of charm. Here in the Marktplatz, the heart of the old city, is the red-brick Gothic **Marktkirche**, containing some lovely 14th–15th-century stained glass and a 15th-century altarpiece, richly carved and coloured; next door is the lofty gabled façade of the **Altes Rathaus** (15th-century), all of mellow dark-red brick, well restored and glow-ingly floodlit at night. The narrow Krämerstrasse is an evening entertainment district, full of lively taverns; it leads to the Holzmarkt and Burgstrasse which have some fine half-timbered or Dutch-gabled houses, notably the Leibnitz Haus, a copy of the tall mansion where the philosopher lived in 1698–1716. Some of the restored *Fachwerk* houses in this Altstadt have been regrouped from other parts of the city since the war, so as to form an ensemble of 'old Hanover' amid all the modernity – an artificial solution, maybe, but an attractive one. In a modern building in Burgstrasse is the **Historical Museum**, whose excellent display includes old maps and pictures of the city, and four state coaches of the Royal House. The nearby half-timbered **Ballhof**, in a delightful little square, was built in 1650 as a badminton hall and now houses Hanover's main repertory theatre. There are many pleasant cafés and pubs in this quiet residential area, around the old Kreuzkirche.

The celebrated **Herrenhausen Gardens**, in the city's western outskirts, are arguably the finest baroque gardens in Germany. There are four of them, the main one being the **Grosser Garten** which was largely the work of Princess Sophie – she called it 'my very life'. It contains a maze, a formal French pleasure garden with white statues, and various fountains which sometimes are illuminated and set playing; the main one, the Grosse Fontäne, has the highest jet in Europe (82m). There are firework displays in summer, and classical plays and concerts (see above), with Handel's *Water Music* suitably in evidence. The smaller botanical **Berggarten** has a wealth of tropical plants and flowers. Nearby was the royal palace of the House of Hanover, almost entirely destroyed in the war (save for one gallery, with Italian frescoes). The royal mausoleum survives, containing the tomb of George I (odd to think that the RAF was bombing one of its own kings!). In the Georgen Garten is the little **Wilhelm Busch Museum**, devoted to the poet and cartoonist (1832–1908) who was born near Hanover and remains hugely popular in Germany for his illustrated comic tales such as *Max und Moritz*: he was an originator of the comic-strip. The museum has many of his landscapes and genre paintings, as well as cartoons; also many drawings by the Berlin satirist Heinrich Zille (see p. 296), but these are not on show when there's a special exhibition of some other well-known cartoonist, as is often the case.

To the east of the city is the large Hanover zoo, on the edge of attractive Eilenriede forest, a popular recreation area.

TOURIST OFFICE
Ernst-August-Platz, tel 1 68 23 19.

Accommodation, Eating and Drinking (Postcode 3000, area tel code 0511)

(H)**Kastens Hotel Luisenhof**, Luisenstr. 1, tel 1 24 40. Stylishly traditional but well modernized; used by visiting celebrities such as opera stars. Very central. Music and dancing; international cuisine. Rooms (250) A–B. Meals (cl July, Aug, Sun) A–B.

(H)**Mercure**, Am Maschpark 3, tel 8 00 80. Modern, cheerful and French; near museums and park. Rooms (141) B. Meals B–C.

(H)**Georgenhof**, Herrenhäuser Kirchweg 20, tel 70 22 44. So unlike the downtown business hotels: a delightful little country house, newly renovated, out near the famous gardens; superb food in its **Stern's** restaurant, served on a terrace in summer. Rooms (17) B. Meals A.

(H)**Loccumer Hof**, Kurt-Schumacher-Str. 16, tel 32 60 51. Traditional, near station. Rooms (70) C. Meals (cl Sat) B–C.

(H)**Inter-City**, Ernst-August-Platz 1, tel 32 74 61. At the main station. Rooms (57) C. Meals C.

(H)**Wülfeler Brauereigaststätten**, Hildesheimerstr. 380, tel 86 50 86. In southern suburbs; generous local cooking. Cl 2 weeks Aug. Rooms (36) D. Meals C.

(R)**Witten's Hop**, Gernsstr. 4, Bothfeld, tel 64 88 44. In north-east suburbs, a converted 17th-century farmhouse, now elegant and pricey; cooking refined and reputed. Meals A. Cl lunch weekdays.

(R)**Ratskeller**, Köbelinger Str. 60, tel 1 53 63. A useful address below the old Rathaus. Cl Sun dinner. Meals B–C.

(R)**Altdeutsche Bierstube**, Lärchenstr. 4, tel 34 49 21. Friendly, atmospheric old downtown pub; good local cooking. Cl Sun. Meals C.

(R)**Härke-Klause**, Ständehausstr. 4, tel 32 11 75. Another lively beer restaurant. Cl Sun. Meals C–D.

(R)**Zum Ochsen**, Kramerstr. 10, tel 1 39 12. Ox and duck specialities in an Altstadt tavern. Meals C–D.

(R)**Kleines Schlemmerlokal**, Kramerstr. 19, tel 32 76 70. Small, cosy, friendly; beamed ceiling and dim lights. Copious home cooking. Meals D.

(C)**Tee Stübchen**, Ballhofstr. 10, tel 1 80 90. Romantic, relaxed, comfortable; pretty décor; outdoor terrace in a lovely square.

Celle, Lüneburg Heath and Cuxhaven

The flattish region between Hanover and Hamburg is notable mainly for the broad expanse of the Lüneburg Heath, which has its own quiet beauty. The town of Lüneburg is lovely too.

CELLE (pop. 71,500), one of the noblest old towns in north Germany, was from 1378 to 1705 the seat of the Lüneburg branch of the Guelph dynasty, distant relatives of the British royal family. The Guelph princes' elegant white Schloss (closed Sat pm) is girt by a moat where swans glide: its state rooms are in Italian baroque style, and its beautiful 15th-century chapel has ogive vaulting and Renaissance décor. The château's theatre (1674), oldest of its kind in Germany, is still used for performances of the classics. Celle's Altstadt, nearby, is a grid of streets lined with 16th to 18th-century red-and-white timbered and gabled houses, some of whose upper floors overhang, as though leaning forwards. This area, though mainly a pedestrian zone, is rather too full of shops and commerce to have much charm. The Rathaus (1579) has a greyish painted façade with a *trompe-l'oeil* effect. In the picturesque Kalandagasse is the Lateinschule (1602), a former college whose decorated façade is inscribed with biblical quotes. The nearby Stadtkirche, dimly lit, is Gothic with baroque additions: daily at 7.30am and 6.30pm the town bugler climbs its tower's 235 steps to sound his horn. The region of Celle grows orchids and breeds horses: there's a stallion parade through the town in late September and early October.

To the north-west, beside the big British army barracks at Bergen-Belsen, is the former **Belsen** concentration camp where 50,000 Nazi victims died, 30,000 of them Jewish. A small museum, open daily, gives harrowing details of these events. You can also inspect the heather-covered mounds above the mass graves, and the obelisk memorial to the victims inscribed in 13 languages. It was near here that on 4 May 1945 the German High Command signed its unconditional surrender, in Montgomery's presence. The area has since been a forward zone of the British Army of the Rhine, and there are various NATO camps, today being phased down.

Bergen is just inside the **Lüneburger Heide** (Lüneburg Heath), a vast and strangely beautiful region that stretches from the river Aller in the south to the Elbe in the north. At any season it is worth exploring this gently rolling and variegated landscape, where grassy prairies full of sheep alternate with marshy ponds, low valleys and forests rich in game. But the

---

Nuns' Mediaeval Nail-files at Wienhausen

South-east of Celle, the large Cistercian abbey of Wienhausen is a most remarkable place, all mellow 13th-century red-brick and full of mediaeval atmosphere. Since the Reformation its sole occupants have been an autonomous community of lay Protestant ladies, mostly elderly: they are *not* nuns (some are widows) but run the abbey as a kind of retirement home. Their superb mediaeval tapestries are displayed to the public only once a year, for ten days around Whitsun. But on other days, April to September, they will show you around. The chapel, lined with 14th-century murals (restored) holds a Gothic wooden shrine; in other rooms are such treasures as a 14th-century cupboard, a stone statue of the abbey's founder (1280), and an armless wooden sculpture of Christ (1390). Most startling, the little museum has a collection of ancient nail-files, thimbles, knives, scissors, notebooks, spectacles, even eggs: all were found under the chapel floorboards in 1953, and are thought to have been dropped or hidden there by nuns in pre-Reformation days, when Wienhausen was still a convent. Nuns in those days were forbidden by the Pope to have spectacles. So probably they were kept hidden.

---

heath is at its best in August/September when the heather is in bloom and the juniper plants are in leaf. In its nature reserves, cars must stay on the main road: but you could hire a bicycle, horse or horse-and-cart, to go exploring them down well-signposted tracks. This is also ideal terrain for hiking, and there is cross-country skiing in some places.

A detour west from Bergen will bring you, just beyond Fallingbostel, to the memorial tomb of Hermann Löns (1866–1914) who wrote sentimental poetry about the glories of the Heide. And just north of Walsrode, is the large **Vogelpark Walsrode** (open mid-Mar to Oct), where some 900 species of bird from all over the world live and fly in freedom – ostriches and parrots, cranes and flamingoes, and many tropical birds. There's a children's playground, too.

The Heath's central nature reserve lies just west of the Hanover–Hamburg *Autobahn*, north of Soltau. There are various entry points: one of the best is the hamlet of **Döhle**, where you can park and then strike west, on foot, horse or bicycle, into the undulating heathland, covered mainly with heather, but also with oaks, birches, pines and red-berried junipers. There are big thatched sheepfolds, old and smelly, where the sheep spend the night after browsing on the heather. Further west is the **Wilseder Berg**, a hill (169m) that offers a wide view of the heath: on a clear day the spires of Hamburg are visible through field-glasses. Another good walk to this hill is from **Undeloh** to the north, a picturesque village accessible by car. Many villages on the edge of the reserve have stalls selling heather bouquets and every kind of kitschy heather ornament; there may even be live sheep for sale, too. At the charming townlet of **Egestorf**, east of Undeloh, heather is again the theme, for in season it decorates the altar of its Protestant church, the Heidekirche. This curious half-timbered church looks more like a dwelling from outside.

East of Egestorf is the very handsome old town of **LÜNEBURG** (pop. 60,000), which grew rich from its salt deposits in the Middle Ages, selling salt to the Baltic cities and Scandinavia. A legacy of that time is the big yellowish Rathaus, 13th- to 16th-century, whose sumptuous interior should not be missed – notably the Gothic Fürstensaal, with lamps made from stags' antlers, and the *Grosse Ratsstube* (council chamber), c. 1566, a Renaissance masterpiece with delicate wood-carvings by Albert von Soest. The city centre has many fine old red-brick buildings, typical of the region – notably Am Sande, a broad street fronted by tall houses with quaintly-shaped stepped gables; some façades still have their old iron bars for lifting

furniture as in Holland. It all looks like a stage-set (pity about McDonald's). The nearby Wasserviertel is delightfully picturesque: here by the river is a half-timbered millhouse, a gabled Renaissance brewery, and an 18th-century crane once used to lift an English-made locomotive for the Brunswick railway. From Lüneburg you could make a detour south to **Ebstorf**, where the remains of a 14th-century Benedictine abbey (open daily) contain a 13th-century map of the world (it's a copy: the original was destroyed in the war).

From Lüneburg, our route runs via industrial Harburg, a suburb of Hamburg, then into a very different landscape – the charming **Altes Land**, along the south bank of the broad Elbe. This is a gently pastoral region of old timbered farmsteads and apple and cherry

---

The Eccentric Artists of Worpswede

All lovers of *fin-de-siècle* art should visit Worpswede, an unusual and fascinating village north of Bremen. Here a group of talented young writers and artists, tired of life in Munich and Berlin, began to settle in the 1880s and 1890s, drawn by the sombrely beautiful moorland scenery. They were influenced by the Pre-Raphaelites and William Morris, whose aesthetic ideas they more or less shared; and their leader was Heinrich Vogeler, a cranky romantic poseur. But after a while the vogue for Worpswede faded, the artists left, and the bizarre houses they had built began to decay. Only recently has it been restored, and is now modishly touristy.

The quirkily asymmetrical buildings, the Villa Mackensen, Bahnhof, Brunjeshof and others, were mostly designed by Bernhard Hoetger, leading architect of the group. Outside the village is his Niedersachsenstein, a bizarre stone monument; his cheeky statuette of a smiling bonze stands in the garden of his exotic Kaffee Worpswede, still in use as a café today. The excellent museum beside it has many originals of the group's work – poetic local landscapes of moonlight, sunset and storm, by Otto Modersohn and Fritz Mackensen; studies of poverty-stricken women by Paula Modersohn-Becker, the most socially-conscious of the group (and today the most highly-rated as an artist); haunting canvases by Vogeler such as his *Wintermärchen* and Rossetti-like portraits of scantily-clad young women. The best known of the group's paintings is Vogeler's luminous study of some friends on the curving white balustrade of his home in Worpswede.

An 18th-century crane and other old buildings in Lüneburg's 'water district'.

orchards, at their best during spring-time blossom. Further west is the attractive old Hanseatic port of **Stade** (pop. 45,000), something of a show-piece. Its small curving harbour, no longer in use, has been well restored and is lined with fine houses, notably the pink-and-white Renaissance one at no 23. Note the strange wooden crane, once used for unloading wheat.

West of Stade the road crosses the flat Friesian plain (see p. 244) on its way to **Cuxhaven** (pop. 64,000) at the mouth of the Elbe. This is Germany's second largest fishing-port, a major seaport too, and a modest beach resort. From its main jetty, oddly called the *Alte Liebe* ('old love'), you get a good view of shipping passing up and down the Elbe, to and from Hamburg. Nearby is the Kugelbake, a tall disused beacon on stilts.

TOURIST OFFICES

CELLE: Schlossplatz 6a, tel (05141) 2 30 31.

LÜNEBURG: Rathaus, Marktplatz, tel (04131) 3 22 00.

STADE: Bahnhofstr. 3, tel (04141) 40 15 50.

CUXHAVEN: Lichtenbergplatz, tel (04721) 3 60 46.

Accommodation, Eating and Drinking

CELLE 3100:

(H)**Fürstenhof**, Hanoversche Str. 55, tel (05141) 20 10. Converted 17th-century palace, formally elegant, with modern bedroom annexe. Rooms (75) A–B. **Endtenfang** restaurant reputed for duck and lamb dishes, A–B; **Kutscherstube** (cl lunch and Sun), C.
(H)**Nordwall**, Nordwall 4, tel (05141) 2 90 77. Central. No restaurant. Rooms (20) C–D.

EGESTORF 2115:

(H)**Hof Sudermühlen**, 3km to NW in Sahrendorf, Nordheide 1, tel (04175) 14 41. Friendly and tranquil. Rooms (50) C. Meals C.

BENDESTORF 2106:

(H)**Meinsbur**, Gartenstr. 2, tel (04183) 60 88. Delightful little rural hotel on edge of Lüneburg Heath. Meals served in garden in summer, by log fire in winter. Cl Jan, Feb, July. Rooms (15) C. Meals B–C.

LÜNEBURG 2120:

(H)**Residenz**, Münstermannskamp 10, tel (04131) 4 50 47. Modern hotel in S outskirts, near Kurpark. Good food; lavish breakfast buffet. Rooms (35) C. Meals B–C.
(H)**Wellemkamp's**, Am Sande 9, tel (04131) 4 30 26. Old post-house in Altstadt; good cooking. Rooms (45) C–D. Meals B–C.
(R)**Zum Heidkrug**, Am Berge 5, tel (04131) 3 12 49. Atmospheric old Gothic mansion (1455) in Altstadt. Good home cooking. Cl Jan 4–16. Meals B–C.

CUXHAVEN 2190:

(H)**Strandperle**, Duhner Strandstr. 7, tel (04721) 4 00 60. Modern beach hotel in Duhnen, 6km to NW. Sauna, indoor pool; 4 restaurants. Cl 15 Jan–Feb. Rooms (65) B–C. Meals B–D.
(H)**Seepavillon Donner**, Alten Liebe 5, tel (04721) 3 80 64. Lovely setting by Alte Liebe lighthouse, with sea views. Modern rooms; good restaurant. Rooms (47) C. Meals B–C.

WORPSWEDE 2862:

(H)**Eichenhof**, Ostendorferstr. 13, tel (04792) 26 76. Delightful old country house, nicely furnished. Cl mid-Dec to mid-Jan. No restaurant. Rooms (16) C.

East Friesland, Oldenburg and Emden

Friesland is the island-girt strip of coast that runs from the Danish frontier down to the the Zuider Zee. It has its own distinctive character and culture, even language. This route takes in so-called East Friesland (*Ostfriesland*), a flat stretch between the Weser and Ems estuaries, crowned to the north by a string of islands whose wide sandy beaches and bracing climate make them popular as summer resorts; some are also bird sanctuaries. With its dykes, windmills and Friesland cows, the coastal area is very like Holland – not surprisingly. And like other Frieslanders the people tend to be reserved and laconic, much addicted to strong brown tea. This route also goes inland to the city of Oldenburg and the open-air museum at Cloppenburg.

OLDENBURG (pop. 139,000) is a river port and the market centre of a prosperous farming and horse-breeding region; it also has a small new university and a lively festival in October, the Kramermarkt. It's a modern, spread-out town: but the small moated Altstadt, most of it traffic-free, retains a few interesting buildings such as the 15th-century Lappan Tower and the Gothic church of Lambertikirche, much rebuilt. There are three museums. The Landesmuseum, housed in the former ducal palace, has notable works by Tischbein, and some reconstructed interiors of local rural dwellings; in the Augusteum are paintings by the Worpswede school (see p. 241); the natural history museum includes corpses found in local peat-bogs, some over 2,000 years old.

To the west is **Bad Zwischenahn** (pop. 24,000), a large summer resort and fashionable spa, set attractively by a broad lake ideal for water-sports. In the middle of its elegant lakeside gardens, rather incongruously, is an open-air rural museum with old cottages and a windmill. Its main exhibit is a stately red-brick farmhouse (c. 1605) from the Ammerland plain nearby, consisting of one enormous room where humans and animals cohabited: it has been well restored, with handsome furniture and panelling. Even more impressive is the lovely old church of St Johann, also by the lake: it has a superb carved and painted altarpiece (1480), a vaulted ceiling with 16th-century frescoes, and charming paintings on the wooden gallery above the pretty white-and-blue pews. At **Ocholt**, to the west, you will find the picturesque old Howieker watermill.

To the north across the Friesian plain lies the big port of **Wilhelmshaven** (pop. 97,000), built as a naval base by Wilhelm I in the 1850s, then a key U-boat base in World War II. Today it receives tankers and supplies the Ruhr with oil down a pipeline. It has an aquarium (open daily), and a coastal museum (*Küsten-Museum*) that gives details of local geography and history. To the west is the very interesting old town of **Jever** (pop. 12,000), whose neat pink hunting-Schloss holds one of North Germany's finest local museums, with a richly varied collection of farm tools, furniture, costumes, clogs, even old toys and games, as well as mementoes of the castle's history. These include portraits of Catherine the Great, for the castle once belonged to the Tsars. Part 18th-century, part much older, it has carved oak beams and is set in a pleasant little moated park. On the outer wall of the café by its gates is an old glockenspiel whose figurines of the castle's former owners perform hourly (Catherine looks most gloomy). Jever's Altstadt is also worth a look, though a bit spoilt by cars and new shops: in the Marktplatz is the red-brick Rathaus (1609), and an unusual modern church whose separate belfry contains a splendid Renaissance sarcophagus adorned with white marble statues. In Jever's suburbs are the three glass towers of its huge modern brewery: it has long been a beer town, and Jever Pilsener is widely sold all over the region.

Go north-west from Jever through pastoral country and you'll come to the sea at **Neuharlingersiel**, a picturesque old fishing-port, now a lively resort. There are good beaches all along this coast, but ugly caravan-sites too. The coastal road goes west through flat, green country just like Holland – windmills, dykes, and masses of black-and-white Friesian cows. I even saw cows and sheep standing on the dykes, maybe enjoying the view. Offshore is the chain of seven inhabited East Friesian islands, all popular in summer, all reachable by ferry, and some with very odd names – Wangerooge, Spiekeroog, Langeoog. Spiekeroog has the highest dune of the chain (75m) and an old church with souvenirs of the Spanish Armada; Langeoog has a well-known bird sanctuary. Borkum and Juist, to the west, are busy resorts in the short summer season.

NORDERNEY, the most developed and populous (8,000) of these islands, has been a resort since 1797: its history and folklore can be studied in its little Fischerhaus museum. Today it's a fair-sized resort with lots of amenities, such as concerts in summer, a nine-hole golf-course, horse-riding, and a heated seawater pool with wave-machine. The bracing air is used for treating eczema and asthma: Norderney has boarding-schools for children with these complaints, and spa facilities for adults on cures. The casino with its formal flower-garden, lit up at night, looks elegant: but unlike Sylt (see p. 276), Norderney is not a 'smart' venue. Its hotels and other buildings are grouped into a town at the west end, while the rest of the island is a 12km stretch of rolling dune, mostly covered with scrub or wild grass. In its wild interior, where the sea is invisible behind the dunes, it has a desolate feel: but the long sandy beaches are superb. In summer they are studded with hooded wicker chairs as protection against the relentless wind, which also causes beach erosion. This is being combatted by the building of breakwaters. Norderney is served by regular ferries from Norddeich: these will take private cars, but the fares are kept high so as to deter motorists, and it could be best to park at Norddeich, then walk or take taxis on the island.

Back on the mainland, Norden has an impressive old Rathaus (c. 1500), while Greetsiel to the south-west is a picturesque fishing-village (very touristy), and the church at Pilsum has a remarkable 15th-century bronze baptismal font. But apart from a few treasures of this kind, the villages and towns of this part of flat, windswept Friesland tend to be modern and charmless. This is true of **Emden** (pop. 50,000) a big seaport on the Ems estuary that today serves the industrial Ruhr via the Dortmund–Ems canal. Emden is a major herring-fishing centre: this industry, and local history, can be studied in the Ostfriesisches Landesmuseum, which also has a magnificent collection of old arms and armour, and some Dutch paintings.

East of Emden, on the plain south of Aurich, is the curious windmill country of **Grossefehn**, with old wooden bridges across quiet canals, and five handsome 19th-century mills. One is still in use for grinding corn – the Dutch-type mill at **Spezterfёhn**, whose very friendly owner shows visitors round for free (weekends only) and will take them up to the gallery to inspect the metal sails. He claims that his mill is economically viable (but the *Land*, for touristic reasons, does provide a subsidy). The nearby mill at Bagland has been restored and will soon be working, too. These are the only working windmills left in Ostfriesland.

Some way south-east, down at **Cloppenburg** (pop. 22,000), is one of the very best of German outdoor rural museums, the Niedersächsisches Freilichtmuseum (open daily), set in a spacious park. Here farmhouses and other buildings, 16th- to 19th-century, have been reassembled from all over the Land. They include a manor with painted cupboards, a tiny, quaint village school with an abacus, a little Catholic church from near Hildesheim, and an old pub still in active use by visitors. A baker sells old-style country bread; live ducks and geese, and sheep in a fold, all embellish the scene. The aim is to show the full range of former rural life; and more than most German museums of this kind, this one has been set out to look like a real village.

To the east of Cloppenburg is an area of Stone Age megaliths, on Ahlhorn heath near Visbek, just south of the motorway. Here a ten-minute walk through woods will bring you to the so-called **'Visbeker Bräutigam'** ('Visbek bridegroom'), a long low double line of granite blocks forming a funeral chamber and monument; the nearby **'Visbeker Braut'** ('Visbek bride') to the east is much the same only smaller. Stone Age man assembled these boulders left by Ice Age glaciers. Though among Germany's most important prehistoric remains, they are pretty feeble compared with Stonehenge or Carnac (Brittany). From here it's only a short drive back to Oldenburg.

TOURIST OFFICES

OLDENBURG: Lange Str. 3, tel (0441) 2 50 96.

WILHEMSHAVEN: Börsenstr 55b, tel (04421) 2 62 61.

NORDERNEY: Bu,ulowalle 5, tel (04932) 5 02.

EMDEN: Feuerschiff im Ratsdelft, tel (04921) 3 25 28.

Accommodation, Eating and Drinking

OLDENBURG 2900:

(H)**Heide**, Melkbrink 49, tel (0441) 80 40. In residential area; indoor pool; good food. Rooms (91). Meals C.

(R)**Sartorius Stuben**, Herbartgang 6, tel (0441) 2 66 76. In old building; rustic ambience. Cl Sun. Meals B–C.

BAD ZWISCHENAHN 2903:

(H)**Romantik-Hotel Jagdhaus Eiden**, tel (04403) 10 22. By the lake, near casino, an old half-timbered hunting-lodge, now a lovely smart hotel. Indoor pool; excellent Friesland dishes (eel, etc); also 'gourmet' **Apicius** restaurant (cl Mon, 3 weeks Jan). Rooms (59) B–C. Meals A–C.

(R)**Der Spieker**, Kurgarten, tel (04403) 234. Picturesque old red-brick *Fachwerk* building near the lake. Meals C–D.

WIESMOOR-HINRICHSFEHN 2964:

(H)**Blauer Fasan**, Fliederstr. 1, tel (04944) 10 47. Charming rural place, secluded amid fields and flowers. Cl Jan Feb. Rooms (26) C. Meals (cl Mon winter) B–C.

WILHELMSHAVEN 2940:

(H)**Kaiser**, Rheinstr. 128, tel (04421) 4 20 04. Modern and central; good cooking. Rooms (80) C–D. Meals C–D.

NEUHARLINGERSIEL 2943:

(H)**Jansen's**, Am Hafen 7, tel (04974) 224. Right on the pretty harbour: modest but attractively rustic. Good for local fish. Cl mid-Nov to mid-Feb. Rooms (23) D. Meals C–D.

NORDERNEY 2982:

(H)**Georgshöhe**, Kaiserstr. 24, tel (04932) 89 80. Near beach; pool, sauna, tennis, solarium etc. Cl 2 weeks Feb, 2 weeks Dec. Rooms (76) B. Meals (dinner only) B–C.

(H)**Golf-Hotel**, Am Golfplatz 1, tel (04932) 89 60. Cheerful modern hotel beside golf-course, amid fields. Rooms (35) B–C. Meals B–C.

VISBEK:

(R)**Engelmannsbäke**, tel (04445) 806. At the Visbeker Bräutigam, by a little lake. Good food served outdoors. Meals D.

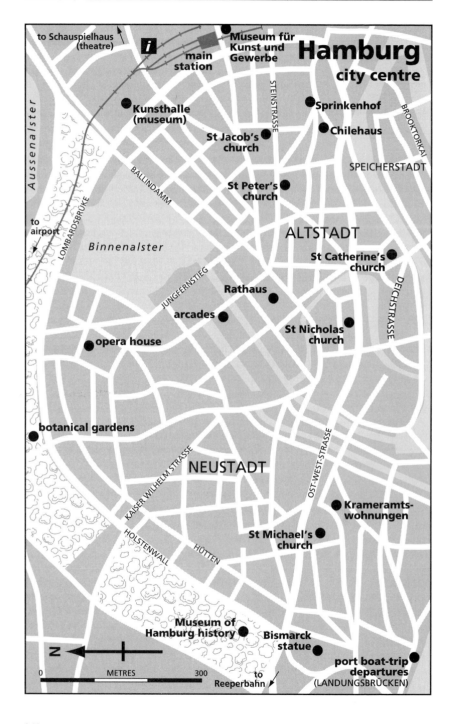

to Schauspielhaus
(theatre)

i

**Museum für
Kunst und
Gewerbe**

main
station

Hamburg
city centre

STEINSTRASSE

BROOKTORKAI

**Kunsthalle
(museum)**

Sprinkenhof

Chilehaus

**St Jacob's
church**

SPEICHERSTADT

Aussenalster

BALLINDAMM

**St Peter's
church**

ALTSTADT

LOMBARDSBRÜKE

to
airport

Binnenalster

**St Catherine's
church**

DEICHSTRASSE

JUNGFERNSTIEG

Rathaus

arcades

**St Nicholas
church**

opera house

botanical gardens

KAISER WILHELM STRASSE

NEUSTADT

OST-WEST-STRASSE

**Krameramts-
wohnungen**

HOLSTENWALL

HÜTTEN

**St Michael's
church**

N

**Museum of
Hamburg history**

**Bismarck
statue**

0   METRES   300

to
Reeperbahn

**port boat-trip
departures**
(LANDUNGSBRÜCKEN)

CHAPTER EIGHT

Hamburg

GERMANY'S LEADING PORT and second biggest city (pop. 1,580,000) stands on the river Elbe some 100km upstream from its mouth. Water is its element – the broad Elbe, the miles of quays and canals, and the large and lovely Alster lake in the very heart of town, a shimmering focus of local life. Hamburg's rough red-light seaport reputation is only a small part of its reality: this is an exceptionally graceful and civilized town, serene and spacious, warmly liked and admired by almost all who know it. Compared, say, with Munich, it may have few buildings of individual distinction: but overall it is harmoniously handsome – from the stately red-brick warehouses by the port, to the line of church spires seen from the Alster, and the noble villas that the merchants built around this lake. Hamburg is heir to a great mercantile seafaring tradition, dating from Hanseatic days and from the time when it was the Continent's busiest port and Germany's richest city. Its people, reserved and prudent in the northern manner, do not burst into easy song like Bavarians: but they are not unfriendly, and theirs is a strongly liberal, outward-looking spirit, cosmopolitan and anglophile.

First settled in the ninth century, Hamburg became a registered port in 1189; soon afterwards it joined the Hanseatic League under Lübeck's leadership, and developed a thriving commerce. Germany's first stock exchange was founded here in 1558. In 1618 it became a Free Imperial City (today it still uses the title 'Free and Hanseatic City'), and then managed to stay out of the ruinous Thirty Years' War. In the later 19th century, new trade with the Americas brought fantastic boom and growth: shipbuilding flourished, and the Hamburg–America-Linie became the world's largest steamship company. After 1933, this liberal city was less welcoming to the Nazis than any other, and Hitler never staged big rallies here. But more than most others it then suffered fearfully from RAF bombing.

Hamburg today is a *Land* on its own, a semi-autonomous city-state. It has been ruled almost continually since the war by moderate pragmatists of the SPD: typical of them is the best-known living Hamburger, ex-Chancellor

Helmut Schmidt, a former city senator. It is hardly their fault that the local economy has run into difficulties in recent years, making this no longer the wealthiest German city. Its shipbuilding has shared in the general European crisis and some yards have closed; its giant port has suffered from competition with Rotterdam, which is better situated for the Atlantic trade; the focus of German industry has been shifting southwards (see p. 101); and the 1945–89 division of Europe cut Hamburg off from its natural hinterland in East Germany and Poland. Today, however it is expecting to benefit hugely from the re-opening of those markets, and from the new German unity. And its port, if past its prime, is still the fourth in Europe, with an annual traffic of some 60 million tonnes. Industry, after a bad patch, is also recovering, especially in aeronautics: Lufthansa's repair yards employ 7,000, while another 7,000 work for MBB, making Airbus components and other aircraft. High-tech electronics firms such as Philips are also active. But the leading shipyard, Blohm und Voss, has been obliged to diversify into building tanks and military vessels for export – to the indignation of the Left.

The great shipping merchants may have lost their dominant role, but there's still a lot of wealth in Hamburg – and visibly so. It is a very stylish city, if in a more discreet way than Munich. It is also truly cultured, with a musical tradition: Germany's first opera house was opened here in 1677, and Johannes Brahms was born and spent his youth in Hamburg. Ever since the war the opera company has been on balance Germany's best, notably under its great Swiss manager, Rolf Liebermann, recently retired; the ballet, under John Neumeier, is in the same league; and the leading State theatre has excelled under Peter Zadek and now under Michael Bogdanov, from London. Small theatres are numerous. But Hamburg has few great museums, for its merchant rulers were much less interested than the South German monarchs and princes in amassing great art collections. The city however is Germany's foremost Press and media capital. Its daily papers do not have the rank of those in Frankfurt or Munich: but the TV news programmes are edited here, the DPA Press agency is here, as are most of Germany's leading weekly magazines, including *Die Zeit*, *Der Spiegel* and *Stern*, and the biggest record companies.

Hamburgers do not flaunt their money as in Munich or Düsseldorf; but they have real style. Many are the northern blond type, tall and lean, and they stride their streets in a lordly way; some men wear those blue Hamburg sailors' caps beloved of Helmut Schmidt. Yet there's little of the exuberant, emotional folklore that you find in Bavaria or the Rhineland. Hamburgers are direct, polite, businesslike. Though affable to visitors, they make friends slowly and their inner social circles are hard to penetrate. They are stiffer than the British. Yet the breezy tolerance and understatement of Hamburg has an English affinity; and this is known as the most 'English' of German towns, alike in its looks and manners. It remains proud of the close historic trade links: 'When it rains in London, Hamburgers put up their umbrellas', is an old saying. But today Hamburg has become less inclined to follow London's lead: the England that it admires and imitates seems to be mainly the old pre-war England of claret-drinking,

Hamburg: the port and city centre, with the Alster lake behind

blue blazers and bespoke tailors. And if Hamburg in some ways looks like London, it's because both cities have the same heritage of tall brick mansions amid lawns and trees, and trim suburban cottages.

Hamburg's **festivals** include the ballet festival (May); a big popular festival in the port (7 May and the following weekend); horse-riding and show-jumping in Klein Flottbek (June); the *Hummelfest* (folk festival, July/Aug); and the Alster folk festival (first weekend Aug). There is a lively **market** every Sunday morning at Fischmarkt, St Pauli. Schauspielhaus and Thalia are Hamburg's main 'straight' **theatres**. Kampnagel is good for avant-garde

productions, Fabrik for the fringe (concerts etc); Schiff is a lively satiric cabaret, on a boat; the Ohnsorg theatre in St Pauli does plays in *Plattdeutsch* dialect.

Hamburg is delightfully spacious, with broad streets and many parks and gardens; within its broad borders you'll find leafy lanes, old timbered farmsteads, country houses with neat lawns. Nearer the centre, residential areas such as Winterhude and Eppendorf have brick houses with charming *Jugendstil* wrought-iron balconies, plus the odd splash of colour from a new pop-art mural on a blind wall. Some streets still keep their odd ancient names – Ole Hoop, Hopfensack. And this watery metropolis holds the world record for bridges – 2,195, compared with Venice's 400.

Central Hamburg is nicely planned. If it has few lovely or picturesque buildings, it's for three main reasons. First, this merchant town was never a major centre of Church or aristocracy, so has no legacy of palaces or mighty churches. Second, much of its mediaeval nucleus was destroyed in a great fire in 1842, and the city was then rebuilt on the spacious pattern it retains today. Thirdly, the RAF fire-raids of 1943 repeated the destruction process: these wiped out much of the port and the working-class and factory districts east of the main station. Post-war rebuilding was then better done than in most big German towns, and very spaciously. The downtown business area, rebuilt mainly in local red-brick style, is not beautiful, but it avoids the hard concrete brashness of many German cities; and in the centre there are no skyscrapers to mar the graceful skyline of green-copper spires and domes. Traffic jams are few and parking fairly easy: so you can tour the main sights by car.

You could, however, begin with a guided boat-tour of the **port**: boats leave from the Landungsbrücken, near the domed entrance to the old St Pauli Elbtunnel (a new motorway tunnel has been built further west). You will see the 42 miles of quays, the ultra-modern terminals, the two-and-a-half-mile Köhlbrand suspension bridge, opened in 1975, and the protection walls built against a recurrence of the 1962 floods that claimed 350 lives. This is a tidal port, taking ships of up to 110,000 tons. Its terminals can load or unload very fast, using only a small workforce. This suits the owners of the big container ships, for harbour dues are high: but it has put many dockers out of work.

Beside some canals near the eastern end of the port is the **Speicherstadt**, a massive ensemble of tall gabled red-brick warehouses: they were erected in the 1880s when Hamburg became a free port, and are still used for storing tobacco, silk, spices, etc. To make room for them, the baroque homes of merchants and the tenements of workers were pulled down, and some 170,000 people were rehoused. Cross one of the bridges here and you'll come to what remains of the **Altstadt**. The brick church of St Catherine, Gothic with a baroque tower, looms above the water-front. Just inland is the tall slim spire of St Nicholas: the church itself, badly bombed, has been left in ruins as a war memorial. Here some nicely-restored gabled warehouses front the curving banks of the Nikolai-fleet canal; and the narrow Deichstrasse is lined with handsome 17th-century merchants' houses, many of them now used as 'old Hamburg' restaurants (see p. 257). This is one of the few corners of the Altstadt that gives an idea of what it must have been like before the fire of 1842.

To the north is the huge high-towered **Rathaus**, erected in 1897 in pompous neo-Renaissance style, to replace the one destroyed in the fire. Its lavish interiors and heavy leather furnishings are symbolic of the city's pride and power at that time (there are guided tours when the Senate is not in session). The Rathaus faces a big square with attractive modern glass structures, and a canal bordered with graceful arches. Cross this, and you'll come to one of the most amazing sights of modern Hamburg – six big new **shopping-arcades**, all built since 1979 and among the most luxurious and stylish in Europe. Galleria and Hanseviertel are the most striking, with domed glass roofs. Their boutiques sell things you do not need, like rare teas, and toys and clothes for cats and dogs, and their window-displays are the apogee of arty provocation – for example, a jeweller's bedecked with broken egg-shells. Even in serious Hamburg, these shops apparently do well.

East of the Rathaus, St Peter's church has a tall tower dating from the 14th century, while St Jacob's is a fine example of a northern late-Gothic hall-church. Near by are two curious office blocks, the Chilehaus and Sprinkenhof, designed in the 1920s by the Expressionist architect Fritz Höger. Cross the busy ring-road and you'll come to the Hauptbahnhof with its vast glass vaulted roof, and close to it the **Museum für Kunst und Gewerbe** (Arts and Crafts Museum), notable for its collections of Renaissance furniture, 18th-century porcelain, *Jugendstil* ornaments, and Greek, Egyptian and oriental artworks: you can even attend a genuine Japanese tea-ceremony in an authentic tea-house. Just behind the station is the city's main theatre, the Schauspielhaus.

Between the station and the Alster is the city's principal art museum, the huge **Kunsthalle**: though badly and confusedly laid out (the best paintings are on the first floor), it is full of good things. The fine collection of North German primitives includes three retables by Master Bertram. Rembrandt, van Dyck and Jan Steen are represented in the Dutch and Flemish section, Tiepolo and Canaletto in the Italian, Claude Lorrain in the French. But the Germans hold pride of place: among them, charming genre paint-

ings by Balthazar Denner (18th century), scenes of Hamburg by Jacob Gensler and country scenes by Christian Morgenstern (both 19th). Dreamily romantic works by Caspar David Friedrich include his famous *Wanderer above the Clouds*. Manet's *Nana*, and a Renoir of women riding in the Bois, dominate an otherwise humdrum Impressionist section; Munch, Dix and Liebermann are all in good form, as are the three Ks, Klee, Kandinsky and Kokoschka.

The **Alster** lake is divided into two. The smaller Binnenalster is a focus of the city's business life, surrounded harmoniously on three sides by 19th-century office blocks. Across a main road is the much larger Aussenalster, surely one of Europe's loveliest city lakes. Here Hamburgers take their civilized recreation. Long-legged Nordic types with scarves and capes go striding along its shore-paths with their bounding, barking dogs, while sails glide against a backdrop of weeping-willows, stately villas, and the line of graceful spires. In summer people sit in outdoor waterside cafés. In a hard winter, the lake freezes over so thick that cars drive across it, and stalls selling hot *Glühwein* are set up on the ice (despite police warnings of danger). You can hire sailboats on the lake, or go windsurfing, or take a regular motorboat excursion round it, to admire the gentle vistas.

On the west side of the lake is the elegant residential district of Harvestehude: here the attractive little 'village' of **Pöseldorf** has become a focus of the *Schickeria* and media trendies, a mini-Chelsea of slick bars and bistros – rather fun. The nearby **Museum of Ethnology** (*Völkerkunde*) presents collections of Third World art and folk-art,

---

St Pauli's Reeperbahn

The suburb of St Pauli used to be a fishing-village and working-class district. Since then, its notorious main street, the Reeperbahn, has undergone *three* metamorphoses. First, in the late 19th century when the transatlantic passenger trade boomed, a large entertainment district grew up, mostly quite respectable, to cater for people waiting often some days for their sailings: there were theatres, terrace-cafés with live orchestras, and a few smart brothels too. The sailors' pubs and whorehouses were in side-alleys. Then after the war times changed. The posh liners vanished, the sailors became fewer as the port modernized; the Reeperbahn slid down-market into the sex-and-voyeurism industry, catering mainly for provincial businessmen and tourists. In the erotic cabarets, the live sex-act came in every shape and style; in the neat brothels of the Herbertstrasse, the girls sat in ground-floor windows in a lurid pink glow. Some civic worthies were upset that Hamburg's worldwide reputation should be identified with the Reeperbahn: but this is a tolerant city.

Since the late 1980s things have changed again, partly under the impact of the AIDS scare. The biggest brothel, the huge Eros Centre, has closed down and become a respectable hotel. The sex-industry is retreating into the side-streets, where the Herbertstrasse still ticks over. And the Reeperbahn itself is again mainly an entertainment centre, still garish and vulgar-looking, but smart restaurants are creeping in, as St Pauli moves back up market.

---

brought back to Hamburg by old-time explorers: the Javanese shadow-puppets and pre-Colombian jewellery are notable. Here you are right beside the University, one of Germany's largest but dating only from 1919. Beyond it is the 271-metre TV tower (splendid view from its observatory: open daily); also two of the city's best parks, the Botanical Gardens (interesting Amazonian water-lilies) and the famous **Planten un Blomen** flower-park. Here, after dark in summer, the coloured illuminated fountains perform a ballet of light and music.

Back near the centre is the rebuilt Opera House. Here the main ring-road leads west along the line of the old city walls (hence its names, Holstenwall, Gorch-Fock-Wall, etc). It passes the law courts, to reach the rather disappointing **Museum of Hamburg History**, whose main thrust is technical and industrial, rather than socio-cultural. It has models, paintings and photos of old Hamburg and the port, and a big model railway that will please children. Just to the south, you cannot fail to notice the statue of a swaggering Bismarck, high on a pedestal with his spiked helmet and sword. More edifying is the handsome baroque church of **St Michael** (1762), light and spacious, built for the Lutherans: its tall greenish tower, known as 'Michel', is a city landmark, and from its platform (open daily) you get a fine view of town and port. Behind the church, the archway at 10 Krayenkamp leads to a picturesque alley of 17th-century brick-and-timber almshouses, the **Krameramtswohnungen**, some now housing cafés and galleries – as charming a corner of 'old Hamburg' as you'll find.

To the west is the famous **St Pauli** district whose gaudy main street, the Reeperbahn, is known the world over for its erotic nightlife. St Pauli's **Hafenstrasse**, high on a terrace above the Elbe, has also achieved notoriety recently, for in the mid-1980s some of its decaying old houses were taken over by squatters who formed a militant commune and violently resisted police attempts to evict them. The conflict dragged on for years, polarizing city opinion and making national headlines. The squatters painted aggressive murals and slogans on the blind walls ('We unite in the Struggle against Renovation, Fascism and the Police State!'), clearly visible from any ship entering the port. The Leftists were crusading against moves to redevelop this prime site above the river by removing its old working-class population and building smart flats and office blocks.

Undeterred by these events, the traditional St Pauli **fish-market** is still held down on the quayside here – every Sunday from five to ten am, when it must close promptly under an old law forbidding it to compete with church services. All year, this big delightful market is lively with buyers and sellers of all sorts – a brave sight at daybreak with the seagulls flying. It is now mainly a food-cum-flea-market, selling anything from potted palms to caged birds. Some fish is still sold too – notably by the bouncy 'Eely Dieter' whose fast-patter line in eels draws the crowds. Late revellers from the Reeperbahn descend on the market, too, blearily sozzled or sated. And at 6 am in the popular Fischerhaus restaurant you can sit down to a Hamburg breakfast of soused herring, eel-and-plum soup and beer, amid accordion-

ists, tipsy sailors, whores, tourists, and necking couples in evening dress.

Here you enter the city's most important suburb, **Altona**, which belonged to Denmark until 1864 and was not made part of Hamburg till 1937: it still has the feel of a separate town, with its own stately character. The street oddly called Palmaille is lined with elegant white patrician houses, c. 1790–1825, while the 'Altona Balcony' in front of the Rathaus provides a noble view down over river and port. Best of all, the local museum, the **Norddeutsches Landesmuseum**, is much the most attractive in Hamburg – a bright modern building devoted to the life and history of Altona and its Schleswig hinterland. It was badly damaged by fire in 1980 and not all exhibits are yet restored. But you can admire the remarkable array of 18th- and 19th-century ships' figureheads. There are also old fishing-boats, models of sailing-ships, and lovely local costumes. Of the many paintings of Schleswig scenes, note Rudolf Jordan's famous *Marriage Contract in Heligoland*, and a charming portrait of tourists at Wyk by the Danish artist David Jacobsen (1821–71). Upstairs, some rooms have been furnished as traditional rural interiors: one attractive 'farmhouse' serves as a café/restaurant for visitors.

Övelgönne, on Altona's western fringe, is a delightfully rural stretch of riverside, where you can stroll under avenues of trees or loll in waterside cafés – Hamburg at its most idyllic. Here some old boats have been grouped to form a 'museum harbour'. The main road, the Elbchaussee, leads west from Altona along the river, past handsome villas in big gardens and fine old timbered mansions: this is the wealthiest part of Hamburg, also the loveliest, in a semi-pastoral style, and it's hard to believe you are still inside a huge city. In the nicely landscaped Jenisch Park, the white neo-classical **Villa Jenisch** (1831), open to visitors, has sumptuously furnished interiors from the Renaissance to the *Jugendstil* periods; the adjacent **Ernst-Barlach House** contains works by the distinguished modern sculptor of that name, who came from nearby Wedel. The Elbchaussee will then take you to the former fishing village of **Blankinese**, now a select suburb-cum-resort, with steep alleys and big villas on its hillside; it's an enchanting place, with some good riverside pubs and restaurants. Beyond the city borders is the old port of **Wedel**, where passing ships are saluted on a high dais, with the raising of their national colours and the playing of their anthem.

In the north-west suburb of Stellingen is the large privately-owned **Hagenbeck Zoo** (open daily), one of the first to pioneer the modern practice of letting wild animals live in comparative liberty. It also trains animals for circuses. Lastly, it can be well worth following the pretty river Alster upstream through the northern suburbs, to Wellngsbüttel and Mellingburg, where attractive old houses grace its banks.

TOURIST OFFICES
Hachmannplatz 1 (main station), tel 30 05 12 45; airport (Halle 3), tel 30 05 12 40.

Accommodation, Eating and Drinking (Postcode 2000, area tel code 040)

(H)**Atlantic-Hotel Kempinski**, An der Alster 72, Hamburg 1, tel 2 88 80. Dating from 1909, a famous, classic and elegant 'grand hotel', facing the lake. Beer-tavern, nightclub, massage, roof swimming-pool. Rooms (259) A. Meals (cl Sat lunch) A.
(H)**Prem**, Am der Alster 9, Hamburg 1, tel 24 54 54. Facing the lake, stylish and quite small. Noted French restaurant, **La Mer**. Rooms (52) A. Meals (cl lunch Sat, Sun) A–B.
(H)**Vier Jahreszeiten**, Neuer Jungfernstieg 9, Hamburg 36, tel 3 49 40. Facing the inner Alster: family-run, superlatively gracious, intimately club-like, very distinguished. Noted **Haerlin** restaurant. Rooms (175) A. Meals (cl Sun) A–B.
(H)**Abtei**, Abteistr. 14, Hamburg 13, tel 44 29 05. In quiet Harvestehude: tiny, elegant and beautiful. Superb breakfasts. No restaurant. Cl Christmas, New Year. Rooms (12) A–B.
(H)**Hanseatic**, Sierichstr. 150, Hamburg 60, tel 48 57 72. Converted villa 4km N of centre. Select, very personal; delightful owner. No restaurant. Rooms (13) A–B.
(H)**Bellevue**, An der Alster 14, Hamburg 1, tel 24 80 11. Facing lake; stylish and efficient. Good food. Rooms (80) B. Meals B–C.
(H)**Mellingburger Schleuse**, Mellingburgredder 1, Hamburg 65, tel 602 40 01. In NE suburb of Sasel: 18th-century thatched farmhouse, nicely converted, with rustic furnishings. Good regional cooking. Rooms (34) B. Meals B–C.

(H)**St Raphael**, Adenauer-Allee 41, Hamburg 1, tel 24 82 00. Near station. Good swimming-pool and breakfast buffet. Rooms (135) B–C. Meals (cl Sat, Sun) C.

(H)**Hafen Hamburg**, Seewartenstr. 9, Hamburg 11, tel 31 11 30. Classic maritime hotel near the port, with river views. Rooms (252) C. Meals B–C.

(H)**Baseler Hof**, Esplanade 11, Hamburg 36, tel 35 90 60. Central, near inner Alster, well run. Rooms (160) C. Meals C–D.

(H)**Eden**, Ellmenreichstr 20, Hamburg 1, tel 24 84 80. Near station. Modern, friendly. No restaurant. Rooms (63) C–D.

(H)**Wedina**, Gurlittstr. 23, Hamburg 1, tel 24 30 11. Near Alster and station. Garden, pool, good breakfasts. No restaurant. Cl mid-Dec to mid-Feb. Rooms (23) D.

Of the many restaurants with a typical 'old Hamburg' atmosphere and local cooking, some of the best are to be found in the narrow Deichstrasse, near the port.

(R)**Landhaus Scherrer**, Elbchaussee 130, tel 880 13 25. Hamburg's best restaurant: charming old house near the Elbe, with superb cooking and atmosphere, some regional dishes. Cl Sun. Meals A–B. Bistro, lunch only, meals B–C.

(R)**Fischereihafen**, Grosse Elbstrasse 143, tel 38 18 16. In old house on Elbe, with fine views; quite smart. Excellent for fish dishes of all kinds. Meals A–B.

(R)**Zum Alten Rathaus**, Börsenbrücke 10, tel 36 75 70. Intimate, sophisticated: first-class Franco-German cooking. Cl Sun. Meals B. Jollity and song in its **Zum Fleetenkieker** cellar tavern.

(R)**Ratsweinkeller**, Grosse Johannisstr. 2, tel 36 41 53. In vaulted cellar of Rathaus; huge, sedate. Cl Sun. Meals B–C.

(R)**Old Commercial Room**, Englische Planke 10, tel 36 63 19. Good Hamburg cooking and a whiff of the sea. Meals B–C.

(R)**Alt-Hamburger Aalspeicher**, Deichstrasse 43, tel 36 29 90. One of the best in this street. Eel a speciality, smoked, grilled, roasted, etc. Meals B–C.

(R)**Schmitz**, Marie-Luisenstr. 3, tel 48 41 32. North of the Alster: cosy, reliable. Cl Sat, 3 weeks July. Meals B–C.

(R)**Zum Brandanfang**, Deichstr. 25, tel 36 55 20. Small, cosy, with typical Hamburg cooking. Meals C.

(R)**Fischerhaus**, St Pauli-Fischmarkt 14, tel 31 40 53. By the fish market; popular with sailors, night-lifers, bohemians. An institution. Fish very fresh. Meals C–D.

(R)**Kanzelmeyer**, Englische Planke 8, tel 36 48 33. Animated and genuine; near St Michael's church. Meals C–D.

(R)**Kartofeller**, Deichstr. 21, tel 36 55 85. Charming, lively, cosy and original: girls in elegant potato-sacks serve elegant potato-snacks, of every kind. Meals D–E.

(P)**Weinstube zur Traube**, Karl-Theodorstr. 4, tel 390 93 47. Pleasant wine-pub in Altona. Some snacks.

(C)**Wiener Café Boheme**, Milchstr. 1, tel 45 07 83. In Harvestehude. Elegant *Jugendstil* furniture.

(C)**Loft**, Galeria-Passage, Grosse Bleichen 21. Trendy musical café in smart arcade, in city centre.

(D)**Café Keese**, Reeperbahn 19–21, tel 31 08 05. Famous dance-hall, respectable, though ladies do the inviting. Jackets and ties.

(D)**Die Insel**, Harvestehude Weg. The best disco, smart and expensive – a villa with red carpets, balcony.

CHAPTER NINE

Bremen

BREMEN (POP. 522,000), Germany's oldest port and its largest after Hamburg, is a most beguiling old city with an exuberantly individualistic spirit. Like Hamburg, its mighty rival, it has a long and proud Hanseatic tradition of independence and so is allowed to be a *Land* on its own (forming an enclave within Lower Saxony, comprising also Bremerhaven).

Like Hamburg, it is a town of merchants and seafarers, with strong English connections and a liberal, outward-looking ethos. But its style is different: whereas Hamburg is rather sedate and serious, Bremen is more intimate and provincial, with a cheeky, folklorish eccentricity that I find delightful. Its tall gabled town houses wear a Dutch look, and the men who stride its cobbled streets have long weather-beaten faces, very Nordic. There's a strong sense of local community (no less than 200 annual street-festivals) and a devotion to old local customs – such as the fraternity dinner for local shipowners and other bigwigs, that has been held every year since 1545 in the Great Hall of the Rathaus. Outside in the Marktplatz, you may sometimes find a chorus of men in nautical dress singing sea-shanties. And there's a custom whereby a man still unwed on his 30th birthday must sweep rubbish from the cathedral steps, attired in top hat and tails, then marry the first pretty girl who kisses him. Typical Bremen.

The town was made a bishopric by Charlemagne in 787. It joined the Hanseatic League in 1358, in partnership with Hamburg and Lübeck, and in 1646 became a Free Imperial City. In the 19th century its port developed hugely, becoming a centre for cotton and coffee imports. Though 60km upstream from the mouth of the broad Weser, the port is accessible to ocean-going ships and it still handles a large part of German traffic in raw materials. But today the port is in difficulty, for much the same reasons as at Hamburg (see p. 250). The local shipyards, too, have been suffering badly from Far Eastern competition, like so many in Europe: in the mid-1980s Bremer Vulkan, largest of all German shipbuilding firms, was forced to shed a third of its workforce and had to be baled out by the City of Bremen, which

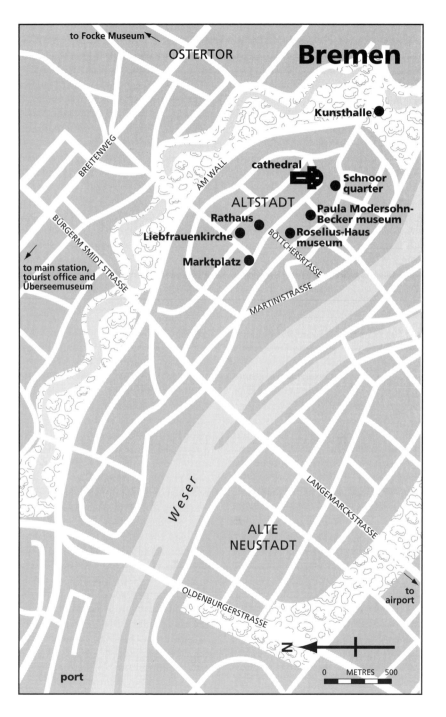

to Focke Museum

OSTERTOR

Bremen

Kunsthalle ●

cathedral

Schnoor quarter

ALTSTADT

Rathaus

Liebfrauenkirche

Paula Modersohn-Becker museum

Roselius-Haus museum

Marktplatz

BREITENWEG

AM WALL

BÜRGERM SMIDT STRASSE

BÖTTCHERSRTASSE

MARTINISTRASSE

to main station, tourist office and Überseemuseum

Weser

LANGEMARCKSTRASSE

ALTE NEUSTADT

OLDENBURGERSTRASSE

to airport

N

port

0   METRES   500

now owns 40 per cent of its shares. Some new modern replacement industries have arrived, notably in electronics and aerospace (MBB): even so, local unemployment is above the West German average.

This largely working-class city has been ruled without a break since 1945 by the moderate wing of the SPD, whose leaders have warmer relations with the local merchants than in Hamburg. If Bremen recently has won the reputation of being the most politically avant-garde of big German towns, this has been due less to the SPD than to the influence of its 'Red' university, founded by the *Land* Government in 1971. This was forged from the ideals of '1968' as a new-style democratic venture, and it filled up with Left-wing teachers and students. The result: it had the lowest academic standards in Germany, and many graduates found it hard to get good jobs. It has now become more moderate, but without entirely giving up its innovations, some of them unusual in Germany – for example, inter-disciplinary studies, and organic links with local trade unions. Bremen's star *Land* prime minister since the war has been the astonishing Hans Koscknik (in office 1967–85), an amiably flamboyant demagogue with the kind of tongue-in-cheek mock-arrogance that is far commoner in France than in a Germany full of boringly decorous local bigwigs. He talked to me with a twinkle about 'my city', 'my shipyards', 'my university', and added: 'I enjoy being first in Bremen. Or rather, I'm second – my wife is stronger.'

Bremen's two main **festivals** are the ice-sports (*Eiswette*) on 6 January, and the *Freimarkt* (last two weeks in October).

Much of the city's architecture fits in with the local quirky ethos. In residential districts you'll find *Jugendstil* villas in various pastel shades, with a medley of oddly-shaped gables. Right in the city centre, an old windmill stands high on a grassy hill formed from the old ramparts; within these is the Altstadt, with many tall old mansions in local Weser Renaissance style, well restored after the bombing. For a northern city, Bremen's level of colourful outdoor vitality is remarkable, and its central streets are always full of stalls, markets, buskers, and strollers in odd clothes.

Apart from the port and some museums, Bremen's main points of interest all lie compactly within the Altstadt, parts of it closed to traffic. At its heart is the lively **Marktplatz**, where two curious statues – both expressive of local spirit – stand outside the Rathaus. One is a giant 10-metre figure of the knight Roland, Charlemagne's nephew, erected in 1404 as an emblem of the city's independence. The other is a modern bronze pyramid of a cock standing on a cat standing on a dog standing on a donkey, representing the Street Musicians of Bremen from the famous Grimm folk-tale. The magnificent arcaded **Rathaus**, Gothic (1405) with an ornate Renaissance façade added in 1612, was undamaged in the war: inside (guided tours daily) you can see the elegant banqueting hall (see above) and its lovely carved spiral staircase. The basement Ratskeller (see p. 263) serves German wines only, no French (a hangover from the time of anti-Napoleonic protest). It has charming little 17th-century cubicles for private parties – and even today the tradition is still observed that a cubicle's door must be kept open if a man and a woman are alone in it.

Facing the Rathaus, the twin-towered **cathedral** (Protestant), rather sombre inside, represents various styles from Romanesque to late Gothic and has been much rebuilt. Note the 16th-century organ gallery with its statues and, in the 11th-century crypt, the fine 13th-century bronze font. Next to the flower market, the Liebfrauenkirche is a beautiful hall-church with one Romanesque and one Gothic tower.

Leading south from the Marktplatz is the curious **Böttcherstrasse**, an alley rebuilt during the 1920s in sort-of *art nouveau* style by the Bremen coffee magnate Ludwig Roselius: he used the talents of the eccentric Worpswede architect/sculptor Bernhard Hoetger (see p. 241). The tall red-brick gabled houses of this delightful *Jugendstil/* neo-Gothic fantasy today form a pedestrian shopping-arcade, lined with stylishly offbeat boutiques selling handmade toys and ornaments. A porcelain musical clock chimes thrice daily. There are also two small museums: one is devoted to the Worpswede artist Paula Modersohn-Becker; the other, the Roselius-Haus, not a 1920s building but a 16th-century merchant's house, contains mediaeval art and furniture collected by Roselius (paintings by Cranach, etc). To the south-east near the Weser is the charming village-like **Schnoor** quarter – a network of narrow flowery streets lined with former fishermen's cottages, 15th- to 19th century, now housing cafés, bistros, toyshops, antique and craft shops – all very twee and touristy, but fetching.

Bremen's three main museums all lie outside the Altstadt. The **Kunsthalle**, in a park just to its east, has a rich collection of paintings, ranging from old German masters (Altdorfer, Cranach) via Rubens, Breughel, Rembrandt, etc, to the French 19th-century (excellent Delacroix) and German artists such as Liebermann, Beckmann and the Worpswede group. Picasso, too. The **Überseemuseum** (overseas museum), near the station, has an array of interesting ethnographic exhibits from Asia and Africa, including art objects collected by Bremen traders in those parts. Before the war the museum had a somewhat racist colonial bias: now the city's rulers have inverted this, to put the accent on the ill effects of colonialist exploitation! The large and spacious **Focke Museum**, out in the north-eastern Schwachhausen district, charts Bremen's long history through maps, scale models, paintings and photos, all well laid out and explained. It has models of ships, portraits of great merchants, romantic canvases of old Bremen, and a prehistoric section with Bronze Age tools and ornaments.

Of Bremen's residential districts, Ostertor, east of the Altstadt, is lively and bohemian, full of cafés and pubs, strong on night-life. The post-war suburb of Neue Vahr, further east, has some striking white modern tower blocks. Finally, it's well worth taking a boat trip (Apr–Oct) round the port of Bremen with its miles of masts and funnels, cranes and refineries. The handsome schooner *Deutschland* is now a naval training-ship.

The *Land* of Bremen includes another big port, **Bremerhaven** (pop. 133,000), 60km downstream at the mouth of the river Weser. It was founded in 1827 as Bremen's deep-sea port: transatlantic liners used to set sail from the Columbuskaje, where ferries and cruise ships now berth. Bremerhaven is Germany's busiest fishing

Bremen's Marktplatz: the Rathaus, with the statue of Roland in front.

port, and has what is claimed to be Europe's largest fishing harbour. The impressive *Deutsches Schiffahrtsmuseum* (navigation museum) traces German maritime history from ancient to modern times: it has models of old harbours and boats, and a real Hanseatic trading ship from 1380, dredged up in Bremen port in 1962. Historic vessels such as whalers are moored outside. There's also a fisheries museum, an aquarium, and an open-air (*Freilicht*) museum, with 17th-century peasant houses.

TOURIST OFFICE
Bahnhofsplatz, tel (0421) 30 80 00

Accommodation, Eating and Drinking
(Postcode 2800, tel code 0421):
(H)**Mercure-Columbus**, Bahnhofsplatz 5, tel 1 41 61. Opposite station. Good restaurant, tavern. Rooms (153) B. Meals B–C.

(H)**Munte**, Am Stadtwald, tel 21 20 63. By a park in N suburbs; rustic-style restaurant. Rooms (64) B–C. Meals C–D.

(H)**Uberseehotel**, Wachtstr. 27, tel 3 60 10. Central, near Marktplatz; unlovely but useful. No restaurant. Rooms (126) C.

(H)**Landhaus Louisenthal**, Leher-Heerstr. 105, Bremen 33, tel 23 20 76. In NE suburb of Horn, near Autobahn, but quiet. An 18th-century mansion in a garden, now a stylish family-run hotel. Simple cooking. Rooms (60) C–D. Meals C.

(H)**Heldt**, Friedhofstr. 41, tel 21 30 51. In quiet residential area; friendly, well run. Rooms (43) D. Meals (dinner only) C–D.

(R)**Grashoff's Bistro**, Contrescarpe 80, tel 1 47 40. Small and modest-looking, but the food's superb, notably fish. Lunches only; cl Sun. Meals A–B.

(R)**Flett**, Haus St Petrus, Böttcherstr. 3, tel 32 09 95. Local worthies come to eat good local dishes (eel soup, etc) at this famous historic place. Cl Sun. Meals B–C.

(R)**Ratskeller**, Am Markt, tel 3 29 09 10. Even more famous (see above), dating from 1408. Notable German wines (over 600). Real Bremen ambience. Meals C–D.

(R)**Deutsches Haus**, Am Markt 1, tel 3 29 09 20. Charming old merchant house opposite Rathaus; good for fish. Meals C.

(R)**Schnoor 2**, Schnoor 2, tel 32 12 18. In picturesque old house. Meals C–D.

(T)**Schnoor-Teestübchen**, Wüste Stätte, tel 32 60 91. Famous old tea-house in Schnoor quarter; snacks.

BREMERHAVEN 2850:

(H)**Nordsee-Hotel Naber**, Theodor-Heuss-Platz 1, tel (0471) 4 87 70. Modern, central. Rooms (101) B–C. Meals B–C.

(H)**Geestemünde**, Am Klint 20, tel (0471) 2 88 00. Near station. No restaurant. Rooms (14) D.

(R)**Seute Deern**, Am Alten Hafen, tel (0471) 41 62 64. An old three-masted ship by the naval museum; good for fish. Meals C.

CHAPTER TEN

Schleswig~Holstein

THIS, THE MOST northerly of the *Länder* (pop. 2,614,000), is made up of the two former dukedoms of Schleswig and Holstein. Schleswig in particular was contested between Denmark and Germany for hundreds of years, often with war and bloodshed, and did not finally become a Prussian province until 1864. In 1920 the mainly Danish population of north Schleswig voted by referendum to join Denmark, and this area remains Danish today. On the German side of the border, in Flensburg and other towns, there is still a sizeable Danish minority, who have a guaranteed seat in the Landtag and defiantly assert their rights.

After 1945 Schleswig and Holstein were amalgamated to form one *Land*, which is mainly rural and conservative and until 1987 was firmly in CDU hands. But then came the notorious 'Barschel affair'. Uwe Barschel, the CDU *Land* Prime Minister, was charged with conducting a slanderous smear campaign against his SPD rival. He committed suicide, thus tacitly admitting his guilt; and in the ensuing *Land* elections the voters showed their disgust by removing the CDU from power – a remarkable victory for morality over self-interest. The *Land* capital is the big port of Kiel. But the *Land*'s second city, Lübeck, former leader of the Hanseatic League, is far more interesting and attractive.

There are other towns of character, too, such as Eutin, Husum, and Schleswig city: this flattish *Land* may not be scenically exciting, but it is full of cultural and historical interest. Every June to August there's a big international music festival, held in several venues at once, some of them town churches, others castles in rural settings such as Glücksburg and Wotersen. Most of the older rural buildings are red-brick, often half-timbered and sometimes with stepped-gable façades; there are some thatched cottages too. The farms tend to be large and prosperous, especially on the wheat-growing plains of Holstein.

Forming an isthmus between North Sea and Baltic, this is the most sea-oriented of the major *Länder* and has the longest coastline. But its two coasts are very different. The shore of the Baltic

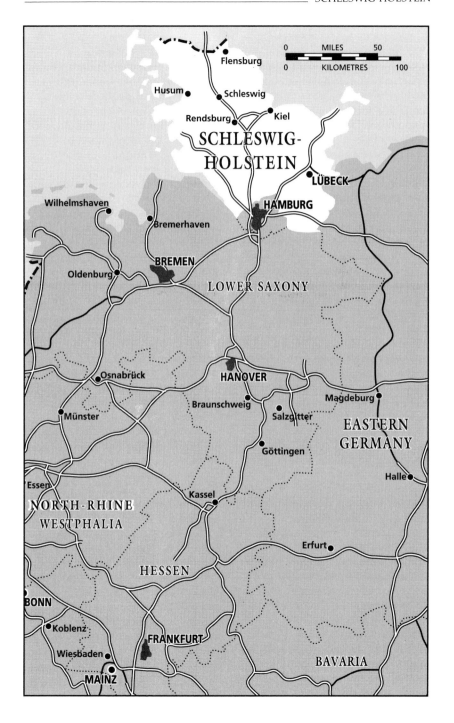

(which the Germans call the *Ostsee*, eastern sea) is prettily pastoral and backed in places by gentle wooded hills; it is also cut by deep low estuaries and lined with bathing-resorts. But the North Sea coast is much flatter and more austere. Here for centuries wind and storm have steadily been eroding the shoreline; recently however, as in Holland, some land has been reclaimed by creating polders (here called *Köge*, singular *Koog*) protected by dykes. This area, known as North Friesia, is given over to sheep-breeding. And they are an odd people, these Friesians, stubborn and taciturn, still using their own dialect, *Plattdeutsch*, which is virtually a separate language. Maybe it is the incessant storms and howling winds that serve to make them so depressive: rates of suicide, divorce, alcoholism and indeed incest are well above the German average. However, in sharp contrast, the North Friesian islands just offshore are happy summer holiday venues – in particular, trendy Sylt.

Lübeck

This grand old Hanseatic city (pop. 211,000) – where Thomas Mann set *Buddenbrooks*, the story of his own Lübeck merchant family – was in the Middle Ages the largest German town after Cologne and the chief business centre of northern Europe, 'the Queen of the Hanse'. Its oval-shaped mediaeval centre lies compactly between two arms of the river Trave, just above its estuary on the Baltic; and though it was heavily bombed, many splendid buildings survive as witness of its wealthy heyday, while its dignified streets still evoke beautifully the memory of a great Hanseatic capital. Many of the old houses have the distinctive Lübeck brickwork (alternating layers of black glazed and red unglazed brick); some also have the high zigzag gabled silhouette that we think of as Dutch, though in fact this style was invented in Lübeck and later copied by Dutch towns.

Lübeck's early trading prowess was helped by its position as a port on the Trave, accessible to sea-going ships. It became a Free Imperial City in 1226 and was one of the earliest German self-governing towns, ruled by its own merchants. In the 13th century it took the lead in developing the Hanseatic League, that club of German, Dutch and Baltic cities which dominated North European trade for three centuries. But as world trade patterns changed, the power of the League declined in the 16th century, and so did that of Lübeck: the Hanse's last meeting was held in the city in 1669. Later Lübeck lost ground heavily as a German port to Hamburg and Bremen on the North Sea; and unlike them it failed to preserve an autonomous Land status, being incorporated into Schleswig-Holstein in 1937. Its former glory is today vanished. Yet it remains an active cargo and ferry port, and an industrial centre (hospital equipment, etc). It was the only big German town right on the former East German border, and this led it to absorb some 100,000 refugees in the years after 1945. During the Cold War, this frontier position was an economic handicap, for firms were reluctant to invest in Lübeck, which was also cut off from its Mecklenburg hinterland. Unemployment was well above average. Today, unification has brought brighter prospects.

One great Lübecker of modern times is Willy Brandt, born there in 1913. Others were the brothers Heinrich and Thomas Mann (see feature). They came from one of the mighty merchant families who ruled Lübeck for so long – cultivated patrician families typifing the 'Hanseatic spirit' that coupled trading enterprise with cosmopolitan liberalism and keen local pride. A few of these families still thrive today, such as the Drägers, makers of medical goods and generous philanthropists. But they no longer dominate the SPD-led city council. So what today remains of the famed Hanseatic spirit? Maybe an unusually high degree of civic pride. And a certain natural grace and civilized good manners, obvious as you walk the streets of this austerely lovely Nordic city. It's a relaxed, breezy place, full of culture and restrained self-confident good taste.

Foremost among local **festivals** is the Schleswig-Holstein summer music festival (see p. 264), which always begins in Lübeck. Markt Anno Dazumal, a traditional fair, is held in the Rathausmarkt in May; and there's a Volksfest in July.

The pleasingly harmonious Altstadt, within the waterways, is best visited on foot. Some of its little streets have odd

In Hanseatic Lübeck: frescoes in the 13th-century chapel of the Heiligen-Geist-Hospital.

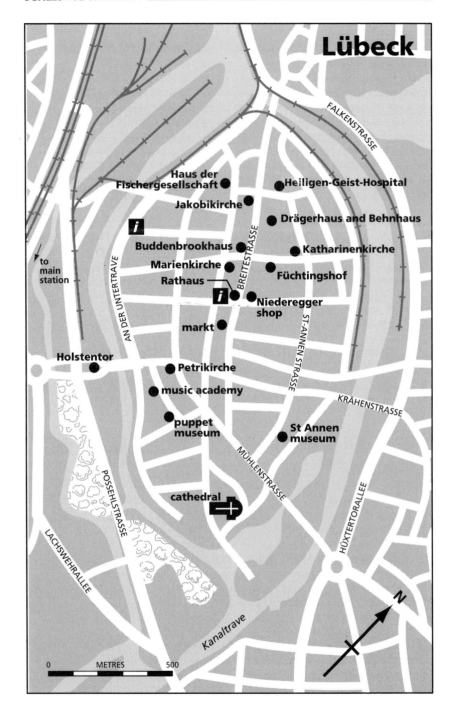

names like Kolk and Schrangen. To the west of its main Breitstrasse is the old patrician quarter of grand houses; to the east, that of artisans. A good entry point to the Altstadt from the west is past the **Holstentor** (1477), a massive reddish twin-towered gateway that contains an historical museum (good model of Lübeck in 1650). On the river beside it, note the fine old gabled warehouses, 16th/17th century, built to store salt from the Lüneburg mines on its way to Sweden. Across the river you'll come first to the Gothic Petrikirche (good view from its tower); close to it, in the narrow Grosse Petersgrube, is the lovely Music Academy, formed out of 22 old merchant homes, a handsome setting for the concerts often held here. Round the corner in narrow Kolk, do not miss the remarkable puppet museum and marionette theatre (shows daily): this private venture is the largest puppet collection in Germany, and has superb exotic puppets, notably from the Far East.

At the top of the broad Holstenstrasse is the Markt (lively market here on Mon, Thur), surrounded on two sides by the remarkable **Rathaus**, begun in 1250. With its Gothic blind arcades and Renaissance additions (e.g. the outside staircase), this building is notable for its dark glazed brickwork, some of it original 14th-century but most added in c. 1880. Go inside (tours daily) to see the council chamber, the paintings of old Lübeck and of local worthies, and the plaque honouring eight citizens shot for defying Hitler. Just opposite in Breitstrasse is the large and famous Niedereggar marzipan store, selling marzipan in every fancy shape: this delicacy has been made in Lübeck since the Middle Ages, from imported Italian almonds.

Beside the Rathaus is the lofty twin-spired **Marienkirche** (1250–1440), said to be Germany's oldest Gothic church built of brick, and to have the highest brick nave in the world. In Lübeck's heyday this was the main church of the merchant rulers, while the bishop was relegated to the cathedral at the south end of town (both churches are today Protestant). St Mary's was very badly damaged in the war (vivid photos of this are on display), but this did make it possible to restore the interior in something near to its original style: the whitewashing and baroque additions were not replaced, while the original Gothic frescoes that had long been covered up were found and refurbished. So the high brick nave with its fine ribbed vaulting again looks much as it did when first built. Behind the high altar is a lovely carved and gilded altarpiece of Mary, made in Antwerp in 1518; a huge mechanical clock parades its figures at noon; and in a side-chapel are the ruins of the great bells that crashed down from the roof in the air-raid.

Opposite St Mary's is Mann's Buddenbrookhaus (see feature). Here the broad Breitstrasse, rebuilt and lined with modern shops, leads down to another interesting old Gothic church, the little **Jakobikirche**, long used by mariners: it has splendid carved 16th/17th century organ lofts, while its chapel dedicated to the shipwrecked holds a lifeboat from a 1957 sea disaster. Lübeck's marine history emerges too in the **Haus der Fischergesellschaft** just opposite: this tall step-gabled Renaissance mansion, built for the fishermen's guild, has long been a popular tavern (see restaurants, p. 272), atmospherically decked out with ships' models and copper lamps.

All famous visitors, such as Prince Charles, pay a ritual visit – and so do all the package tours. Also much visited is the nearby **Heiligen-Geist-Hospital** (Hospice of the Holy Spirit), gabled and turreted, built c. 1280 and for centuries used as an old people's home. You enter straight into its lovely vaulted Gothic chapel, with 14th/15th-century frescoes and altar screen, all much restored. The huge hall at the back, where the elderly once lived, is now the venue of a lavish pre-Christmas market (local crafts, etc). In the cellars are two fine restaurants (see p. 272), one of which offers 'mediaeval' banquets for groups; and at the back is a beautiful little garden. A few pensioners are still housed in this glorious hospice.

Down the Königstrasse, two adjacent patrician houses of great elegance, the **Drägerhaus** and **Behnhaus**, are now small museums, both furnished in the style of 18th-century merchants' homes. The former, restored by the Dräger industrial family, includes a collection of souvenirs of the Manns; the latter has paintings by Edvard Munch, Kirchner and others. The Katharinenkirche, now a museum, bears nine notable modern statues on its 14th-century façade (the three on the left are by the great Ernst Barlach). Behind the church, down the Glockengiesserstrasse, is the remarkable Füchtingshof, a posh almshouse built in 1639 for the widows of merchants; the simpler Glandorpshof in the same street performed this function for craftsmen's widows. These estates of

little houses around quiet courtyards are still the homes of genteel elderly people. This part of the Altstadt has a number of mews-like alleys lined with small houses backed by gardens – behind its brick street-façades, Lübeck is secretly a very green city, full of enclosed gardens, like Oxford.

In the south part of the Altstadt, a former monastery houses the St Annen Museum: it has details of old Lübeck, much religious statuary, and a remarkable triptych of the *Passion* by Memling (1491). The twin-towered cathedral, dating from 1173, is a Romanesque structure with a Gothic chancel added later, and is notable for its huge triumphal cross by Bernt Notke (1477).

Lastly, a worthwhile excursion south from Lübeck will bring you to **Ratzeburg** (pop. 13,000) a charming old town on a lake near the former East German border: there's a good view of the area from the tower in nearby woods. The 12th-century red-brick high-towered Romanesque cathedral, set amid parkland outside the town, has a lovely 15th-century altarpiece. **Mölln** (pop. 16,500), further south on the old Salt Road from Lüneburg, is somewhat similar – a lakeside setting, an old brick church, a 14th-century step-gabled Rathaus. The practical joker Till Eulenspiegel is said to have died of the plague at Mölln in 1350, and is allegedly buried below the church tower. His statue stands in the market-place: touching its thumb, as thousands do, is said to bring good luck.

The Lübeck of Thomas Mann's *Buddenbrooks*

One of Thomas Mann's best-known novels is *Buddenbrooks*, his saga of the slow decline of a Lübeck merchant dynasty in the 19th century, based on his own family experience. This great Nobel-Prize-winning writer (1875–1955) was born in Lübeck, the son of a rich grain-dealer and city senator. The family left for Munich when he was 16, and there he spent the next 42 years, until he moved to Switzerland to escape the Nazis. *Buddenbrooks* (1901) was the novel that made his name, as a young man. It gives a vividly detailed picture of Lübeck's patrician milieu, and is a major social document as well as a poignant study of human frailty. Its main characters were mostly based on real people, including his own family – and this did not please Lübeck. When in 1955, months before his death, he was finally awarded the 'freedom of the city', the town council agreed to this by a majority of only one vote.

Mann, who became an American citizen, died in Zürich. His elder brother and fellow writer Heinrich, more Left-wing in his views, wrote *Professor Unrat*, a novel also set in Lübeck and later famously filmed by von Sternberg as *The Blue Angel*.

The stately house where the family lived in 1841–91, the model for the *Buddenbrookhaus*, at Mengestrasse 4, opposite the Marienkirche, was bombed in the war: little but its façade survives, and the interior has been rebuilt to house a bank (alas). The museum in the Drägerhaus (see opposite) has many photos and souvenirs of the Manns, including a scale model of the *Buddenbrookhaus*'s interior, and a fascinating display of how the real people in Mann's life relate to his fictional characters. The city's best restaurant, the *Schabbelhaus* (see below), is furnished in elegant *Buddenbrooks* style and will even serve, to order, a 'Buddenbrooks menu', based on the dinner that the family serve their guests at the start of the novel.

TOURIST OFFICE
Markt, tel (0451) 122 81 06, Beckergrube 95, tel 122 81 09.

Accommodation, Eating and Drinking (Postcode 2400, tel code 0451)
(H)**Kaiserhof**, Kronsdorfer Allee 13, tel 79 10 11. Old patrician villa, luxuriously furnished. No restaurant. Rooms (75) B–C.

(H)**Jensen**, Obertrave 4, tel 7 16 46. Traditional atmospheric dark-panelled hotel facing Trave; good food in elegant setting. Rooms (46) C. Meals B–C.

(H)**Lindenhof**, Lindenstr. 1a, tel 8 40 15. Near main station. No restaurant. Rooms (54) C.

(H)**Alter Speicher**, Beckergrube 91–93, tel 7 10 45. In old town, new and spruce. Rooms (55) C–D. Pub with snacks.

(R)**Das Schabbelhaus**, Mengstr. 48, tel 7 50 51. Old merchant's house, now a lovely elegant classic restaurant, furnished in Lübeck style. Cl Sun dinner. Meals A–B.

(R)**Schiffergesellschaft**, Breitestr. 2, tel 7 67 76. Very famous, in a 16th-century house built for seamen (see p. 269). Touristy but atmospheric; good local dishes. Cl Mon. Meals B–C.

(R)**Lübecker Hanse**, Kolk 3, tel 7 80 54. Charming, cosy and classic, with dark panelling. Franco-German and local dishes. Cl Sun, 1–8 Jan. Meals D (lunch), B–C (dinner).

(R)**Historischer Weinkeller**, Koberg 6–8, tel 7 62 34. In cellars of Heiligen-Geist-Hospital (see p. 270), 12th-century wine-tavern, excellent food. Meals C–D.

(R)**Café Niederegger**, Breitestr. 89, tel 7 10 36. In the marzipan shop (see p. 269); good light meals. Cl dinner. Meals D.

(B)**Brauberger**, Altstrasse 36, tel 7 14 44. Atmospheric old brewery and pub; light snacks. Meals D.

Kiel and Rural Schleswig-Holstein

Just north of Lübeck is Germany's leading Baltic resort, **Travemünde**, facing former East Germany across an estuary. It was a highly fashionable place in the days when the young Thomas Mann used to stay here (see p. 271), and today the imposing Kurhaus-Hotel survives from that era. With its large casino, tidy public gardens and broad promenade, this 'Deauville of the Baltic' still has some classic elegance; and it is crammed with activity in summer, when the beach gets so full that making sandcastles is *verboten*. There's a colourful market on Monday and Thursday mornings. To the north is a string of family bathing resorts with good beaches, notably Timmendorfer Strand and Scharbeutz.

Inland, to the north-west, is the area misleadingly known as the **Holsteinische Schweiz** (Holstein Switzerland). It was given this nickname in the 19th century by some local dignitaries who wanted to exploit its tourist potential: but its gentle wooded hills are hardly Alpine (the highest attains a mere 168m). Yet in its quiet way it's a very pleasant region, marked by a network of pretty lakes, popular for bathing, sailing and windsurfing. The woods with their well-marked paths are good for walking. **Eutin** (pop. 16,000), the main town, was the birthplace of the composer Carl Maria von Weber (1786–1826), whose operas are performed in summer in the pink courtyard of its fine old baroque Schloss, moated and bronze-cupola'd. Nearby is the charming little lakeside resort of **Malente**, where water-galas with lit-up boats and fireworks are sometimes held in summer. **Plön** (pop. 12,000), an old town on an isthmus with lakes on all sides, is crowned by a huge white baroque castle that once housed a Prussian military cadet school. Today it's a private boarding school and is not open to visits: but you can walk up to its terrace for a wide view of the lakes. Or you can tour these by boat-trip. To the north, the gentle Baltic coast east of Kiel has several modest bathing-resorts, popular with older people and families. The biggest is **Hohwacht**, where a long line of thick trees has been planted on a ridge behind the beach, to protect the new holiday homes from the importunate north winds.

Just before you come to Kiel, at **Laboe** by the mouth of its wide harbour, you will find Germany's leading naval war memorial – a tall dark-brick tower shaped like a ship's stern. Beside it, a U-boat built in 1943 is a memorial to the U-boat dead of two wars. The tower's roof-terrace provides a fine view over Kiel sound and the distant Danish coast. And its base holds a museum (open daily) of modern German naval history, with a scale model of the Battle of Jutland, and a memorial to the 2,000 sailors who were drowned with the *Scharnhorst* in 1943. On it is the ambiguous inscription, *'Sie starben für Uns, den Lebenden zur Mahnung'* ('They died for us as a warning to the living') – and I fell to reflecting on the strange logic of that phrase, and on how difficult it is for Germans today to honour their war dead humanely without thus condoning the Nazi cause in which they died.

KIEL (pop. 245,000), Schleswig-Holstein's capital, is set at the end of a broad sound always busy with shipping. It used to be Germany's leading naval base, and so was very heavily bombed in the last war. Few of its notable buildings have since been rebuilt, apart from the *Jugendstil* Rathaus (1907–11) with its high 106m tower (fine view from top platform). The university is the oldest in North Germany (1665). The modern town is of little interest, but Kiel is still an important shipping centre. The sailing events of the 1936 and 1972 Olympics were held in its sound, which in the last week of June is the venue of Kiel Week, one of the world's biggest and most fashionable regattas. The 100km **Kiel Canal**,

linking the Baltic to the North Sea, was opened in 1895 and is still the world's busiest, taking more than 50,000 ships a year, more than the Suez or Panama canals. The passage of ships through the Holtenau locks, where the canal enters Kiel sound, is worth watching.

Just south-west of Kiel, at Molfsee, is one of the best of Germany's open-air museums of traditional rural life, the **Schleswig-Holsteinisches Freilicht-museum** (open daily, July–mid-Sept; daily ex. Mon, Apr–mid-Nov; Sun and hols only the rest of year). Some 30 old farmhouses and other buildings from all over the region, most of them red-brick and half-timbered in the North German style, have been regrouped in a lovely park – among them, cottages with box-beds, a working watermill and three windmills, a vicarage (1569), and an 18th-century manor with oak-panelling, chandeliers and a fascinating 1817 school timetable. Visitors can see potters, carvers, bakers and other craftsmen at work, and can buy their wares. All a bit contrived, maybe, but intriguing.

An Autobahn leads west from Kiel into Schleswig, to the old fortified town of **Rendsburg** (pop. 32,000), beside the Kiel Canal. In its Altstadt is the 13th-century Marienkirche and 16th-century timbered Rathaus. Of even more interest are the wonders of modern engineering close by – the broad canal; the railway bridge over it, that was built high enough for shipping to pass beneath, and so has to perform a great loop so as to get back to ground level at Rendsburg station; and the four-lane road tunnel beneath the canal, with a parallel pedestrian tunnel that is reached by Europe's longest escalator (1,278m).

From Rendsburg a road winds across Schleswig's dull central plain to **Friedrichstadt**, a charming little town of canals, cobbled streets and Dutch-style stepped gables – it was built by Dutch Protestant refugees whom Duke Friedrich III of Holstein permitted to settle here in 1621. To the west is the Eiderstedt peninsular, where the health resort of St Peter-Ording is noted for its broad sandy beaches and its sulphur cures. And to the north is **Husum** (pop. 24,000), a handsome old harbour town by the North Sea. Its Nissenhaus museum (open daily, cl Sat in winter) evokes the history of the nearby polders, with details of land reclamation and storm havoc; there is also a small museum in the home of the aptly-named writer Theodor Storm (1817–88), whose poems and novels hauntingly evoke this strange region. North-west of Husum, around Bredstedt, you can drive down side-roads to explore typical *Köge* such as Sönke-Nissen or St Cecilien.

Further north is Niebüll, where the motorail shuttle leaves for Sylt. North again, amid flat fields near the Danish border, is the former home of the Expressionist painter **Emil Nolde** (1867–1956): it's now a museum full of his vivid, disturbing canvases, plus some of the watercolours that he did secretly when the Nazis had forbidden him to paint. If his work is not to your taste, you might still enjoy the pretty garden.

Cut back east across Schleswig, through pleasant rolling country, and you'll come to **Flensburg** (pop. 86,000), on a fjord by the Danish border. When this was a Danish city, it grew rich as a merchant centre for the Caribbean sugar trade: today rum-making is still a major local activity, and the town still has a Danish 'feel',

together with some handsome old buildings such as the 16th-century Nordertor (north gate). The nautical museum and the Städtisches Museum are both good on local history. What's more, the famous Beata Uhse, that life-long crusader against German sexual inhibition and hypocrisy, creator and owner of most German sex-shops, has her large and very hygienic factory here.

To the north-east is the lovely white-walled Renaissance castle of **Glücksburg** (closed Jan, Feb), strikingly located out on the fjord, with water all round. It has a fine banqueting-hall and Gobelin tapestries, and souvenirs of its formers owners, the Dukes of Oldenburg, related to the Danish royal family. From here a scenic road winds round the easterly part of Schleswig, known as **Angeln**: it has given its name to England, for it was from here in the fifth and sixth centuries that the Angles came, our early colonizers. In the old town of **Kappeln**, by the Schlei estuary, the distinctive long wooden fences in the water are still used for catching herring.

The appealing old maritime city of **SCHLESWIG** (pop. 28,000) may appear on the map to be well inland, but in fact it's on a fjord called Schlei, full of sailing-boats. In its high-towered red-brick Gothic cathedral is the superb Bordesholm Altar (1521). The suburb of Holm, close by, has some streets of old fishermen's cottages, attractively restored. The town's chief distinction is the majestic white water-girt **Schloss Gottorf**, 16th–18th century: it has a magnificent Renaissance chapel with ducal gallery, a sumptuous Gothic hall with painted ceiling, and a regional museum (ceramics, costumes, etc). Housed next door is one of the

16th-century Glücksburg Castle on a fjord outside Flensburg, by the Danish border.

world's oldest surviving boats, the astonishing fourth-century **Nydam boat**: this 21-metre oaken rowing-boat, well preserved, was found in 1863 in the marshes just inside Denmark. In the same building are the equally notable 'moor corpses' – 2,000-year-old skeletons of people who as a punishment were tied up, blindfolded and left out in the marshes to die slowly. At Haithabu, south of the city, is an interesting new museum of Viking history and culture.

Out in the North Sea to the west is the tiny island of Heligoland, which was British until 1890. There are daily boat services from Cuxhaven. The island is worth visiting for its red sandstone cliffs, good sea bathing, pure air – and duty-free shopping.

The Fashionable Island of Sylt

Of the North Friesian islands off the west coast of Schleswig, the largest and best-known is Sylt. This narrow strip of land, 40km long, is linked to the mainland by a causeway that carries a railway but no road: cars must be put onto the train shuttle at Niebüll. Fares are kept high, to deter motorists from invading Sylt.

Its windy but invigorating climate has long made it fashionable as a resort. Thomas Mann and Marlene Dietrich were among those who holidayed here. In the 1960s it became 'the St-Tropez of the North' – a much-publicized haunt of film-stars and rich playboys such as Gunter Sachs. That era has waned: but Sylt is still popular with top politicians, editors, bankers and tycoons, who come seeking privacy. Like many islands, Sylt has a special ambience. Though flat it has a strange beauty, for the insistent wind from the North Sea whirls the clouds into bizarre shapes, with ever-changing patterns of light. The two coastlines are different. The eastern one facing the mainland is more sheltered and varied, while the North Sea coast offers one unbroken line of broad sandy beach, backed by dunes in the form of low reddish cliffs. Sylt is a paradise for health freaks and sport-lovers. Tall blonde muscular Northerners can be seen everywhere – riding, cycling, jogging, surfing, or doing aerobic PT in unison on the beach.

Of Sylt's nine separate resorts, the biggest but not the smartest is **Westerland**. To its south a long tongue of land leads to Hörnum village. And to its east is the pretty showpiece village of **Keitum**, full of galleries, boutiques and thatched holiday-cottages. The Altfriesches Haus, an old farmhouse, is now a museum of local lore history: in fact, this Friesian island has a history far pre-dating tourism, as you can see from Keitum's 12th-century church that stands alone to the north of the village, on the road to the former port of Munkmarsch. The road goes on to **Kampen** village, for some 30 years the principal venue of Sylt's showy smart set. One short street, Stron Wai, is known as 'Whiskystrasse': its neat modern thatched villas have been bizarrely converted into bistros, night-clubs, and boutiques with such names as Jil Sander and Cartier.

TOURIST OFFICES

TRAVEMÜNDE: Kurverwaltung, Strandpromenade 1b, tel (04502) 80431.

KIEL: Sophienblatt 30, tel (0431) 6 22 30.

HUSUM: Grossstr. 25, tel (04841) 66 61 33.

FLENSBURG: Norderstr. 6, tel (0461) 2 30 90.

Accommodation, Eating and Drinking

TRAVEMÜNDE 2400:

(H)**Kurhaus-Hotel**, Aussenallee 10, tel (04502) 811. The stately 19th-century resort hotel that Mann knew, now well modernized; good food in its **Buddenbrooks Restaurant**. Rooms (104) A–B. Meals B–C.
(H)**Strandhaus Becker**, Strandpromenade 7, tel (04502) 7 50 35. By the beach, near casino (all rooms have sea view); sympathetic ambience, good cooking. Rooms (34) C. Meals C.

TIMMENDORFER STRAND 2408:

(H)**Yachtclub**, Strandstr. 94, Niendorf, tel (04503) 50 61. By the sea, elegantly furnished; pool, sauna; ambitious restaurant. Cl Jan. Rooms (60) B. Meals A–B.

SCHARBEUTZ 2409:

(H)**Martensen – Die Barker**, Strandallee 123, tel (04503) 71 17. Smartly attractive seaside hotel; heated pool, good fish and Holstein dishes. Mar–Oct. Rooms (36) B. Meals C.

EUTIN 2420:

(H)**Wiesenhof**, Leonhardt-Boldt-Str. 25, tel (04521) 27 26. Outside the town, by a lake; a modern hotel, quiet and select; lovely garden, heated pool; diet-slanted meals. Mar–Oct. Meals for residents only. Rooms (35) C–D.

PLÖN 2320:

(H)**Fegetasche**, Fegetasche 1, tel (04522) 90 51. Lakeside hotel with pleasant terrace, good local food. Mar–Nov. Rooms (20) D. Meals C.

HOHWACHT 2322:

(H)**Schlampmühle**, Seestr., tel (04381) 53 10. Thatched inn, unpretentious and friendly. Rooms (25) D. Meals D.

PANKER 2322:

(R)**Forsthaus Hessenstein**, tel (04381) 416. Cosy, modest-looking old *Gasthaus* with distinguished Holstein cooking. Frequent closures (check). Meals B; **Bistro**, C.

KIEL 2300:

(H)**Kieler Kaufmann**, Niemannsweg 102, tel (0431) 8 50 11. In a quiet setting near sea and park, a nicely furnished old building; good service and food. Rooms (48) B–C. Meals B–C.
(H)**Kieler Yacht-Club**, Hindenburgufer 70, tel (0431) 8 50 55. Modern hotel right by the sea; nautical flavour, good views. Rooms (60) B–C. Meals B–C.

(H)**Dietrichsdorfer Hof**, Heikendorfer Weg 54, tel (0431) 26108. In eastern suburbs. Italian restaurant next door. Rooms (28) D–E.

(R)**Im Schloss**, Wall 80, tel (0431) 9 11 58. By the port, in 16th-century cellars of former castle. Cl Sun dinner. Meals B–C.

(R)**Friesenhof im Ratskeller**, Fleethörn 9, tel (0431) 9 54 94. In the Rathaus; local ambience and dishes. Meals C.

ALT-DUVENSTEDT 2371:

(H)**Töpferhaus**, Am Bistensee, tel (04338) 333. Stylish modern rural hotel beside a lake; excellent food. Cl Jan; restaurant cl Mon. Rooms (12) C. Meals B–C.

FRIEDRICHSTADT 2254:

(R)**Holländische Stube**, Am Mittelburgwall 24, tel (04881) 72 45. 17th-century Dutch-style inn, charmingly quaint; good Dutch and Schleswig dishes. Meals, C. 7 rooms too, D.

WITZWORT-ADOLFSKOOG 2251:

(R)**Roter Haubarg**, tel (04864) 845. Converted 18th-century farmhouse, serving good local dishes. Cl mid-Jan to mid-Feb. Meals C–D.

BARGUM 2255:

(R)**Andresen's Friesenstuben**, tel (04672) 10 98. Charming rural inn with beamed ceilings; excellent cooking. Cl 3 weeks Jan, 2 weeks Feb, Mon. Meals A–B. 5 rooms too, D.

FÖHR (island):

(H)**Landhaus Altes Pastorat**, Süderende 2270, tel (04683) 226. Delightful country house with pretty garden; good food. Mid-Apr to Sept. Meals for residents only. Rooms (5) B.

SYLT (island) (tel code 04651):

KAMPEN 2285:

(H)**Hinchley Wood**, Kirchenstieg. tel 4 15 46. An elderly ex-RAF officer, Sam Smith, runs this offbeat private hotel. Rooms C–D.

(R)**Gogärtchen**, Strönwai, tel 4 12 42. Chic and celebrity-studded. Easter to mid-Oct. Meals A–B.

(R)**Kupferkanne**, Stapelhogawai, tel 4 10 10. Converted wartime bunker on the cliffs, once very trendy. Disco, restaurant; large, attractive garden-café. Meals B.

(R)**Lysieffer**, Strönwai, tel 1773. Upmarket bistro-coffeeshop, currently trendy. Superior snacks. Meals C–D.

(R)**Dorfkrug Rotes Kliff**, Alte Dorfstr. 1, tel 4 35 00. A big thatched house; traditional and popular. Meals C–D.

KEITUM 2280:

(H)**Romantik-Hotel Benen-Diken-Hof**, Süderstr., tel 3 10 35. Handsome and well furnished, in Friesian style. No restaurant. Rooms (38) A–B.
(C)**Café Kliffruh**. Serves excellent *Friesentorte* (plum tart).

WENNINGSTEDT 2283:

(R)**Hinkfuss**, Am Dortteich 2, tel 54 61. Serious cooking, pleasant setting. Cl mid-Jan to mid-Feb, Mon. Meals A–B. 3 rooms too, C.

WESTERLAND 2280:

(H)**Vier Jahreszeiten**, Johann-Möller-Str. 40, tel 2 30 28. On the beach; well run. Cl Nov to mid-Jan. Meals for residents only. Rooms (26) B.
(H)**Roth**, Strandstr. 31, tel 5091. Close to beach; modern, comfortable; superb breakfast buffet. Rooms (55) B–C. Meals B–C.
(H)**Gästehaus Hellner**, Maybachstr. 8, tel 69 45. Mar–Oct. No restaurant. Rooms (19) C.

FLENSBURG 2390:

(H)**Am Stadtpark**, Nordergraben 70, tel (0461) 2 49 00. In quiet street, with view over fjord. Rooms (22) D. Meals C.
(R)**Borgerforeningen**, Holm 17, tel (0461) 2 33 85. Central, in old merchants' house; some local dishes. Cl Sun. Meals C–D.

OEVERSEE 2391:

(H)**Historischer Krug**, tel (04630) 300. 16th-century rural inn, stylishly modernized, a bit pretentious; good for game and fish dishes. Rooms (44) B–C. Meals B–C.

TARP 2399:

(H)**Bahnhofshotel**, Bahnhofstr. 1, tel (04638) 358. Modest, family-run, pleasant. Rooms (52) E. Meals C–D.

STEINBERG 2391:

(H)**Norderlück**, tel (04632) 75 95. Old farmhouse (1778), nicely converted. Meals for residents only. Rooms (14) C.

SCHLESWIG 2380:

(H)**Strandhalle**, Strandweg 2, tel (04621) 2 20 21. Lively hotel with nautical décor, by a marina on the Schlei. Outdoor terrace. Rooms (28) C. Meals C.

TREIA 2381:

(H)**Osterkrug**, Treenestr. 30, tel (04626) 550. Cosy old rustic guesthouse; good local cooking. Rooms (8) D. Meals C.

CHAPTER ELEVEN

Berlin, the Reunited City

BERLIN, THE WORLD'S most talked-about city of recent years, exerts an hypnotic effect. From 1945 until 1989, it stood as a daunting symbol of the division of Europe and the Cold War: the eastern part was made the capital of the German Democratic Republic, while the western part was isolated 120 miles inside the borders of that Communist territory. After the Wall was built in 1961, visitors to West Berlin would come to see the sad little flower-decked crosses marking the spots where East Germans died while trying to escape across it. Then in November 1989 the Wall was thrown open, the GDR regime crumbled, and now the city is again the capital of a united Germany, though not yet its seat of Government.

If Berlin hypnotizes, this is due partly to its strange post-war history, but also to its own very special quality, dating back long before the war; and to the spirit of Berliners, sharp, sardonic, creatively unconventional, full of wry humour. The city has long been a centre of avant-garde culture and cheeky satire, and since the 1960s West Berlin has become a magnet for Germany's 'alternative' scene. It has been the least conformist of German towns, a place of cultural innovation and social mix, sometimes of violence: 'Berlin', they say, 'lets it all hang out.' Even in the years of isolation, West Berlin retained something of its cosmopolitan capital-city spirit and stayed the prime centre of German culture, just ahead of Munich. The town is no beauty: alike

in the prosperous West and the still down-at-heel East, it is one sprawling jumble (apart from the severe grandiosity of the Unter den Linden area). But it is full of fascinating insights into history; and in the West at least it has an electric vitality, which may soon infect East Berlin too.

This is quite a young city. It grew from two Spree-side fishing-villages to become in 1470 the main residence of the Hohenzollern rulers. Wrecked in the Thirty Years' War, it was then built into a proper town by Friedrich Wilhelm the 'Great Elector' (1640–88) whose supreme merit was to welcome thousands of French Huguenot refugees, after the Revocation of the Edict of Nantes in 1685: these artists, scholars and technicians were to make a

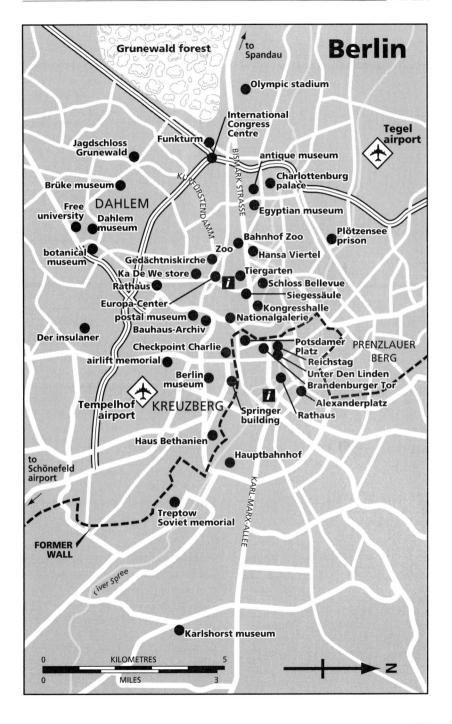

Berlin

Grunewald forest

to Spandau

Olympic stadium

International Congress Centre

Funkturm

Tegel airport

Jagdschloss Grunewald

antique museum

BISMARK STRASSE

KURFÜRSTENDAMM

Charlottenburg palace

Brüke museum

DAHLEM

Free university

Dahlem museum

Egyptian museum

Bahnhof Zoo

Plötzensee prison

botanical museum

Zoo

Gedächtniskirche

Hansa Viertel

Ka De We store

Tiergarten

Rathaus

Schloss Bellevue

Europa-Center

Siegessäule

postal museum

Kongresshalle

Bauhaus-Archiv

Nationalgalerie

Der insulaner

Checkpoint Charlie

Potsdamer Platz

PRENZLAUER BERG

airlift memorial

Reichstag

Unter Den Linden

Berlin museum

Brandenburger Tor

Tempelhof airport

KREUZBERG

Alexanderplatz

Springer building

Rathaus

Haus Bethanien

Hauptbahnhof

to Schönefeld airport

KARL-MARX-ALLEE

Treptow Soviet memorial

FORMER WALL

river Spree

Karlshorst museum

0   KILOMETRES   5

0   MILES   3

N

vital contribution to the development of the city. Friedrich I, the first King of Prussia, then erected Charlottenburg Palace; his grandson Frederick the Great endowed Berlin with its stately monuments along the Unter den Linden and built it up as a manufacturing town and leading centre of culture. The university was founded in 1810, relatively late.

Berlin's major growth as an industrial city came in the mid-19th century; Werner von Siemens founded his electrical engineering firm in Kreutzberg, and it grew into one of the world's greatest. Soon afterwards, the unification of Germany under Prussia, with Berlin as its capital, gave a further big boost to its development: in the years after 1870 known as the *Gründerzeit* (foundation time), its population doubled to reach 1.9 million by 1890, as peasants poured in for factory work and were housed in grim tenements with dank inner courtyards, many still visible today in poor districts such as Wedding and Neukölln (the satiric artist Heinrich Zille poignantly portrayed their plight).

By 1920 the city's population was over 4 million, larger than Paris at that time (today it is only one-third the size of Greater Paris, with some 2 million people in former West Berlin, 1.1 million in former East Berlin). The 1920s were a troubled time of unrest and high inflation, but also an exciting period culturally, with some great theatre and film-making (Brecht, Reinhardt, Lang, Pabst, etc) and brilliant satiric songs and cabaret. Hitler put an end to this: he ruled from Berlin, though its sceptical citizens never gave him much support, and he always preferred Munich where Nazism had been born.

Berlin was mostly reduced to rubble by the war, then hurriedly and gracelessly rebuilt or left as messy wasteland. From 1945 the post-war division of Germany put it in an odd situation, deep inside the Russian zone but protected by the four Allied Powers under a special statute. The Russians, who had one of its four military sectors, made a bid to gobble up the other three: but their ten-month blockade of West Berlin in 1948–49 was foiled by the Allied airlift (200,000 flights brought in 1.5 million tons of supplies) and by Berliners' courage. After this, as the GDR was created and the Cold War raged, the two halves of the city grew steadily apart. In August 1961, in order to stem the growing exodus of refugees, the GDR built its 75-mile concrete Wall round West Berlin, sealing it off from all contact with the east; many families were sundered. So the 1960s were a sad and lonely time, when West Berliners were grateful for any morale-boost, such as President Kennedy's rousing words on his visit in 1963: 'All free men . . . are citizens of Berlin . . . *Ich bin ein Berliner.*'

However, Chancellor Brandt's *Ostpolitik* in 1969–71 finally led to *détente* with the Soviet Union and new guarantees of security for West Berlin. This proved a turning-point. Optimism returned, the drain of population slowed as people became readier to settle and West German firms more willing to invest; new high-tech enterprises began to boom, in what is still Germany's leading industrial town, in terms of jobs. But, physically so isolated, it continued to depend heavily on subsidies from Bonn, which in 1989 were still accounting for over 50 per cent of the city's budget. And West Berlin still had an odd status, not officially part of the Federal Republic and still juridically under the control of the British, French and US 'occupying' forces which retained huge reserve powers, albeit tactfully used. In practice, however, West Berlin was governed as a city-*Land* like Hamburg, with a parliament and senate; its various excellent mayors since the war, some SPD, some CDU, have included Brandt himself and today's Federal President, Richard von Weizsächer.

Meanwhile, away on that distant planet beyond the Wall, the GDR illegally built up the Russian sector as its state capital, and did all it could to ignore and denigrate what it called 'Westberlin'. It put up grandiose public buildings in the central area (the division of the city had given to the East the historic centre and former government district), but the war-scarred suburbs it left woefully neglected, apart from the building of monstrous high-rise housing estates. East Berliners remained sullenly passive – until, in the autumn of 1989, taking their cue from Poland and Hungary, and then from nearby Leipzig, they began to rebel. Finally on 9 November (certain to become one of the key dates in European history) the tottering GDR government removed all travel restrictions – and so a cascade of East Berliners swept through the wall into the West, to sightsee, to shop, or just to drink and rejoice with their re-found fellow citzens, amid scenes of excited emotion unequalled in Europe since 1945. Soon after this, large sections of the Wall were torn down and grabbed for souvenirs, scores of new border crossings were opened, and on 1 July 1990 the currency union between the two Germanys ended all barriers between the two Berlins. Then on 2 December the first pan-Berlin elec-

tions fully reunified the city. But today the two parts of the city still remain very different, in looks and in living standards, in lifestyles and psychology, and it will take some years to heal the wounds caused by Communism.

Berlin, like Paris, is a town that inspires an intense local patriotism, expressed in many a cabaret song that mixes self-irony with sentimentality. One of these is about the famous *Berliner Luft* (Berlin air), headily invigorating, a product less of climate than of the temperament of Berliners, restless, witty, mercurial, quick at repartee. In many ways they are more like Parisians or New Yorkers than, say, staid Hamburgers. And their city lives late, more so than most in northern Europe: at 2 am the Ku'damm is still thick with crowds and cars, its cafés and eateries full. And all day too the people on many central streets are an odd mixture, few in normal city dress – bohemian students and trendy mannequins, coxcomb punks and gawping tourists, and wizened old bourgeois ladies in flowery hats. Long a melting-pot, West Berlin is more socially informal, even eccentric, than other German cities, capital not only of the 'alternative' scene (centering mainly on the Kreuzberg district) but also of Germany's gay scene – as you can tell from the zany films of that queen of Berlin gays who calls himself Rosa von Praunheim. It's a town of transvestite bars, way-out art galleries, struggling fringe theatres, innumerable 'happenings', and over 1,000 rock groups (but, alas, satiric cabaret is not what it was, killed in part by TV). Even the 'pop' culture is well subsidized by the city Senate (helped by Bonn), which has also poured funds into the high-level classic culture – as witness the superb Berlin Philharmonic orchestra, conducted by von Karajan until his death in 1989, the Schaubühne theatre company which under Peter Stein was so dazzling, the annual Film Festival in February, the September Arts Festival, the November Jazz Days, and much else.

All the above applies to West Berlin. In the East, life was much more subdued: but this is now changing. And it's true that the GDR did do much for 'official' culture, with some good opera, concerts, theatre and museums. So now, as the city reunites and again becomes Germany's capital, will it become a duller place, as it loses the creative tensions of its abnormal situation? Or on the contrary, will it become the vibrant cultural metropolis of Central Europe, upstaging even Paris and London? Time will tell. It now faces the huge challenge of imaginative architectural planning to utilize the wide open spaces astride the old Wall. This may give it rather more of the grace and dignity of a great capital city, which it lacks at present. Even in the wealthy west, much of the building is either old-tatty or new-ugly – a legacy in part of bad 19th-century housing that survived the bombing, in part of too-hurried utility post-war rebuilding. Berlin is a giant jumble of styles and epochs, with touches of baroque, plenty of *Jugendstil*, much tawdry 1950s, but flashes of brilliant modern, and some streets enlivened by zany modernistic sculptures or by lively pop-art murals on blind walls. It was built on a very spacious pattern, and its borders are far-flung: this greatly helped West Berliners to endure the isolation of the Walled-in years, for within their domain were big forests, lakes and rivers, and true countryside

including 80 farms. Rural West Berlin was a reality, often overlooked by those intent on portraying it falsely as a pent-in, claustrophic place.

The main sights of former East Berlin are closely grouped around the Unter den Linden and can be toured on foot. In the west, the sights are much more scattered and need to be explored by car or public transport (parking is not too hard, except in the central area). A circular tour could maybe start in the Ku'damm area, which includes the memorial church and the Zoo; then go out to Charlottenburg Palace and Spandau Citadel; then down via Grunewald forest and the broad Havel river to Glienicke Bridge; then cut back to the Dahlem museums, Schöneberg Rathaus and Kreuzberg; then return to the Ku'damm via the extraordinary sector along the former Wall between Checkpoint Charlie and the Reichstag, an area that also includes some notable museums.

Kurfürstendamm and Tiergarten

Laid out under Bismarck in 1871, the two-mile **Kurfürstendamm** boulevard (known to Berliners as the Ku'damm) was before the war the city's entertainment district, some way west of the centre. Then it became the main focus of West Berlin, but is still given over mainly to pleasure, lined with smart hotels, cafés, shops, cinemas and nightclubs; it gets more down-market as it goes west. The Ku'Damm Karree at no. 206, a modern glass-domed arcade with amusing pubs and antique shops, even has a teddy-bear museum. Here too is theatreland, including the Komödie and Schaubühne, while the Savignyplatz area just to the north has the best range of attractive bohemian pubs and bistros.

In the broad piazza at the top of the Ku'damm rises the unmistakable gaunt silhouette of the **Gedächtniskirche** (memorial church), built in 1891 to the memory of Kaiser Wilhelm I: it is now a memorial of a different kind, to wartime suffering, for only its tower survived the bombs and this is carefully kept as a ruin, and a much-photographed emblem of the city. Berliners, with typical droll humour, call it 'the Gaping Tooth', and have given the nicknames 'Powder-Box' and 'Lipstick Tube' to the two modern church buildings (1961) beside it. Of these, the octagonal campanile has impressive blue stained glass made in Chartres. The skyscraping Europa-Center nextdoor offers a good panoramic view from its observation platform. Down Tauentzienstrasse is Berlin's largest department store, **Ka De We** (*Kaufhaus des Westens*), whose enormous superopulent food section outdoes Harrods': it was much frequented by privileged GDR Party leaders' wives (you could see their chauffeur-driven Volga limousines parked nearby), while in East Berlin the hoi polloi queued for stale cabbages.

Berlin's large **Zoo** is spacious and full of greenery, and the 1,800-odd species are pleasantly housed. I enjoyed especially the amorous hippos, white fluffy wolves, wild cats and majestic condors. There are few bears, although these are Berlin mascots; and the zoo's last two pandas died in 1984. But many animals are born here each year, their birth-rate being nearer to local Turkish than German levels. The **Bahnhof Zoo**, West Berlin's main station, has long been a haunt of drugaddicts and other sad social cases. At least it has now been spruced up and repainted.

South-east of the Zoo you'll find the **Postal Museum**, with a lively display of the growth of communications since the 17th century; and the **Bauhaus-Archiv Museum** (closed Tue, open Mon), showing details of the influential Bauhaus design movement (see Dessau, p. 317) and works by the artists it influenced, housed in a building designed by the Bauhaus' founder, Walter Gropius. At the Nollendorfplatz, a disused overhead U-Bahn station now contains an intriguing fleamarket (*Flohmarkt*) whose charming 1920s-ish pub-café has live music at weekends.

The 630-acre **Tiergarten**, largest and oldest of central Berlin parks, stretching two miles from the Brandenburg Gate to the Zoo, was laid out originally for royalty, and has been much rewooded after wartime damage. In its middle is the 67-metre **Siegessäule** (victory column), built in 1873 to commemorate the defeat of the Austrians and French. The view from the top (285 steps) is quite dramatic. Below it is the 18th-century neo-classical **Schloss Bellevue**, which since 1959 has been an official residence of the Federal President and is likely to see this role increased when Berlin is again the capital; its interiors, much restored since the war, can be visited when the President is not there. Nearby, the 1960s **Kongresshalle** with its curly lopsided façade is known to Berliners as 'The Pregnant Oyster' or else as 'Jimmy Carter's Smile'. Less ludicrous is the **Hansa Viertel**, a model housing estate designed in the 1950s by several leading architects.

Before exploring the eastern end of the Tiergarten, towards the Brandenburger Gate, we shall make a great round trip through West Berlin, via

Charlottenburg, the Havel, Dahlem and Kreuzberg.

Charlottenburg Palace and Spandau

Charlottenburg, a big residential district west of the Tiergarten, has as its main point of interest the huge and stately **Schloss** of that name, which will take the best part of a day to visit properly. Begun in 1695 as a country home for the future Queen Sophie-Charlotte, wife of Friedrich I, and later much expanded, it is is fronted by a superb bronze equestrian statue of the Great Elector, Friedrich Wilhelm, by Andreas Schlüter (1703). The guided tour of the interior (much restored after wartime damage) will take you through suites of rather gloomy state rooms hung with royal portraits and tapestries; but the Queen's rooms, sumptuously furnished, are more cheerful. The porcelain room, and the chapel with its portrait of the Queen as the Virgin, are notable. The west wing, a former orangery, houses a museum of pre-history and special exhibitions. The east or **Knobelsdorff wing**, added in the 1740s, contains a stunning collection of German 19th-century Romantic paintings, by Caspar David Friedrich, Karl Friedrick Schinkel (note his colourful fantasies, e.g. *Gothic Church on a Seaside Buff* and *Vision of the Golden Age of Greece*) and others. Upstairs are two brilliantly ornate rococo rooms, somewhat over-restored – the Golden Gallery with its gilt and pale green marble, and the Banquet Hall whose ceiling fresco dates from 1973, replacing the bombed original. Paintings by Watteau and Chardin are in the small gilded room beyond.

In front of the palace, two former guards' barracks now house notable museums (closed Fri, open Mon): the Egyptian Museum with its marvellous painted bust of Nefertiti (c. 1350 BC), and the Antique Museum holding vases, jewellery, gold and silver from Scythian, Greek and Roman times. The beautiful gardens behind the palace were laid out in an English landscaped manner but have since been partly transformed in baroque style. In them are: the Schinkel Pavilion (1824), built in the Pompeian mode then fashionable; a mausoleum containing Prussian royal tombs; and over by the Spree a belvedere with a lovely watery view. To the north-east, beyond a canal, is the former **Plötzensee prison** where the Nazis executed over 2,500 political opponents: after the July bomb plot, 89 suspects were hanged in agony here on piano wires, on Hitler's orders. The prison now holds a memorial museum, simple and moving. To the west, the modern Catholic church of Maria Regina Martyrum is also a memorial to victims of Nazism.

The Eiffel-like **Funkturm** (radio tower), built in 1928, rises to 130m and offers a broad view of the city from its upper platform (open daily). Below it are the exhibition grounds and the huge new silvery **International Congress Centre**, seating 5,000, which has enabled Berlin to become a leading European convention city. To the west stands the massive **Olympic Stadium**, built for 1936 Olympic Games that Hitler used as a showpiece of his new order. Further on is yet another reminder of the Hitler period in this part of Berlin: **Spandau Citadel**, where Nazis awaiting trial were held after 1945. Its one final inmate, up until his suicide there in 1987, was Rudolf Hess (or rather, according to one theory, a

A street-café on the Kurfürstendamm, principal avenue of former west Berlin: the Wilhelm memorial church rises behind.   Tony Stone Photolibrary

man masquerading as Hess). The imposing moated citadel was built on the site of a 12th-century fort whose keep, the Julius Tower, is still there. Across the road the Nikolaikirche, a 15th-century brick hall church, has a fine Renaissance altar.

Grunewald Forest and Havel River

This forest in the western suburbs, and the broad lake-like river beside it, lined with sandy beaches, were a great solace to West Berlin during its decades of isolation behind the Wall: without these wide expanses of nature, much used for hiking, boating, bathing and picnicking, Berliners' sense of claustrophobia would have been far greater. Largest of Berlin's forests, the **Grunewald** was for centuries a royal

hunting preserve, where today wild boar and deer still roam free amid its beeches, oaks and pines. Beside the tiny Grunwaldsee is the former royal hunting-lodge, **Jagdschloss**, a fine half-timbered Renaissance building (1542), with baroque 18th-century additions and a pretty cobbled courtyard. The museum inside has details of the history of Grunewald hunting, also paintings by Rubens, Cranach the Elder and others. Berlin riding clubs sometimes hold meets here, as blowing their horns they go off to chase boar in the forest.

The river **Havel**, a tributary of the Elbe, broadens into what is virtually a lake, one to two km wide, along a 15km stretch between Spandau and Potsdam. Excursion boat-trips leave from several points. Spandau too has a forest, to its north, and here a little car-ferry across the Havel leads to Tegelort, a quiet village beside the **Tegelersee**: this is a real lake, branching off the Havel, and very pretty it is with its islets and wooded shores, and the coloured sails of the yachts and windsurfers. South of Spandau, the eastern shore of the Havel has yacht marinas and beaches of fine natural sand, unusual so far inland: they are packed in summer, especially the nudist (FKK) ones. In winter the river gets frozen over, attracting crowds of skaters, and stalls are set up to sell them hot *Glühwein*. The tiny resort of Schild-horn, in a cove full of pleasure-boats, is an elegant and secluded spot; the nearby Grunewaldturm, an old stone watchtower by the lake, provides a splendid view over this verdant, watery side of the city, for those who care to climb its 200 steps.

On little Schwanenwerder island, reached by a causeway, some wealthy people such as Axel Springer's family have villas. Beyond is the deep bay of the Grosser Wannsee with its big boating marina. Next you'll come to the very curious **Pfaueninsel** (Peacock Island) just offshore (frequent boat services). It was landscaped in the 1790s as a fantasy paradise by Friedrich Wilhelm III, who brought in not only tropical animals, birds and plants but also 'exotic' live pygmies and negroes from Africa whom he paraded to amuse his guests. The peacocks, palms and cacti are still there, plus some intriguing follies – a fake Roman wall, a high fountain, a strange house with church-windows and battlements, and the façade of a half-built Schloss that typifies the 18th-century love of false ruins (see Bayreuth, p.

197). A so-called 'Gothic farm', with old cart-houses, is still operative. A good example of Rousseau-inspired Romantic landscaping, this very rural island is also a delightful spot for a picnic or sunbathing.

Souvenirs of the Prussian royalty are numerous in the lovely wooded riverside stretch between here and Glienicke Bridge, for it is by the old road from Potsdam to Charlottenburg. On a hill above the river is the strange **Blockhaus Nikolskoe**, an ornate Russian-style wooden chalet that Friedrich Wilhelm III built in 1819 for his daughter Charlotte (she married a Russian prince who later became Tsar Nicholas I). It is now a restaurant (see p. 298). The pink onion-domed Russian church in the woods nearby, also built for Charlotte, is still used for worship. In a nicely landscaped park by the river is the newly restored Schloss Glienicke, a former summer home of the Prussian rulers; and across the main road is their hunting-lodge by the water, now used by the European University summer school. This south-west corner of West Berlin is steeped in post-war as well as Prussian history, for the Havel here formed the old border with the GDR, just opposite Potsdam: **Glienicke Bridge**, carrying the main road over the river, was famous as the scene of high-level 'spy swaps', i.e. exchanges of freed prisoners, between the Russians and Americans. Today all the controls are gone, and you drive straight across into Potsdam (see p. 305). Gone too are the GDR armed patrol-vessels, and the line of white buoys marking the actual border, which a western boat crossed at its peril.

The Dahlem Museums and Schöneberg Rathaus

Dahlem is a quiet suburb of tree-lined avenues and big houses, where many well-to-do Berliners live. Here a group of distinguished museums hold superb art treasures inherited from the Prussian kings. After 1939 the Nazis removed these royal collections from Berlin and scattered them around Germany, where the Americans and Russians seized them. In the 1950s these two Powers agreed each to give back its own share of this loot to 'its' Germans. So some treasures are now in East Berlin, while others, the major part, were inherited by the Federal Republic which decided to put them in West Berlin – a bold decision, at a time when the city's future looked so precarious.

Of the six departments of the huge **Dahlem Museum**, much the most important is the **Painting Gallery** (*Gemäldegalerie*) whose vast collection is one of the world's most wonderful, deserving a whole day's visit. What's more, the room attendants are unusually helpful and erudite. The pictures are laid out chronologically and by nation. Among the highlights of the German section are the 14th-century *Madonna of Graz*, works by Altdorfer, Dürer and Holbein, and Cranach the Elder's astonishing *Fountain of Youth*, showing wizened hags descending into a pool, to emerge on its far side as pretty girls (only women use this magic fountain: maybe men get rejuvenated by being with a young woman?). The Dutch and Flemish rooms take in Hieronymus Bosch, Van Dyck, Ruysdael, lots of Rembrandts (including his *Man with a Golden Helmet*), some splendid works by Vermeer and Franz Hals, a lovely village scene by the little-known Sebastian Vranex, and Breughel the Elder's teeming, vivid canvas of a hundred *Proverbs*. France contributes a charming *Peasants Eating* by de La Tour, as well as some Watteau and Chardin. The many Italians include Botticelli, Tizian, Tiepolo, and a stunning set of Canalettos.

The **Sculpture department** ranges from third century Byzantine to 18th-century baroque. Two fine Riemenschneiders are in the German mediaeval section; among the Italian Renaissance works, Donatello impresses most. The Drawings and Prints Department includes Dürer and Rembrandt; the Museum of Oriental Art has bronzes, lacquer ware, porcelain and painted miniatures from many parts of Asia. The **Ethnographic Museum** is notable for its South Seas section: painted masks, sailing-boats, etc, some of them collected by Captain Cook. Lastly, Germany's own folk art is well displayed in the German Folklore Museum – painted cupboards, wedding costumes, some big lavishly furnished dolls' houses, and much else.

Dahlem has two other lesser museums. The **Brücke Museum**, on Bussardsteig, is devoted to the 'Brücke' (bridge) group of Expressionist painters, led by Karl Schmidt-Rottluff and E.L. Kirchner, who flourished in Berlin and Dresden before the 1914–18 war. The **Botanical Museum** is next to the pleasant Botanical Gardens, with 15 hothouses full of tropical plants. Nearby is the **Free University** of Berlin, which itself was a major hothouse of student revolt in the late 1960s. After the war it split off from the non-free Humboldt University in East Berlin (see p. 293) to become West Berlin's main higher education establishment.

Schöneberg, a district north-east of

Kreuzberg

Just south of the former Wall is notorious **Kreuzberg**, a sprawling borough of old tenement blocks and other mixed housing, much of it very run-down. In the 1960s Turkish immigrants settled here in large numbers, and they make up a quarter of the population. Drop-outs, squatters, bohemian intellectuals and artists also moved in, so Kreuzberg has become the capital of Berlin's huge 'alternative' scene. An abandoned factory known as **Mehringhof**, at Gneisenaustrasse 2, has been taken over by a network of small co-operatives and is dubbed 'the Alternative Rathaus': it has vegetarian stores, a bike-shop, a sort-of theatre, a sort-of publishing house, and a messy kindergarten run by parents.

This is one focal point of a varied Kreuzberg scene, rich in romantic squalor and quirky self-expression – provocative graffiti such as *'Raus mit dem Schweine-Schwanz System'* ('Away with the swinish penis system') scrawled by feminists, and blackened bomb-scarred buildings beside bright pop-art façades newly painted by squatters. Veiled Turkish women crouch on the steps of a neo-Byzantine church; sinister black-jacketed punks hang out around the Kottbusser Tor; drugged weirdies and sad-looking drop-outs haunt the night-bars of the Oranienstrasse, high-street of the local 'scene'.

Kreuzberg in the early 1980s was the scene of violent battles between squatters led by militant Leftists, who took over 170 empty tenement blocks, and police who came to evict them. Today the militants have mostly gone, the remaining squatters have been legalized – and Kreuzberg is generally quieter. Relations between Germans and the local Turks have also much improved since the 1970s, when rival gangs of youths fought each other nightly. The district since then has become more like Greenwich Village, filling up with middle-class Greens, Leftish intellectuals and the kind of radical-*Schickeria* who like to live in a racially-mixed area. And today, as the developers get to work on the former desolate areas by the Wall, Kreuzberg is due for more massive change.

Dahlem, is best known for its **Rathaus** which since 1948 has been the seat of the West Berlin Parliament and governing Senate. Here each day at noon the Liberty Bell rings out, a copy of America's Liberty Bell, donated to the city by the US in 1950. And, as a plaque recalls, it was from the balcony of this Rathaus that in June 1963 President Kennedy proclaimed: *'Ich bin ein Berliner.'* Further south, in Steglitz, is **'Der Insulaner'**, one of several artificial hills built in Berlin after the war to dispose of rubble from the bombing: rising to 79m, it now has an observatory on top. **Tempelhof Airport**, used mainly by the US Air Force since the war, was the principal venue for the Allied Airlift in 1948–49: the 75 airmen who died in this operation are honoured at its entrance by a monument whose three arcs symbolize the three air corridors.

West of the Old Wall: Checkpoint Charlie to Reichstag

This is one of the most strange and haunting parts of Berlin, around the Potsdamer Platz which was once the teeming core of the busy city, but then became a huge desolate empty zone, dissected by the Wall. Today, with the Wall gone, it is being grandly and stylishly replanned, so it won't haunt for much longer.

Checkpoint Charlie, near the western edge of Kreuzberg (see feature), used to be the only entry point into East Berlin for foreign motorists. It is now gone: but some chunks of graffiti-daubed Wall remain, chipped at by souvenir-hunters. And you can still visit **Haus am Checkpoint Charlie** (open daily), a startling museum of the Wall's history and of the various escapes and attempted escapes, in which 75 people were killed by GDR border guards. Right beside the Wall here is the 19-storey newspaper block that **Axel Springer** defiantly erected in 1959, with a neon sign beaming out eastwards from its roof, *Berlin bleibt frei*. To the south at Lindenstr. 14 is the excellent **Berlin Museum**, which uses paintings, prints and scale models to relate the city's history: note the cartoons of Berlin life by Zille.

To the west near the Wall are more strange and diverse places that reek of recent history. The black façade of the old Anhalter railway terminus stands alone, a wartime ruin. But the **Martin Gropius Bau** has been gracefully restored: designed in 1877 by the uncle of Walter Gropius the Bauhaus leader, this palace with its sumptuous colonnaded interior is used for big special exhibitions of modern art. Upstairs is a permanent collection of works by Jewish artists, including Dix and Grosz (the Carl Hofer paintings are hallucinating); and a **Jewish Museum** that gives sobering details of Berlin Jewish families under the Nazis. More sobering still, and right next door, is **The Topography of Terror** (open daily), a

museum housed in cellars that were the torture chambers of the Gestapo: the museum uses photos and texts to relate the grim story of the Gestapo and SS, whose headquarters were in a now destroyed building upstairs. Across the street, where the Wall stood, the old Prussian Parliament building looms up. 'Here', said one Berliner, 'you have the whole history of modern Germany encapsulated in a hundred square metres.'

The sector just south of the Potsdamer Platz has remained a strange lunar landscape, a wasteland partly covered by shacks, rubbish dumps and parking lots. For various reasons, West Berlin did not want to rebuild here, though in other parts of this western fringe of Kreuzberg some attractive new housing and office blocks were erected in the 1980s, under the programme of the International Building Exhibition that involves 40 architects. And just south of the Tiergarten, an ensemble of major cultural buildings and museums was created back in the 1960s, designed by top architects. The **National Library**, one of the world's biggest, with some three million books, and the peculiar orange tent-like **Philharmonie** concert hall, home of the Berlin Philharmonic, were both the work of Hans Sharoun in 1963. The **Kunstgewerbemuseum** (decorative arts) holds European treasures from mediaeval to Art Deco times: look out for the Guelph reliquary (1175), the 16th-century gold and silver plate from Nuremberg, and the 20th-century Bauhaus jewellery and furniture. There's also a museum of musical instruments, from the 15th century till today.

The most important of the museums

here is Mies van der Rohe's glass-and-steel **Nationalgalerie** (1968). Taking over where the main Dahlem museum ends, it has a splendid array of 19th- and 20th-century painting and sculpture, mostly German and French. There are German Romantics (Friedrich, Böcklin, etc) and some French Impressionists; also Dix and Grosz, and works from the Expressionist, Brücke, Bauhaus and Surrealist movements.

The **Potsdamer Platz**, before the war Berlin's busy Piccadilly Circus, then became an empty no-man's-land cut by the Wall; now, at the very heart of the city, it will come into its own again. Here Roger Waters' mammoth outdoor rock opera *The Wall* was staged on 22 July 1990. Just to the north, a discreet mound marks the site of the **bunker** where Hitler and Eva Braun committed suicide on 30 April 1945. Further on, the Strasse des 17 Juni in the Tiergarten is named after those who died in the GDR workers' revolt of 1953. Beside it is the Soviet War Memorial which the Russians erected just inside the British Sector before the city was divided. Indeed, recent history here rises up at every step you take: just beyond the Brandenburg Gate is the massive neo-Renaissance hulk of the **Reichstag**, built in the 1890s to house the German parliament, then burned out in January 1933 (almost certainly by the Nazis), then bombed, then restored. Ceremonial meetings are still held here, and it may now again become the seat of the German parliament. The museum it holds, 'Questions on German History', is forceful on the Nazi period.

The **Wall** ran right behind the Reichstag, and right in front of the Brandenburg Gate (see opposite), just a few metres away in East Berlin. It is sobering today to see how very close were these two great buildings, long divided by a crazy Wall that has now been completely removed in this area. But a few simple crosses remain as memorials to those here shot dead while trying to escape. At various points beside the Wall you can find other such crosses – notably at Bernauerstrasse to the north, where in August 1961 some people tried to jump to freedom from upper floors, as militiamen erected the Wall just in front of their homes. One of those who died in the process was Olga Segler, aged 80. Daubed on the Western side with psychedelic frescoes and with graffiti in many languages, political, erotic or comic (e.g. 'What are you gawping at, haven't you seen a wall before?', or 'Darling, we love each other – why worry about the Wall?'), this barrier has now passed into history. But the suffering it caused needs to be remembered by these sad little crosses.

East of the Old Wall: Unter den Linden and Alexanderplatz

The old pre-war heart of Berlin, where imperial palaces, ministries and great cultural monuments stood either side of the broad Unter den Linden avenue, was almost all in what was to become East Berlin. Here the GDR regime purposely left as a semi-derelict wasteland the areas closest to the Wall, towards the Potsdamer Platz: but the great buildings around the Unter den Linden, nearly all of them wrecked in the war, it either meticulously restored or replaced with grandiose new ones. These massive modern edifices, some with gleaming façades of bronze-coloured glass, rose as assertive symbols of the GDR's ambitions as a modern state. And so today the Unter den Linden area, severe but neat and spacious, does have the look of an important capital city – much more than any part of West Berlin.

On the broad Pariser Platz at the bottom of the avenue, where the Wall used to run, stands the majestic **Brandenburger Tor**, as emotive and history-laden a building as any in Berlin. This triumphal gate with six Doric columns was erected in 1789, modelled on the Propylaea of the Parthenon; it is topped by the famous Quadriga sculpture of four horses drawing a chariot, reconstructed after the war. Prussian troops used to hold victory parades through the gate, then it was a focus for Nazi torchlit rallies, then it became a prime symbol of the Divided City: here the concrete blocks of the Wall were specially strengthened to prevent any GDR tanks from trying to make a dash for freedom during the military parades. Amid emotional scenes, the gate was finally reopened on Christmas Eve 1989 and the Wall there torn down. Today it is a tourist haunt, surrounded by stalls selling souvenirs such as old GDR flags and uniforms.

Fashionable new Western boutiques line the lower stretch of Unter den Linden, ironically just opposite the heavily-guarded Soviet Embassy. Higher up, a left turn will bring you to the huge and gloomy Friedrichstrasse S-Bahn station which until 1989 was the sole entry point by rail from West Berlin. Beyond, along drab Friedrichstrasse, is the famous Distel satiric cabaret which managed to keep some criticism alive during the dark decades of censorship; and the Berliner Ensemble theatre that still keeps the Brecht flag flying, though in recent years its productions of the great man's plays have been fustily mediocre.

Continuing up Unter den Linden, the first restored historic building that you come to, on the Left, is the baroque Old Library; next to it is the headquarters of Humboldt University, which Wilhelm von Humboldt founded in 1809. The temple-like **Neue Wache** (1818) is one of several neo-classical buildings in this area designed by one of Berlin's great architects, Karl Friedrich Schinkel: the GDR regime turned it into a Memorial to the Victims of Fascism and Militarism outside which, with unintended irony, steel-helmeted goose-stepping soldiers would grimly change guard – a crassly tactless sight to present to tourists. The Zeughaus (former arsenal), a very fine baroque building (1706), houses the **Museum for German History**: it contains some fine warrior masks by Schlüter, but it also gave until recently an inevitably propagandist GDR-style version of modern German history; in 1990, plans were afoot to restore a more truthful balance.

Across the road, the **State Opera House** designed by Knobelsdorff (1743) has been superbly restored and stages notable productions. Behind it is the cathedral of St Hedwige (1747), used by Berlin's Catholic minority. Here you are close to the elegant traffic-free **Platz der Akademie** where three more of Berlin's classic buildings have been well restored – Schinkel's neo-classical Schauspielhaus (theatre), now rebuilt as a concert hall, and two matching 18th-century churches that face each other: the so-called 'German' and 'French' cathedrals. The former was built for Lutherans; the latter, also Protestant, holds a museum of the influential French Huguenot refugee immigration to the Berlin area in the 17th–18th centuries.

On the so-called 'museum island', between two arms of the river Spree, is a cluster of old museums, gloomy and decrepit-looking from outside but full of interest. The **Nationalgalerie** has 20th-century works by Dix, Barlach and the *Brücke* and *Blaue Reiter* schools, as well as mediocre 19th-century paintings from the Kaiser's collection. The **Altes Museum** was used by the GDR regime to show post-war state-sponsored art: but this may now be changed. The **Bode Museum** has Egyptian, Byzantine and early Christian items, including a sixth-century mosaic from Ravenna. But the glory of Museum Island is the huge **Pergamon Museum** (open daily), built in the 1900s to house treasures brought back from the ancient world by German archaeologists. Its centrepiece is the Pergamon Altar (180–160 BC), a massive temple dedicated to Zeus and Athena, dug up near Smyrna in the 1880s. Placards give full details, including photos of the excavations. There are other bits of Greek temples, and a stately Roman gate from Miletus (AD 120). Even more impressive than the Pergamon temple, to my mind, is the vast Ishtar Gate from Babylon, built under Nebuchadnezzar II in c. 604–562 BC – a wall of dark-blue brick decorated with animal motifs. Parts of the throne room, and of the processional street leading to the palace, are also on show. The museum's Islamic and East Asian sections are worth a look.

Back on Unter den Linden, the high-domed **Dom** (Protestant cathedral), built by the Kaiser in 1894–1905, has recently been renewed and reopened. Across the road is the **Marx-Engels-Platz** (how long will it retain that name?), at the centre of an open space in the heart of this spacious city. Here the Royal Palace stood, bombed and then razed; here now stand some enormous modern buildings put up by the GDR regime, notably the white rectangle of the former Foreign Ministry, and the brown-glass hulk of the Palast der Republik, which housed the parliament. In the park across the Spree is a double statue of Marx and Engels, no doubt pondering on why it all went so wrong.

This part of central Berlin was carefully tidied up and renovated for the city's 750th birthday celebrations in 1987. The banks of the Spree were neatly grassed over. And around the twin-towered Gothic red-brick **Nikolaikirche**, well restored, a new show quarter was built, the **Nikolaiviertel**. With its cobbled pedestrian alleyways and pleasant low-rise housing, it was an attempt to recover some of the flavour of pre-war Berlin, and it marked a complete break with the GDR's earlier monumentalist style. Even before the 1989 Revolution it had filled up with chic boutiques, pubs and cafés, appealing to tourists – a sign of the way things were moving, even in 1987. It remains a very pleasant place.

The huge late-19th-century Italianate building next door is the town hall, long known as the '**Rotes** (red) **Rathaus**' – because of its bricks more than its politics. The 13th-century Gothic **Marienkirche** nestles below the giant 365-metre **TV Tower**, East Berlin's most dominant landmark. For a sweeping view on a clear day, you can go up by lift (daily) to its globe-shaped revolving observation tower (and café), from where East Berliners used to gaze wistfully down at the lights of

The Unter den Linden in former East Berlin: Protestant cathedral and TV tower. Spectrum

the forbidden Ku'damm. The adjacent **Alexanderplatz**, scene of Alfred Döblin's raffish novel of the 1920s (filmed by Fassbinder), was rebuilt by the GDR as the main shopping and entertainment centre of East Berlin – a vast piazza enclosed by department stores and skyscraper hotels in brutalist style. It is no beauty, but lively: music plays, fountains splash, and in the middle the curious 'world clock', giving the time in various cities around the globe, is a favourite meeting-place. Eastwards stretches the long and pompous **Karl-Marx-Allee**, lined with giant 1950s blocks of workers' flats. Its sheer scale is impressive – a kind of Stalinist Champs-Elysées.

The pleasant banks of the Spree, to the south-west, are more rewarding. Here are some finely restored old mansions, and interesting museums – above all the **Märkisches Museum** (details of Berlin history, and of the work of the radical satiric artist Heinrich Zille who portrayed Berlin poverty in the early part of this century). The **Otto-Nagel-Haus**, whose tub-thumping 'proletarian-revolutionary' slant may now be modified, is devoted to the Leftist 1920s painter Otto Nagel, and to radical-humanist artists of that time such as Dix and Barlach.

The Suburbs of Former East Berlin

Stray only a few yards from the showpiece sector around Unter den Linden, and you will enter a still very drab city, with pot-holed side-streets and miles of decaying apartment blocks and workshops, victims not of the bombing but of long neglect. At least there are lots of children's playgrounds, and barrack-like premises housing youth clubs, old people's day-care centres and other symptoms of the GDR's all-enveloping welfare state; and here and there new Western-style shops bring a touch of vitality. But it will take many years before former East Berlin is properly renovated. The task is enormous.

There are some places of interest in these suburbs. In Oranienburger Strasse, just north of Museum Island, is the former central **Synagogue**, burned out by the Nazis on Kristallnacht, 9 November 1938 (yes, *another* 9 November). Its ruins survive as a grim memorial. Chausseestrasse 125,

Brecht's last home before his death in 1956, is now a modest museum. The **Dorotheenstädtische Friedhof** (cemetery) next to it holds the graves of Brecht and his wife, also of Heinrich Mann, Hegel and other luminaries. Over to the north-east is **Prenzlauer Berg**, East Berlin's counterpart to Kreuzberg – a former working-class district where in the 1980s some young people tried to live the life alternative, not so easy in the old GDR. Some of its bohemian bars, pubs and galleries are well established, others are now burgeoning in the new free climate. One small street of *Jugendstil* houses with balconies, **Husemannstrasse**, was already well restored by the old régime: it has antique shops and two curious museums, one devoted to hairdressing, the other (possibly closed by now) holding a collection of photos of 19th-century Berlin working-class life.

In the southern suburbs, in Treptow Park, is the towering **Soviet Memorial** to the Russians killed in the 1945 battle for Berlin (5,000 of them are buried here): the 11-metre statue is of a Russian soldier with his sword on a smashed swastika. The HQ of the Soviet garrison in Berlin, now on its way out, is at nearby **Karlshorst**, a suburb that was virtually a Russian colony, full of Russian shops. Here the Red Army's Berlin-Karlshorst Museum gives the Soviet version of World War II.

Further to the south-east is **Köpenick**, an old town on a tiny island where the Dahme river joins the Spree: it was the setting for Carl Zuckmayer's well-known satiric comedy *The Captain of Köpenick* (1931). Its moated baroque riverside Schloss has a museum (closed Mon, Tue) of old porcelain, jewellery, furniture, etc.

Further on is much the largest of East Berlin's lakes, the **Grosser Müggelsee**, popular at weekends for boating and bathing. On a ridge in the forest to the south, the Müggelturm observation tower offers a wide view over this south-eastern sector of the city which, like the Havel and Grunewald in the west, is largely made up of unspoilt woodland and rivers as wide as lakes.

East Berlin took far less trouble with the upkeep of its rural areas than West Berlin, and much of this area is still messy: but some spots have their charm. At the quiet riverside village of **Grünau**, the idyllic banks of the broad Dahme are lined with weeping-willows, dinghies moored by landing-stages, and handsome *belle époque* mansions whispering of the old Berlin. Regattas are still held here. In Grünau forest, you can walk through the trees to lovely Schmöckwitz bridge, with its rural riverside vistas. **Rauchlangswerder**, at the extreme edge of the city limits, is a village secluded on two tiny peninsulas, with swans on the river, quaint old cottages, and moored motor-boats. In this intimate paradise, the rest of workaday East Berlin seems very far away.

TOURIST OFFICES
West: Europa-Center, tel 262 60 31; Tegel airport, tel 41 01 31 45.
East: Alexanderplatz 5, tel 221 50.

Accommodation, Eating and Drinking
FORMER WEST BERLIN:
Hotels tend to be full (and rather expensive): you should book well ahead if possible. The best areas for lively inexpensive restaurants and typical Berlin pubs are the Savignyplatz district and Kreuzberg.

(H)**Bristol Kempinski**, Kurfürstendamm 27, Berlin 15, tel 88 43 40. Berlin's premier hotel, rebuilt in 1952 but with old-style luxury, service and comfort. Rooms (325) A. 3 restaurants, A–C.

(H)**Ambassador**, Bayreutherstr. 42, Berlin 30, tel 21 90 20. Central, with 2 good restaurants, lovely pool, solarium. Rooms (200) A. Meals A–C.

(H)**Berlin**, Lützowplatz 17, Berlin 30, tel 260 50. Huge, no beauty but well run; fairly central. Rooms (537) A–B. Meals A–B.

(H)**Alsterhof**, Augsburgerstr. 5, Berlin 30, tel 21 99 60. Stylish and personal; heated pool; central. Rooms (144) B. Meals B.

(H)**Hecker's Deele**, Grolmanstr. 35, Berlin 12, tel 889 01. Just off Ku'damm, friendly; excellent traditional Westphalian-style restaurant, good value. Rooms (54) B. Meals B–D.

(H)**Residenz**, Meinekestr. 9, Berlin 15, tel 88 28 91. *Jugendstil* building, full of comfort; high-quality exclusive restaurant, **Grand Cru**. Rooms (85) B. Meals A–B.

(H)**Seehof**, Lietzensee Ufer 11, Berlin 19, tel 32 00 20. Sedate and stylish, by a small lake near TV tower and fair grounds. Dining-terrace, pool, solarium. Rooms (77) B. Meals B–C.

(H)**Schlosshotel Gehrhus**, Brahmsstr. 4–10, Berlin 33, tel 826 20 81. In quiet suburban Grunewald, a converted private palace with sumptuous public rooms, much
used for society functions. Garden. Food rather dull. Rooms (35) B–C. Meals B–C.

(H)**Rheinsberg am See**, Finsterwalderstr. 64, Berlin 26, tel 402 10 02. By a small lake
in N suburbs; garden terrace, 2 heated pools. Good cooking. Rooms (80) C. Meals
B–C.

(H)**Igel**, Friederikestr. 33, Berlin 27, tel 433 90 67. In quiet NW suburb of Tegel;
small, friendly. Nearby riverside restaurant. Rooms (48) C. Meals C–D.

(H)**Ibis**, Messedamm 10, Berlin 19, tel 30 39 30. Beside fairgrounds. Modern, serviceable; no restaurant. Rooms (191) C.

(H)**Belvedere**, Seebergsteig 4, Berlin 33, tel 826 10 77. In the smart, leafy
Grunewald suburb, a villa in a garden, discreet and quiet. Light cold meals to order.
Rooms (19) C–D.

(H)**Pension Dittberner**, Wielandstr. 26, Berlin 15, tel 881 64 85. Just off the
Ku'damm, a quaint but comfortable old *pension* that Herr Issyvoo might have rel-
ished. No restaurant. Rooms (21) D.

(H)**Hospiz Friedenau**, Fregestr. 68, Berlin 41, tel 851 90 17. In southern Berlin, near
Schüneberg; quiet, simple and friendly. No restaurant. Rooms (16) D.

(R)**Rockendorf's**, Düsterhauptstr. 1, tel 402 30 99. In N suburb of Waidmannslust:
Berlin's finest cooking in an elegant setting. Cl 3 weeks July–Aug, 22 Dec–6 Jan,
Sun, Mon. Meals A.

(R)**Alt Luxemburg**, Pestalozzistr. 70, tel 323 87 30. In Charlottenburg; distinguished cuisine. Cl lunch, Sun, Mon, 2 weeks Jan, 3 weeks June–July. Meals A–B.

(R)**Castel Sardo**, Hagenstr. 2, tel 825 60 14. In Grunewald; good Italian cooking. Cl
Mon. Meals B.

(R)**Mövenpick**, Europa-Center, tel 262 70 77. Large Swiss-owned multiple modern
eatery; slick service. Meals B–C.

(R)**Paris Bar**, Kantstr. 152, tel 313 80 52. Popular with media people, writers; good
French cooking. Cl Sun. Meals B–C.

(R)**Zlata Praha**, Meinekestr. 4, tel 881 97 50. Reliable Czech-Hungarian cooking.
Intimate. Meals C.

(R)**Joe am Ku-Damm**, Kurfürstendamm 225, tel 883 62 73. Lively and popular; traditional Berlin food; dancing. Meals C–D.

(R)**Blockhaus Nikolskoe**, Nikolskoer Weg, tel 805 29 14. Russian-style 1819 chalet
overlooking Havel river, lively and popular; outdoor terrace. Cl Thur. Meals C–D.

(R)**Hardtke**, Meinekestr. 27, tel 881 98 27. Typical, animated Berlin eatery with
good local fare, large helpings. Meals C–D.

(R)**Weissbierstube in Berlin Museum**, Lindenstr. 14, tel 251 40 15. Good Berlin
cold buffet. Open when the museum is. Meals D.

(R)**Cour Carree**, Savignyplatz 5, tel 312 52 38. Lively and bohemian, French and
German cooking. Meals D.

(R)**Max und Moritz**, Oranienstr. 162. Old-fashioned bohemian Kreuzberg *Kneipe*;
simple, hearty Berlin fare. Meals D.

(R)**Zillemarkt**, Bleibtreustr. 48, tel 881 70 40. Charmingly quirky pub near
Savignyplatz; youthful ambience, food so-so. Meals D.

(R)**Ömur Grill**, Oranienstr. 6, tel 618 72 12. Authentic Turkish restaurant in

Kreuzberg. Meals D.

(R)**Spatz**, Kurfürstenstr. 56, tel 261 27 57. Basement pub, lively, youthful, very cheap. Meals E.

(P)**Dicke Wirtin**, Carmerstr. 9, tel 312 49 52. Delightful bohemian Savignyplatz pub, often crowded; good snacks.

(P)**Zwiebelfisch**, Savignyplatz 7, tel 31 73 63. Popular with artists, intellectuals; atmospheric. Some simple dishes.

(C)**Kranzler**, 18 Kurfürstendamm. Large well-known terrace-café, now rather touristy. Good cakes.

(C)**Einstein**, Kurfürstenstr. 58, tel 261 50 96. Atmospheric Viennese-style literary café. Garden. Good snacks.

(C)**Café Schildhorn**, Havelchaussee, tel 304 41 05. Unusual, fashionable, charming, with outdoor terrace by Havel river.

FORMER EAST BERLIN:

The relatively few hotels in this half of the city were all state-built and state-run, large, modern and efficient but characterless; since currency union, they are also very expensive. Smaller private medium-priced hotels will now emerge, but it will take time. Meantime, if you do not fancy the high prices, it might be best to seek bed-and-breakfast accommodation (see p. 17) or stay at a cheaper hotel on the western side. Restaurants are plentiful, but since the DM arrived they too have ceased to be good value; and generally the cooking remains indifferent and menus restricted. Private restaurants will now grow in number and improve in quality, but this too will take time. For a good Berlin meal, the best bet for the moment is to go to the west.

(H)**Palasthotel**,Karl-Liebknechtstr., tel 24 10. Huge, modern, well-equipped, pricey.

(H)**Stadt Berlin**, Alexanderplatz, tel 21 90. Huge, modern, slightly cheaper.

(h)**Unter den Linden**, Unter den Linden 14, tel 220 03 11. Huge, modern, again slightly cheaper.

(h)**Müggelsee**, Am Grossen Müggelsee, tel 652 10. By the lake in the suburbs, modern, upper-medium.

(R)**Ermeler-Haus**, Märkisches Ufer 10, tel 279 40 28. By the Spree: elegant, French and expensive, but with cheaper basement Stube serving German food.

(R)**Operncafé**, Unter den Linden 5, tel 200 02 56. In former palace, stylish, upper-medium.

(R)**Sofia**, Leipzigerstr. 46, tel 229 18 31. Bulgarian, with music, upper-medium.

(R)**Zur Letzten Instanz**, Waisenstr. 14, tel 212 55 28. Historic pub, lively ambience, cheapish.

(R)**Zum Nussbaum**, Am Nussbaum 3, tel 21 71 33 28. In Nikolaiviertel, historic pub, rebuilt; mainly for drinks, but some snacks.

(R)**Aphrodite**, Schönhauser Allee 61, tel 448 17 07. Charming little place in Prenzlauer Berg, medium.

(R)**Metzer Eck**, Metzerstr. 32, tel 448 25 55. Classic arty Prenzlauer Berg pub; simple inexpensive food.

(R)**Café Liebig**, Regattastrasse 158, tel 681 68 69. In Grünau village, sympathetic, privately owned, good value.

CHAPTER TWELVE

Eastern Germany

The North: Rostock, Schwerin and Stralsund

THE NORTHERN PART of the former GDR is a mainly flat region, but not without its own quiet beauty. There are numerous lakes, bordered by woodlands, while avenues of trees line many of the country roads. Along the Baltic coast, sand dunes alternate with chalky cliffs: here the collectivized trade-union bathing-resorts are now aspiring again to capitalist chic. The western part of this region comprises the former duchy of Mecklenburg, with Schwerin as its old capital and Rostock as its biggest town and seaport: it is now again a *Land* in its own right, proudly flying its blue-yellow-and-red flag, which you see everywhere. The area to the east, around Stralsund, is part of the former Prussian province of Pomerania. Much of this Baltic coastal region was for centuries under Swedish possession. It is also marked by its Hanseatic past, and the distinctive Hanseatic architecture of tall houses with curly step-gabled façades still survives in some of the old towns, just as in Lübeck.

S et back from the coast on the estuary of the Warnow, **ROSTOCK** (pop. 223,000), was a key Hanseatic trading city in the Middle Ages and its university (1419) is one of the oldest in northern Europe. Badly bombed in the war, the town was then built up as the leading seaport and shipyard centre of the GDR. Much of it is still a mess, but parts of the Altstadt have been well restored: it is a town of great civic pride, and despite the blight of Communism it has retained traces of the same breezy, elegant patrician quality that you find in Lübeck or Bremen.

On the Ernst-Thälmann Platz, the broad main square, stands the very curious Rathaus, whose seven-towered original Gothic structure peers up behind the baroque façade added in 1727. The nearby Marienkirche, a towering Gothic red-brick hall-church, has interesting features in its sombre interior – a font from 1290, a Gothic triptych, and a complex astronomical clock (1472) where the apostles parade at noon. The 13th-century Nikolaikirche, in a derelict part of the Altstadt to the east, is being restored. West from the Rathaus leads the main traffic-free

boulevard, Kröplinerstrasse, today lined with modern shops and some nicely painted old gabled mansions: it has more than a touch of grace. Here a lively modern bronze fountain, and a statue of the greatest of native Rostockers, Marshal Blücher, Napoleon's foe, stand outside the university and the former baroque palace of the grand dukes of Mecklenburg.

Round the corner, in a serenely secluded corner of mediaeval Rostock, is a 13th-century former Cistercian convent, the Kloster zum Heiligen Kreuz, now housing a museum of local history and culture. On my visit late in 1990, this large and fascinating museum was in a curious state of transition, like so many in the GDR: the propagandist captions to the exhibits, relating Rostock history in terms of the Struggle of the Working Class, had not yet been removed, but the staff had cleverly introduced some anti-Honecker exhibits too (art objects that he had corruptly hoarded). Rostock's main history museum, housed in a former city gate, the Kröpliner Tor, was also in the grip of the 1989 Revolution and had been closed down for de-Marxification. The most handsome of the old city gates is the Steintor, near to the interesting Museum of Shipping.

Down on the coast, beyond some titanic new workers' high-rise housing estates, the Rostock suburb of **Warnemünde** is a most appealing fishing-port-cum-bathing-resort. Its broad sandy beach is backed by a towering State-built hotel, the Neptune; but go to the east end of the classic promenade and you'll find a charming and lively old quarter of fishermen's cottages, now full of small restaurants and cafés, with fishing-boats lining the quays.

Bad Doberan, just west of Rostock, has a famous 14th-century Gothic minster church set amid beechwoods, with lovely altars and statues; it was part of a Cistercian monastery, some of whose old buildings still survive. The civic museum gives details of the town, which the Mecklenburg dukes made into a fashionable spa in the late 18th century, with mud baths as a speciality. Its race-track was the first on the Continent, dating from 1807. Further west, the old Hanseatic seaport of **Wismar** (pop. 57,000) belonged to Sweden from 1648 till 1803 and retains traces of that influence. Today it is a very dreary-looking, run-down place: but a few fine old buildings survive, notably around the broad market square – the 14th-century *Alter Schwede* (Old Swede) building with its striking step-gabled façade, the Renaissance copper-domed fountain just in front of it, the lofty red-brick tower of the Marienkirche (1339), and the high-naved Gothic Nikolaikirche with a richly decorated south gable.

Schwerin (pop. 121,000), dating from 1160, is an historic capital city that will be impressively handsome when it has been better restored and cleaned up. It has a lovely setting beside a big lake, amid forests. It was a cultural centre from the 16th century and from 1815 the seat of the Mecklenburg grand dukes, who resided in the mighty castle on a small island in the lake. A castle has stood here since the Middle Ages, but the present grandiose high-pinnacled building dates from the 1840s, a mix of mock-Gothic and mock-Renaissance. You can visit the restored throne room and other state rooms, dark-panelled and a bit gloomy. Across the causeway from the island is a broad square lined with stately buildings, one of them an art museum whose mainly Dutch and Flemish paintings, poorly hung, I found disappointing. The soaring Gothic cathedral, the Altes Rathaus and the museum of prehistory (in the castle) are all worth a look, while at Muess just outside the town there's a Freilichtmuseum in the form of a reconstructed village. To the south, **Ludwigslust** has a majestic baroque ducal palace and a temple-like church whose two nearby bell-towers are in ancient Egyptian style.

Güstrow, another historic town, has an ornate Gothic cathedral and a superb Renaissance palace (1559–98), while restored gabled houses like the market square. The great radical humanist sculptor Ernst Barlach, persecuted by the Nazis, lived and worked in Güstrow from 1910 till his death in 1938: some of his finest works are on view in his former workshop at Heidberg 15, and in the 15th-century Gertrudenkapelle.

South-east of Güstrow lies the Mecklenburg lake district, a wide and beautiful area containing over 1,000 lakes, many of them suitable for bathing, boating or fishing, with low wooded hills and heathland all around. The largest lake, the Müritzsee, has a bird sanctuary, with eagles, cranes and ospreys. To the east is **Neustrelitz** with its stately park; and the former women's concentration camp at **Ravensbrück**, where a memorial and museum record the sufferings of the 92,000 who died there. **Neubrandenburg** (pop. 79,000), to the north, is an ancient fortified town whose Altstadt was largely destroyed in the war: but the 13th-century ramparts survive, with their four quaint brick Gothic gateways, nicely restored. One of these, the Treptower Tor, now houses a local history museum. And tiny half-timbered houses are built into the ramparts at some points; one is now a bookshop. The town also has three interesting old churches.

Greifswald (pop. 61,000), an old university and Hanseatic town close to the sea, was little damaged in the war and many of its fine buildings are intact – the 14th-century cathedral with its baroque tower added later, the 14th-century Rathaus rebuilt in Renaissance style, and the handsome gabled houses lining the Markt. The Romantic landscape artist Caspar David Friedrich was born in the town in 1774 and spent much of his life there: many of his canvases depict its pastoral surroundings, including notably the ruined Eldena monastery. To the east is the flat island of Usedom, whose sandy beaches are popular summer resorts.

The old Hanseatic port of **Stralsund** (pop. 75,000), part of Sweden from 1648 to 1814, has a delightful water-girt setting and a lively little harbour. Many of its fine old step-gabled houses are dirty and crumbling, sorely in need of restoration: but the handsome red-and-black-brick Gothic Rathaus is worth a look, and so are the two towering Gothic churches of St Mary and St Nicholas, the latter with an ornate interior and a five-metre-high crucifix. Of the two excellent museums in the Katharinenkloster, one is devoted to tropical fish, the other deals with local culture and history, and has impressive collections of tenth-century jewellery, religious art, Delft porcelain and old toys.

To the west of Stralsund are the primeval forests of the Darss peninsular; and to the north-east, across a causeway, the large island of **Rügen**, very popular in summer. Binz and Sellin are its main resorts, close to the towering white Granitz hunting-lodge, a bit of a 19th-century folly. Sassnitz in the north, in a region of high chalk cliffs in odd shapes, is a ferry port for Sweden and Denmark: Brahms and Lenin both stayed here. West of Rügen, the long, thin island of **Hiddensee** was until 1939 the fashionable beach-resort for Berliners: famous artists, writers and stage and screen stars, such as Marlene Dietrich, used to come here (the playwright Gerhart Hauptmann is buried in its cemetery). Then under Communism the island was given over to trade union collective holidays, like so many GDR Baltic resorts. But today, as Berlin recovers its old role, so indeed may Hiddensee.

TOURIST OFFICES

ROSTOCK: Schnickmannstr. 13/14, tel 226 19/ 346 02.

SCHWERIN: Markt 11, tel 86 45 09.

NEUBRANDENBURG: Ernst-Thalmannstr. 35, tel 61 87.

GREIFSWALD: Strasse der Freundschaft 126, tel 34 60.

Accommodation, Eating and Drinking

ROSTOCK 2500:

(H)**Warnow**, Hermann-Duncker-Platz, tel 37381. Large, modern, upper-medium.
(H)**Am Bahnhof**, Gerhart-Hauptmann-Str. 13, tel 363 31. Simpler, cheaper.
(R)**Fünf-Giebel-Haus**, Universitätzplatz, tel 221 62. Medium.
(R)**Gastmahl des Meeres**, August-Bebelstr. 111, tel 22301. Medium, good for fish.
(R)**Zur Kogge**, Wokrenterstr. 27, tel 344 93. Lively old sailors' tavern, touristy but fun; mainly for drinking, but a few light fish dishes too; cheapish.

WARNEMÜNDE 2500:

(H)**Neptun**, Seestr., tel 58 31. Large, modern, expensive.
(R)**Fischerklause**, Am Strom 123, tel 525 16. Nautical ambience, good fish; medium.
(R)**Teepott**, Am Leuchtturm, tel 54020. Odd modern building by beach; medium.

BAD DOBERAN 2560:

(H)**Kurhaus**, August-Bebelstr. 2, tel 30 36. Upper-medium.

WISMAR:

(R)**Alte Schwede**, Markt. Pleasant; upper-medium.

SCHWERIN 2700:

(H)**Stadt Schwerin**, Grunthalplatz, tel 5261. Large, modern, expensive.
(H)**Polonia**, Grunthalplatz 15, tel 864 05. Cheaper, simpler.
(R)**Weinhaus Uhle**, Schusterstr. 13, tel 86 44 55. Classic wine tavern, upper-medium.

GÜSTROW 2600:

(H)**Stadt Güstrow**, Markt 2, tel 4841. Simple, cheapish; night bar.

NEUBRANDENBURG 2000:

(H)**Vier Tore**, Ernst-Thalmannstr., tel 5141. Ugly but serviceable; good breakfasts; not cheap.
(R)**Blumenborn**, Ringstr. 5, tel 68 03 10. Elegant, upper-medium.

GREIFSWALD 2200:

(H)**Boddenhus**, Karl-Liebknecht-Ring 1, tel 5241. Medium.

STRALSUND 2300:

(R)**Bacchus zum Kurhof**, Kneiperwall, tel 2130. Pleasant wine tavern, fairly cheap.

SASSNITZ 2355:

(H)**Rügenhotel**, Seestr., tel 320 90. Large, modern, upper-medium.
(R)**Gastmahl des Meeres**, Strandpromenade 2, tel 223 20. Good for fish; medium.

Around Berlin: Potsdam, Frankfurt, the Spreewald

Now that the Wall is down, royal **POTSDAM** (pop.. 131,000), so close to Berlin, is again the favourite excursion-point from the city, for the palace and its gardens are among the loveliest in Germany. Potsdam has a pleasant setting beside the broad Havel and its lakes, and it was this that led the Prussian rulers in the 17th century to choose it as their seat, when Elector Friedrich Wilhelm built it up as a centre of culture, welcoming Hugue-nots fleeing from France. Then Frederick the Great, that arch-francophile, built Sans Souci Palace and its park on the model of Versailles, and endowed the town with baroque buildings.

Not that Sans Souci is on the grand scale like Versailles: this long one-storey rococo building is quite small and intimate. Inside you can visit the marble hall, the concert room, and the room where Friedrich's friend Voltaire used to stay; the adjacent picture gallery has works by Van Dyck, Rubens and Caravaggio. The most striking feature of Sans Souci is the series of broad south-facing terraces where Friedrich planted vines, with the aim of producing wine as good as French: soil and climate were against him and he failed, but some of the vines are still there, and their rows of green-framed protective glass screens are a curious and unique sight. They slope down to a high fountain, and beyond is the big park, a beguiling mix of the formal and informal. Dotted around in it are various buildings – Schloss Charlottenhof, Roman baths, the Chinese tea-house (a delightful round pavilion decorated with gilded oriental statues) and the Dragon House, also oriental. The huge late-baroque New Palace (1763) was the summer home of Kaiser Wilhelm II until he was deposed in 1918. The towering Orangerie was built in Italian Renaissance style; and the *Neue Kammern* (new chambers), also built as an orangerie, is a graceful summerhouse with sumptuous rococo décor.

The town of Potsdam, once so elegant, was badly bombed and has mostly been clumsily rebuilt – save in one or two spots, such as the traffic-free Klement-Gottwald-Strasse with its restored 18th-century houses. The Dutch Quarter is an ensemble of brick Dutch-style houses built c. 1740 for immgrants from Holland; the *Alexandrovka Siedlung* (settlement) is a group of wooden Russian-style houses built in 1826 for Russian singers who had come to Potsdam. The Orthodox church nearby still has services in Russian, attended by some soldiers from the local Soviet garrison.

The main residential palace of the German Emperors, beside the Havel, was badly damaged in the war, as was the Garrison Church nearby. The Communist regime then decided not to restore these 'symbols of imperialist militarism', so they were razed, and the towering Interhotel Potsdam now stands on the site of the palace. However, the neo-classical Nikolaikirche in the Alter Markt has been well restored, as has the former town hall next door, now an arts centre. But alas the Honecker regime in its final years decided to build in front of them a high concrete blockhouse of a theatre – 'The Communists wanted to block the vista of a Christian church', said one sceptic. Today the new regime is not sure what to do with this monstrous half-built theatre, planned for Potsdam's 1000th anniversary in 1993. Across the road is the National Film Museum, a reminder that Potsdam used also to be Germany's Hollywood. In the suburb of **Babelsberg**, many great films were made between the wars at the UFA studios which later became the GDR's main production centre. Nearby, facing Glienicke Bridge, is the grandiose neo-Gothic Schloss Babelsberg (under restoration), containing a museum of early history.

Last but not least, in a pleasant lakeside park just north of the town is the famous **Cecilienhof**, an English-style mock-Tudor mansion (1913) where the Potsdam Agreement between the four Allied Powers, on the future of Germany, was signed in August 1945, and where the control commission charged with carrying out that agreement has met ever since – until reunification brought its demise. You can visit the room where the 1945 conference was held (the rest of the building is now a hotel). A walk through the park leads to the lakeside *Marmor Palais* (marble palace), housing a GDR Army Museum that today – happily – has become as superfluous as the Potsdam Agreement itself.

Brandenburg (pop. 95,000), an

industrial town on the Havel river west of Potsdam, began life as a Slav fortress and later was capital of the Mark Brandenburg region. The Romanesque/Gothic cathedral, built on an island, has a lavish interior; worth noting also are the churches of St Gotthart and St Catherine, and the 15th-century Rathaus, fronted by a 5-metre statue of Roland (1474). East of Berlin, by the Polish border, **Frankfurt an der Oder** (pop. 80,000) is also industrial. Its brick Gothic town hall contains a large gallery of modern art, some of it 'proletarian revolutionary'. Nearby is a research centre devoted to the playwright Heinrich von Kleist, born in the town in 1777. He committed suicide in Potsdam at the age of 34.

The textile-making town of **Cottbus**

(pop. 113,000) has some attractive classical and baroque buildings, notably the Schloss Branitz, while the Oberkirche contains a remarkable altarpiece by Andreas Schulze of Jonas and the whale. North-west of the town is the delightful and unusual **Spreewald**, a flat watery region where the Spree divides into countless streams, amid meadows, orchards and market gardens. Many of the inhabitants are a local Slav minority, the Sorbs, who have their own culture, and their own language similar to Polish. They still use flat punt-like boats as transport, and sometimes still wear local costume. Tourist boat trips of the region, crowded in summer, leave from Lübbenau.

TOURIST OFFICE

POTSDAM: Friedrich-Ebert-Str. 5, tel 230 12.

Accommodation, Eating and Drinking

POTSDAM 1500:

(H)**Potsdam**, Lange Brücke, tel 46 31. Large, modern, pricey.
(H)**Schloss Cecilienhof**, Neue Garten, tel 231 41. Cosy, nice garden; upper-medium.
(H)**Touristen und Congresshotel**, Otto-Grotewohl-Str. 60, tel 865 15. Medium.
(R)**Kloster-keller**, Friedric-Ebertstr. 94, tel 215 84. Large, varied prices.
(R)**Minsk**, Max-Blankstr. 10, tel 236 36. Russian cuisine.
(R)**Ufergaststätte**, Auf dem Kiewitt 39, tel 241 32. Outdoor riverside terrace.
(R)**Froschkasten**, Kietzstr. 3, tel 213 15. Beer-tavern.

FRANKFURT 1200:

(H)**Stadt Frankfurt**, Karl-Marxstr. 193, tel 38 90. Upper-medium.

COTTBUS 7500:

(H)**Lausitz**, Berliner Platz 1, tel 30151. Medium.

Dresden and the Elbe valley

DRESDEN (pop. 516,000), the old capital of Saxony, used to be one of the loveliest cities in central Europe – 'Florence on the Elbe' it was called. It has never really recovered from the massive Anglo-American air-raid of February 1945 and still wears a stunned, blackened look: but enough of its art treasures and fine baroque buildings remain for it to be much sought out by tourists, and in a macabre way it is hauntingly impressive.

It was an important town by the 13th century, and in the 15th the princes (later kings) of Saxony made it their capital, which it remained till 1918. It was the Elector Friedrich August I, known as August the Strong (he is said to have had 365 children, almost all illegitimate), who in the early 18th century endowed Dresden with its greatest baroque buildings, such as the Zwinger and the cathedral. It also became a major cultural centre with a noble opera house, attracting Wagner, Strauss and other composers. The air-raid of 1945, the most intensive of the war in Europe, killed 35,000 civilians and left mountains of rubble. Much of the centre of town has since been rebuilt in graceless modern style. Some of the old buildings have been patiently restored, notably the Zwinger and Opera House; others, such as the mammoth Schloss in the heart of town, are still gaunt ruins. And so fierce was the heat of the fire-bombing that much of the old stone, once golden, is now blackened irretrievably – a grim sight by day, but strangely beautiful at night when skilful floodlighting lends these scorched façades a ghostly silvery grandeur. A walk through the city centre makes for an awesome encounter with the changing moods of history – from the majestic 18th century via wartime horror and Socialist drabness to today's more hopeful era, when new paint and chic are appearing in the streets and shops and Germany's second largest bank, the Dresdner, is again joyfully present in the city where it was born in 1872.

Most historic buildings are close together beside the Elbe and can easily be toured on foot. The high-towered **Hofkirche** (court cathedral, Catholic), Saxony's largest church, was built in 1738–51 in Italian baroque style and has a fine Silbermann organ; from its parapet, 78 statues of saints look down accusingly on the havoc wrought in the city. Across the square is the stately **Opera House** (1838–41), known as the Semperoper after its architect Manfred Semper. Some Strauss works had their world premières here. Much bombed, the opera was reopened in 1985. The splendid baroque **Zwinger** (1710–32), Dresden's most famous building, has also been well restored: it consists of seven linked pavilions around a wide courtyard, approached through the stately Kronentor (crown gate), and it includes three museums, of porcelain, science and zoology. Opposite, the vast royal castle of the Saxon rulers, built in phases between 1530 and 1701, was never restored by the GDR regime and is still mainly in ruins; the new regime now has plans to rebuild it. Behind it, the *Langer Gang* (long passage), built in 1586, consists on its inner side of an elegant white pillared arcade in Italian style, while outside is a huge frieze of Saxon princes (1874–1908). Close by, devoted to transport and geology, are two of the city's 20 museums.

Much the most important of these museums is the Albertinum, a big 16th-century building that was once the arsenal. Its Picture Gallery of Modern Masters takes in Friedrich, Dix, Liebermann and other German artists, as well as many French impressionists. It also houses temporarily some of the Old Masters normally in the Zwinger's gallery (under restoration) – a marvellous collection whose many great Dutch and Italian works include Canaletto's views of Dresden and Raphael's *Sistine Madonna*. The museum's *Grünes Gewölbe* (green vault) contains many precious items of silver, gold and jewellery from the Saxon royal collections, mostly 15th to 18th century: star exhibit is *The Court of Delhi on the Birthday of the Great Mogul* (1701), with some 132 gold or painted figures.

The most evocative of Dresden's ruins is the **Frauenkirche** in the Neumarkt, whose two stunted towers rise above a heap of weed-covered rubble: like the Gedächtniskirche in West Berlin, it has been preserved as a memorial to the bombing, and it contrasts starkly with the glossy modern buildings beside it, one a luxury hotel. The Neumarkt used to be loveliest part of old Dresden, and the Frauenkirche was the city's symbol. To the south rise the tall black towers of the Neues Rathaus (1907–10) and the rebuilt Kreuzkirche, known for its boys' choir and its five huge bells. It stands by the Altmarkt which used to be bustling heart of the city and is now a wide empty space, flanked by the GDR regime's brash modern Palace of Culture. The main modern shopping street, the traffic-free Pragerstrasse, leads from here to the central station. Further out from the centre, the zoo, the Grosser Garten park, and the

baroque Japanese Palace are all worth attention.

On the Elbe north-west of Dresden, the historic old town of **Meissen** (pop. 40,000) was undamaged in the war and so has kept its attractive market-place and two grand hilltop buildings, the cathdral and the Albrechtsburg castle. The former, begun in 1270, has monuments to early Saxon rulers and an altarpiece by Cranach. The latter, a splendid feudal hulk built in 1471–85, was long a seat of the Saxon princes and is full of their souvenirs, including some lively 19th-century murals depicting the castle's varied history. One of Europe's oldest porcelain factories, using local china clay deposits, was created here by August the Strong in 1710: the factory was in the castle itself until 1864, when it moved to its present larger premises in the town's outskirts. Here it still produces Germany's most prestigious porcelain, with its distinctive blue pattern. Visitors who take the guided tour can watch craftsmen at work, and see a lavish display of Meissen china and painted figures, old and new. The vineyards of the region are among the few in east Germany that produce good wine.

Beside a lake in the woods to the east is the imposing ochre-coloured **Schloss Moritzburg**, built as a hunting lodge for the Saxon princes in the 16th century and much enlarged by August the Strong. Baroque music plays as you stroll through its rooms full of hunting trophies and family portraits. Two small rooms are devoted to the radical artist Käthe Kollwitz, who came to Moritzburg to escape the Nazis soon before her death in 1945. In the grounds is the rococo Pheasant Palace, full of stuffed birds.

The baroque Zwinger palace in Dresden, fastidiously restored after the 1945 bombing.
Spectrum

Out on the south-east side of Dresden the Elbe passes some varied and interesting places. **Schloss Pillnitz** is an attractive ensemble of pleasure-pavilions beside the river, built for the Saxon rulers in the 18th and 19th centuries. The Wasserpalais and the Bergpalais, both in ornate oriental style, face each other across a formal flower-garden, linked by the Neues Palais. You will find also a more informal 'English garden', and a 'Chinese garden' with a Chinese-style pavilion. Further upstream is the curious scenic area known as **Saxon Switzerland** (*Sächsische Schweiz*) where high sandstone hills have been eroded into odd rocky shapes. The favourite beauty-

spot is the **Bastei**, where from the crests of huge jagged rocks you can survey the winding Elbe far below, and a romantic landscape of other rocky hills beyond. Across a high stone viaduct a path leads down to an open-air theatre amid the rocks, where plays are held in summer. The Lilienstein crag is another fine viewpoint in the area.

To the east, **Hohnstein** with its half-timbered houses is an unusually trim and cosy village by GDR standards: its castle, now a youth hostel, was used as a political prison by the Nazis in 1933–34, and its small museum recalls that time. Bad Schandau, on the river near the Czech border, is a spa town that has known better days: but the scenery all around is lovely and unspoilt. Returning towards Dresden on the left bank of the Elbe, you could pay a visit to **Königstein**, a massive mediaeval fortress built on a rocky plateau, its thick walls merging with the rock.

Bohemian kings and Saxon princes built it as an impregnable stronghold; more recently it was used as a political prison for Left-wingers, including in 1899 the writer Frank Wedekind.

TOURIST OFFICES

DRESDEN: Pragerstr. 10, tel 495 50 25.

MEISSEN: Willy-Ankerstr. 32, tel 44 70.

Accommodation, Eating and Drinking

DRESDEN 8000:

(H)**Bellevue**, Köpckestr., tel 566 20. Modern, lavish, pricey.

(H)**Newa**, Leningraderstr., tel 496 71 12. Large, near station, upper-medium.

(H)**Gewandhaus**, Ringstr 1. Cheaper, central.

(R)**Meissner Weinkeller**, Strasse der Befreiung 1b, tel 558 14. Classic wine cellar.

(R)**Oberlausitzer Töpp'l**, Strasse der Befreiung 14, tel 556 05. Attractive, medium.

(R)**Kügelgenhaus**, Strasse der Befreiung 11, tel 527 91. Large atmospheric pub, varied prices.

(R)**Maygarten, Linie 6**, Schaufusstr. 24, tel 302 68. Amusing, lively, original, with tramway décor, whistling waiters.

(R)**Luisenhof**, Bergbahnstr. 8. On hill above city, upper-medium.

MEISSEN 8250:

(H)**Goldener Löwe**, Rathenau-Platz 6, tel 33 04. 16th-century house, upper-medium.

(R)**Vincenz Richter**, An der Frauenkirche 12, tel 32 85. Historic wine-tavern.

BASTEI 8351:

(R)**Berghotel Bastei**, tel Wehlen 406. At viewpoint, large, touristy, medium.

Leipzig and the Erzgebirge

Famous for its trade fairs, and for its connections with Bach and Goethe, the second biggest city of the old GDR (pop. 560,000) has been a major commercial and intellectual centre since the Middle Ages. Its university, founded in 1409, was a literary focus of the German Enlightenment in the 18th century, at a time when Leipzig was also known as 'the market-place of Europe'. Its great Trade Fair, held each spring and autumn, kept going during the dark GDR decades as Europe's foremost business meeting-point for East and West, and was used by the regime as a shop-window for its goods. You see its distinctive 'MM' logo everywhere.

From the 18th century until 1945 Leipzig was also the major publishing and printing centre of the German-speaking world, with at one time about 900 firms involved in book making and selling. Germany's leading annual book fair (now in Frankfurt) used to be here, and even in the GDR years Leipzig retained a sizeable output of state-censored books. A major library, the Deutsche Bücherei, is here. The city's strong musical tradition dates back to Bach, who lived and worked here from 1723 until he died in 1750; Wagner was born in Leipzig in 1813, Mendelssohn and Schumann were active here, and today Leipzig is still renowned for the St Thomas's Choir and the Gewandhaus orchestra under musical director Kurt Masur.

However, the city's past prosperity has depended also on its surrounding heavy industry, which the GDR regime allowed to grow into a cesspit of pollution, so that the Leipzig' air today is chokingly foul – and this may take years to clear up. In many ways Honecker exploited Leipzig, for the benefit of Berlin: local resentments built up, and this helps to explain why in 1989 the town was the motor of the Revolution. Protest groups first met covertly in the Nikolaikirche, then took courage and instigated the great mass rallies in the Karl-Marx-Platz which finally toppled the regime. Many Leipzigers today are proud of this. It is not a lovely town, to say the least: in fact, many parts of it hideously dirty and derelict, even by GDR standards. But the jumble of the much-bombed Altstadt, where a few old buildings remain intact, has an animated cosmopolitan ambience with touches of sophistication – due maybe to the trade-fair links with the world, to the huge university right in the centre, and to the lively temperament of the Saxon inhabitants, very different from the severe Prussians to the north. There are lots of neat cafés, bookshops, boutiques, art clubs; and two satiric cabarets, the Pfeffermühle and Akademixer, somehow kept going during the Honecker years. They have now had to find entirely new targets.

If much less spectacular than in Dresden, a few buildings in the Altstadt are worth seeing. In the broad square (*Markt*) is the gabled old weighhouse (*Alte Waage*, 1555), looking across to the handsome Altes Rathaus, originally Renaissance but much rebuilt since: its local history museum has been closed 'for technical reasons'. The nearby Naschmarkt contains a statue of Goethe as a student, in front of the baroque Alte Börse. Down a covered arcade is Leipzig's historic restaurant, the Auerbach's Keller, where Goethe set a scene from *Faust*:

lively statues of Faust and Mephistopheles guard its entrance, but its gloomy décor is unworthy of its renown. The Nikolaikirche, dating from the 12th century but remodelled in classical style, with a spacious white interior, pillared and galleried, is not only a handsome church but has earned its place in post-war history as surely as any building in Germany: today, under democracy, it still keeps up its famous Monday meetings, now focussed on the peace movement. The broad Karl-Marx-Platz to its east, where the 1989 rallies were held, is bordered on one side by the rebuilt Opera House, on another by the Neues Gewandhaus concert hall of unusual modern design. Also on the square is Karl-Marx University whose 34-floor skyscraper (1967) earns its nickname of 'the jagged tooth' from its uneven pointed summit (there's a fine view from the café near the top). Below it, the Moritzbastei is a lively student club and cultural centre, built in the bowels of the old city ramparts.

To the west, the grimy hulk of the Neues Rathaus (1899) stands next to a big building that the Deutsche Bank has now taken over – appropriately, for who can doubt that the great Frankfurt banks are now the true owners of East Germany? Across the ringway is another grimy hulk, that of the Imperial Court (*Reichsgericht*) where the supreme judiciary of the Reich sat from 1895 to 1945: here in 1933 the Reichstag fire trial was held, where the Nazis tried unsuccessfully to frame the Bulgarian Communist leader Georgi Dimitrov for starting the fire. The GDR regime then of course made a meal of this, turning the Court into a highly propagandist museum extolling the Communist and Working-Class

Struggle Against Nazism. Mercifully now toned down, this Dimitroff Museum is still open. Part of the building is an art museum with some good Dutch and German works (Ruysdael, de Hooch, Thoma, Friedrich, Spitzweg, etc), but second-rate French ones.

On a quiet square north of the Rathaus, facing two discreetly civilized cafés, is the 15th-century Thomaskirche where Bach was organist and choirmaster; his *St Matthew Passion* had its first performance here in 1729. His tomb is in the choir, and a statue to him stands outside. It is not a notable church to look at. But its organ and choir recitals are reputed – and it can be wittily critical on current issues. On my first visit in 1985, I found daringly displayed inside it a quotation from Luther, 'A Christian is a free man in all things and no man's slave'. That was about as far as dissent could go, in those days. Returning in July 1990, just after currency union with West Germany, I found this poster replaced by another, of a man blindfolded by a DM 100 banknote, with coins covering his eyes and the words, 'Man does not live from money alone'. Nearby, the pleasant *Kaffeebaum* (coffee tree) is an 18th-century coffee-hause once patronized by Goethe, Liszt, Wagner, Schumann and others. It is still a literary club, though part is open to the public.

North of the Altstadt is Leipzig's zoo, noted for its breeding of wild animals (lions, tigers, etc). North again you'll find the Gohliser Schlösschen, a small baroque palace once an intellectual centre, now sometimes used for concerts; and the farmhouse where Schiller wrote his *Ode to Freedom* (it is now a museum). In the south-east suburbs, beyond the Trade Fair grounds, there rises up a huge, incredibly hideous memorial, the *Völkerschlacht-denkmal* (Massacre of the People Memorial). Despite its name, this is not Socialist art but Wilhelmine: it was completed in 1913 to mark the 1813 Battle of the Nations at Leipzig, when Napoleon and the French were decisively defeated by the Prussians, Russians, etc – but 100,000 perished. At least the 1989 Battle of Liberation shed no blood at all.

A tour south-east from Leipzig will bring you first to the little town of **Colditz**, dominated by its notorious castle. In 1939–45 this was a maximum security prison for Allied officers who had already made escape attempts elsewhere. It was claimed to be escape-proof, but this did not deter the truly daring: some 300 were caught trying to break out, 130 others managed to get away but were captured on German soil, while 30 made it back to their home countries. The Dutch were the most skilful and brave escapers. The 16th-century hilltop castle, a former seat of the dukes of Saxony, has been a hospital since the war, but there are now plans to turn it into a hotel and museum. Meanwhile, a modest but fascinating museum of the escapes, full of souvenirs, is just up the road: its guides will take you to the castle, to see one of the former escape tunnels.

Heavily industrial **Chemnitz** (pop. 318,000), known for its machine tools and textile machinery, was called Karl-Marx-Stadt under the GDR regime but in 1990 reverted to its proper name. In the main Karl-Marx-Platz the regime in 1971 placed a titanic Soviet-made bust of the eponymous bearded Socialist, in front of a wall bearing in four languages his clarion call, 'Working Men of all Countries Unite!'. The new town

council in 1990 began trying to sell the bust – but whether to Albania, or Highgate cemetery, or some nutty American collector, was not clear. Chemnitz, as you might expect, is no beauty spot: but a few fine old buildings have survived the war, such as the partly 12th-century Red Tower, the Altes Rathaus with its Renaissance portal, and some churches. The municipal museum has paintings by Friedrich, Liebermann, Dix and other well-known German painters, and details of Chemnitz's star curiosity – a petrified forest of 250-million-year-old silicified tree-trunks, standing just outside the building. Just east of the city, the attractive townlet of **Augustusburg** has an imposing Renaissance hilltop castle with lots to see including two museums and a chapel with a Cranach altarpiece.

All around Chemnitz is a region of antiquated factories and open-cast mines, near the top of the European pollution league. Along the Czech border run the **Erzgebirge** ('ore mountains'), really little more than rolling hills, still mined for their tin, silver and other mineral deposits. The spas and other resorts have not been made more attractive by the pollution – and the local people seem notably surly, as well they might be. Yet this was one of the GDR's four main holiday areas, along with the Baltic coast, the Harz and the Thüringer Wald. It does in fact have some appealing curiosities. One is the village of **Seiffen**, where the traditional cottage-industry of wooden toy-making is still very active, turning out hand-carved Christmas pyramids, wooden nutcracker figures in local costume, and much else. You can watch the craftsmen at work, and see fascinating details of the industry and

The much-restored Altes Rathaus in the centre of Leipzig. Ellerbrock & Schafft/Bilderberg/ Network

its social history in the large local toy museum. The small octagonal baroque church is also worth a look.

Annaberg and Schneeberg are two former ore-mining towns where the miners used to turn to wooden toy-making as a hobby. This is related in the miners' folk-art museum at **Schneeberg**, while at **Annaberg** the impressive hall-church of St Anne has an astonishing Breughel-like altarpiece (1521) of mediaeval silver-miners at work. Note also the elaborate painted font and the vivid painted frieze of biblical scenes. Just outside Annaberg, the Frohnauer iron tilt-hammer was used as a forge from 1692 to 1904 and is now a museum of technology.

At the summer and skiing resort of **Oberwiesenthal**, by the Czech border, a cable-car will take you up to the Fichtelberg, highest point in the old GDR (1,214m) where the view is splendid on a clear day. Further west, **Klingenthal** and **Markneukirchen** are little towns devoted traditionally to the making of musical instruments, including violins and accordions: the museum in the latter has over 2,000 instruments on display. From here you could return to Leipzig via industrial **Zwickau** (pop. 122,000), Schumann's birthplace, where the notorious and smelly little Trabant ('Trabi') car has been made. You might find it more edifying to stop off at **Altenburg** (pop.

55,000), a fine old town with a Renaissance Rathaus, an 18th-century castle on a rock and, surprisingly, a museum with a big collection of early Italian paintings. Altenburg also makes playing-cards and has a notable museum devoted to that subject.

TOURIST OFFICES

LEIPZIG: Sachsenplatz 1, tel 795 90.

CHEMNITZ: Strasse der Nationen 3, tel 620 51.

ALTENBURG: Markt, tel 31 11 45.

Accomodation, Eating and Drinking

LEIPZIG 7000:

(H)**Merkur**, Gerberstr., tel 79 90. Huge, modern, pricey.

(H)**Stadt Leipzig**, Richard-Wagner-Str. 1, tel 28 88 14. Central, modern, upper-medium.

(H)**Parkhotel**, Richard-Wagner-Str. 7. Fairly cheap.

(R)**Auerbachs Keller**, Grimmaischestr. 2, tel 20 91 31. Historic; upper-medium.

(R)**Panorama**, Karl-Marx-Platz 9, tel 74 60. Skyscraper-top view; upper-medium.

(R)**Ohne Bedenken**, Menckestr. 5, tel 557 34. Charming old pub in Gohlis suburb, with beer-garden; inexpensive.

(R)**Café Concerto**, Thomaskirchhof 13, tel 20 43 43. Small, quiet and civilised.

(R)**Kaffeebaum**, Kleine Fleischergasse 4, tel 20 04 52. Famous literary haunt; light inexpensive meals.

CHEMNITZ 9000:

(H)**Chemnitzer Hof**, Theaterplatz 4, tel 68 40. In Bauhaus style; large, upper-medium.

(H)**Moskau**, Strasse der Nationen, tel 68 10. Cheaper.

Halle, Magdeburg and the Harz mountains

This route takes us west and north from Leipzig – first to **HALLE** (pop. 232,000), an important town in mediaeval times thanks to its saltworks, and still industrial today. It was the birthplace of the composer Händel in 1685, who studied law at the university and was also cathedral organist. There's a statue of him (1859) in the market square; his family home is a museum, with a large collection of musical instruments. Halle's other sights include the *Roter Turm* (red tower), the Marktkirche, a late Gothic hall church, and in the Alter Markt a fountain of a boy with a donkey, the town's historic symbol.

WITTENBERG (pop. 54,000), officially designated 'Lutherstadt Wittenberg', is a town of exceptional interest for students of the Reformation. In 1508 a young Augustinian monk named Martin Luther became a professor of theology at its newly-founded university, and in 1517 he nailed his famous 95 theses of anti-Papal protest to the doors of the Schlosskirche – thus sparking off the Reformation in Germany. He then travelled widely, but spent much of his later life in Wittenberg; he and his ally the humanist theologian Philipp Melanchthon lied buried in the church, while statues of them stand outside the 16th-century Rathaus. Luther lived for some years in the Augusteum, a Renaissance building later remodelled in baroque style: it now holds an important museum of Reformation history, with paintings by Cranach the Elder (another supporter of Luther) and many early editions of Luther's works and other souvenirs of the great man. Melanchthon's birthplace, a well-preserved Renaissance house, is also an interesting museum. The twin-towered 15th-century Stadtkirche, where Luther often preached, has paintings by Cranachs both Elder and Younger, and a bronze font (1457) by Vischer. Here Luther was married and his children baptized. Non-Luther features of Wittenberg include the local history and ethnology museums in the Schloss.

DESSAU (pop. 103,000) is associated with another great reformer and innovator – not an old-time theologian but a modern architect and designer: Walter Gropius. He had launched an architectural school in Weimar called the Bauhaus, which in 1925 he transferred to Dessau: here he constructed a special building, also called Bauhaus, which exemplified his philosophy of design, using glass, steel and concrete, with modern techniques that were to have huge influence on architecture worldwide. Gropius was hated by the Nazis who closed down his school: but since 1977 the Bauhaus has been open again as a cultural centre. It is notable for its huge glass façade and unusual rectangular design. In the Törten district of Dessau is an estate of 316 villas built also on Bauhaus principles of aesthetic modern engineering. Architecture from earlier periods is represented in Dessau by the neo-classical Schloss Georgium (1780) with its lovely park, and the baroque Schloss Mosigkau south-west of the town.

The large industrial town of **MAGDEBURG** (pop. 289,000) was heavily smashed up in the last war and has been gracelessly rebuilt – apart from the Alter Markt and baroque Rathaus, neatly restored. The cathedral survives, Germany's oldest Gothic church (its interior has notable sculptures, pews and pulpit); so does the fine Romanesque monastery church of Unser Lieben Frauen. The Kulturhistorisches Museum contains the remarkable Magdeburger Reiter, an equestrian statue dating from 1240; also lively details of the work of the town's great 17th-century scientist, Otto von Guericke, pioneer of the 'two hollow hemispheres'. At **Eilsleben**, west of Magdeburg, the houses where Luther was born and died both now hold museums devoted to him.

South-west of Magdeburg, **Halberstadt** is notable for its Gothic cathedral and museum of ethnology (some 16,000 stuffed birds). Beyond lie the **Harz mountains**, astride the former border with West Germany (see p. 227): they are nowhere very high, but their wooded scenery is varied and beautiful, with an abundance of wild flowers and bird and animal life. It is excellent walking country. And the villages and small towns, with their narrow winding alleys and mediaeval half-timbered houses, are among the most picturesque in all Germany, relatively untouched by the blight of Socialist neglect that has afflicted most of the former GDR. **Quedlinburg** and **Wernigerode** are two of the prettiest places. In the former, one 14th-century

house is now a museum of timberframing; the Gothic/Renaissance Rathaus is charming, while near the old castle is a museum devoted to the poet F.G. Klopstock, born here in 1724. Wernigerode also has enchanting *Fachwerk* houses, with ornately decorated façades: most notable is the quaint gabled Rathaus. The massive hilltop castle above the town is not so old (1881), but it contains a museum of feudal society.

The **Brocken** (1,142m), highest point of the Harz, is in the former 'forbidden zone' close to the old border and was long out of bounds: but now you can again walk to its top, for a fine view. South of the town of Thale, the scenery is spectacular. Here you can explore the beautiful Bode valley, where the huge caves at Rübeland have remarkable stalactites and stalagmites. Or you can take a chair-lift up to the rocky Rosstrappe cliffs, or a cablecar to the high *Hexentanzplatz* (Witches' Dance Floor) where Goethe set a scene in Faust. Goethe and Heine both wrote well-known poems about journeying through the Harz – before the days of the scenic narrow-gauge steam railway that since 1899 has transected these mountains from Wernigerode to Nordhausen.

TOURIST OFFICES

HALLE: Kleinschmieden 6, tel 233 40.

WITTENBERG: Collegienstr. 8, tel 22 39.

DESSAU: Friedrich-Naumannstr. 12, tel 46 61.

QUEDLINBURG: Markt 12, tel 28 66.

WERNIGERODE: Breitestr. 12, tel 30 35.

THALE: Rathaustr. 1, tel 25 97.

Accommodation, Eating and Drinking

HALLE 4000:

(H)**Stadt Halle**, Ernst-Thalmann-Platz 17, tel 380 41. Modern, upper-medium.
(H)**Rotes Ross**, Leipzigerstr. Simpler, cheaper.
(R)**Zum Roland**, Am Markt 23, tel 241 91.

WITTENBERG:

(H)**Goldener Adler**, Markt 7. Cheapish.
(R)**Schlosskeller**, tel 23 27. In castle vaults; medium.

DESSAU 4500:

(H)**Stadt Dessau**, Wilhelm-Pieckstr. 35. Upper-medium.
(R)**Ratskeller**, Am Markt, tel 46 92.

MAGDEBURG 3000:

(H)**International**, Otto-von-Guericke-Str. 87, tel 38 40. Modern, upper-medium.
(R)**Buttergasse**, Alter Markt, tel 347 48. Old cellar wine-tavern; upper medium.

QUEDLINBURG 4300:

(H)**Motel**, Wipertistr. Medium.
(R)**Münzenberger Klause**, Pölle 22, tel 29 28. Medium.

WERNIGERODE 3700:

(H)**Weisser Hirsch**, Markt 5, tel 324 34.

Thuringia: Erfurt, Weimar and Eisenach

Now again a *Land*, as it was in pre-war days, Thuringia is a pleasant region full of character and tradition, lying at the heart of the old Germany. Its main towns, Erfurt, Weimar and Eisenach, have all played quite a role in German history and culture. And the range of wooded hills that runs along its southern flank, the Thüringer Wald, has some of Germany's most attractive scenery, not unlike parts of the Black Forest and Eifel. Here the villages with their grey slate house-façades are much better tended than most in the old GDR; and some small towns still practise traditional craft industries, e.g. glass-blowing in Lauscha, gun-making in Suhl. For the visitor, hiking, swimming, fishing, and skiing in winter, are all possible. Lying right next to Bavaria and Hesse, Thuringia suffered severely from the post-war division of Germany, but its people have now eagerly renewed contacts across the former border.

ERFURT (pop. 212,000), the capital, has many fine historic buildings and will again be charming place when it has been cleaned up and made more cheerful-looking. Its long history dates from 742 when the English monk St Boniface founded a bishopric there. It was a key trade centre in the 14th–15th centuries; its university, where Martin Luther studied, was founded in 1392 but closed in 1816. Today Erfurt is known especially for its permanent exhibition of horticulture.

The big cathedral, on high ground facing a big square, dates from 1154: it is notable for its Romanesque altar, 14th-century choir stalls, 15th-century stained glass, and huge bell. Next to it is the handsome tripled-spired church of St Severus, 14th-century, with a fine sarcophagus of the saint. In the little streets of the old town, restoration work is going on, especially in and around the Fischmarkt where some Renaissance buildings have superb ornate façades. The nearby Krämer Bridge, 15th-century, consisted of a row of 33 picturesque half-timbered houses straddling two streams, some now converted into art boutiques. This is claimed to be the only extant Ponte-Vecchio-style bridge of houses north of the Alps. Of the town's museums, best is the Anger Museum on the broad pedestrian square called Anger: it has a collection of mediaeval art and some more modern works too.

Whereas Erfurt under the GDR regime, and even still in 1990, was a distinctly drab, depressing and lifeless town (in my own view), **WEIMAR** (pop. 64,000) managed to remain a haven of civilized serenity, perhaps because of its cultural heritage which is much the strongest in all Germany among towns of its size. In the 16th century it became a residence of the Saxon rulers, and Cranach was among the great artists who came to work in the town; it also became capital of the duchy of Saxony-Weimar and stayed so until 1918. These cultured dukes promoted it as a centre of the arts. Germany's first opera house was opened here in 1696; Bach was a resident in 1708–17; the writer Wieland became a tutor to the duchess Anna Amalia's sons in 1772; and, to cap it all, in 1775 the Duke Carl August invited the great Goethe to Weimar where he then spent most of the rest of his life. The town in that period was Germany's cultural capital: writers such as Herder and Schiller were drawn there, and later on composers such as Liszt and Richard Strauss. In the 20th century a school of painting grew up in Weimar, which was also the original home of Gropius' Bauhaus movement (see p. 317). Politics have played their part, too: in 1919 the new German parliament met here to escape from Leftist unrest in Berlin, and drew up the constitution that then gave its name to the Weimar Republic (but the deputies soon moved back to Berlin, so Germany was never ruled from Weimar).

Not much bombed in the war, Weimar is a charmingly graceful little town packed with interesting buildings, museums and cultural souvenirs, all of them easily accessible on foot from the centre. The GDR regime treated it with respect and did not try to exploit its heritage for propaganda effect. It remained quiet, a bit seedy, not too tourist-ridden, full of a suitable poetic melancholy. Now, however, commercial mass-tourism is arriving, and there could be a danger of Weimar becoming engulfed in the manner, say, of Florence or Stratford-upon-Avon.

A tour on foot of the main sights could well begin at the house where

Goethe lived for 50 years, from 1782 until his death in 1832. In this neat, green-shuttered baroque building, kept much as it was in his day, you can visit his library, study, and the room where he died, then stroll in his beloved garden where he tried without much success to grow grapes for wine. Goethe's interests extended beyond literature into science and agriculture, and the museum next door has details of his experiments in these fields, plus many other souvenirs. Goethe was an advocate of German unification, as a quote posted up in the hall of the house records: 'I am not worried that Germany should be one especially if it is done with mutual love, and that German coins should have the same value in all the Reich.' My visit was in July 1990, the very week of economic union between the two Germanies, and that quote had an uncannily topical ring.

Nearby is the house of Charlotte von Stein, the high-born married lady who for years was Goethe's close and loving friend. And beyond it is the beautiful park where you can visit Goethe's simple garden house, furnished with some of his own possessions. Here he came to write, and to meet Frau von Stein and other loves. Also in the park is a statue of Shakespeare (1904) beside the little river Ilm. You could walk back into town via the house where Franz **Liszt** lived in 1869–86: it is beautifully kept as a museum, with his grand piano and many portraits, music scores and other mementoes in his cosy salon. Also on the edge of the park are the Renaissance Green Palace housing the Central Library of German Classics (splendid rococo hall) and the Grand Ducal Palace (*Residenzschloss*) which contains the magnificent Weimar Art Collections (from Cranach to Klee, via Veronese, Rubens, C.D. Friedrich and a host of other great names). Beyond, in the elegant Kegelplatz is a memorial to Albert Schweitzer.

From here it's a short walk to the **Herderkirche**, named after the great theologian and philosopher who was pastor in Weimar in 1776–88; he lies buried in this lofty baroque church, which also has a fine Cranach altarpiece. The adjacent Kirms-Krackow-Haus holds a Herder museum. In the Markt is the Renaissance **Lucas-Cranach-Haus** where the painter lived; here the graceful traffic-free Schillerstrasse leads past the **Schillerhaus**, where the poet lived in 1802–5 (a small museum records his link with Weimar). A famous double statue (1857) of Goethe and Schiller clasping hands stands in front of the **German National Theatre**, which has had a momentous history. Goethe was its manager in 1791–1817, in which period several of his own and Schiller's plays were premièred here. Burned down in 1825, it was swiftly rebuilt, and staged the première of *Faust* in 1829 and of Wagner's *Lohengrin* in 1850. In 1907 the theatre was again totally rebuilt, on a grander scale, and in 1919 it was here that the Weimar Constitution was adopted by parliament. Badly bombed in 1945, it was then rapidly rebuilt yet again, and reopened in 1948 with a new *Faust*. What other theatre in Europe has had such an amazing record? Also worth seeing in Weimar are the house of the poet Wieland, the Wittumspalais where Duchess Anna Amalia lived (the mother of Goethe's patron), and the Jakobskirche where Goethe was married.

A traditional market scene in Erfurt, beside the cathedral and St Severus church.
Spectrum

In grim contrast to this blessed cornucopia of culture, on a hill a few miles north of Weimar is the site of one of the most notorious of Nazi concentration camps: **Buchenwald**, where in 1937–45 some 240,000 prisoners from 35 nations were held and 56,000 of them died. Rather as at Dachau (see p. 177), the camp has been turned into a memorial and museum. You can see the place where 123 Polish patriots were locked in a wire cage and left to die slowly of cold and hunger, and the spot where Ernst Thälmann, the German Communist leader, was killed; there are memorials to Jews and British servicemen who died, and to Soviet soldiers. During the GDR years, the museum's guides and placards put the accent firmly on the gallantry of German Communist anti-fascists and of the Russians, and suggested that the 'bourgeois' elements now in West Germany had abetted Nazism. This bias shocked many visitors from the West. But in 1990 moves began to install a more balanced version and to stress the bravery and sufferings of other anti-Nazis such as Christians and Jews. In 1945 the Red Army took over the camp and used it as a prison for Nazi suspects, many of them innocent, whom they rounded up in the area. The Russians in their turn used torture

and brutality, and the screams were audible as far as Weimar. Mass graves of their victims have been found nearby. These are not facts that were ever told to the GDR public – and certainly not to the young conscripts of the GDR Army who regularly were brought to Buchenwald to swear an oath in front of the towering monument that looms up on the hilltop.

North-east of Weimar is the old town of **Naumburg**, whose fine Romanesque cathedral is noted for 12 vividly life-like sculptures (1250) by an unknown artist of genius. The gabled late-Gothic Rathaus is imposing. **Jena** (pop. 104,000), just inside Saxony, has an old and renowned university where Schiller briefly taught history. Jena is also the home of the great optical

---

Goethe in the Roman Countryside: the original of Tischbein's famous painting is in the 'Städelsches Kunstinstitut', Frankfurt.   Joachim Blauel/Artothek, Peissenberg

instruments firm founded in 1846 by Carl Zeiss, who was soon making microscopes and lenses. After World War II the owners moved to West Germany, but the factory in Jena went on with optics production under State ownership, using the name Zeiss, and this led to many lawsuits. Happily, in 1990 the two rival firms began to reunite. Jena has an optical museum and the famous Zeiss Planetarium, oldest of its kind in the world.

Going south from Weimar you will enter the **Thüringer Wald** around Rudolfstadt, where the narrow winding Schwarza valley leads idyllically to **Schwarzburg**, an unspoilt holiday village of *Fachwerk* houses. Nearby **Saalfeld** (pop. 34,000) has a folk museum and a fine baroque church, St John's; on the outskirts are the so-called 'fairy grottoes' whose stalactites are naturally illuminated by minerals in the caves, providing beautiful coloured effects. The village of **Lauscha**, to the south, is typical of Thuringian cottage-industry: long a glass-blowing centre, it invented Christmas-tree decorations in 1848 and is still producing them today. The story is told in the local glass museum, where you can watch blowers at work.

Suhl (pop. 50,000), chief town of the Thüringer Wald massif, has attractive old *Fachwerk* buildings. It has long produced hunting rifles and other firearms, as the local Weapons Museum relates. To the north, on a plateau amid splendid scenery, is the large summer and skiing resort of **Oberhof**, a workers' collective paradise of trade-union holiday flats and modern utility hotels – no Baden-Baden! What will now happen to it under capitalism? But all around this part of the Thüringer Wald the wide vistas are so bracing, the for-

ested heights and upland meadows so lovely, that one can almost forget politics. Down on the plain to the north is **Arnstadt**, where Bach was organist in 1703–07 at the church now called the Bachkirche (a small museum relates this). The baroque Neues Palais has a remarkable collection of 400 dolls made locally in the 18th century at the suggestion of a princess. **Gotha** (pop. 58,000) has a pleasantly restored Altstadt with a Renaissance Rathaus, and an interesting baroque castle. A local firm used to publish here the famous *Almanach de Gotha*, an annual guide to the nobility not unlike Britain's *Debrett*. Ironically, the town was also a foyer of the German Socialist Workers' movement which here adopted the Gotha Programme in 1875.

EISENACH (pop. 51,000), close to the former West German border, has links with Bach and Luther, and several picturesque houses in its well-restored old quarter – for example, the red Rathaus with its curious slanting black tower, and the baroque Schloss now housing a museum of Thuringian arts and crafts. One old house is now a museum of the life and music of Johann Sebastian Bach and his family: he was born at Eisenach in 1685. Another prettily restored 15th-century house is where Luther stayed as a student in 1498–1501: it too is now a museum, devoted to Luther's life and work, including details of his translation of the Bible.

Luther came back to Eisenach in 1521–22, when he spent a year seeking refuge from his persecutors in the Wartburg, the splendid mediaeval castle that sits on a hill outside the town. This former seat of the Landgraves of Thuringia dates from 1067 and was a major cultural centre in the 12th–13th centuries: here in 1207 was held the famous 'Contest of Minnesingers' (minstrels, including the great Walter von der Vogelweide) that Wagner took as a subject of *Tannhäuser* (he himself stayed at the Wartburg in 1842). Built in the 11th to 16th centuries, and much restored in the 19th, the Wartburg is not awesomely feudal but invitingly cosy, with half-timbered buildings set around two courtyards. Here are splendid rooms – the Romanesque knights' hall, the minstrels' hall and banqueting hall, and the Elisabeth gallery decorated with 19th-century frescoes by Moritz von Schwind that depict the life of St Elisabeth (this great 13th-century lady of charity spent her early years in the castle before moving to Marburg, see p. 219). The many works of art include paintings by Cranach, and 14th-century frescoes in the chapel. Visitors are shown Luther's room, kept as it was when he worked here on his translation of the New Testament. The Wartburg has also given its name to a small saloon car that has been manufactured at Eisenach since 1898. In 1990 the local Wartburg factory had a workforce of 9,000, three times more than needed for profitability; and the polluting little cars were no longer saleable, for most East Germans were now buying Western models. Mass unemployment loomed.

The old Hanseatic town of **Mühlhausen**, North of Eisenach, was in 1525 the scene of the martyrdom of the theologian Thomas Müntzer, leader of the Peasants' Revolt. The GDR regime saw Müntzer as an early Christian Communist and built him up as a national hero: Mühlhausen has two museums devoted to him and to the revolt, one in the former Marienkirche where he was briefly a priest. At the Müntzer memorial in **Bad Frankenhausen**, over to the east, the Leipzig artist Werner Tübke in 1990 finished work on a giant painting of the Peasants' Revolt, measuring 123m by 14m. It is claimed to be 'the biggest picture in the world'.

TOURIST OFFICES

ERFURT: Bahnhofstr. 37, tel 262 67.

WEIMAR: Marktstr. 4, tel 21 73.

JENA: Neugasse 7, tel 246 71.

SAALFELD: Blankenburgerstr. 4, tel 39 50.

SUHL: Steinweg 1, tel 200 52.

EISENACH: Bahnhofstr. 3–5, tel 48 95, 61 61.

Accommodation, Eating and Drinking

ERFURT 5000:

(H)**Erfurter Hof**, Am Bahnhofsvorplatz, tel 511 51. Near station, modern, medium.

(R)**Gildehaus**, Fischmarkt 13, tel 232 73. Old building, lively, popular, medium.
(R)**Hohe Lilie**, Domplatz 31, tel 225 78. Elegant, in historic building, upper–medium.

WEIMAR 5300:

(H)**Elephant**, Markt 19, tel 614 71. Famous inn, described by Thomas Mann in *Lotte in Weimar*; upper–medium.
(H)**Einheit**, Brennerstr. 42. Simpler, cheaper.
(R)**Zum Weissen Schwan**, Frauenplan. Old inn beside Goethe's house, upper–medium.

JENA 6900:

(H)**International**, Ernst-Thälmann-Ring, tel 88 80. Modern, upper–medium.

SUHL 6000:

(H)**Thüringen Tourist**, Ernst-Thälmann-Platz, tel 56 05. Large, with nightclub, good food; upper–medium.
(R)**Goldener Hirsch**, An der Hasel 11, tel 220 48. Historic; upper– medium.
(R)**Ratskeller**, Meiningerstr. 89, tel 227 09. Classic, medium.

EISENACH:

(H)**Auf der Wartburg**, Auf der Wartburg, tel 51 11. In castle, good food, upper–medium.
(H)**Parkhotel**, Wartburgallee 2, tel 52 91. Medium.
(R)**Berghof**, An der Göpelskuppe 1, tel 37 46. Medium.

LAUCHRÖDEN 5900:

(R)**Zur Krone**, Eisenacherstr. 2, tel Unterellen 351. Old family-run village inn.

Acknowledgements

Among the many people who helped us to prepare this book, I should like to thank especially Gunter Nischwitz and Agathe Süss of the German National Tourist Office in London; Hans Wörndl and Ron Shaw of the DER Travel Service, Richard Day of Scandinavian Seaways, and the Romantik Hotels Association, all for facilities kindly provided; also a vast number of local tourist offices in Germany, particularly those in Berlin, Bonn, Cologne, Düsseldorf, Frankfurt, Freiburg, Hanover, Heidelberg, Kassel, Konstanz, Lübeck, Mainz, Munich, Nuremberg, Regensburg and Würzburg.

My thanks also must go to my editor, Richard Wigmore at Simon & Schuster, and of course to my wife Katinka who was also my consultant, research assistant and companion on the entire project.

The publishers would also like to thank the German Tourist Board and the following tourist offices for their generous help in providing pictures: Cologne, Lübeck, Düsseldorf, Dortmund, Bonn, Trier, Mainz, Heidelberg, Stuttgart, Freiburg, Bodensee, Munich, Regensburg, Augsburg, Nuremberg, Bamberg, Frankfurt, Wiesbaden, Hanover, Lüneburg, Hamburg, Bremen and Kiel.

Some Further Reading ════════

Germany and the Germans, *John Ardagh* (Penguin, 1991 revised version) (comes first purely for alphabetical reasons!).
The Germans, *Gordon A. Craig* (Penguin, 1984).
Atlas of German Wines, *Hugh Johnson* (Mitchell Beazley, 1986).
Your Swabian Neighbours, *Bob Larson* (Stuttgart, 1980).
History of Germany since 1789, *Golo Mann* (Penguin, 1987).
The New Germany, *David Marsh* (Century, 1990).
The Oxford Companion to German Literature (OUP, 1986).
The German Food Book, *Judy Ridgway* (Martin Books, 1983).
Lowest of the Low, *Günter Wallraff* (Methuen, 1988).

Index to Place Names

(Individual buildings inside towns are not indexed, nor are names of people)